Managing Fast Growing Cities

New Approaches to Urban Planning and
Management in the Developing World

Edited by Nick Devas and Carole Rakodi

Longman
Scientific &
Technical

Copublished in the United States with
John Wiley & Sons, Inc., New York

Longman Scientific & Technical,
Longman Group UK Ltd,
Longman House, Burnt Mill, Harlow,
Essex CM20 2JE, England
and Associated Companies throughout the world.

Copublished in the United States with
John Wiley & Sons, Inc., 605 Third Avenue, New York, NY 10158

First published 1993

ISBN 0–582–09304–X

British Library Cataloguing in Publication Data
A catalogue record for this book is available
from the British Library

Library of Congress Cataloging-in-Publication Data
A catalogue record for this book is available
from the Library of Congress

Set by 3 in 10/11 pt Palatino

Produced by Longman Singapore Publishers (Pte) Ltd.
Printed in Singapore

Contents

List of Figures

List of Plates

List of Boxes

List of Contributors

Mr Jim Amos, Senior Fellow, Institute of Local Government Studies, University of Birmingham

Dr Richard Batley, Reader in Development Administration, Institute of Local Government Studies, University of Birmingham

Professor Kenneth Davey, Professor of Development Administration, Institute of Local Government Studies, University of Birmingham

Mr Nick Devas, Senior Lecturer, Development Administration Group, Institute of Local Government Studies, University of Birmingham

Mr Michael Mattingly, Lecturer, Development Planning Unit, University College, London

Professor Patrick McAuslan, Land Management Advisor, UNCHS (Habitat), Nairobi

Dr Carole Rakodi, Senior Lecturer, Department of City and Regional Planning, University of Wales, Cardiff

Preface and Acknowledgements

In September 1989 an international workshop took place near Birmingham, UK, under the title 'Planning and Management of Urban Development in the 1990s: New Directions for Urban Development in Rapidly Urbanising Countries'. The aim of the workshop was to bring together a number of leading practitioners and specialists in the field of planning and management of urban development, to review what has been learnt from the experience over the last two or three decades, and to identify what may be the most promising approaches for tackling the great challenges which face the planners and managers of the world's fast growing cities in the future.

The workshop was the outcome of an initiative of the Royal Town Planning Institute, as part of the celebration of its 75th Anniversary. It was organised jointly by the Development Administration Group of the Institute of Local Government Studies and the Centre for Urban and Regional Studies, both of the University of Birmingham, and the Development Planning Unit, University College, London. Funding for the workshop was provided by the British Government's Overseas Development Administration (ODA) and the Herbert Manzoni Trust. The occasion brought together a number of senior government officials responsible for managing urban development, from India, Philippines, Brazil, Jamaica, Nigeria and Zimbabwe, together with a number of consultants and urban specialists from Britain and representatives of several donor agencies – the World Bank, UNCHS (Habitat), ODA, USAID, and GTZ of Germany.

This book is an outcome of that workshop. It is not, however, a collection of workshop papers. Each of the chapters in this book has been written specifically for this volume, drawing on the ideas and papers presented at that workshop, together with the authors' own insights and experiences. A number of the original workshop papers, by both practitioners and consultants, are to be published in a forthcoming issue of *Habitat International*.

We wish to acknowledge the support provided by the funding agencies which made the workshop possible, and the contributions of all those who prepared papers for and participated in that workshop.

We would also wish to thank those colleagues who provided technical and secretarial support, and who contributed comments on early drafts of chapters. In particular, we are grateful to David Pasteur for his very thorough review of the draft manuscript. We would like to acknowledge the use of photographs supplied by Richard Batley (Plates 1 and 7) and David Pasteur (Plates 10, 12, 23, 28, 29, 31, 32 & 38).

Finally, we would like to acknowledge sincerely the contribution of Michael Safier of the Development Planning Unit. Michael played a major part in initiating and organising the workshop, stimulating discussion during that event in his own inimitable way, and contributing many of the formative ideas contained in this book.

Nick Devas
Carole Rakodi
March 1992

CHAPTER 1

The urban challenge

Nick Devas and Carole Rakodi

The planners and managers of the cities of the developing world face an enormous task. The world's urban population is growing at a phenomenal rate: in some cities more than a quarter of a million people are added to the total each year, overwhelming all the efforts to improve conditions, while cities which are already larger than any known in the past continue to expand without any apparent limit. This poses a huge challenge to those responsible for the management of urban development and the provision of services.

Unfortunately, all the evidence suggests that city planners and managers have failed to meet this challenge. Large numbers of citizens are left without adequate shelter and without access to safe water or sanitation, while the haphazard patterns of urban growth have caused economic inefficiency, environmental degradation and human misery. Over the years, city planners and managers have made attempts to bring the situation under control, but with few exceptions their efforts have proved totally inadequate. In this book we examine these attempts which have been made to plan and manage the cities of the developing world, and we seek to draw lessons from that experience as a basis for identifying new approaches to the planning and management of the world's fast growing cities. In this first chapter, we look at the scale of that urban challenge, and its implications for city planners and managers.

Exploding cities?

The dramatic growth of the cities of the developing world has become something of a cliché. Yet this growth is a basic fact which city planners and managers must come to terms with if they are to have any impact on the situation. In this section, we review briefly the recent trends in urban growth and consider some of the implications.[1]

Between 1950 and 1990 the world's urban population more than trebled, from 730 million to 2.3 billion (Figure 1.1). Between 1990 and

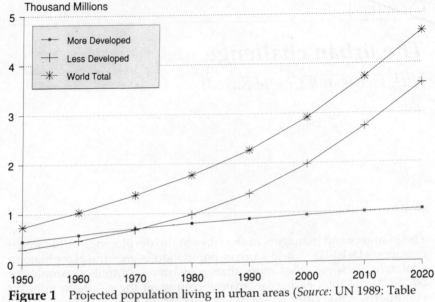

Figure 1 Projected population living in urban areas (*Source:* UN 1989: Table A-3)

2020 it is likely to double again, to over 4.6 billion. A staggering 93 per cent of this increase will occur in the developing world. That means more than 2.2 billion people will be added to the already burgeoning cities of the Third World – an increase of 160 per cent.

At present, around 43 per cent of the world's population lives in urban areas. In the developed world, that proportion is around 73 per cent; in the less developed world it is around 34 per cent (Figure 1.2). However, such averages disguise huge variations – from over 90 per cent in Belgium, UK, Hong Kong and Singapore, to under 10 per cent in Nepal, Uganda, Rwanda and Burundi. The growth rate of the urban population worldwide during the period 1970–80 was around 2.5 per cent per annum, but that comprised growth rates of under 1 per cent in the developed world and 3.7 per cent in the developing world (Table 1.1). In more than a dozen countries, mostly in Africa, the growth rate of the urban population is thought to have exceeded 7 per cent per year in the early 1980s (see Table 1.2).[2]

The total size of the urban population in the developing world overtook that of the developed world in the early 1970s, and now stands at around 1,400 million, compared to around 900 million for the developed world. The rate of growth of urban population has slowed somewhat since the 1950s, both in the developed world (substantially) and the developing world (marginally) – see Table 1.1. Nevertheless, the huge size of the world's urban population means that, even at these somewhat reduced rates of growth, the urban population will continue to increase dramatically, and that growth may start to slow down significantly only well into the twenty-first century.

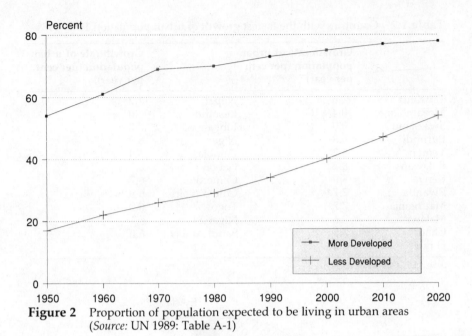

Figure 2 Proportion of population expected to be living in urban areas
(*Source:* UN 1989: Table A-1)

Table 1.1   Growth of urban population 1950–2020

	Average growth rate of urban population (per cent per year)		
	More developed regions	Less developed regions	World total
1950–1960	2.46	4.88	3.46
1960–1970	2.04	3.93	2.92
1970–1980	1.33	3.71	2.56
1980–1990	0.94	3.60	2.48
1990–2000	0.76	3.60	2.58
2000–2010	0.61	3.32	2.51
2010–2020	0.45	2.79	2.21

Source: UN 1989: Table A-2

Such broad aggregations mask some very significant differences between countries and regions (Figures 1.3 and 1.4; Table 1.3). The following are some of the principal regional trends.

China: the vast size of China's population means that urbanisation in
that country has a significant effect on the world totals. During the 1970s
and 1980s China has pursued vigorous policies to limit urban growth, as
a result of which urban population growth dropped from over 8 per cent
per year in the late 1950s to just 1.4 per cent in the early 1980s. Despite
this very low growth rate (one of the lowest in the developing world),
and the still relatively low level of urbanisation (only 21 per cent of the
population lived in urban areas in 1985), China's urban population is
still huge: in 1985, China accounted for nearly one-fifth of the urban

Table 1.2 Countries with the fastest growth of urban population 1980–1985

	Growth rate of urban population (per cent per year)		Growth rate of urban population (per cent per year)
Tanzania	11.6	Nepal	7.2
Mozambique	10.4	Lesotho	7.0
Swaziland	9.0	Libya	7.0
Burundi	8.8	Niger	6.9
Yemen	8.2	Zambia	6.9
Botswana	8.2	Gabon	6.7
Kenya	8.0	Cameroon	6.7
Rwanda	7.7	Côte d'Ivoire	6.6
Mauritania	7.7	Togo	6.2
Malawi	7.6	Nigeria	6.1
Chad	7.5	Saudi Arabia	6.0
Benin	7.4		

Source: UN 1989: Table A-2

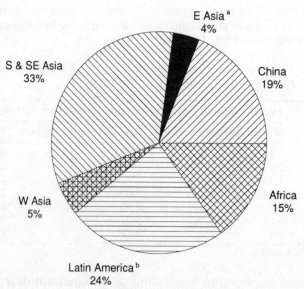

Figure 3 Share of developing world urban population 1985 (*Source:* UN 1989: Table A-3) (*Notes:* [a] Excluding Japan and China, [b] Including Caribbean)

population of the developing world, and ranked second to India in terms of the absolute increase of the urban population in the period 1970–85 (Table 1.4). In view of the economic changes which have been initiated, it seems unlikely that the government of China will be able to maintain quite such tight control over urban population growth in the future: this could have significant implications for world urbanisation levels in the twenty-first century.

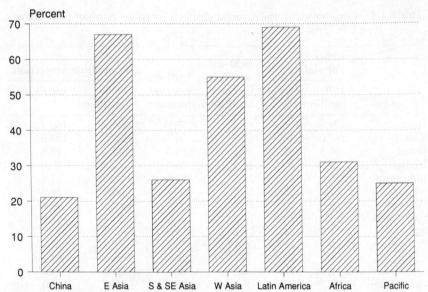

Figure 4 Share of urban population in total population 1985 (*Source:* UN 1989: Table A-1)

Table 1.3 Urban population changes by region 1970–2000

	Urban population 1985 (millions)	Urban population growth rate 1970–85 (per cent)	Projected urban population 2000 (millions)	Projected urban population growth rate 1985–2000 (per cent)
China	219	1.8	322	2.6
East Asia[a]	46	4.4	68	2.6
South and South East Asia	377	4.1	694	4.2
West Asia	63	4.6	109	3.7
Latin America[b]	279	3.6	417	2.7
Africa	174	5.0	361	5.0
Pacific	1	4.2	2	4.7
Total	1,158	3.7	1,972	3.6

Notes: [a] Excluding Japan and China
[b] Including Caribbean
Source: UN 1989: Table A-1

South and South East Asia: this region, which accounts for one-third of the developing world's urban population, experienced quite rapid growth of urban population – somewhat over 4 per cent per year from 1970 to 1985. On average, 26 per cent of the region's population lived in urban areas in 1985. India, which accounts for over half of this region's share of urban population, was quite close to the average for the region.

Table 1.4 Countries with the greatest absolute increase in urban population 1970–1985

	Urban Population		1970–85 absolute increase (millions)	1970–85 per cent increase	Population projection	
	1970 (millions)	1985			2000 (millions)	increase
India	109.6	196.2	86.6	79%	356.9	160.7
China	167.0	218.6	51.6	31%	322.1	103.5
Brazil	53.5	98.6	45.1	84%	148.4	49.8
Mexico	31.1	55.3	24.2	78%	82.9	27.6
Indonesia	20.5	42.2	21.7	106%	76.0	33.8
Nigeria	11.4	29.6	18.2	160%	68.9	39.3
Pakistan	16.4	30.8	14.4	88%	61.4	30.6
South Korea	13.0	26.8	13.8	106%	38.7	11.9
Iran	11.6	24.7	13.1	113%	45.5	20.8
Philippines	12.4	21.8	9.4	76%	38.0	16.2
Egypt	14.0	22.1	8.1	58%	36.5	14.4
Colombia	11.9	19.4	7.5	63%	28.6	9.2
Venezuela	7.7	15.2	7.5	97%	23.2	8.0
Bangladesh	5.1	12.0	6.9	135%	27.4	15.4
South Africa	10.8	17.7	6.9	64%	28.1	10.4
Argentina	18.8	25.6	6.8	36%	32.2	6.6
North Korea	7.0	13.0	6.0	86%	20.5	7.5
Iraq	5.3	11.2	5.9	111%	20.9	9.7
Turkey	13.6	19.5	5.9	43%	36.2	16.7
Peru	7.6	13.3	5.7	75%	21.0	7.7
Saudi Arabia	2.8	8.5	5.7	204%	16.9	8.4
Thailand	4.8	10.2	5.4	113%	18.7	8.5

Source: UN 1989: Table A-1

Because of the massive size of India's population, it contributed the largest absolute increase in urban population of any country in the world during the period 1970–85 – 87 million.

Latin America, including the Caribbean: this is the most urbanised region of the developing world, with nearly 70 per cent of the region's population living in urban areas, although there are considerable regional variations within that. The urban population is still growing quite rapidly (3.6 per cent per year in the period 1970–85), but this rate of growth has already started to decline. Nevertheless, the region contains some of the world's largest cities, and these can be expected to continue to grow very substantially in the future. Overall, this region accounts for 24 per cent of the urban population of the developing world.

Africa: Africa is the most rapidly urbanising continent, with an average rate of growth of urban population of 5 per cent per year from 1970 to 1985. Even so, the urban population still represents only 31 per cent of the continent's total population, and only 15 per cent of the world's urban population. Nevertheless, if this rapid growth continues, the urban population in Africa will treble before the year 2020, in a part of the world which is probably least able to meet the costs of such growth.

Other regions: the remaining 9 per cent of the developing world's urban population is located in Western Asia (5 per cent), Eastern Asia excluding Japan and China (4 per cent) and the Pacific (0.1 per cent). The first two are both relatively urbanised (55 per cent and 67 per cent of total population, respectively), the Pacific much less so (25 per cent). In all three cases, the urban population is growing quite rapidly – over 4 per cent per year between 1970 and 1985, although in the first two cases that rate can be expected to decline in the near future.

The effects of urban population growth can perhaps be seen most dramatically by looking at the growth of the largest cities (Figure 1.5). In

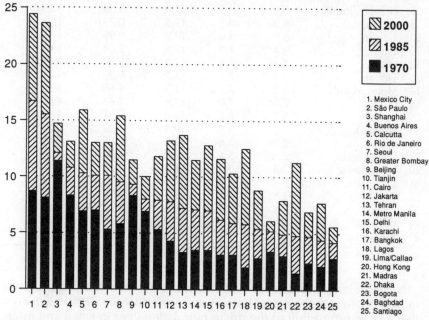

Figure 5   1970, 1985 and projected 2000 population of the largest cities of the developing world (*Source:* UN 1989: Table 6)

1985, seven of the world's ten largest cities were in the developing world. Indeed, Mexico City has probably by now overtaken Tokyo/Yokohama to become the world's largest city. By the year 2000, Mexico City is expected to have a population of over 24 million – vastly bigger than any city yet known. In 1985 there were already 25 cities in the developing world with populations exceeding 4 million (compared to only 12 in 1970), and a further 35 with populations over 2 million. Many of these cities continue to grow at phenomenal rates (Table 1.5): between 1985 and 2000, the 25 largest cities in the developing world will have to accommodate between them an additional 100 million people – almost the combined populations of Britain and France.

Table 1.5 Populations of the largest cities in the developing world 1970, 1985 and 2000

1985 size order	Population (millions)			Growth rate (per cent per year)	
	1970	1985	2000	1970–85	1985–2000
1 Mexico City	8.7	16.7	24.4	4.30	2.56
2 São Paulo	8.1	15.5	23.6	4.38	2.79
3 Shanghai	11.4	12.1	14.7	0.37	1.32
4 Buenos Aires	8.3	10.8	13.1	1.72	1.29
5 Calcutta	6.9	10.3	15.9	2.65	2.92
6 Rio de Janeiro	7.0	10.1	13.0	2.43	1.66
7 Seoul	5.3	10.1	13.0	4.27	1.69
8 Greater Bombay	5.8	9.5	15.4	3.26	3.25
9 Beijing	8.3	9.3	11.5	0.79	1.38
10 Tianjin	6.9	8.0	10.0	0.98	1.49
11 Cairo	5.3	7.9	11.8	2.64	2.64
12 Jakarta	4.3	7.8	13.2	3.93	3.53
13 Tehran	3.3	7.2	13.7	5.23	4.29
14 Metro Manila	3.5	7.1	11.5	4.65	3.32
15 Delhi	3.5	7.0	12.8	4.52	4.06
16 Karachi	3.1	6.2	11.6	4.51	4.20
17 Bangkok	3.1	5.9	10.3	4.22	3.73
18 Lagos	2.0	5.8	12.5	7.08	5.05
19 Lima/Callao	2.8	5.4	8.8	4.33	3.19
20 Hong Kong	3.4	5.2	6.1	2.78	1.10
21 Madras	3.0	4.9	7.9	3.16	3.18
22 Dhaka	1.5	4.8	11.3	7.70	5.74
23 Bogota	2.4	4.7	6.9	4.62	2.54
24 Baghdad	2.1	4.4	7.7	4.88	3.71
25 Santiago	2.8	4.2	5.6	2.66	1.85

Source: UN 1989: Table 6

Nevertheless, attention should not be confined to the largest cities merely because of their size. Hardoy and Satterthwaite (1989a: 260) note that a large proportion of the urban population lives in small and inter-mediate urban centres: 50 per cent of Kenya's urban population (1979), 57 per cent of Colombia's (1985), 62 per cent of Pakistan's (1981) and 76 per cent of India's (1981), for example.

The implications of city growth

The rapid growth of urban population has obvious implications for the infrastructure and service needs of cities. The failure to expand water supplies, sanitation systems, housing supply and transportation to match the growth of population has been a prime cause of misery in the cities of the developing world. The UN Centre for Human Settlements, in its *Global Report on Human Settlements 1986*, estimates that around 30 per cent of the developing world's urban population does not have access to safe water supplies – a figure which rises to over 40 per cent for Africa (UNCHS 1987; Table 5.19). Of the developing world's urban population 40 per cent do not have access to proper sanitation – over 50 per cent in the case of Asia. Table 1.6 provides figures by country and shows that, for example, in Benin and Bangladesh, only a quarter of the urban population have access to safe water, while in Nepal less than one-fifth have access to proper sanitation.[3]

The same report suggests that in many cities of the developing world, 40–50 per cent of the population live in slums and informal settlements – as much as 85 per cent in the case of Addis Ababa, 59 per cent for Bogota and 51 per cent for Ankara (UNCHS 1987: 77). While not all informal settlements provide unsatisfactory living conditions, they are usually inadequately served with essential infrastructure. Extremely high population densities and room occupancy rates, while not proof of unsatisfactory housing conditions, usually do indicate an inadequate supply of housing. In urban India, room occupancy rates *average* 2.8 persons; in Pakistan and Sri Lanka the figure is 2.7, with around half of all dwellings having three or more occupants per room (UNCHS 1987: Table 14). In Greater Bombay, 77 per cent of households (average size 5.3 persons) live in one room (UNCHS 1987: 77).

Other services, too, are generally quite inadequate to meet the rapidly growing needs. UNCHS estimates that, for most large cities in the developing world, only a quarter to a half of solid waste is collected by municipal authorities (UNCHS 1987: 82). Whilst some of the rest may be recycled, much of the uncollected waste ends up on open ground or in water courses, with obvious consequences for public health. Inadequate road networks result in severe congestion as the volume of traffic grows; public transport systems disintegrate through overcrowding and lack of investment. In addition, provision of social services such as health and education lag far behind the needs. While the health facilities for high-income groups may be very good, those for the poor are often so inadequate that their health conditions are as bad as those of the rural population. For example, in Bombay, the crude death rate in Bombay island (the central area) was twice as high as that of the suburbs, and three times as high as that of the extended suburbs where the well-to-do live; in Karachi, in three low-income areas, between 95 and 152 infants per 1,000 live births died before the age of 12 months, while in a middle-class area, the figure was 32 per 1,000 (Harpham *et al.* 1988; Cairncross *et al.* 1990).

The costs of providing satisfactory urban services for all are, of course, enormous. Prakash suggests a per capita cost of US$350–500 at 1977 prices for the most basic urban infrastructure (Prakash 1988: 63); updating these figures to 1992 prices would give a range of $1,400–2,000 per capita. Thus, in order to meet the basic infrastructure needs of the additional urban population between 1990 and 2000 would require developing country governments to spend some $80–120 billion per year; this is just to cater for the additional population, without any provision for improving conditions for the existing urban population. These figures represent about 2.5–4 per cent of the gross national product of

Table 1.6 Urban service indicators 1980

	Water supply (1980)			Sanitation (1980)			Electricity[a]
	Per cent of urban population served by			Per cent of urban population served by			Per cent of urban dwellings with electric light
	house con.	public tap	total	sewer con.	other system	total	
Angola				20	20	40	
Benin	10	16	26	0	48	48	
Burkino Faso	16	11	27	0	38	38	
Burundi	23	68	91	8	32	40	
Egypt	69	19	88	45		45	77
Ghana	26	46	72	4	43	47	
Guinea	16	53	69	13	41	54	
Kenya	59	26	85	49	40	89	
Lesotho	24	13	37	10	3	13	
Libya	95	5	100	44	56	100	
Madagascar	19	61	80	4	5	9	
Malawi				16	84	100	
Mali	20	17	37	1	78	79	
Mauritania	20	60	80	5		5	
Mauritius				55	45	100	
Morocco	44	56	100				82
Niger	29	12	41		36	36	
Rwanda				0	60	60	
Senegal	33	44	77	5	95	100	
Sierra Leone	20	30	50	1	30	31	
Togo	14	56	70	0	24	24	
Tunisia	71	29	100	46	54	100	
Costa Rica	95	5	100	43	50	93	
Dominican Rep.	60	25	85	25		25	
El Salvador	62	6	68	48	32	80	73
Guatemala	51	38	89	35	10	45	68
Honduras	46	4	50	43	6	49	67
Mexico	62	2	64	49	2	51	77
Nicaragua	68	24	92	35		35	90
Panama	93	7	100	62		62	
Trinidad/Tobago	79	21	100	24	71	95	
Argentina	61	4	65	32	57	89	
Bolivia	24	45	69	23	14	37	
Brazil	80		80	32		32	76
Chile	93	7	100	69	30	99	
Colombia	74	26	100	61	39	100	
Ecuador	47	35	82	36	3	39	84
Guyana	90	10	100	27	73	100	
Paraguay	39		39	30	65	95	42
Peru	57	11	68	55	2	57	54
Uruguay	90	7	97	15	44	59	89
Venezuela	82	10	92	60	30	90	

Table 1.6 Urban service indicators 1980 (*continued*)

	Water supply (1980)			Sanitation (1980)			Electricity[a]
	Per cent of urban population served by			Per cent of urban population served by			Per cent of urban dwellings with electric light
	house con.	public tap	total	sewer con.	other system	total	
Afghanistan	7	21	28				
Bangladesh			26			21	
Burma			38			38	
Hong Kong				80	20	100	
India			77			27	
Indonesia			35			29	
Jordan	78	22	100	18	76	94	
South Korea	86	0	86	9	91	100	92
Macau				80	20	100	
Malaysia	90		90	15	85	100	85
Nepal			83			16	
Pakistan	30	42	72			42	54
Philippines	53	12	65	1	80	81	63
Saudi Arabia	35	57	92	20	61	81	
Singapore	100	0	100	80		80	
Sri Lanka			65			80	35
Syria	98	0	98	74	0	74	85
Thailand			65			64	86
Turkey	69	26	95				
Yemen Arab Rep.				10	50	60	
Yemen (Democ.)	80	5	85	50	20	70	

Notes: Blank means no data available
[a] Data for electricity are for various years between 1970 and 1980
Source: UNCHS 1987: Tables 14, 17, 18

the developing countries as a whole, although clearly they would represent a much larger proportion for some countries than for others. In 1985, the Government of India's Planning Commission estimated that Indian cities would need to spend a total of US$25 billion over fifteen years to 2000 (N Harris 1990: 22). For Indonesia, it is estimated that the government would need to invest around US$1.4 billion per year between 1985 and 2000 in order to meet their targets for basic urban services; that represents around one-fifth of the government's annual development budget (Devas 1989b: 244). Of course, such calculations are wide open to challenge, both over the definition of acceptable standards for urban services and over the costing of such provision. Nevertheless, they do indicate something about the scale of the problem.

Whilst progress is being made in some countries towards the target of satisfactory urban services for all, in many developing countries the situation appears to be deteriorating. For example, out of 58 developing countries in the UNCHS survey, 26 showed a lower proportion of the urban population being served with clean water in 1980 than in 1970

(UNCHS 1987: Table 17). The WHO estimated in 1985 that 25 per cent of the population of Third World towns and cities still lacked access to safe water, meaning that 100 million more people were unserved in 1985 than in 1975 (WHO 1987). The situation is particularly bad in Africa, where serious economic problems have greatly reduced the capacity of governments to finance even basic urban services.

Box 1.1   *Deteriorating urban services in Dar es Salaam*

It is estimated that less than 10–15 per cent of Dar es Salaam's population have connections to the central sewerage system. Most middle- and upper-income areas depend on septic tanks, and most lower-income areas use pit latrines. Yet in 1983/4, only two out of the City Council's fleet of 32 cesspit emptying machines were in working condition, and only 8 per cent of the city's estimated production of 6 million litres of liquid waste could be removed. Government records for 1986 show that only 0.3 per cent of 'foul water' produced in the city was being collected. As a result, overflowing latrines are a major problem, particularly during the rainy season. (Information taken from Hayuma 1983 quoted in Stren and White 1989: 43.)

In the case of public transport, UDA, the state transport company for Dar es Salaam, had 205 buses in 1984, of which only 131 were operational. This compares with a 1975 position of 374 buses, of which 257 were serviceable every day, and a consultant's estimate in 1984 that UDA needed to have 305 operational vehicles to meet the demand. As a result, during the morning peak period, 21 per cent of all waiting passengers on the Dar es Salaam routes are left behind because of overcrowding on the buses. (Information taken from Kulaba 1986, quoted in Stren and White 1989: 51–2).

Urban poverty

It might be argued that these problems are an inevitable consequence of the poverty of the countries concerned, and that only substantial economic development – and/or a major transfer of resources from the rich nations – can solve the problems. This may well be true. However, it is one of the purposes of this book to argue that, even with a limited level of economic development, resources can be better managed to provide an improved urban environment for all. Even so, there is an issue of the uneven distribution of resources within a country, and the consequence of that for the poor of the cities.

In the past, most of the poor were to be found in the rural areas, but the shifting patterns of population mean that a growing proportion of the world's poor now live in cities. The World Bank estimates that around 330 million city dwellers or 28 per cent of the developing world's urban population fall below the poverty line (World Bank 1989). This

Table 1.7 Incidence of urban poverty

	Percentage of urban population below poverty level (per cent)[a]	Urban population below poverty level (millions)[a]
REGIONAL AGGREGATES		
Asia (excl. China)	23	136.5
Africa (sub-Sahara)	42	55.5
Europe/Mid. East/N. Africa	34	59.5
Latin America	27	77.3
DEVELOPING WORLD	28	329.8
ASIA		
Bangladesh	86	15.5 (10.2)
India	28 (40%)	63.2 (78.5)
Indonesia	26	14.1 (11.0)
South Korea	18	5.4 (4.8)
Malaysia	13	1.0 (0.8)
Nepal	55	0.9 (0.7)
Pakistan	50 (32%)	12.2 (9.8)
Papua New Guinea	10	0.1
Philippines	32	12.8 (7.0)
Sri Lanka	n/a (26%)	n/a (0.9)
Thailand	15	1.8 (1.5)
AFRICA		
Cameroon	15	0.7
Côte d'Ivoire	30	1.4
Egypt	21	4.9
Ethiopia	60	3.7
Ghana	59	2.8
Kenya	10	0.5
Morocco	28	3.2
Zambia	25	1.0
SOUTH AMERICA		
Brazil	32	34.9
Colombia	32	7.1
Ecuador	40	2.3
Peru	49	7.2
Uruguay	22	0.6

Sources:
Regional Aggregates (1988): World Bank 1989: Table A3
Country data for percentages (column 1) (1979–1988): UNICEF 1991: Table 6 except for Brazil
Brazil (1985): data for 9 Metropolitan Regions derived from Rocha 1988
Country data for numbers in poverty (column 2) (1989): UNICEF 1991: Tables 1 and 5 for urban population multiplied by percentage figure from column 1
Note: [a] Figures in brackets are from World Bank 1985b, where these differ from the above.

represented around half of the world's poor in 1985, and the Bank suggests that this percentage share could increase to 57 per cent by the turn of the century, with the numbers of poor households more than doubling by the year 2000. As Table 1.7 shows, 86 per cent of the urban population of Bangladesh is regarded as being below the poverty line; in

Nepal the figure is 55 per cent and in India 40 per cent (World Bank 1985b). Once again, there are serious problems about how poverty is defined and measured (J Harriss 1989: 187), and about where the poverty line is placed, not to mention inadequacies in the data about household incomes. Nevertheless, the essential point is clear: urban poverty will continue to present a major problem for city managers, and the scale of that problem is likely to grow, in absolute numbers, in most countries, and particularly in South Asia and Africa.[4]

City case studies

Boxes 1.2, 1.3 and 1.4 give thumbnail sketches of three of the world's rapidly growing cities, illustrating the conditions and some of critical problems which cities in the developing world face. They are not intended to be comprehensive or definitive accounts of city life or of planning policies.

Box 1.2 São Paulo

Brazil is a highly urbanised country: 30 per cent of the population live in the eight metropolitan regions, and over half of the population is concentrated in the south-east region of the country. São Paulo is the largest conurbation (Figure 1.6). The Municipality of São Paulo, with a population of around 8.5 million in 1980, is one of 37 municipalities which make up the metropolitan region of Grande São Paulo. The population of Grande São Paulo, 12.6 million in 1980, is projected to reach 23 million by the turn of the century (UN 1989: Table A-9).

The growth of São Paulo has been very rapid. In 1874 its population was a mere 23,000; in 1900 it was 240,000 (Violich 1987: 322). Its growth over the last century has been the result of migration from overseas as well as from within Brazil. The city has a strong economic and industrial base, with one-third of all Brazil's factories, and is probably Latin America's most prosperous city. São Paulo accounts for 40 per cent of the country's electricity consumption. However, as in Brazil as a whole, that prosperity is very unequally divided. It is estimated that, in 1985, 26 per cent of São Paulo's population lived below the poverty line – a significant increase on the figure for 1981 of 11 per cent (Rocha 1988).

Unlike so many other cities, the geographical location of São Paulo presents no serious, natural obstacles to continued outward expansion. However, attempts to plan the growth of the city have been overwhelmed by the forces of the private land market and the pressures for development. Thus, the city has grown through an uncoordinated process of private subdivisions, and continues to do so. As a result, infrastructure and transportation networks are seriously inadequate, incurring huge costs and constraining further development. The high-rise buildings of the central business district are reminiscent of Manhattan. This rather over-developed urban form is at least in part a result of building codes which determine the permitted height of buildings in relation to the width of adjoining streets.

Box 1.2   São Paulo (*continued*)

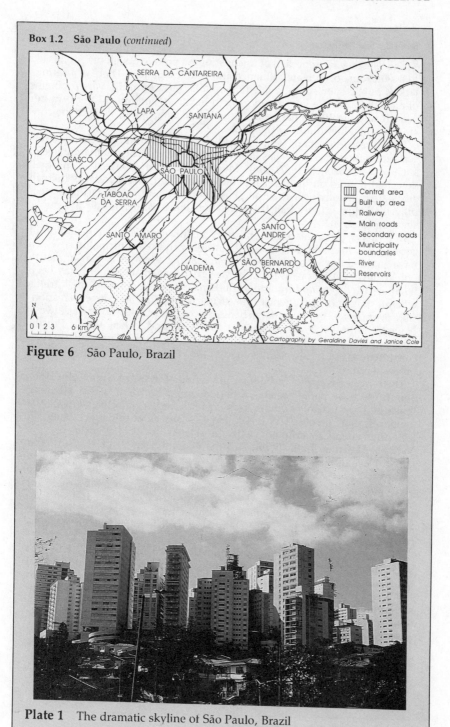

Figure 6   São Paulo, Brazil

Plate 1   The dramatic skyline of São Paulo, Brazil

Box 1.2   São Paulo (*continued*)

The *'laissez-faire'* approach of unconstrained private development has led to a syndrome of 'private affluence and public squalor'. There is a serious lack of public open space, inadequate public services and severe problems of air pollution. The very rapid growth in car ownership (13 per cent per year during the 1970s) has resulted in severe congestion, despite the construction of a metro during the 1970s.

In contrast to so many Third World cities, São Paulo has relatively few squatter settlements or favelas (less than 5 per cent of the population live in such areas – Violich 1987: 346). Most low-income groups live in small detached houses on quasi-legal subdivisions. Housing standards in such areas are generally very low, and basic services and public facilities woefully inadequate. Only half the city's housing is connected to the public sewerage system.

In terms of urban management, the constitution vests responsibility for zoning, building and development control with the municipalities, which have guarded these powers jealously, impeding attempts to plan at metropolitan level (Davey 1989a: 5). However, urban management has been hampered by overlapping and conflicting responsibilities of the various federal, state and local agencies, particularly since the state level is responsible for many of the essential urban services. The city's Mayor has always played a crucial role. Thus, during the 1930s and 1940s, Mayor Prestes Maia implemented impressive public works programmes, particularly road construction, but he also bequeathed to the city a distinctly rigid system of urban planning.

The repressive period of military government in Brazil during the 1960s and 1970s was, paradoxically, a period when Brazilian urban planning flourished, as urban planning was seen as an essential element of the 'modernisation process' (Wilheim 1989). Many new initiatives emerged from the Federal government, with the establishment of agencies like the National Housing Bank (BNH) and the Federal Service for Housing and Urban Development (SERFHAU), and the commissioning of many new city plans. In 1973, the Federal Government established the São Paulo Metropolitan Region (Grande São Paulo) with an office responsible for metropolitan planning (EMPLASA). According to Violich, the transition to an effective system of metropolitan administration progressed far more rapidly in São Paulo than elsewhere in Brazil or indeed Latin America (Violich 1987: 360).

The 1988 constitution has a strong decentralist emphasis. This has strengthened the powers of municipalities and given them additional local tax resources. However, problems of overlap and competition between states and municipalities remain. The recent disbanding of the metropolitan authority for São Paulo has resulted in serious problems of co-ordination between the many municipalities which make up the São Paulo metropolis.

The experience of urban development in São Paulo is well summed up by Francis Violich:

Although unchanneled market forces and private enterprise have brought forth a higher quality of individual dwelling than one finds elsewhere in . . . Latin Amer-

---

Box 1.2 São Paulo (*continued*)

ica, the overall urban pattern still remains inadequate for community needs. This demonstrates that . . . in Latin America, private economic development alone is not sufficient to generate resources to meet all urban development needs. Without the guidance of public policy to influence provision of the entire range of infrastructure requirements – social, physical and institutional – the basic social advantages of growth are dissipated and the full advantages of a free enterprise economy are lost. (Violich, 1987: 346)

Box 1.3 Jakarta

Jakarta may be regarded as somewhat typical of the vast and rapidly growing cities of Asia. Although its history can be traced back 500 years, its growth really started when the Dutch colonial settlers made it their capital. Batavia, as the Dutch called it, was established round the port on the north coast of Java (Figure 1.7). The settlement which the colonial power built to serve its trading purposes and to house its personnel stretched through the swampy coastal area to the slightly higher ground which the Dutch called Weltevreden. Little or no account was taken of the housing needs of the indigenous population, who accommodated themselves as best they could in kampungs (traditional settlements) built on the surrounding agricultural land.

When Indonesian Independence was declared in 1945, the city had a population of 600,000. Forty years later, the population had multiplied thirteen fold to 7.8 million. Indeed, the real population of the city is now probably substantially greater, since a significant proportion of Jakarta's recent growth has taken place beyond the city's boundaries. Estimates made for the Jabotabek (Greater Jakarta) Metropolitan Development Plan in 1981 indicated that the population of the city region could reach 25 million by 2000.

This rapid growth of population has not been matched by the development of infrastructure. Much of the increased population has been accommodated in informal settlements or kampungs in and around the city. These settlements generally lacked even basic services, although considerable improvements have been made in their condition as a result of the Kampung Improvement Programme. In the first ten years of that programme basic services were provided to kampungs containing around 3 million people (Devas 1980: 34). However, these services were very basic, and improvements to city-wide infrastructure tended to lag far behind. Thus, even by 1989, only 14 per cent of the city's population was served with piped water, the rest depending on private pumps and wells (52 per cent), private water vendors (32 per cent), and heavily polluted rivers and canals (2 per cent) (Struyk *et al.* 1990: 52). There is still no sewerage system in the city, and despite the construction of pit latrines and other private sanitation systems, the bulk of human waste goes into the city's rivers and canals. Less than half of the city's refuse is collected by the municipal waste

Box 1.3   Jakarta *(continued)*

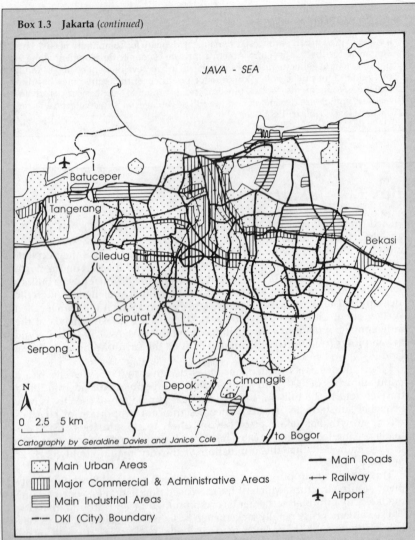

Figure 7   Jakarta, Indonesia

disposal service, much of the rest ending up in the rivers and canals or on open ground. The accumulation of waste in the watercourses adds to the already severe problem of flooding caused by the low level of the city, with obvious consequences for public health and property, particularly for the poor. The continued extraction of water from the ground has caused sea-water to be drawn in under the city, polluting the available supplies and damaging the foundations of high-rise buildings. Meanwhile, the rapid growth of the city southwards has meant the development over the city's water catchment zone, causing further pollution of the water supply.

Box 1.3 Jakarta (*continued*)

Plate 2 Jakarta: informal kampung housing overshadowed by the modern offices and hotels on Jalan Thamrin. Compare this picture, taken in 1987, with that in the frontispiece, taken from the same position in 1992 and note how 'improvements' to the city's infrastructure have resulted in the removal of many of these homes.

Despite a major programme of road building, traffic congestion is a serious problem, as car ownership has increased dramatically: the number of private cars quadrupled in the fifteen years 1970–85 (DKI Jakarta 1979 and 1986). Public transport, which is mainly in the form of buses and minibuses, is severely overloaded, and competes for the same limited road space with private vehicles. Air quality has deteriorated markedly in recent years, particularly as a result of vehicle emissions.

Jakarta is governed by a single-tier provincial authority, the Special Region of Jakarta (DKI), covering some 650 km^2, although much of the recent development has taken place in the surrounding districts within the province of West Java. Despite having a powerful and relatively well-financed unitary authority for the city, with responsibility for urban planning, there does not appear to have been an effective system of planning control. Whilst the city has long had development plans on paper, the means with which to implement these plans seem to have been lacking. Thus, informal settlements develop wherever land is available, without regard to long-term consequences. Even housing constructed by public

Box 1.3   Jakarta (*continued*)

sector agencies and by real estate developers, with high on-site specifications, is often located in areas with totally inadequate vehicular access
and without connections to main public services. Much strategically
located land is held back from development by influential landowners,
resulting in a sporadic and inefficient pattern of development. Meanwhile,
the poorest occupy what space they can on the sides of canals and railway
tracks, and under motorway flyovers – at least until they are removed by
the authorities.

Box 1.4   Dar es Salaam

Dar es Salaam, the largest city in Tanzania, had a population of 1.22 million
in 1988, sprawling over a radius of about 10 km to the north, west and
south of its harbour. It is a run down city, with deteriorating buildings and
little new investment in its central business district, totally inadequate
infrastructure and services and a largely uncontrolled pattern of urban
expansion. Symptomatic of its problems is that the most recent adequate
map dates from 1978 (Figure 1.8).

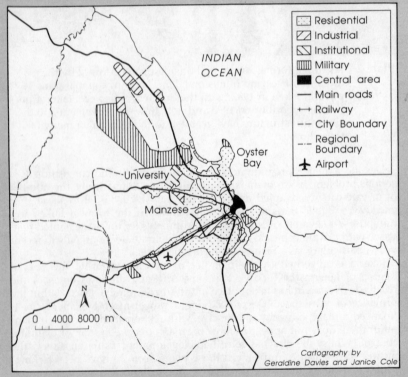

Figure 8   Dar es Salaam, Tanzania
(*Source:* Derived from maps in Marshall, Macklin, Monaghan
(Ltd) 1979 Dar es Salaam Master Plan)

Box 1.4   Dar es Salaam (*continued*)

The physical infrastructure installations are old and poorly maintained. Daily supply of water is less than 70 per cent of demand, water shortages are common, only 20 per cent of households have individual piped water and 32 per cent have a shared supply. Average water consumption is only 26 per cent of the suggested international standard and the operation of factories is adversely affected. In 1979, more than 80 per cent of the urban population used pit latrine sanitation and the situation had deteriorated by the later 1980s, with the city disposing through waterborne systems or cesspit emptying of 'a derisory 0.3 percent of its foul water' (Kulaba 1989: 239).

As a result of the lack of refuse trucks, only 22 per cent of solid waste was collected in 1986. Most urban roads are in very poor condition and storm-water drainage channels blocked, mainly because of the shortage of construction and maintenance equipment and finance. Dar es Salaam City Council had an approved budget equal to 0.41 per cent of its needs for road maintenance in 1986/7 (Kulaba 1989). The poor infrastructure, services and road network adversely affect the efficiency of industry and living conditions for residents and exacerbate the problems of public transport.

Operating failures, cumulative deterioration and failure to extend services to keep pace with urban growth are accompanied by an urban development process which is largely unregulated. Although, through land nationalisation in 1969, the Tanzanian government intended to make access to building land a relatively easy matter, the administrative allocation mechanism is very bureaucratic. As a result, much land is subdivided and developed informally, with neither official registration of ownership nor approval through the development control system (Kaitilla 1987). Today only about 35 per cent of the houses are on authorised plots (Rakodi 1990c).

Public programmes to provide infrastructure, service plots and upgrade squatter areas have been limited in extent. Although informal subdivision is the main urban development process, many plots remain unoccupied because of the absence of services, giving rise to unplanned sprawl. Serviced plot programmes have been limited in scale, relatively high standard and unaffordable by the majority (Campbell 1988). While very basic infrastructure has been installed in Manzese, the largest squatter area, the poorest are driven to squat on areas of marginal land – steep slopes or areas liable to flooding (Mosha 1988).

Explanations for Dar es Salaam's pattern of development and its poor living conditions can be found both in its colonial past and in post-independence policy. The settlement which became Dar es Salaam was one of many small coastal towns established centuries ago on the East African coast by Arab traders. Chosen as his coastal base by an Omani Sultan of the island of Zanzibar in the 1860s because of its good natural harbour, the city was essentially a planned trade and administrative centre from the outset. Despite the Sultan's death in 1870, Dar es Salaam continued to grow and was adopted as the headquarters of, successively, the East Africa Company and the German and British colonial governments. High-quality residential and administrative areas were developed around and to the north of the harbour, and separate Asian and African commercial and residential areas to the north-west and west respectively, establishing a pattern of

> **Box 1.4 Dar es Salaam** (*continued*)
>
> segregated areas of widely differing standards which was reinforced by
> early town planning (Segal 1979; A Armstrong 1987).
>
> By 1957, the centre's population had reached 129,000 and its already pre-
> eminent position among Tanzania's small and scattered urban areas was
> reinforced by independence in 1961. Its population grew by 7.8 per cent
> per year between 1957 and 1967, and even faster (9.8 per cent per year)
> over the next decade, to 769,000 in 1978, despite being replaced as capital
> by Dodoma, in the interior, in 1975 (O'Connor 1988).
>
> Although Dar es Salaam's municipal council had been established in
> 1949, on the British model, its financial and administrative capacity was
> limited at independence. Political changes eroded its autonomy and the
> abolition of poll tax in 1969 eroded its financial base, until in 1974, as part of
> national administrative reorganisation, urban councils were abolished and
> urban areas integrated into supposedly decentralised regional administrat-
> ive structures. Development strategy and allocations were biased towards
> rural development, to the extent that, by 1978, 'there was a public outcry
> over the deterioration in urban conditions. In particular . . . basic services'
> (Kulaba 1989: 221). Although a City Council was re-established·in 1978,
> worsening economic recession, failure to establish local government and
> urban management on a sound basis and resource shortfalls resulted in the
> continued deterioration of services. Dar es Salaam's growth rate slowed
> between 1978 and 1988, and attempts at planning were embodied in devel-
> opment plans prepared by Canadian consultants in 1968 and 1979 (A
> Armstrong 1987). However, Tanzania's worsening economic circum-
> stances and limited resources, ineffective planning procedures, and anti-
> urban policies for much of the post-independence period, have resulted in
> failure to control the direction and pattern of urban development, to
> provide residents and enterprises with adequate services, or to establish a
> local government system with the financial and administrative capacity to
> manage urban growth.

Why do cities continue to grow?

In the past, rapid urban growth was attributed mainly to migration.
Migration still accounts for a substantial proportion of urban population
growth in the developing world, but the natural growth of the existing
urban population accounts for an increasingly large share of the total.[5]
For example, in the Philippines, the in-migration rate to urban areas was
1.8 per cent per year during the 1970s, out of a total population growth
rate of 3.9 per cent; for other countries during that period figures were
comparable – Brazil: in-migration of 2.2 per cent out of a total urban
growth of 4.4 per cent; Indonesia: 2.7 per cent out of 5 per cent; South

Korea: 2.9 per cent out of 5.3 per cent; Kenya: 4.6 per cent out of 8.5 per cent (UN 1988: Table 79 and Table A-1). Thus the growth of cities can no longer be regarded simply as a 'problem of migration': cities will continue to grow rapidly even if there is no further migration. Of course, the young age of most migrants (well over half of urban migrants are under 24 years of age in most developing countries – UN 1988: 199) tends to increase the natural growth rate of the urban population.

Much has been written on the subjects of urbanisation and urban migration (Friedmann and Wulff 1976; Castells 1977; Gilbert and Gugler 1982; Renaud 1981; Drakakis-Smith 1986; Fuchs *et al.* 1987; Gugler 1988; to name but a few), and the intention here is not to add to that literature. Nevertheless, since migration continues to be a major factor in urban growth, it is useful to consider briefly why people migrate, and in particular to consider the paradox of why people continue to migrate to cities when there appears already to be widespread unemployment, underemployment and poverty there.

Urban migration has often been explained in terms of the lure of the 'bright lights' and the tales of 'city streets paved with gold', contrasting so vividly with the meagre conditions in the rural areas. Inappropriate styles of education, which equip people for non-existent white-collar jobs, have also been blamed. Shortages of rural land and increasing numbers of landless households, particularly in Asia, may have forced many to seek alternative livelihoods in the cities. In Latin America and in parts of Asia, such as the Philippines, the problem has not been so much a shortage of land as a lack of access to it, since so much of the available land is owned (and often under-utilised) by large landowners. In Africa, there has generally been no shortage of land, but the productivity of much of it has been eroded by drought and creeping deserts, while the returns to farming have often been reduced by heavy taxation of produce and controlled prices of crops. In a number of countries, these problems have been compounded by civil wars which have driven people off the land to seek refuge in the cities.

It is now generally acknowledged that 'bright lights' theories do not really explain migration. For one thing, most migrants are far too poor to take advantage of such facilities. Tolley argues that even the push factor of land shortages may not be all that significant, since investment can often increase the effective supply of land and its carrying capacity (Tolley and Thomas 1987: 18). However, although this may be true in aggregate, it seems unlikely that such investment will significantly improve the situation of the poor, who are the potential migrants, since the poor may be excluded from access to land, may be adversely affected by environmental problems, or may lack the investable resources to make their holdings viable.

The evidence available shows clearly that the prime motivation for migration is economic – the need to earn a higher income. Thus, intending migrants make choices, based on their perceptions of what they will earn if they stay in the rural area compared to the wages they hope to earn if they move to the city. However, since there is generally a serious shortage of jobs in the urban formal sector, many migrants end up scratching a living from casual labour or in the informal sector. J R Harris and Todaro (1968) suggested that intending migrants discount expected urban formal sector incomes by the probability of finding proper employment, allowing for a period of low initial earnings. Since potential lifetime earnings are perceived to be higher in the urban areas, the risk is worth taking and the migration decision is rational. This early formulation of a model of migration behaviour has been subject to modification in order to explain migration patterns in particular developing countries (Woods 1982; Ogawa and Suits 1985).

Such a model has been criticised for being too simplistic. In particular there are questions about the reliability of the information on urban income opportunities available to intending migrants, about the difficulties of estimating future earnings, and about family needs factors which constrain migration decisions, particularly for women. The process of migration is often more complex than a once-for-all decision, and may involve circular or chain migration patterns. It appears that in some cases rural families may adopt quite sophisticated risk-minimising strategies by 'placing' family members in different labour markets (World Bank 1990b: 62). The evidence does suggest, however, that the vast majority of migrants consider that they have improved their situation, even if not as much as they might have hoped (Gugler 1988: 83).

The above discussion has assumed that the decision to migrate is essentially an individual or family one. However, such an analysis cannot offer a complete explanation for migration, since it is the political-economic system which generates the inequalities to which migrants respond. The penetration of capitalist production since colonial times has both created a demand for labour and has led to fundamental changes in the agrarian economy (Standing 1985). Colonial powers often devised mechanisms such as taxation, some of which are still in place today, to ensure an adequate supply of labour, to encourage the cultivation of cash crops, or to alter systems of land rights, in order to further their interests. Colonial and capitalist exploitation, it is argued, has created such an uneven pattern of development, both within and between sectors, that migration is an inevitable part of the process of extracting the surplus value from the periphery (van Binsbergen and Meilink 1978; Swindell 1979; Gilbert and Gugler 1982; N R Shrestha 1988).

The patterns of urbanisation are also influenced by the way in which the economy is organised and how the country interacts with the global economy. Cities offer advantageous conditions for capital, and so encourage concentration of financial, commercial and industrial power, as well as the expansion of markets through the dissemination of tastes and consumer habits. Much of the surplus produced outside the cities is channelled into consumption, speculation and property development in the largest cities, or is expatriated by transnational corporations. Meanwhile, the informal sector persists because it is functional to the further development of the capitalist system. The alliance between local dominant classes and international capital reinforces the unequal distribution of wealth and power, leads to a polarised pattern of urban places, and facilitates the flow of surplus to advanced capitalist countries (W Armstrong and McGee 1985: 33).

Thus, 'urban areas can be understood only in terms of the conflict between classes which are a direct outcome of the operation of the capitalist mode of production; . . . space is socially determined: the outcome of conflicts between different social classes' (Gilbert, referring to Castells' analysis, in Gilbert and Gugler 1982: 2). The logical implication of such an analysis is that the problems of urban migration and urban development can be solved only through revolutionary change and the introduction of socialism. Yet experience suggests that even that may not resolve the underlying pressures. China, for example, although it has achieved much in redressing urban–rural inequalities, continues to face huge pressures of urban migration.

Is the growth of cities a good thing or a bad thing?

Opinions differ sharply on whether urban growth is a good thing or not. The popular perception is that it is certainly a bad thing, conjuring up images of appalling slum conditions and human misery. On the other hand, many see cities as symbols of prosperity and civilisation, and as the 'engines of economic growth'.

Historically, cities have grown as the centres of trade. The concentration of activities in cities permits specialisation and exchange – processes which are essential to economic growth. Commerce and industry are located in cities because of the existence of external economies of scale: pools of skilled labour, access to capital, availability of information, common services, markets for products, and sources for inputs. Such interdependencies mean that urban areas have a clear comparative advantage for industry and commerce: few industries can survive in isolated locations.[6]

In the now developed nations, it has been the growth of industry which has been the key to economic growth. This is because of the higher income elasticity of demand for manufactured products compared to agricultural products. Thus, W Arthur Lewis, in his labour-surplus theory of economic growth, suggested that the path to prosperity for the under-developed countries of the world is to invest in industry, which would draw surplus and underemployed labour out of the subsistence agriculture sector (Lewis 1954). Through such a process, Lewis argued, total output of the economy could increase without loss of agricultural production.

Unfortunately, this process has rarely occurred as Lewis had envisaged. For one thing, in many countries, labour was not really 'surplus' in the agriculture sector, particularly at peak times of harvesting and planting, so that migration often did result in a drop in agricultural output. For another, the industrialisation process has tended to be slow, with a highly protected and capital-intensive form of production, creating relatively few jobs. The resulting pattern of development in many countries has been a dualistic one, with a protected formal sector offering relatively high wages, alongside a low-income informal sector. A recent study found the urban labour market in India to be highly segmented and stratified, with access to formal sector jobs being highly discriminatory (J Harriss 1989: 190). It has also tended to be the service sector rather than industry which has grown to absorb any 'surplus' labour from the agriculture sector: for developing countries as a whole in 1980, 22 per cent of the labour force was employed in the service sector, compared to only 16 per cent in the industrial sector (World Bank 1988: Table 31).

Nevertheless, there has been, in most developing countries (though in some far more than others), a process of increasing labour productivity associated with industrialisation and with urbanisation. As Nigel Harris notes:

> the heart of the process of economic development is the establishment of mechanisms for a continuing rise in productivity of the factors of production. This involves radical changes in the structure of an economy and the quality and composition of the labour force. The sharp difference in productivity between sectors and subsectors of the national output are key factors in producing or enhancing territorial differentiation (and territorial differentiation in turn enhances the growth of productivity). The sectorally different potential for scale economies generates and sustains different sizes of settlement. (N Harris 1990: 10)[7]

Harris shows that there is a fairly clear relationship between a country's level of development (defined by GNP per capita) and the proportion of national population which is urbanised (N Harris 1990: 3).[8] He also quotes figures for India which suggest that the value added per worker in the urban areas is around three times that in the rural areas, and evidence from the World Bank that nearly 60 per cent of the GNP (and 80 per cent of the increment in national output) of developing countries derives from urban areas, even though the urban population accounts for only around 30 per cent of the population (N Harris 1990: 10). However, any such global figures must be treated with caution, since they disguise huge variations between countries: there is obviously the world of difference between the situation in the newly industrialising countries (NICs) of East and South East Asia and that in sub-Saharan Africa.

In contrast with this positive view of urbanisation, there is a substantial body of opinion which regards urban growth as highly undesirable, and views cities as parasites extracting surplus from the agricultural sector. Perhaps the best known exponent of this view is Michael Lipton, whose book *Why Poor People Stay Poor: A Study of Urban Bias in World Development* opens with these words:

> The most important class conflict in the poor countries of the world today is not between labour and capital. Nor is it between foreign and national interests. It is between rural classes and urban classes. The rural sector con-

tains most of the poverty, and most of the low-cost sources of potential advance; but the urban sector contains most of the articulateness, organisation, and power. So the urban classes have been able to 'win' most of the rounds of the struggle with the countryside; but in doing so they have made the development process needlessly slow and unfair. (Lipton 1977: 13)

In the view of Lipton and others, cities have managed to extract most of the resources from the rural areas, and have spent them on high levels of urban consumption. It is certainly true that in many countries the rural sector has been exploited through low product prices and high taxation, while resources have been wasted on over-blown bureaucracies and on prestige projects in capital cities. Protection of manufacturing sectors has also distorted patterns of development in favour of cities. But resources may also flow the other way: cities produce essential inputs for agriculture; migrants send remittances home to the rural areas; and the bulk of national tax revenue in most countries is generated in the cities. There does not appear to be any clear evidence whether, overall, there is a net transfer of resources from rural areas to the urban areas or vice versa.

The anti-urbanists also point to the very distorted nature of the urbanisation process in most developing countries: highly dependent on foreign capital, over which decisions are made far away; protected and capital-intensive industries in countries which are short of capital; as a result, serious problems of urban unemployment, underemployment, and a large, low-income informal sector; the need for cheap food for the urban masses, effectively subsidised by the rural poor or else imported; the huge costs of meeting the needs for housing and urban infrastructure of the new city dwellers (the costs of which would probably have been much lower had they remained in the rural areas); highly unequal patterns of income and wealth, with public resources being wasted on providing high standards of facilities for the urban elite; serious problems of congestion, pollution and environmental degradation in the cities; the loss of cultural and spiritual values and traditions within the 'urban melting-pot'; and the ever-present threat of civil disorder from a discontented urban population.

Much of this is, of course, true. In some countries, there have been serious distortions within the economy which have encouraged excessive migration to the cities, and have impoverished the rural areas. In some cases, urban migration has caused a loss of agricultural production, as a result of labour shortages at critical periods, although it must also be noted that in almost all countries, the rural population has continued to grow despite urban migration (UN 1988: 180). Certainly there are major questions about how resources are used in the cities, and how the needs of the growing urban population can be met without squandering scarce resources: indeed, these are major themes of this book.

But the anti-urban school has overstated its case. As we have already noted, all the evidence shows that the vast majority of urban migrants consider that they have improved their situation by the move. While the quality of life in cities may leave a lot to be desired, the very fact that population is concentrated means that there are likely to be greater income-earning opportunities, and that many services can be provided better and more cheaply. Just one statistic illustrates this: average infant mortality rates are generally significantly lower in urban areas than in rural areas (Gilbert and Gugler 1982: 53; World Bank 1990b: 30).[9] Nor, with a few exceptions, is there clear evidence that the improvements in the living standards of the urban migrants (and the rest of the urban population) have been achieved at the expense of reduced living standards for the rural population.

It is our view that urbanisation is inherently neither good nor bad. It is not, in itself, a cause of economic growth: rather it is a response to it. Nor does it necessarily disadvantage those outside the cities. There are often, of course, biases in favour of cities, particularly the capital city, not least because this is where political and economic power and decision-making are concentrated. Such biases also occur because of an inadequate consideration of alternative patterns of spatial development (such as small towns and intermediate cities, for example), and because of the unintended consequences of other, non-spatial policies. As Renaud has suggested, government policies should, for the most part, seek to be neutral as between urban and rural areas, neither deliberately encouraging nor discouraging urbanisation (Renaud 1981).

In the now 'developed' world, the process of urban development has long been accepted. The principal objection to the urbanisation process in the developing world has arisen because of the failure to cope with its effects – the failure of governments to meet the basic needs for land, shelter and services of the growing city population. Thus, it is not urban growth itself which is the problem, but the rapid rate of growth, which outpaces the institutional, administrative and financial capacity to cope with it. It is our view that this challenge must be met without wasting resources or distorting the pattern of national development. Continued urban growth in the developing world – and continued rapid growth – is inevitable. What matters is how governments and municipal authorities cope with it. That is the subject of this book.

Can urban growth be controlled?

Whatever the merits of the arguments presented above, most governments have taken the view that they need to control the process of urban growth. Many governments have adopted specific policies to this end, but few, it seems, have achieved any real success.

For many years, South Africa has pursued a strict policy of controlling the movement of the black population. The motive for this policy has much more to do with the government's philosophy of racial superiority than with containing urban growth, but the effect certainly has been to stem the migratory flows. During the period 1970–85, South Africa's urban population grew at the rate of 3.4 per cent per year, significantly

Plate 3 Jakarta from the air: it is not urbanisation itself which is the problem, but the ability or otherwise of governments to cope with it, in terms of ensuring access for all to land, shelter and essential services.

slower than most other African countries. However, the policy has required a very repressive system of 'Pass Laws' for its implementation, with huge political and social costs. Even so, it seems that the controls were far from effective – half of the population of Soweto is said to live there illegally (Gugler 1988: 59).

During the 1970s, the Government of Indonesia attempted to control the growth of Jakarta by the use of residence permits, but with little success it seems. Cambodia, under the brutal Khmer Rouge regime, succeeded in reducing the urban population from 800,000 in 1970 to 650,000 in 1980 (UN 1989: Table A-1), by a policy of enforced rustication – not to mention genocide.

Perhaps the only real 'success story' of urban population control has been China, but even there the experience is quite mixed. A number of policies are involved. First, strict control over family size – the national one-child policy – which has been rigidly enforced, especially in urban areas. Second, an emphasis on development in the rural areas, through investment in agriculture, the location of places of employment outside the major cities, and the planned provision of public services such as education and health. Third, and most significantly, the effective control which the state has over where people live. Since the state controls virtually all employment, as well as most housing and a large part of the essential food supply, it can effectively determine where people live. If people seek to move from their appointed place they risk losing not only their source of income and their housing, but also their food rations and access to services such as education and health. Thus illegal (ie unregistered) residence in an urban area is extremely difficult. In addition to these three policies, there have also been periods, notably during the Cultural Revolution, of enforced rustication of students, intellectuals and other politically suspect groups.

The combined effects of these measures has been to keep urban population growth between 1965 and 1985 down to 2 per cent per year – a remarkable achievement. Indeed, during the 1970s, some cities, such as Shanghai, experienced a reduction in their population (Whyte 1988: 256). Such results have been achieved at considerable costs to society and to individual liberty. Nor is the story entirely one of success even in its own terms. It appears that, despite all the controls, many unemployed young people migrated back to the cities during the 1970s. More recently, with the renewed emphasis on industrialisation and the liberalisation of the economy, the state is no longer able to wield such total control, and the indications are that migration has started to rise sharply (Kirkby 1985). Thus, as in other socialist states, a contradiction is revealed: urban population growth can be limited effectively only by totalitarian controls, yet such controls inhibit the initiative and dynamism which is required for economic growth; liberalisation of the economy inevitably undermines the social, economic and political controls which contained urban growth.[10]

Aside from these special cases, the conventional wisdom in most of the developing world has been that urban migration can be stemmed only by improvements in the standards of living of the rural population. Thus, investment in agriculture, increased prices for agricultural crops, rural land reform, improved access to education and health services, improved rural infrastructure and transport, all have been advocated. In some countries, real progress has been made in these areas, although the investment costs are huge. But it is not clear that such policies necessarily reduce the flow of migrants. Whilst they may improve the quality of rural life, improved rural communications and education, and even increased rural incomes, may in fact increase access to the urban job market and hence stimulate migration. At the same time, improvements in agriculture, notably mechanisation, may reduce the demand for labour. Thus, improving rural living standards, whilst justified in its own right, may not reduce migration.

The UN's report *World Population Trends and Policies* (1988: Tables 82 and 83) lists a large number of policies intended to influence patterns of population distribution, and particularly to curb the growth of large cities: controls on industrial location; loans and tax incentives for investors in rural areas; employment subsidies; the development of growth centres and the promotion of other small settlements; land colonisation schemes; and so on. Most governments appear to be adopting at least some of these policy measures, but how far any of them have had any real effect on the pattern of urban growth is unclear. There certainly appears to have been little evaluation of the impact of such policies (Tolley and Thomas 1987: 9).[11]

Should governments intervene in urban development?

As we have seen from the preceding sections, the phenomenal growth of cities in the developing world poses a huge challenge to the governments of the countries concerned, and specifically to the planners and managers of the cities involved. In posing this as a challenge, there is an implicit assumption that governments should somehow intervene in order to control and organise the situation. Yet this begs two fundamental questions. The first is whether governments should, in principle, seek to intervene in the process of urban development, or whether they should simply leave the process to the 'self-regulating forces of the market'. The second is whether governments have the skills and abilities to intervene in the process of urban development in a way which succeeds in producing a better outcome. Casual observation of what happens in many cities in the developing world (and indeed in the developed world) suggests that they may not. Certainly, much government intervention in urban development has been singularly inappropriate and unsatisfactory. However, much has been learnt over the years, and one of the purposes of this book is to review that experience and to try to identify how government intervention can be made more appropriate and effective.

We return, therefore, to the first question: should governments intervene in the urban development process? In one sense, this is a non-issue, since all governments intervene in the process of urban development, whether directly through systems of urban planning and management, or indirectly, through interventions in the wider economic system which have consequences for urban development. Not even the most *laissez-faire* administration in today's world would consider ceasing completely to intervene in the economic system. Nevertheless, the issue of principle still needs to be addressed.

The essential justification for government intervention in urban development, as elsewhere in the economic system, is the failure of the market mechanism to provide an outcome which is satisfactory to society as a whole. Whilst the market mechanism offers considerable benefits as a system of economic management, it frequently does not produce a socially desirable outcome. There are a number of reasons for this. The first is that markets may not be competitive, so that market power rests in the hands of a few – even a single – supplier. In the case of certain urban services, there may be a 'natural monopoly' where competition is unrealistic: piped water supplies are an obvious example. In such cases, it is normally considered unacceptable to allow an 'unaccountable' private supplier to control such services, unless there is an adequate regulatory framework to protect the public interest. Urban land markets may also be highly imperfect, with a limited number of owners able to exert considerable power over the market.

The second reason is the existence of 'externalities'. Externalities arise where the pattern of benefits and costs of a particular activity to the individual(s) concerned do not match the pattern of benefits and costs to society as a whole. These externalities may be negative – one person's activities may adversely affect another, or positive – the benefits to society as a whole of a particular activity may exceed the private benefits. The nature of cities, with their high densities of population, means that negative externalities are likely to be a significant problem. Obvious examples are disposal of waste, atmospheric pollution from industries, traffic congestion, and construction of buildings on neighbouring land. Positive externalities are also common, and when combined with difficulties of excluding non-payers, mean that certain facilities which are vital to society as a whole are unlikely to be privately profitable. As a result, such facilities will not be provided by the private market, at least not on the scale or in the manner required by society. Obvious examples are roads, drainage, street lighting, parks and fire prevention services. Thus, because of externalities, government intervention is generally considered to be necessary, whether in the form of regulatory controls over the private sector, or direct public provision of certain services.

Plate 4   Housing built on 'Smokey Mountain' – Manila's vast refuse heap: it is clear that market forces alone cannot be relied upon to provide basic human needs or to deal with environmental problems.

The third reason relates to the uneven distribution of income and wealth. Within all societies, wealth is unequally distributed, not only in terms of the private ownership of land and capital, but also in terms of the distribution of human skills and capacities. The market mechanism tends to perpetuate these inequalities of wealth, as incomes are distributed according to the marginal products of the factors of production.

Indeed, the market tends to reinforce these inequalities, through the differences in bargaining power which result from differences in wealth and monopoly power over capital. As a result, the poor may become steadily poorer, until they are unable to obtain enough even to survive. Thus, it has generally been seen as the role of the state to protect the poor from being further disadvantaged by the operations of the market, and to redress at least some of the inequalities in income and wealth.

For all these reasons, it is clear that the market on its own will not produce an outcome which is satisfactory to society as a whole. Thus, the question is not whether the state should intervene, but rather to what extent it should intervene, and what form that intervention should take. The extent and nature of intervention in the urban sector will be discussed in the following section. It is not clear, however, that government intervention can actually resolve all the problems created by the failure of the market: hence the second question posed at the beginning of this section – can government intervention in urban development be effective? This is a theme which underlies much of the discussion in this book.

The scope for government intervention in the urban system

Five broad areas of government intervention may be identified. The first is **providing general protection of the public**. This includes such things as maintenance of public order and the rule of law, and the protection of life, human rights, and property rights. No society, and no system of market relations, can function without these things. Such matters are generally regarded as the responsibilities of national governments, and apply equally in rural and urban areas.

The second is **regulating the activities of the private sector** in the public interest. Such regulation is most commonly in the form of administrative controls, but may also include the use of incentives and disincentives, through taxation and pricing systems, to influence private decisions. Within the urban sector, this would include the regulation of the use of land and of the construction and use of buildings. It would also include the control of pollution and other forms of public nuisance. It might also include regulation of private business activities and the protection of consumer interests. Such regulation may be carried out either by national or by municipal authorities, or both, but is generally carried out within a framework of national legislation.

The third area is the **provision of public services**, in those cases where the private sector either does not provide them at all, or does not provide them in a manner which is satisfactory to society as a whole. This may include the provision of infrastructure such as roads, drainage, water, sanitation and housing. It may also include routine services such as public transport, waste disposal, education, health services and recreational facilities. Urban services are most commonly provided by

municipal authorities, but some may be provided by national governments and others by parastatal agencies. However, such services need
not be provided directly by the public sector at all. Instead, the public
authorities may choose to contract the provision of the service to a
private company, or to the local community. Alternatively, it may use its
regulatory powers and/or subsidies to encourage direct provision of an
appropriate type of service by the private sector (Roth 1987).

The fourth area is what might be called the **developmental function**.
Apart from any direct provision of infrastructure and services to meet
intrinsic needs, the government may use its resources instrumentally in
order to promote economic development and employment creation by
the private sector. This development function may include the co-ordination of development activities (both public and private), the use of
regulatory powers to encourage new businesses, and the selective use of
public expenditure in order to lever resources from the private sector. In
the case of urban development, this is essentially the role of the municipal authorities, although national governments may also be involved.

The fifth area concerns **redistribution of income and wealth**. This is
normally a function of national governments through such mechanisms
as progressive taxation and subsidy policies, although local governments may administer social security transfer payments and often have
residual responsibility for assisting the poorest. There are, however,
important distributional implications for urban authorities in terms of
the types of services they provide, to whom they provide them, the
prices which they charge for them and the types of taxes they levy.
Municipal authorities may specifically seek to alleviate poverty by subsidising services consumed by the poor, such as water supply and primary health care. Governments may also seek to legislate to protect the
poor from exploitation in such areas as employment and wages, access
to land and land tenure rights.

One other area of public sector intervention which should be mentioned, because of its significance in certain parts of the world, is that
of **production**. Marxism calls for public ownership of the means of
production, distribution and exchange. Consequently, in many socialist
countries (and in some non-socialist developing countries), a large proportion of the production sector is under direct governmental control,
whether at national or local level. Clearly, such an arrangement offers
the potential for a high degree of public sector influence over the pattern
of development, including the development of cities. However, it cannot be assumed that the objectives of those managing public sector
enterprises will necessarily accord with those of city managers: indeed,
there is enormous scope for conflict here. The dramatic shift away from
public ownership of the means of production in recent years, including
within the former communist countries of eastern Europe, has rendered
this aspect rather less significant than before.[12]

It is clear that each of these areas of government intervention involves
choices: choices about what should be done, about how it should be
done and about who should do it. It is clear, too, that government
interventions do not produce unequivocal results: the outcomes of inter-

vention may be uncertain, and there may be disagreement about the extent of gains and losses which result. Moreover, the consequences of intervention will be differentially distributed: there will be gainers and losers, both in terms of individuals and in terms of groups, social classes and so on. Thus, conflicts, like choices, lie at the heart of public policy-making. Some of these issues will be explored further in Chapter 2, as they relate to interventions in the field of urban development. Before that, though, it is useful to view the debate about government intervention within the context of the changing world economic and political environment.

The changing economic and political context

The principles and practices of government intervention, and their application to the planning and management of cities, have evolved over time. They have evolved within social, economic and political environments which have themselves been evolving. They have also been influenced by changing ideas, ideologies and fashions.

Over the past century – and for much longer than that in many cases – there has been a steady expansion in the role of the state within national economies. In 1932, public expenditure in Britain represented 29 per cent of GNP; half a century later, it represented 54 per cent (C V Brown and Jackson 1986: 2). Similar trends can be found in most countries: not quite so rapid in some other developed countries, but more rapid in most socialist countries. In most developing countries, the share of the public sector in the economy remains much lower (India 18 per cent; Kenya 29 per cent; Chile 33 per cent, for example), but has been growing in most cases, at least until the mid-1980s (World Bank 1990b: Table 11).

In Europe and North America, the growth in the role of the public sector during the second half of the nineteenth century was a response to growing awareness of the failure of the market system to provide satisfactorily for all. In particular, reformers saw the need to provide education and improve public health.[13] Such needs were particularly apparent in the cities, where inadequate housing, sanitation and water supplies caused disease and death. Thus, municipal authorities in these countries were spurred on to invest in water supplies, sewers, roads and, later on, in public housing and town planning.

The authorities which were awakening to the need for public investment at home had rather less concern about conditions in their colonies. For most imperial powers, interest in their colonies was limited to what could be extracted from them through trade. Thus their objectives were to maintain public order, to provide the necessary infrastructure to facilitate trade, and to provide a pleasing environment for the colonial settlers, traders and .administrators. There was generally little concern with the conditions of the indigenous population. In some colonies, there arose a belated recognition of the need for economic development and for services for the local population, but in most cases little was done before the tide of independence swept out the colonial masters.

Newly independent governments faced a huge task of national development, often with very limited financial resources and skilled manpower. In many cases, they inherited a pattern of urban development which was ill-suited to their needs, and often modelled on some far-away city in Europe. Independence also meant, in most cases, the sudden withdrawal of technical skills needed to run the cities, and a dramatic surge in urban population, as a result of the removal of colonial restrictions on movement and the opening up of job opportunities. Infrastructure, designed to serve a small colonial elite, was overwhelmed, and often disintegrated through lack of maintenance. Cities grew without any planned framework, and without the resources to expand basic infrastructure or services. Municipal governments often lost what autonomy they had, as the role of the central state in economic planning and development expanded, with its emphasis on building national unity and central control over the use of scarce resources.

The 1950s and 1960s were decades of confidence in the prospects for economic development in the newly independent nations. There was a strong belief that public sector planning could bring about economic development. Observing the successful transformation of the Soviet economy during the previous half century, development theorists stressed the need for planned investment in industry, particularly state-owned industry, as the key to economic growth.

The late 1960s and the 1970s saw a growing disillusionment with this approach. It became increasingly obvious that conventional economic growth strategies had not resulted in the benefits being enjoyed by all. Excessive centralisation of development effort had created 'apoplexy at the centre and anaemia at the edges' (Rodwin and Sanyal 1987: 10). In many countries, the position of the poor had worsened, and the squalid conditions of city slum-dwellers and squatters were plain for all to see. There followed a shift in thinking away from growth as the primary aim, and industrialisation as the primary strategy, towards an emphasis on equity and redistribution. Poverty-focused aid programmes and 'basic needs' strategies became key approaches for the donor agencies.

At the same time, others (eg Frank 1966; Dos Santos 1970) pointed to the continued dependence of the less developed nations on developed nations, ensuring that their under-developed status was maintained. The experience, particularly in Latin America, of attempts to industrialise through import-substitution had merely reinforced countries' continued dependence on imported capital and technology, and on multinational corporations. For some, this was seen as an inevitable consequence of capitalist exploitation. In a number of countries, revolutionary changes saw the emergence of socialist regimes, for example in Ethiopia, Angola, Mozambique, Nicaragua, Cambodia and Vietnam, although similar movements in other countries (eg Chile, El Salvador, Malaysia, Indonesia) were reversed, with or without external intervention.

The 1980s saw a profound shift to the right in world politics. This shift occurred not only in capitalist, developed countries, but also in both communist states and developing countries. The world recession at the beginning of the 1980s, combined with a growing disillusionment with the results of state intervention, led to significant reductions in the scale and nature of public sector activities in many countries. National economic planning went into abeyance, public sector industries were privatised, public spending was reduced, and many of the controls on the private sector were removed (Toye 1987; Aylen 1987). Of course, the pace and extent of change has varied enormously from one country to another. The obsessive ideological commitment in Mrs Thatcher's Britain to free enterprise and the market has not been matched in other European countries. For many of the developing countries, reductions in state intervention have been forced on them by financial collapse and by international institutions such as the IMF, themselves committed to the 'new neo-classical economics' (Killick 1989). In eastern Europe, the dramatic collapse of the centrally planned economies at the end of the decade revealed further evidence of the contradictions of extensive public sector control and led to a wholesale rejection of central economic planning.

During the 1980s there also emerged an increasing awareness of the problems of the environment, and of the lasting damage being done to the global ecological system. The problems of atmospheric and water pollution, damage to the ozone layer and consequent global warming, progressive desertification, destruction of the tropical rain forests, and depletion of non-renewable fossil fuels, all threaten the future of life on this earth. Yet so far, little has been done to tackle any of these problems. They pose a direct challenge to the current ideological orthodoxy which favours maximum economic growth and the deregulation of the private sector. A growing recognition of this fact, combined with an increased awareness of the widening gap between the rich and the poor, and of the terrible position of the world's poorest, is beginning to force a rethinking of the orthodoxies of the 1980s (Cornia *et al.* 1987; Onimode 1988; Killick 1989).

In discussing these very broad, global shifts in thinking, it must be acknowledged that there are enormous differences between countries, and even between regions and cities within countries. A few governments (and even some local authorities) have pursued policies and ideologies which are in marked contrast to worldwide trends. However, for cities in the developing world, it is often difficult to resist the pressures exerted by the donor agencies to conform to current fashions. Donor agencies, such as the World Bank, have considerable leverage, especially since they may be the only source for the capital which a city urgently requires in order to undertake essential investment in infrastructure and services. Donor agencies are prone to frequent shifts in fashion. These shifts are not always based on adequate analysis of either the real nature of the problems or of the experiences of past interventions. Indeed, they are more often than not the consequence of changing ideas and political pressures within the donor nations. These changing fashions may also be quite confusing to recipient governments. It is our view that changing ideas and approaches need to be thoroughly evaluated, and that, given the enormous diversity of cultures, conditions, political positions, legal and administrative systems represented among the rapidly urbanising countries of the world, approaches and 'solutions' need to be tailored carefully to particular situations.

The scope of this book

The aim of this book is to provide a bridge between theory and practice; to review the performance of urban planning and management over the years in the light of both theory and comparative experience; and, on the basis of that analysis, to suggest approaches for the future.

In **Chapter 2**, we examine what is meant by urban planning and management, what these tasks involve, and how the performance of these activities can be judged. In **Chapter 3**, we review the evolution of ideas about urban planning and management, and the current conventional wisdom available to city planners and managers.

In **Chapter 4**, Michael Mattingly examines the crucial role of urban land markets, how planning can influence the processes and forces within those markets, and therefore the vital importance of planners and managers having a better understanding of urban land markets. In **Chapter 5**, Jim Amos looks at how urban services are provided and managed, and how the performance of those services can be improved.

In **Chapter 6**, Kenneth Davey examines the alternative institutional arrangements for urban planning and management, and in particular what the role of local government should be. In **Chapter 7**, Richard Batley looks at the political context in which the processes of urban planning and management are carried out, and the question of how political control is exercised over these processes. Carole Rakodi extends this analysis in **Chapter 8** with an examination of the issue of participation (or the lack of it) in the urban planning process, particularly by the poor and by women.

In **Chapter 9**, Patrick McAuslan examines the issues involved in the application of law to urban planning and management: the assumptions and interests which underlie urban law, the role which law plays in shaping the process of urban development, and the principles which should guide urban law reform.

In **Chapter 10**, we seek to draw some conclusions about the current state of the debates about urban planning and management, about what we have learnt from past experience, and about which approaches offer the greatest potential for guiding the planning and management of the world's fast growing cities in the future.

Notes

1. The data in this section are taken from UN sources, notably *Prospects of World Urbanization 1988* (UN 1989). A number of caveats are needed. First, the distinction between 'developing' and 'developed' world is a rather

crude shorthand which is open to challenge. For the purposes of this chapter, 'developing' refers to Africa, Latin America and the Caribbean, the Middle East, Asia excluding Japan, and the Pacific; 'developed' covers Europe (west and east, including the former Soviet Union), North America, Japan and Australasia. However, it must be recognised that there are countries within that definition of 'developing', for example, Hong Kong, Singapore, South Korea, which have significantly higher standards of living than a number of countries classified as 'developed'. Second, the definition of 'urban' is not precise and may vary from country to country, thereby affecting the statistics on urban population. In particular, there is the question of where urban boundaries are drawn, and the effects of changes in these boundaries over time. Third, the statistics on urban population and population growth must be treated with caution, since the national data from which they are derived may be subject to considerable error. In particular, comparative international figures used in UN publications are adjusted to common years by interpolation, while nearly all figures for years since 1981 are extrapolations (see Hardoy and Satterthwaite 1986b for a further discussion of these issues). However, the purpose of this section is to give some broad impressions rather than a detailed examination of statistics.

2. Little is really known about urban growth rates in the 1980s. These figures are based on extrapolations using census data in most cases from 1970/71 and 1980/81. The impact on migration rates of economic difficulties and structural adjustment in particular countries is not known but may have tended to reduce them.

3. The figures in Table 1.6 should be treated with caution, because of variations between countries in the definitions used. Also, since most of the statistics derive ultimately from government sources, one must be sceptical about whether some of the countries recording high levels of access to safe water and sanitation are really achieving the levels they claim.

4. This does not mean, as Gilbert has rightly pointed out (Gilbert and Gugler 1982: 25), that urban poverty is necessarily becoming worse in an overall sense: although the numbers of urban poor have increased, the proportion of the urban population living below the poverty line has decreased in most countries, while living standards for most people – including the poor – in most countries have improved steadily (if very slowly) over the years. There are important exceptions, of course, particularly in certain countries in Africa where real urban incomes have declined in the past decade or so due to economic stagnation and structural adjustment (J Harriss 1989: 187).

5. A proportion of the statistical growth of urban population may also be accounted for by changes in urban boundaries.

6. The comparative advantage of cities may, however, be less significant now than was the case in the past: the advent of new technology and new means of communication, together with emphasis on 'flexible specialisation' in production, have all tended to reduce the importance of physical proximity.

7. Kelley and Williamson also conclude from their statistical analysis that it is the differences in productivity growth between sectors which has been the main determinant of city growth (1987: 43).

8. By contrast, Tolley and Thomas found no statistically significant relationship between the *rate* of growth of per capita income and the *rate* of growth of the urban population during the period 1960–80 (1987: 4).

9. It must be said, though, that the evidence is not unequivocal: for example,

       infant mortality rates in certain city slum areas may be higher than those in rural areas (B Harriss 1987).

10. There is one interesting, and perhaps unintended effect of certain recent reforms in China: the 'responsibility system' in agriculture has resulted in many peasants having a surplus to invest in businesses, and it seems that they tend to locate these business activities in small and medium-sized towns and cities, since they are not permitted to travel to the larger cities.

11. South Korea is a partial exception (see H-Y Lee 1989; Auty 1990). For a fuller discussion on the evidence on the role of towns and secondary cities, and of policies to stimulate their development, see Hardoy and Satterthwaite (1986a); Kammeier and Swan (1984); Rondinelli (1983); UNCRD (1982); and UNCHS (1985).

12. Even in China, where the vast majority of production remains within the public sector, the trend towards decentralised and autonomous management of state enterprises means that the state is no longer able to control all decisions within the production sector.

13. Sceptics might see less altruistic reasons: Marxists would point to capitalism's need for a literate and healthy workforce; 'public choice' theorists would argue that the growth of the public sector has more to do with the coalition of interests between public servants, politicians and certain client groups, rather than with the real needs of society as a whole. These are large areas of debate which are beyond the scope of this volume, but see Briggs (1963); Castells (1977); Niskanen (1971); Tullock (1987a and 1987b).

CHAPTER 2

Planning and managing urban development

Nick Devas and Carole Rakodi

What do we mean by urban planning and management?

This book is about the planning and management of cities. But what do we mean by the terms 'planning' and 'management'? Unfortunately, there are no agreed definitions. Indeed, there is a bewildering array of possible definitions, varying according to the academic or professional background or the particular point of view of the writer. In order to identify some working concepts, it is useful to review briefly the three broad traditions which may be said to make up the current approach to urban management in the developing world. These are town planning, economic development planning and municipal management.

The origins of town planning derive principally from architecture and public health engineering. Historically, town planning was concerned with the orderly, aesthetic and healthy layout of buildings and land uses. Its primary focus has always been a spatial one. Thus Keeble, in a classic textbook, defined town and country planning as 'the art and science of ordering the use of land and the character and siting of buildings and communication routes so as to secure and maximise the practicable degree of economy, convenience and beauty' (Keeble 1964: 1). Although such exclusively physical preoccupations have tended to give way to a wider view of the task, this primary concern with physical development still typifies the planning approach in many countries, particularly many former colonies.

During the 1960s and 1970s, many town planners sought to adopt a more 'rational', systematic and comprehensive approach to the planning tasks and to the evaluation of alternatives. Thus, Davidoff and Reiner refer to planning as 'a process for determining appropriate future actions through a sequence of choices' (1962), while Faludi defines planning as 'the application of scientific method – however crude – to policy-making' (1973: 1).

Over the years, 'town planning' has come to recognise much wider concerns with the economic, social, political factors which affect urban development. Thus, for Franklin, 'Physical planning is concerned with the design, growth and management of the physical environment, in accordance with predetermined and agreed policies, whereby balanced social and economic objectives may be achieved' (1979: 5). More recently, Taylor and Williams (1982) defined planning as 'a mechanism to provide an environment for living which all may desire but which would not be attained through the fragmented decisions of individuals. It is a means to organise the public goods of society' (1982: 23).

The second contributory strand is national development planning. This has its roots in economic theories of development, as well as in economic modelling and 'scientific' planning methodology. This form of planning drew particularly on the experience of the former Soviet Union, and placed great faith in the planner's ability to shape the economy and society ('planning as the purposeful direction of human activity' – Griffin and Enos 1970: 6). Tinbergen identified the 'three chief elements of modern planned economic policy: looking ahead, co-ordination and attainment of deliberate aims' (1967: 44). Waterston defined planning as 'in essence, an organised, conscious, and continual attempt to select the best possible available alternatives to achieve specific goals' (1965: 26), while Franklin defines planning, in this broad sense, as 'a process, flexible and subject to change, which attempts in advance to arrange for the effective deployment of resources in relation to human need' (1979: 8).

Like town planning, national economic planning as it evolved has tended to incorporate broader social and political aspects. It has also developed a spatial dimension in the form of regional planning. Both town planning and national economic planning have moved on from a primary concern with the preparation of plan documents to a broader concern with the implementation of those plans, and with those forces which influence and determine the patterns of development. As a result, 'planning' has come to be more closely related with the third contributory strand: municipal management.

The roots of municipal management lie in the traditions of public administration, and particularly the Weberian ideals of a 'legal, rational, authority' (Wallis 1989: 2). Historically, the main concerns of national public administration were the maintenance of public order and the protection of the interests of those in power. At the municipal level, this was often mixed with elitist and professional concerns with promoting civic improvement and economic prosperity. Gradually, as democratic influences prevailed within western nations, the concerns of public administration widened to a take account of the interests and needs of the ordinary citizens, at least as filtered through the prevailing power structures. Green defines urban administration as 'a system of public organisational interactions, focusing on a single urban area (however defined) that results in the performance of essential/important services and/or functions' (H Green 1975: 353). Sazanami refers to urban management in terms of the mobilization of human and financial resources through government and non-government organisations to achieve societal goals (1984: 6).

Yet the practice of public administration in much of the developing world continues to be dominated by the interpretation and enforcement of legislation, with regulation and control of the activities of the private sector, and with routine procedures about the provision of established services (Sivaramakrishnan and Green 1986: 49). Only recently have new concepts of public sector management, many of them derived from the private sector and particularly from the United States, led to a more positive and innovative approach towards resolving urban problems and improving urban conditions. This more proactive approach calls for the integration of urban planning and management, as indicated by Clarke: 'The management of urban development to meet city level and national objectives of economic growth and improved equity requires an integrated process of planning, investment (public and private), construction, operation, maintenance and rehabilitation' (1989: 9).

Box 2.1 Evolving views of urban planning

'In recent years theory and practice have increasingly concentrated on urban and regional planning as a dynamic, organizational process of pursuing moving goals and objectives in conditions of uncertainty and accelerating change. This perception has encouraged a shift of emphasis from town planning as conventionally understood (that is designing of comprehensive land use plans) towards the initiation of wide-ranging and policy-oriented research and analysis requiring contrasting and changing clusters, patterns and flows of activity not necessarily focused on land uses. This differently orientated activity may in fact be concerned mainly with defining development problems and goals in the economic and social context; such activity includes the design and appraisal of related action projects and extends to learning by assessing performance' (Sivaramakrishnan and Green 1986: 56)

For the purposes of this book, we shall interpret the terms planning and management very broadly, to cover the full range of governmental interventions in the development and day-to-day operations of the city. The purpose of such interventions is, of course, to bring about an improved situation, but that immediately raises some important questions:

1 An improvement compared to what?
2 Who decides what is an improvement?
3 An improvement for whom? (especially since the interventions may result in some losing as well as some gaining)
4 Can we be sure that the interventions will have the outcomes we expect?

We shall not attempt to deal with these questions at this stage since they are the themes which underlie much of the discussion in the rest of this book.

It is apparent from the discussion above that we are not here drawing a clear distinction between the activities of 'urban planning' and 'urban management', but rather using the terms in tandem. If a distinction has to be drawn between urban planning and management, it may be that urban planning is concerned primarily with anticipating and preparing for the future, and particularly with the spatial and land-use dimensions of urban development; meanwhile, urban management is concerned more with the immediate operations of a range of public services, and with a wide variety of public interventions which affect urban conditions as a whole. This distinction is, however, far from being clearcut: what matters more is how these two elements can effectively be integrated.

There is one further element which has yet to be mentioned: that is public policy-making. Policy-making is essentially the process by which decisions are made about the objectives to be pursued and the actions to be taken in order to realise those objectives.[1] Within a democratic system, policy-making is the role usually assigned to elected politicians, while the task of management is to implement those policies and actions. However, the boundaries between planning, policy-making and management are far from precise. They represent, perhaps, different dimensions or aspects of the same general task. Just as traditional urban land-use planning has tended to move into the sphere of urban management, and traditional municipal administration has tended to move into the realm of development planning (Sivaramakrishnan and Green 1986: 50), so both urban planning and management have become increasingly concerned with policy-making. In all cases, though, the essential task is to mobilise and utilise a range of resources (finance, land, personnel and so on) to achieve the objective of improved urban living conditions for all concerned.

Lest it appear that this discussion reduces urban planning to no more than a generalised form of administration applied to cities, it may be worth re-emphasising the traditional concern of urban planning with land and with the spatial dimension. Land is not only one of the key resources to be utilised efficiently, but also a resource in respect of which actions tend to endure. Money may be spent and disappear, but more can always be raised next year. Manpower may be wasted, but mistakes can be rectified next time. But once land is built upon it cannot easily be reclaimed. The problems created by misuse of land remain to haunt us. Hence, a concern with land, its use and its physical development must remain central to the planning and management of urban development.

The planning/policy-making/management cycle

Traditionally, the planning process has been regarded as a linear sequence of survey–analysis–plan–implementation. Clearly, though, such a simple linear process misrepresents what is a considerably more complex, cyclical process. The cycle of activities involved in the planning/policy/management process may include:

Survey and analysis

- estimation of current and projected needs
- survey of the existing situation
- analysis of economic and development potential
- identification of available resources (finance, land, personnel, etc.)
- evaluation of results of past interventions (feedback)
- responses from the public.

Development of strategies and policies

- clarification of goals and objectives
- identification of key issues/problems
- identification of alternative strategies/policies
- analysing the costs and benefits of alternatives
- identification of the likely consequences of adopting the various alternative courses of action
- prioritisation of alternatives
- selection of alternatives which achieve the optimum balance between goal achievement and resource utilisation.

Implementation

- identification of implementing agencies
- mobilisation of the necessary resources
- specification and co-ordination of activities
- specification of programmes and projects
- preparation of programme budgets
- specification of terms for implementation
- specification of performance measures and targets
- supervision of routine operation and maintenance functions.

Monitoring and evaluation

- regular monitoring of performance against targets
- ex-post evaluation of performance and impact
- feedback of results into previous stages through an effective information system.

Three important points should be noted about the above model. First, whilst these various stages may appear to represent a logical cycle of activities, they are not necessarily sequential in practice. In most cases, the process must be an iterative one and may need to involve short-circuits. Given limited resources and the pressure for immediate action, it is clear that it may not be possible to pursue the various stages of survey, analysis, development of alternatives and evaluation to their logical conclusion. Indeed, it may be very important to compress many of these stages in the interests of providing a rapid response to pressing problems. There is, however, a real danger that vital stages in reaching a satisfactory solution are replaced by a series of crisis-responses. Meanwhile, the failure to monitor and evaluate outcomes may mean that mistakes are repeated.

The second point concerns uncertainty. Given the paucity of data available in most developing cities, and the poor quality of much of those data, it may be very difficult to determine the scale of needs, and the level of resources available. It may be even more difficult to predict the precise outcomes of proposed government interventions, or even to assess the outcomes of past or current interventions. Risks of error are very high. It is thus particularly important to incorporate within the planning/management cycle an effective system of monitoring and feedback. This needs to be an integral part of an information system which provides relevant information for policy-making and planning in a timely manner. Given the limited resources available, however, any information system needs to be relatively simple and to concentrate on the key issues. An alternative strategy for dealing with the problems of uncertainty is the adoption of a flexible and incremental approach to problems, which permits not only the steady consolidation of initial success but also modifications to the plan in the event of failure.

The third point concerns choices and conflicts. As we have already noted, public policy-making involves choices about goals, strategies and actions. It also involves conflicts between individuals and groups, particularly between those who gain and those who lose from particular policies or actions. These issues will be discussed further in a later section of this chapter. What matters here is that the existence of such choices and conflicts should be recognised, and that there should be legitimate processes for considering the issues involved and for reaching decisions about the policies and actions to be pursued.

The instruments of urban planning and management

If the ultimate aim of urban planning and management is to improve conditions of life in the city, what instruments do planners and managers have at their disposal to achieve this end? In theory, at least, a wide range of tools is available, as the list in Box 2.2 suggests.

In practice, of course, not all of the tools listed in Box 2.2 will be available in any particular situation, either because the legislative powers do not exist, or because there is no capacity to implement the power. In many cases, tools may exist on paper, but there is insufficient administrative or legal resources, or insufficient political will, to enforce the instruments effectively. It is the task of urban management to mar-

shal the instruments which are available in a way which achieves the
policy objectives most effectively.

Box 2.2   A range of instruments potentially available to the urban planner/manager

- public ownership of land (including open-market land acquisition, compulsory acquisition, land nationalisation)
- legal regulation of private land ownership/tenure
- legal powers to control private use and development of land
- legal powers and fiscal penalties to control public nuisances (pollution and so on)
- legal controls over vehicles and transportation
- government provision of infrastructure
- government construction of housing
- government construction of other public buildings/facilities
- direct government provision of public services (water, refuse
  collection, transport, etc.) or the contracting of these services
  from other agencies/private sector
- regulation of private provision of public services (transport, commercial activities, etc.)
- taxation of land and land development
- recovery of the costs of public services from beneficiaries
- subsidies for public or private provision of public services.

The above instruments could be categorised in terms of function: regulatory mechanisms, fiscal mechanisms (taxation and subsidies), and direct
public provision or ownership. They could also be categorised in terms of
subject area or element: land/land-use, public services and infrastructure.
These alternative classifications are indicated in the matrix below.

| | ELEMENTS | | |
MECHANISMS	Land use	Public services	Infrastructure
Regulation	/	(/)	
Fiscal measures*	/	(/)	(/)
Direct public ownership/provision	/	/	/

/ = conventional mechanisms
(/) = less common methods (although increasingly being used)
* Fiscal measures include the use of subsidies and taxation where the main
  purpose is to influence the decisions through incentives rather than to
  raise revenue.

In the foregoing discussion, 'urban management' has been referred to as
if there were a clearly defined locus of such management authority. In
practice, in many cities in the developing (and developed) world, there
is no clear locus of management authority. Indeed, that is frequently one

of the fundamental problems confronting rapidly growing cities. Responsibility for city management may be divided between a local government (or several local governments), a central government department (or several departments), and a variety of public sector agencies. Private sector and non-governmental organisations may also play a significant role. Institutional arrangements vary enormously, depending on the local context (Rakodi 1990b), and there is no ideal arrangement. The question of institutional arrangements for urban government will be considered in more detail by Kenneth Davey in Chapter 6.

Choices and conflicts

The classical, Wilsonian view of administration is that of the neutral and disinterested execution of decisions made by elected policy-makers (Wallis 1989: 25). Similarly, the traditional view of urban planning is that of a neutral, technical exercise in which the planner is regarded as an objective expert, who is able to recommend professionally determined solutions to technical problems (Keeble 1964: 1). In such a model, the task of making choices belongs to the democratically elected politician, to whom the planner can provide neutral, professional advice on the technical merits of those choices.

Increasingly, though, such idealised models have come to be seen as inadequate (B C Smith 1987; Low 1991). The problems confronting the urban planner and manager are not simply technical ones, to which there is an objective solution. Most of the issues, in fact, involve political choices: choices between competing interests or claims; choices between alternative policies with varying consequences for different groups; choices between alternative uses for scarce resources. Thus, urban planning and management are not about producing a technically perfect plan or devising a policy to bring about an ideal situation in which all will benefit equally. Rather it is about assessing conflicting claims and making choices.

Nor can the urban manager and planner in most developing countries hide behind the protective shield of an elective democracy in which the political choices of the population are transmitted through a decision-making system made up of elected representatives. In many developing countries (and some developed countries too) those in power are not in any real way accountable to the population. Whilst the position of the planner or manager may still be that of a servant of such unaccountable decision-makers, the former cannot claim that the political choices being made by them represent the will of the people.

More than that, the neat division between political decisions on the one hand and the professional advice of the planner and the neutral execution of those decisions by the administrator on the other, which might appear to exist within a western democracy, may not exist in practice in many developing countries. Planners and urban managers in the developing world are likely to be making many of the important choices directly. This may be because of limited resources to examine the various possible alternatives; because of the inadequacies of the mechanisms by which the recognised decision-makers can consider the choices; or because the planner/manager is simply expected to get on and make the decisions anyway. Thus, in practice, such a person is often making the effective choices about resource allocations, about competing claims, and about the distribution of costs and benefits of policies and programmes. In such circumstances, their role cannot be regarded as the exercise of a neutral professional or technical expertise.

In the planning and management of the city, there are clearly many different individuals and groups with interests which compete and conflict. Each may have its own particular agenda, and may pursue policies or actions for reasons which have more to do with their individual or group interests than with the 'public good'.

First, the most obvious area of conflict is within the political arena, between competing ideologies and parties. Even where, as in a one-party state, such conflicts are not explicit, there clearly are differences of ideology, principle and practical policy which emerge and must be resolved if decisions are to be made. Second, there may be conflicts between politicians, both national and local, which may have little to do with ideology or principle, but may instead be conflicts over the distribution of resources – about who gets what. Such conflicts may be entirely legitimate, as politicians seek to represent the interests of their constituents, or they may be more narrowly concerned with personal political power and vested interests. Motives for seeking political office are complex and may influence political actions in contradictory ways. Third, there is the area of conflict between politicians and officials (Menezes 1985: 61). The conflict may be a demarcation dispute over the boundaries between political decisions and execution – boundaries which are often very unclear. Or they may be conflicts about policy: between the advice of the professional and the judgement of the politician. Or they may be conflicts about vested interests in terms of political power, preservation of position, or the division of spoils. Where the military are involved, there may be further areas of conflict between civilian and military interests.

There may be similar areas of conflict between administrators themselves, between different groups of professionals, and between generalist administrators and professionals. A further source of conflict may arise with the involvement of external consultants, whose advice may be different from that of those within the organisation and may therefore be perceived as threatening by them (Clarke 1985: 51). Consultants may also have their own vested interests, such as the renewal of their contracts.

There may be conflicts between agencies and between departments within organisations. There may be conflicts between central and local government. And there may be conflicts between statutory authorities and voluntary (non-governmental) organisations (NGOs). Once again, these may involve differences of ideology, policy or practice (that is, about what is the best thing to do in a particular situation), or they may be demarcation disputes (that is, about who is responsible for doing what). But even with organisational conflicts, the underlying issue may be one of vested interests of the individuals involved: about power and influence in a particular situation, or about the division of spoils. Again, the involvement of outsiders, such as donor agencies, may enlarge the scope for conflict, not only over the choice of policy or practice, but also in terms of the exercise of power and influence. It is important to recognise that donor agencies are not neutral operators but have their own agenda, and their own constituencies which must be satisfied.

At the risk of over-simplification, the principal areas of potential conflict can be summarised as shown in Box 2.3, although the distinctions are rarely clearcut.

So far, our analysis of interests has confined itself to the government sector. The obvious omission from this discussion is that of 'the people'. However, except in popular mythology, there is no such thing as 'the people'. There are individuals, classes, groups, communities, and popular organisations, each of which may have different and competing

Plates 5 and 6   Urban development and redevelopment involves choices and conflicts: China has achieved considerable success in housing its urban population, but not without cost; the street in Shanghai in the first picture is scheduled for demolition because the authorities regard such houses as unsatisfactory, despite having services which are considerably better than in many other countries; the houses are privately rather than publicly owned; they will be replaced with 'modern' government flats like those in the opposite picture.

interests and ideas. Thus, although everyone may be able to agree that the plan is unsatisfactory, they may not agree on why it is unsatisfactory or what should be done about it. It is therefore impossible in most situations to devise any plan upon which everyone can agree.

One may be able to identify broad groups within society, such as the rich and the poor, though such groups are rarely homogeneous, and the

Box 2.3   Major areas of potential conflict

Major areas of potential conflict	ID	PP	BR	VI
Between politicians	/	/		/
Politicians/administrators		/	/	/
Administrators/professionals		/	/	
Between administrators	/	/	/	
Between professionals	/	/		
External consultants/internal		/	/	/
Between departments		/	/	/
Central government/local government	/	/	/	
Statutory body/voluntary body	/	/	/	/
Donor agency/national government	/	/		/
Public authorities/community	/	/		/
Within communities		/		/

Key: ID – ideological differences
PP – differences over practical policy
BR – issues about boundaries of responsibility
VI – vested interests of individuals (or organisations)

distinction is a relative rather than an absolute one. Using the framework of a class analysis, one may be able to identify dominant classes (capitalists, managers, landlords, traders, bureaucratic bourgeoisie) and dominated classes (proletariat, petty commodity producers and traders, tenants, landless), each of which will have different interests in relation to urban development. However, such a crude class analysis rarely provides a sufficiently precise basis for identifying the nature of the claims which the individuals involved represent. There are ethnic and religious differences, which may be very powerful in terms of how their members perceive the outcomes of public policies. Gender, too, has a profound effect in determining perceived needs, priorities and interests.

There is the division between business interests and residents, although again the distinction may be far from clear. Then, there are those who live in a particular area, who will obviously have strong interests in relation to policies and proposals for their area, although that does not mean that they will all agree – far from it, in most cases. And there are the powerful vested interests involved in land ownership, where the scale of profits involved is such as often to distort the decisions made about the use and development of land.

In all this discussion, three aspects need to be emphasised. First, decisions about competing alternatives are fundamental to the whole process of urban development, as to any other aspect of public policy. Because resources are limited, it is not possible to satisfy everyone, and therefore choices have to be made. Any system of planning and management must incorporate some mechanism for reaching decisions between differing views, competing claims and conflicting interests. Second, there is a huge scope for conflict between the various groups, organisations and individuals involved, over issues of principle, practice and priorities, over boundaries of responsibility, and over vested interests. These areas of conflict need to be recognised and mechanisms established to resolve them. Third, such conflicts may not always be apparent or explicit, particularly in certain cultures, or where individuals are pursuing personal interests which may be different from those of the organisations of which they are a part. Failure to address these latent conflicts may mean that plans and programmes which appear to be agreed are not actually implemented.

Box 2.4   Case examples of conflicts

In Trinidad and Tobago ... the problem of planning was perceived by the planners to be a lack of order and discipline especially amongst the rural population who wished, contrary to the National Physical Development Plan, to subdivide their land, build houses on the subdivision to keep the family together in accordance with traditional beliefs, thereby contributing to ribbon development and increasing the cost of providing services. Thus the need was perceived as being for tougher enforcement powers and a way round political and legal blockages to their use. At the same time, at the political level, the problem was perceived as undue rigidity of development control and overmighty planners, so the need was perceived as being one for the creation of mechanisms to enable other political points of view to have an input into the planning system. (McAuslan 1989: 43)

[In the Turks and Caicos Islands] ... On the surface, the issue of a new [town planning] law was discussed in terms of the need for control over the development process, in the interests of the environment and proper land use. The hidden agenda was: who was going to control the control, who would make the decisions in land allocation and applications for development permission? Power and wealth were involved. From the colonial side, it began to emerge that the new law was seen as providing an opportunity to shift decision-making from elected or appointed Belongers to colonial officials. (McAuslan 1989: 15)

In one project we had spent a considerable amount of time trying to improve the hideous lot of the residents of a pretty bad housing area. Self-help had been the major feature of our approach which had resulted in getting people to install a water supply and some drainage. A certain community identity had emerged and even a pride. Some residents planted trees for shade and privacy purposes along a strip of land reserved for a public road, whose construction would be many years into the future. The appearance of the edge of the area improved wonderfully, and we were about to attempt some negotiations with the authorities to legitimise this initative when the local authority with whom we had worked as our clients brought a bulldozer to remove the gardens and then sought to fine the impoverished residents. (R Stewart 1989: 18)

In at least two countries bordering the Mediterranean, tourism interest coupled with some recent economic improvement has fuelled the expectation of every coastal landowner, and many inland, of large profits from land sale or development. So strong and indeed numerous are the interests that planning regulations to prohibit development (for example, for conservation reasons) will not be

---

Box 2.4   Case examples of conflicts (*continued*)

brought forward, and 'control' exercised by the planners is limited effectively to the use of building regulations. (R Stewart 1989: 11)

Politicians at the national level [in Jamaica] are not inclined to share power [with those at the local level] for one third of the total population [in Kingston] unless they can exert control when they wish to do so. Control is exerted by whittling away the functions of the Kingston and St Andrews Corporation on the grounds of inefficiency and inability to perform. The management audit showed, however, that the Corporation could not perform because it was not able to access the resources necessary, and also because its institutional framework was not conducive to effective performance. (Knight 1989: 29)

The standards for housing and other infrastructure services [in Kenya] have been set too high and unrealistic. Most of these standards are set to western expectations and ignore the socio-economic circumstances in the country. It has now been accepted that the standards set by the building code are too high and it has been under review. However, although the housing by-law study was completed at the end of 1980, the recommendations have not been promulgated into a code. This suggests reluctance on the part of the authorities to put into practice the controversial lower building standards. Housing schemes designed for the low income earners end up being too expensive because of the unnecessarily high standards. The Dandora site and service project in Nairobi was originally designed at lower standards. The project came under constant pressure from the authorities to conform to the established higher standards. Consequently, completion of phase two was delayed as it had to be redesigned and this resulted in an increased expenditure of Ksh 25 million. Unnecessarily high standards make the services too expensive for the poor. (Bubba and Lamba 1991: 53)

The broader ideological debate

The whole debate about urban planning and management takes place within the context of a wider political debate about the role of the state and the place of the individual – a debate which has already been referred to in Chapter 1. At the risk of gross over-simplification, this is a debate between those who see the individual and his or her private freedom of choice as being supreme, and those who regard the corporate welfare of society as being paramount, necessitating a surrendering of certain of the individual's freedom of choice to the state. This ideological debate about the role of the state has been amply discussed elsewhere (Higgott 1983; Evans *et al.* 1985; Brett 1988; Low 1991) and will not be rehearsed further here, except to try to identify the position of the discussion about urban planning and management within it.[2]

The traditions of urban planning and management may be regarded as lying somewhere in the middle of this continuum between left and right, but perhaps rather closer to the 'corporatist' end of the spectrum. They would recognise the limitations of the free market to produce a satisfactory outcome for society as a whole from a series of individual decisions (Taylor and Williams 1982: 23). But they would (increasingly) recognise the limitations of the state in bringing about a superior outcome through regulation and control. Safier (1989) has referred to the concept of the 'improving hand' to suggest some middle way between the 'invisible hand' of the free market, and the very visible, but often deadening, hand of state control.

Similarly, Lea and Courtney (1985: 5) distinguish between two approaches to urban management: the 'problem-oriented technocratic' approach, which relies on improved performance of the planning process to overcome urban problems, and the 'structural politico-economic' tradition, which identifies the roots of urban problems within the national and international structures of political and economic power. The 'improving hand' metaphor may suggest an uneasy compromise between these two views. The challenge is to avoid the twin pitfalls of, on the one hand, a naïve technocratic or 'neutral-professional' view which can result from an inadequate analysis of the realities of the political and economic structures of society, and on the other hand an inertia resulting from an analysis which suggests that there are no real solutions short of world revolution.

Criteria for evaluating performance

If we are to evaluate the performance of plans which have been implemented, interventions which are already taking place or policies which are proposed, we need some criteria on which to base our judgements.

It is, however, very difficult to produce a definitive list of criteria. First of all, the range of possible considerations is very large, and it is difficult to do justice to all the possibilities. Second, any criteria are inevitably derived from value systems, cultural traditions and ideologies, and are not, therefore, neutral. What may be regarded as an appropriate criterion in one culture or system may not be regarded as appropriate or important in another. For example, increases in material goods may be highly valued in one culture, but the diminution of spiritual values and cultural identity which often results from the process of economic growth may be considered a much more serious matter in another culture. Much of the value which those in the west place on multi-party democratic decision-making may be much less highly regarded in cultures which value consensus and harmony rather than open dispute. Third, criteria may conflict. It will not be possible to satisfy all the objectives identified below simultaneously, since several are by definition mutually incompatible. Others may prove to be mutually unattainable in practice. Fourth, in order for such a list of criteria to be useful, we really need to know the relative importance or weight to be attached to each one. That, however, would be an almost impossible task in abstract, and could be done, if at all, only in a particular situation, and in relation to a particular plan or set of proposals.

Nevertheless, the exercise is still worthwhile. Unless we can identify the range of possible criteria, we have no way of judging between alternatives and thereby reaching conclusions or making rational choices. In practice, in the absence of explicit criteria, such judgements are often made on the basis of implicit considerations, which may be no more than the personal prejudices of the decision-maker, or the vested interests of those in power.

In what follows, an attempt has been made to arrange the various possible criteria into groups. Within each group there are both broad, long-term goals and more specific criteria, which could be applied to particular plans, policies or projects. In general, the sequence is from the broad to the more specific. However, it must be recognised that any attempt to arrange or rank goals and criteria provides scope for endless debate, and cannot be resolved satisfactorily in a brief section like this.

Improving standards of living

A principal goal in most societies is to improve the standard of living of its members as a whole, through an increase in the production of goods and services. This requires a number of things. First, the diversion of a proportion of resources out of current consumption and into investment, in order to increase productive potential. The greater the proportion of resources devoted to investment, the more rapid the rate of economic growth which could be achieved, other things being equal. Second, wherever possible, there needs to be effective competition between producers, and a real choice of goods and services for consumers. Third, resources should be used in the most economically efficient manner possible. This means achieving the maximum output from a given level of inputs (resource cost), or achieving a specified output or objective from minimum amount (value) of resources. Economists refer to this as Pareto optimality. In practical terms, this criterion of economic efficiency implies the following:

1   that resources should be employed in the most productive and cost-effective way possible
2   that the impact of public interventions (as defined by the objectives for those interventions) should be maximised while the costs, both direct and indirect, of those interventions should be minimised
3   that the pricing of both inputs (resources) and outputs should reflect the true values of those resources to society (ie their 'opportunity costs'), so that the choices made by consumers reflect the true costs of the resources used.

Hence, it is generally considered that, where possible, the costs of public services should recovered from beneficiaries, so that they make choices in the light of the correct ('economically efficient') price signals. This will also mean that additional resources are generated, rather than being used up, thereby permitting activities to continue and be replicated.

There are, however, certain well-recognised limitations to this criterion of economic efficiency. These limitations are essentially the same as the reasons which were used in Chapter 1 to explain the failure of the market mechanism to ensure a socially desirable outcome. These are the fact that markets are frequently uncompetitive so that consumer choice is limited; the existence of both positive and negative externalities; and the uneven distribution of income and wealth which underlies the pattern of prices in the market. Although there are ways of dealing with these limitations, in theory at least, the criterion of economic efficiency must be treated with caution, and cannot be taken as an absolute measure of performance. (For a further discussion of these issues, see Mishan 1981; C V Brown and Jackson 1986, Chapter 3; Musgrave and Musgrave 1984, Chapter 3.)

The goal of improving living standards raises fundamental questions about the distribution of costs and benefits involved in this process, and about the sustainability of ever higher standards of living. These issues are discussed in the next two sections.

Distribution and equity

There is widespread agreement in principle that the benefits, and the costs, of development should be fairly distributed among all members of society. It is, however, much more difficult to reach agreement on what is meant by a 'fair distribution'. Answers may range from total equality of wealth and income on the one hand, to a much more general notion of equality of opportunity within a competitive system on the other. However, given the initial inequality of incomes and wealth in all socie-ties, almost any definition of equity is likely to imply some form of redistribution, in order to improve the situation of the poor and the disadvantaged.

Plate 7   Access to land is one of fundamental aspects of equity: here in Caracas, Venezuela, as in many other Third World cities, the poor have little alternative but to build on steep and dangerous hillsides.

The equity criterion may, in practice, be viewed in a number of ways:

1 the equal opportunity principle which requires that there should not be any barriers of discrimination according to race, gender, class, income, disability or other characteristics
2 equal treatment of all members of society in terms of access to public services (horizontal equity)
3 vertical equity, which requires that those who have greater wealth and income should contribute more towards the costs of public services than those who have less
4 the benefit principle, which suggests that people should contribute in accordance with the benefits they have received.

The criterion of equity may be taken further to require that public sector interventions (and private sector activities) do not disadvantage the poor and other vulnerable groups, that they protect such groups, or even that they are specifically designed to advantage them (positive discrimination). This may mean directing public policies to ensuring that basic physical needs (for food, water, clothing, shelter) are satisfied for all people. However, here again we encounter a problem of defining both the minimum levels and the range of goods and services to be included within this concept of basic needs.

In the end, we are left with the problem that many of the concepts of equity and fairness conflict: what is perceived as being fair depends on one's point of view. It is not logically possible to achieve a system which is totally equitable from everyone's point of view.

Environmental sustainability

Whatever plans, policies and programmes are adopted, these must be sustainable in terms of both the global and the local ecological systems, and the resource base on which cities depend. Resources such as water, air, energy, food and fuel not only are vital for the survival of the cities themselves but also may have profound implications for the surrounding rural areas. All forms of government intervention must therefore be judged in terms of whether they[3]:

1 conserve scarce, non-renewable resources (eg fossil fuels), and use renewable resources (water supplies, forest wood) in a sustainable way
2 minimise the impact of development and activities on ecologically fragile situations (eg land liable to erosion, habitats of endangered species, drainage of wetlands)
3 minimise the risk of irreversible changes in the condition of the planet (eg damage to the ozone layer and global warming caused by carbon dioxide emissions; local climatic changes caused by flooding, draining or deforesting large areas of land)
4 minimise (or ideally reverse) the pollution of air, land and water
5 ensure adequate and sustainable supply systems for the resources on which the cities depend: food, water, building materials and so on.

Plate 8 In many developing countries, the volume of traffic has grown
extremely rapidly in recent years: continued growth at this rate is
certainly not environmentally sustainable.

Fundamental rights, freedoms and personal needs

The UN Charter of Human Rights identifies a host of basic human
rights. For the purposes of this analysis, some of the key human needs,
rights and freedoms which any system of government must seek to
protect and enhance are:

1 freedoms of thought, belief, speech, worship and assembly
2 freedoms of individual choice about the use of time and money,
   about what to consume, where to work, where to live, and so on
3 personal, social and spiritual well-being, including individual self-
   fulfilment, self-realisation, self-esteem and dignity, creativity, cultural identity, community values and mutual support
4 political values, including the distribution of political power within
   society, the opportunity for expression of alternative political ideas
   and for exercising political choices, and the opportunity to influence
   political decisions affecting one's life and community
5 safety of life and security of property, including individual property
   rights.

These concepts are fundamental to human life and well-being, but many
of them are hard to define, and harder to quantify. In many cases there
would be disagreement over what was meant, and about the relative
importance of particular elements. Many of the concepts cannot be
treated as absolutes: freedom of choice about how to use one's money
clearly has to be constrained in the interests of society as a whole. Also,
there may be situations where these values come into conflict with other
goals: freedom of political choice may be seen in some cases as being in
conflict with economic growth; protection of private property may be in
conflict with objectives of wealth redistribution; freedom about what to
consume may conflict with environmental sustainability.

Nevertheless, in terms judging government policies and programmes in the urban sector, we may derive a number of practical criteria:

1   plans and public sector actions should seek to minimise the infringement of any of the freedoms and basic human rights identified above
2   where individual choices and freedoms have to be restricted in the interests of the wider community, such decisions should be taken in a manner which is open to public scrutiny
3   decisions concerning people's lives and communities should be made in such a way that those affected have the opportunity to influence those decisions; this may be through some form of democratic election, or through formal or informal processes of public participation/consultation; either way, those making decisions should be in some way accountable to those who are affected
4   systems of urban planning and management should be designed to enable individuals and communities both to improve their own living situations, in ways which match their own objectives, and to enhance their personal, social and spiritual well-being.

Effectiveness and the ability to implement

However good a plan, policy or programme may be in terms of all the above criteria, it will not be effective if it cannot be implemented. There are two broad aspects to this. The first is administrative capacity, the second is political will.

Those institutions which have to implement the plans, policies and actions must have the administrative capacity to do so. This requires technical skills, financial resources, management competence and legal powers. It also requires that the capacity of the institution is not diverted by competing private interests – in other words, corruption. In many countries, it is the lack of an honest, efficient and competent administration which means that even the best laid plans and programmes are not implemented, or not implemented satisfactorily. Therefore, plans and policies have to take realistic account of the institutional capacity to implement them, and of the factors which constrain that capacity.

If plans and policies are to be implemented effectively, they also require a commitment of political will. If that is to occur, plans and policies must somehow be acceptable to those in positions of political power. Hardline determinists might argue that, since those in power always have a vested interest in the status quo, significant reforms can never be implemented. But this is not necessarily the case. Those in power are not (generally) a homogeneous group, but rather a variety of individuals and groups with different objectives and agenda. Some will have achieved their positions as a result of a commitment to change. Others can be persuaded that changes will be in their interests. Some may even recognise the need for changes in the interests of society – in other words, they may not be motivated solely by self-interest. Clearly, political situations are never static, and windows of opportunity may open unexpectedly which can be exploited for good or ill.

However, this consideration of political will does imply that, in the

absence of dramatic or revolutionary political changes, plans and policies which are directly opposed to the vested interests of those in power
are unlikely to succeed. It also implies that it is not sufficient for
planners and urban managers merely to devise plans and policies. It is
necessary for such plans and policies to be 'sold' to those in power, or at
least to someone or some group which has sufficient influence within
the power structure to be able to put the proposals on the political
agenda and to generate the necessary political will. This requires that
the urban planner/manager is able to exercise political as well as technical and managerial skills.

Conflicts and uncertainty

We have already noted that there are conflicts between some of these
criteria. Both economic growth and the pursuit of equity may necessitate
some surrendering of individual freedoms. Pursuit of economic growth
is likely to threaten environmental sustainability. One of the most
obvious conflicts is that between equity and efficiency, with the self-
evident trade-off between redistribution of income and incentives to
work, save and invest. Thus, a balance has to be struck between these
conflicting objectives. These are fundamental political choices. In some
cases, however, careful policy design may permit improvement on more
than one front – in economists' jargon, moving to a higher Pareto optimum. For example, provision of public standpipes which provide cheap
(or free) water to low-income groups could increase economic efficiency
(by reducing the time wasted in collecting water and reducing health
losses caused by consumption of polluted water), as well as improving
the position of the poor and hence achieving greater equity.

One particular problem in applying any system of criteria to judge
either past performance or future proposals is that of uncertainty. In the
case of past performance, there are two main problems: first, obtaining
sufficiently accurate data on the outcomes, and second, determining the
nature of the relationships between cause and effect. In the real world of
public administration it is rarely possible to conduct controlled experiments. In judging future actions, though, the problem of uncertainty
about outcomes is compounded. In a complex system such as a city,
many things can change, either independently, or as an unanticipated
consequence of policy interventions. Thus, using criteria to appraise
plans or programmes may also necessitate the use of techniques such as
risk analysis or sensitivity analysis, to estimate the likelihood of particular outcomes, and to estimate how variations in the pattern of outcomes
will affect the results of our appraisal.[4] Not all activities, however, are
susceptible to such an analysis.

Notes

1. For a fuller discussion of the field of public policy analysis, see Dror (1983;
    1986); Wildavsky (1980); Hogwood and Gunn (1984); Quade and Carter
    (1989); Grindle and Thomas (1991).

2. This debate is, of course, not simply about whether there should be more or less state intervention, but also about the nature of that state intervention. There is, for example, the 'entrepreneurial state' model, in which the state, or the local authority, intervenes very explicitly within the market system in order to provide a framework or 'climate' for constructive private sector action. (See the example of Birmingham in Box 3.5, p. 79.)
3. It is not only direct interventions by governments which must be judged according to such criteria, but also non-interventions, since in most cases it is the actions of individuals and businesses, unconstrained by effective government controls, which continue to threaten the environment.
4. For a fuller discussion of such techniques, including the Planning Balance Sheet and Logical Framework approaches, see Pouliquen 1970; Lichfield *et al.* 1975: 60–2, 78–97; Carley 1980: 106–8; Bracken 1981: 76–9; Cracknell and Rendall 1986; Overseas Development Administration 1988.

CHAPTER 3

Evolving approaches
Nick Devas

The present form of cities in the developing world is the result of the interaction over the years of countless decisions by individuals, households, businesses and organisations on the one hand, and, on the other, a variety of governmental interventions designed to influence or control those decisions. The nature of governmental interventions has changed over the years as both circumstances and ideas have evolved. In this chapter, we trace some of the main factors and ideas which have influenced public sector interventions in city development.

The inheritance

The colonial inheritance

For many of the cities of the developing world, colonialism played a dominant role in shaping their urban form. As the European nations competed with each other for overseas territory and for domination over international trade, they established urban centres to serve their needs. In many cases, these centres were based on existing settlements, although sometimes they were established from scratch. Their purpose was to serve as trading posts or as centres for the administration of the surrounding territory, in order to facilitate the economic exploitation of the hinterland (Drakakis-Smith 1981: 19).

The founding fathers of these cities were concerned primarily or solely with the interests of the colonial powers. Cities were laid out (inasmuch as they were consciously laid out) to serve the needs of trade and territorial administration. In practice, that meant creating a secure, comfortable and healthy environment – as far as that was possible in an alien climate – for the colonial settlers, traders and administrators. The colonial city builders were in no way concerned with the native population, who were generally required to live outside the city limits, or to exist 'invisibly' within the city as servants of the colonial settlers.

The predominant concern in the planning of these settlements was with public health. This meant developing, where possible, a spacious layout to permit the passage of air, and segregating the colonial settlers from the native population, often with a 'cordon sanitaire' of open land in between (Mabogunje 1989: 6; Wekwete 1989: 7). The colonialists imposed alien systems of private property rights which facilitated the expropriation of land from the indigenous population (Mabogunje 1989: 18; van Westen 1990: 87). In order to create a congenial environment, the settlers often brought with them replicas of European architecture and urban form which they deposited on a tropical landscape: elaborate Spanish and Portuguese churches and public squares in Latin America, Dutch canals and town houses in Batavia (Jakarta) and monumental English Victorian civic architecture in Calcutta and Colombo.

Plate 9   Penang City Hall, Malaysia: in many cities of the developing world, the colonial heritage is very evident.

For many cities in the developing world, the present urban form is still dominated, at least in the central part of the city, by this colonial inheritance (G B Lee 1991). In some cases, such as Zimbabwe, the interests of the settler population have continued to dominate the pattern of urban development until very recently, and in South Africa they still do. But in many of the newly independent countries, the new local elites, having developed a liking for European culture and architecture, often sought to maintain the pattern of urban development inherited from the colonialists, and to protect themselves from the 'lower orders' by perpetuating the social segregation of residential areas (Bolaffi 1989: 1; Wekwete 1989: 23).

Box 3.1 A colonial view of town planning

Where the colonial authorities did exhibit any concern for the layout of native settlements, the emphasis was on public health and the potential effect on the European community. Thus, in 1919 Lord Lugard issued guidelines for the layout of Native Reservations:

> Streets in the Native Reservations should be broad and parallel, or at right angles to each other, and the main street should run in the direction of the prevailing breeze so as to promote a free current of air. Overcrowding of the Native Reservation must, for reasons of health, be prevented. . . . The number of occupants of a plot must not exceed ten. Houses should have mud walls (if not burnt bricks), with non-inflammable roofing, if possible. A large and adequate market should be provided with permanent stalls open to the air. (Lord Lugard, Eleventh Memorandum, 1919)

Traditional systems of planning

It would, of course, be quite wrong to suggest that colonialism was the only influence on urban form in the developing world. In many countries there were well-established traditions, cultures and architectural styles which have influenced urban form. There were the ancient civilisations of Central and South America, West Africa, the Middle East and China, each of which had distinctive urban forms, although in most cases relatively little remains of these. For much of North Africa and the Middle East, Islam has had a profound effect on architectural styles, on the relationship of buildings to each other, and on the patterns of urban land development (Hourani and Stern 1970; Serageldin and El-Sadek 1982). Throughout much of Africa there were well-developed traditional systems of land allocation. These tended to shape the way in which settlements developed, for example, around the residence of the chief. Such land allocation systems were often undermined – indeed often deliberately destroyed – by the colonial administrations. Similarly, the so-called informal housing, which emerged in many developing countries as a response to the constraints placed by the authorities on the housing options for the poor, often reflected traditional concepts of land development and housing patterns.

The post-colonial British town planning legacy

Because of the extent of her colonial possessions, Britain had a major influence in shaping the pattern of urban development in many parts of Africa and Asia in the immediate pre- and post-independence period.

Many of the ideas and principles which have been applied in city development in the Third World during this period were derived from the practice of town and country planning in Britain. Indeed, many of the practices were transferred from Britain with little or no adaptation to local conditions.

The history of British town planning has been well documented elsewhere (Cherry 1974; 1988; Hall 1982; Cullingworth 1988) and so will be reviewed only briefly here. The origins of present-day British town planning may be traced principally to the concern among reformers of the mid-nineteenth century about the living conditions of the working classes. Their concern was both altruistic and self-interested. Like the colonial settlers, Victorian reformers were concerned about the risks of disease and fire spreading through the city. They were also concerned to maintain a healthy and productive labour force. But there was much genuine concern too about the well-being of their fellow citizens (Cherry 1988).

Box 3.2   Engels on Manchester

Engels' description of a slum in Victorian Manchester has obvious parallels with the conditions in many cities in the developing world today:

> Passing along a rough path on the river bank between posts and washing lines, one penetrates into the chaos of little one-storied, one-roomed huts. Most of them have earth floors; cooking, living and sleeping all take place in one room. In such a hole, barely six feet long and five feet wide, I saw two beds – and what beds and bedding – that filled the room, except for the doorstep and fireplace. In several others I found absolutely nothing, although the door was wide open and the inhabitants were leaning against it. Everywhere in front of the doors was rubbish and refuse. It was impossible to see whether any sort of pavement lay underneath this, but here and there I felt it out with my feet. This whole pile of cattle-sheds inhabited by human beings was surrounded on two sides by houses and a factory and on a third side by a river ... a narrow gateway led out of it into an almost equally miserably-built and miserably-kept labyrinth of dwellings. (Frederick Engels, *The Condition of the Working Class in England in 1844*, translated by W O Henderson and W H Chaloner, Oxford, 1958)

This concern with the conditions in which the working classes lived resulted in the introduction during the latter part of the nineteenth century of by-laws to control the construction of housing so as to create a safer and more healthy environment. Gradually this led to the development of an embryonic system of planning control over new development. This was consolidated in the Town Planning Acts of 1919 and 1932. The latter part of the nineteenth century also saw an upsurge in civic pride and civic enterprise, particularly in the major cities: roads, water mains and sewers were constructed, municipal gas undertakings were established, public parks were laid out, and slum housing was cleared.

But the Victorian reformers tended to display a distinct anti-urban bias. The contrast was frequently drawn between the appalling conditions in the slums of the city and a romantic image of the healthiness of life in the rural areas. The very size of cities was regarded as evil, and the spreading of the city over the surrounding countryside was seen as something which had to be prevented. As long ago as 1821, William Cobbett had referred to London as 'the great wen'. Thus, when Ebenezer Howard described his vision of 'garden cities', in which everyone would have easy access to the countryside, he found a ready acceptance (Howard 1898). Similar concepts were already being applied by enlightened industrialists like Cadbury, Rowntree and Lever, who wished to create healthy housing environments for their workers. Howard's ideas led to the development of garden cities at Letchworth and Welwyn in the early years of the twentieth century, and had a profound effect on British thinking about urban development during the first half of the twentieth century. The garden city concept provided the basis for the post-war plan for a series of new towns around London and elsewhere, and to the establishment of green belts around the major cities.

Victorian concern about the housing conditions of the working classes also led to the construction of 'improved industrial dwellings' and 'model cottages' by enlightened private landlords, housing associations and local authorities. The first local authority housing was built during the 1890s. During the years between the wars, local authority housing was constructed on a large scale to accommodate the 'war heroes', as well as providing a means of reducing unemployment. In the post-war period, the policy of demolishing inner city slum housing (most of which was privately rented) and replacing it with local authority housing estates, resulted in the share of the public sector in the total housing stock increasing from about 15 per cent in 1945 to a peak of 31 per cent in the mid-1970s.

As far as town planning itself was concerned, the Town and Country Planning Act 1947 is generally seen as a watershed in the development of town planning in Britain. For the first time, planners had effective powers to control development of all types. Under this Act, development plans were prepared for all urban areas, and an effective system of development control was established. The late 1940s and the 1950s was a period of great confidence in the capacity of the public sector, and of the planning profession in particular, to deliver an improved living environment. The role of the public sector in all spheres of life increased significantly over the three decades following the Second World War.

The approach to planning during the post-war period was based on a number of precepts:

1 that the public sector should play a key role in promoting and developing a satisfactory urban environment
2 that private rights to develop and use land could and should be restricted in the public interest
3 that the professional planner, as a 'neutral' adviser to the local authority, should act as an unbiased referee between competing interests in the control of land development

4   that the size of the major cities should be limited and 'urban sprawl' over surrounding countryside should be prevented by the use of green belts, new towns and regional policies to disperse development around the country
5   that land uses should be separated, particularly industrial and residential uses (Keeble 1964: 1)
6   that visual order and 'tidiness' are of great importance, and that the professional planner should be the arbiter on such matters (Keeble 1964: 323)
7   that the growing volume of vehicular traffic should be accommodated, where possible, by separation of vehicles from pedestrians.

Central to this British system of town planning was the role of local government. Local governments, with their elected councils and their cadres of professional officers, were well established by the beginning of this century as the primary vehicle for providing local services. The role of central government in the planning system was limited to broad policy guidance, approval of development plans, and adjudicating on appeals from applicants over refusal of planning permission. At the heart of this model of local government were certain important principles: elected local democracy; a high degree of local autonomy; and the clear distinction between elected members and paid officials. The last of these implied, in theory at least, that the elected members would set the broad goals and the direction of policy for the local authority, and would make the key decisions, while the officers would implement these in a politically neutral way.

The profession of town and country planning in Britain developed predominantly within this local government context. It drew on – and competed with – a number of related disciplines and traditions:

1   the **architectural tradition**, from which many town planners were drawn, with its roots in the great civic architecture of previous centuries, and with its emphasis on urban form and 'civic design'
2   the **engineering tradition**, with its broad responsibilities for the provision and maintenance of municipal infrastructure, for highway design, and for traffic management; in many local authorities, town planning was regarded as merely a branch of the Municipal Engineer's Department
3   the **legal profession**, whose involvement derived from the fact that town plans were statutory documents and development control involved legally binding decisions
4   the **economists**, whose involvement was generally limited to consideration of the industrial and employment implications of large-scale development plans and regional policies, but whose role has grown as planning has become increasingly concerned about issues of economic growth and employment
5   the **sociologist**, whose involvement was generally limited to commenting upon the impact of redevelopment on local communities, and researching into the growing problems of urban deprivation

6   the **public housing suppliers and managers**, with their shared roots
    in the Garden City movement, also played a key role since much of
    the work of urban development and redevelopment was concerned
    with the provision of public sector housing.

The prestige which 'rational' and technocratic planning enjoyed in
Britain and elsewhere during the 1950s began to wane in the 1960s.
Unsympathetic slum clearance and city centre redevelopment schemes,
and poor quality housing developments which were unpopular with
their residents, contributed to public disillusionment. There was a growing realisation that there are no simple technical solutions to conflicting
needs, interests and priorities. Perhaps most important, though, was
the retreat from public sector intervention, and the re-emergence of
private sector and market solutions which accompanied the 'Thatcher
revolution' of the 1980s. These themes will be discussed at greater
length later in this chapter.

   For better or for worse this legacy of British town planning has been
passed on to many developing countries (Franklin 1979). In particular,
many countries were provided with planning legislation based on (and
often directly copied from) British planning legislation (McCoubrey
1988). For example, the Nigerian Town and Country Planning Ordi-
nance of 1946 was directly based on the British Act of 1932 (Mabogunje
1989: 9). Little consideration was given to the capacity to prepare the
range of development plans required or to control development effectively. Institutions were also transferred, notably the system of local
government, with its assumptions about local autonomy and local
democracy and about the clear division of roles between elected
members and officers (El Shakhs and Obudho 1974: 10).

Alternative planning legacies

Clearly, there have been many other 'planning traditions', such as the
French, Spanish, Portuguese, Dutch and American, which have
influenced the pattern of urban development in different parts of the
world through the process of colonialism and neo-colonialism.

   The American planning tradition, for example, has been particularly
influential in the Caribbean, Central America and the Philippines. The
American planning system is based on two key elements: land-use zoning and land subdivision regulations. In origin, these were concerned
primarily with protecting private property rights and values against
incursions into the local community, and with ensuring that adequate
public services were provided for land that was being developed. (For a
fuller discussion of these issues, see So and Getzeis 1988.) Thus,
whereas the roots of the British planning system lay with public concern
about conditions in the urban slums, the American system is firmly
embedded in the private property ideology and the urban expansionist
context of the United States. As Guarda (1989: 5) has commented, the
American system views land-use control mainly as a local, voluntary

device to protect individual property rights and to promote development, while the European (notably British and French) approach
involves a greater (and more centralised) degree of public interference,
which requires government permission for any kind of land development initiative.

Another influential legacy is that of the great architect planners such
as Haussmann in Paris, L'Enfant in Washington and Wren and Nash in
London.[1] The development of the town planning in France in particular
was heavily influenced by the *Beaux Arts* tradition of grand civic architecture. This legacy of 'monumental' civic design has clearly had its
influence on the developing world, notably in the construction of new
capital cities such as New Delhi and Brasilia.

Perhaps the most notable exponent of the architectural tradition of
city building to have put his stamp on a Third World city was Le Corbusier in his building of Chandigarh. Le Corbusier was a visionary architect who had a profound effect on contemporary ideas about architecture and urban form. However, his visions were imposed upon a
recipient population (whether in Europe or elsewhere) of whom he
seemed to have little understanding. His writings display a determinism
about how people relate to architecture which appears to be contemp-
tuous of the realities of human life. Thus, in his planning schemes he
developed models, hierarchies and urban forms which bore little relationship with the real needs and aspirations of those who would have
to live in them. Le Corbusier described his plan for Chandigarh as a
'radio-concentric city of exchanges', with a hierarchy of seven road
types, and sectors 'of harmonious dimensions' (derived mainly from a
Spanish land unit) as 'the container of family life' (Sarin 1973: 15). In
order to implement the plan, a strict system of development control was
required to force the functioning of the city into Le Corbusier's rigid
plan. Whatever may be the architectural merits of this project, Sarin
concludes that 'The planned development of Chandigarh has not
catered for the needs of the deprived newcomers to the city, and has
been wasteful of scarce resources in a number of ways' (Sarin 1973: 18).

The dominance of master planning

Traditional planning practice is often referred to as 'master planning',
and this is the term we shall use here, although the issues involved are
clearly much broader than simply the type of plan produced. Box 3.3
contains a caricature of such planning practices in a fictitious city in the
developing world. It could fairly be argued that such practice does not
exist in reality anywhere. Alas, though, at least some of the characteristics described here do exist in most planning systems.

Box 3.3   Master planning in Erewhon: a cautionary tale

Traditional master planning practice in Erewhon is concerned first and foremost with the production of a plan. The nature of the plan is that of an end-state 'blueprint', seeking to specify how the city will look at some date in the future. A principal objective of such a plan is to limit the growth of the city, since the city is seen as being essentially unhealthy and parasitic, and rapid urban expansion is seen as being dangerous and undesirable.

Because there are limited resources of skilled urban planners in the country, the urban planning function is located in the central ministry. From there, staff are sent out to the cities concerned to collect the information on which to prepare their master plans. The planners, therefore, are unlikely to have a detailed working knowledge of the city for which they are planning nor are they part of the local decision-making and management system for the city. In particular, it is difficult for them to be aware of the problems faced by the poor in that city.

Because the task of producing a master plan is a very substantial one, the available personnel are entirely taken up with the process of plan production. This process lasts several years. When complete, the plan is submitted to the appropriate government authority, which spends several more years considering whether or not to approve it. However, because of changes in political control, there is a problem that no one in government is willing to be responsible for either accepting or rejecting a plan prepared under a previous regime.

By the time the master plan has been produced and considered by government, the city of Erewhon has changed considerably. Much – perhaps most – of that change is not in conformity with the plan. But the plan is rigid and so cannot easily be adapted to fit the changed circumstances.

The plan calls for massive investment in land acquisition, infrastructure development and improved service provision. It also calls for a large amount of good quality housing to be built. Unfortunately, the resources available to the municipal authority are but a small fraction of what is called for in the plan, while the State Housing Authority has succeeded over the last ten years in constructing in the city only a tiny fraction of number of the houses needed.

The city's Public Works Department, together with the various service departments, has drawn up an investment programme for the municipality, but this has been prepared without the benefit of the master plan, since that was not yet available. This investment programme is being implemented through the annual capital budget prepared by the Treasurer. In neither process have the urban planners played any significant part.

The city's population has doubled in size during the time taken for plan preparation. It has, in fact, already reached the population level predicted for the end of the plan period, twenty years hence. This is in spite of the recommendations in the plan that in-migration should be controlled. Much of this additional population has been accommodated in unplanned and unserviced settlements beyond the municipal boundaries, and therefore

> **Box 3.3 Master planning in Erewhon: a cautionary tale** (*continued*)
>
> outside the scope of the plan. In addition, many low-income households have squatted on vacant land which was zoned in the plan for other uses. Squatting has also taken place on land which the plan identified as being unsuitable for development (river banks, unstable hillsides, aquifer recharge zones, etc.). The city is therefore faced with a choice between upgrading such areas, however unsuitable, or trying to resettle a very large proportion of the city's population in peripheral housing schemes.
>
> The system of planning is based directly on legislation in use (or rather, formerly in use) in a developed country. This legislation specifies a strict land-use zoning for all parcels of land, together with a system of control for all land development, defined as both new construction and any material change of use. Unfortunately, the bulk of development has taken place without the benefit of planning approval, and the city lacks the staff to take enforcement action. Even if enforcement action were taken, delays in the courts would mean that cases might not be dealt with for several years. Even then, it is doubtful whether there is the required political will to enforce any penalties imposed.
>
> Meanwhile, those occupying the illegal squatter settlements are suffering severe hardship because of the lack of infrastructure and services, as well as uncertainty over their tenure rights. Ad hoc action by politicians and/or officials has enabled certain communities to obtain essential services, but this has generally occurred only after the extraction of some form of payment, either in terms of votes or cash.
>
> In addition, environmental conditions in and around the city are deteriorating rapidly, with high levels of atmospheric and water pollution, excessive extraction of ground water, uncollected domestic refuse, untreated human waste and toxic industrial waste, and degradation of the surrounding land which is subject to speculation. However, most of these problems are not regarded as part of the urban planners' brief, and they have neither the powers nor the resources to deal with them.

The weaknesses of master planning

The tale of master planning in Erewhon illustrates some of the obvious shortcomings of the master planning approach:

1 the concern with the preparation of a plan document rather than with achieving any effect on the ground (Rosser 1970)
2 the attempt to be too comprehensive, covering all possible aspects, ' like a mini national development plan, rather than focusing on key issues (Ahmed 1989: 8)
3 the dominance of spatial and land-use issues compared to social, economic or environmental issues
4 the negative view of urban growth, leading to an objective of limiting urban growth regardless of whether that is either appropriate or achievable

5   as a result, unrealistic projections are made of urban population growth
6   projections of public investments requirements also tend to be unrealistic, given the sort of resources which are likely to be available
7   the separation of the plan-making process from decision-making process about budgets, infrastructure development and service provision
8   the absence of any effective mechanism for controlling land development, whether because of legislative weaknesses, bureaucratic failures, corruption, or simply the absence of an adequate mechanism of relating the plan to the development control system; examples abound: Jakarta (Douglass 1989: 231); Mexico City (Aguilar 1987: 31; P M Ward 1986: 231); Delhi (Mitra 1990); Nairobi (Yahya 1990)
9   the production of a detailed, rigid, zoning plan which is unrelated to the forces which really shape the city (economic, social and political), and which is too inflexible to be adjusted in the light of the realities of the situation.

Why master planning continues to be the dominant approach

Given the very obvious weaknesses of master planning, it seems odd that such an approach still appears to dominate urban planning in so many countries. Of course, it must be acknowledged that the Erewhon case is a caricature: in no situation would one expect to find all those weaknesses, and in many countries there have been sustained attempts to move away from such an inappropriate approach. Nevertheless, aspects of the master planning approach continue to dominate the urban planning systems of many developing countries. Why is this?

There are a number of reasons. First, there is the professional training and ideology of planners. Most of those at the top of their profession were trained many years ago, often in planning schools in Europe or North America. Such schools were (and often still are) dominated by the cultural values and concerns of the countries in which they are located, and often by strong architectural and spatial planning traditions. The architectural and planning ideology that inspired cities like Chandigarh and Brasilia was a visionary one which was profoundly unconcerned with the details of the real world (Sarin 1973; Gosling 1979). Such traditions die hard, particularly in countries where such 'visionary professional expertise' is accorded a high status. The professional ideology also emphasises high standards – the most laudable aim of providing the struggling masses with 'proper standards' of housing and services. Such notions are incorporated into a professional rhetoric which is hard to challenge: who wants to be seen to be advocating poor housing and low quality services? Yet the reality is that such standards are almost invariably unattainable, given the limited resources of the developing countries. But planners are often unwilling to surrender this commitment to high standards and may as a result be unable to achieve anything.

Second, there are the professional vested interests: the vested interests of professional planners, who do not wish to compromise their professional status by involvement in the minutiae of development control or construction on the ground; the vested interests of the firms of consultant planners, both domestic and international, whose principal aim is to ensure their future work (Bolaffi 1989: 7); the vested interests of the administrator who administers and polices the development control process and who does not want his empire threatened by interference from the planner; similarly, the public works engineer and the finance director, who between them programme the infrastructure development, prefer to keep the planner at a distance; so do the managers of the various city services, who consider that they know well enough how their services should be provided without advice from the planner (Clarke 1985: 51).

Third, the mere preparation of plan documents can serve the interests of the politicians and the donor agencies, without these plans necessarily having to be implemented. A large and well-illustrated plan document can look very impressive in the politician's office, and can give the impression that action is on the way (Aguilar 1987: 26). The action need not, of course, be related to the plan – after all, only the planner knows what is in the plan! The donor agency, too, needs a plan document to provide a basis for drawing up its aid programme and to provide the necessary information on which to design its projects. So long as its own projects are implemented, though, the donor agency is little concerned about whether or not the rest of the plan is carried out.

Fourth, the legislative basis for planning may be totally inappropriate, in terms of both the types of plans which are required to be prepared, and the mechanisms for plan implementation. As we have noted already, planning legislation inherited from colonial powers is often rigid and inappropriate, but for many reasons it may be difficult to change this legislation.

Box 3.4   Bombay's Development Plan

Bombay's First Development Plan (1964–81) was approved in 1964. In accordance with the Maharashtra Regional and Town Planning Act, this plan regulated the use of each plot of land in the city and prescribed detailed rules for development. Referring to this First Plan, D'Souza comments:

> In most senses it was a dismal failure, because scarcely any of the several items of development it envisaged actually materialised. Moreover, the municipal body could not find the funds to buy more than a tiny fraction of the land the Plan had reserved for public amenities. In fact, the owners of such lands generally lost interest in protecting them, so that most of them were overrun by squatters. The

---

Box 3.4 Bombay's Development Plan (*continued*)

Plan had estimated the cost of its implementation, but had made no serious assessment of the municipality's ability to meet that cost. (D'Souza 1989: 2–3)

In 1977, Bombay Municipal Corporation set about revising the First Plan. The Planning Cell was composed mainly of engineers and architects, without city planners, geographers, economists or sociologists. The Municipal Corporation submitted the draft Second Plan to the Maharashtra State Government in 1985. In 1989, twelve years after starting the Plan preparation, the State Government was still considering it (D'Souza 1989: 1).

The Planning Cell's Report which accompanied the land reservation maps for the Second Plan and which sought to spell out the policy for the city's future was 600 pages long. According to D'Souza:

It contained information on Bombay's history, climate and rainfall, velocity and direction of wind, and many other features, most of them peripheral in comparison to the economic condition of the people, on which there was very little in the Report. The Report did make some attempt at a 2001 population forecast, but could not quite choose between a 12 or 14 million low and a 19 million high. So it decided on 9.87 million as a target figure for 2001! It explained this by pleading that the city would not be able to provide the amenities required for a population level realistically estimated, so 9.87 would be a sensible target to work on. At the time the Report came to the Government, Bombay's population was already 9.5 million, and growing by a quarter of a million yearly. (D'Souza 1989: 5)

Before submission to the State Government, the recommendations in the draft Plan were reviewed by a Planning Group established by the elected members. According to D'Souza:

The Group's scrutiny of the suburban [part of the] Plan focused chiefly on individual designations of plots rather than on the important prescriptions in the Plan, the policies proposed, the targets adopted, the rules to regulate building, the resource requirements, the municipal resources, and plenty more that a prudent planner for a large city might consider. Its obsession with reservations gave rise to strong suspicions about its integrity, suspicions that were strengthened by the quality of the recommendations it made to its parent body, the Corporation. Land values are very high in Bombay, and pressure to escape an inconvenient reservation is correspondingly heavy. Landowners are often quite ready to reward those who aid such escapes. (D'Souza 1989: 3–4)

(Material taken from J B D'Souza: 'Will Bombay have a plan? Are planners and their plans irrelevant?' Paper presented to the International Workshop on Planning and Management of Urban Development in the 1990s, University of Birmingham, September 1989, and forthcoming in *Habitat International* 1992.)

Are there success stories?

The traditional approach has not, of course, been a total failure. There have been some notable success stories. Hong Kong and Singapore are obvious examples, where conventional town planning has been carried through to its logical conclusion, with high standards of public services and public housing, and a firm control over land development (Yeh 1986; Yeung 1987; K Watts 1989: 3). However, these two cities seem to be the exceptions to most generalisations about development. Their status as city states makes them unusual, and permits national resources to be concentrated on the cities' problems. Both economies have prospered, and living standards now exceed those in several European countries. This has allowed substantial resources to be put into urban development. In addition, in both cases all the citizens are acutely aware of the very limited amount of land available and are therefore willing to accept tough controls over land development.

Zimbabwe might also be regarded by some as a successful example of the traditional approach to town planning. The cities of Zimbabwe are generally well laid out, and private development has, for the most part, been controlled effectively. However, many would question whether the Zimbabwean case really represents success. The orderly development of cities was largely the product of a colonial-style minority government which continued to exist until the end of the 1970s. Such a government was able to use the resources of the country to build an elegant environment for the white city dwellers, and to exert tough controls on African urban development. It is not hard to see that such an approach offered few benefits for the majority community (Wekwete 1989), and it is questionable whether it can be sustained in a changed political environment.

Influences on the evolution of urban planning and management

Over the past three or four decades there have been many ideas, theories and approaches which have influenced the evolution of urban planning and management in practice. These influences have not generally been sequential, but have had different impacts at various times and in various places. Many of the ideas have themselves evolved over time. Some remain very influential, others less so. In identifying these various influences, we do not imply that they are separate and isolated: many of them are highly interrelated, and it is often difficult to distinguish one influence from another.

The concern with national patterns of urban development

The thinking about urban development at both national and local level in the Third World has been heavily conditioned by a traditional, anti-urban view. Just as in Victorian times, cities have been perceived as unhealthy and dangerous, as parasitic on the national economy, as wasteful of agricultural land, and as a haven for the unemployed, the feckless and the criminal. The very rapid migration from the rural areas has been perceived as the prime cause of 'overcrowding' of cities and the overloading of urban services (Amis 1990: 12; Franklin 1979: 9).

Thus, limiting city growth became a major objective. City plans were tailored to the size of population which the planners thought could be accommodated (A Turner 1989: 7; D'Souza 1989: 5). Squatter settlements were destroyed and new housing provision kept to a minimum in order to discourage migrants from the rural areas. In Indonesia, the Governor of Jakarta declared a 'closed city' policy, in which no one was to be allowed to settle without permission. Whilst this policy was notably unsuccessful in Jakarta, in China the government was able to use its control of employment, food supplies and housing to prevent migration to the cities, but even there such control measures have ceased to be so effective in the more liberal atmosphere of the 1980s and 1990s.

Such negative views of 'urban problems' have been reinforced by concepts such as the 'optimum size' of cities (Spengler 1967: 77). This theory suggests that further growth beyond a certain optimum size would result in diminishing returns, due to congestion and overcrowding. Failure to control urban growth would result in increased economic and social costs, and lead eventually to a complete breakdown in city life and to civil disorder. A similar concern was expressed about the 'rural–urban balance', with the continued growth of cities being seen as upsetting the natural balance between urban and rural areas (Taylor and Williams 1982: 18). What was needed, it was suggested, was to promote rural development and to provide greater employment opportunities in the rural areas (for example, President Nyerere of Tanzania, quoted in El-Shakhs and Obudho 1974: 24).

Faced with the perceived problems of rapid growth of their major cities, many governments sought to adopt European and North American models of new towns and growth centres as a way of redirecting urban growth away from the primate cities (Appalraju and Safier 1976; K Watts 1989: 17; A Turner 1980). However, these have not generally had much success in altering the pattern of urban migration, and in some cases planned new towns failed to gather the required momentum (A Turner 1989: 4). Nevertheless, the debate over decentralisation of urban development is far from over, and there is a renewed interest in the development of secondary and medium-sized cities as an alternative to metropolitan growth (Rondinelli 1983; Hardoy and Satterthwaite 1986a). As a number of cities in the developing world reach mega-city status, and apparently continue to function despite their size, the debate moves on from prophecies of doom to a more reasoned analysis of the most effective way to accommodate urban expansion (Government of Indonesia 1985; N Harris 1989: 180).

The city economy and the discovery of the informal sector

A parallel debate, already alluded to in Chapter 1, has been that over the role of the city in economic development. The 1950s and the 1960s were the ascendant years for national economic planning. Planning was seen to be the key to economic growth and 'modernisation'. In most devel-

oping countries, national planning agencies were set up and development plans produced, recommending large-scale investment in both
industry and agriculture. There was, however, little relationship between such national economic planning and urban planning. Whilst
much of the industrial development was inevitably located in the major
cities, investment in urban infrastructure tended to be seen as unpro-
ductive ('social overhead capital' was a common phrase).

Much of the industrial development of that period tended to be capital-intensive, with the result that few jobs were created. Meanwhile, a
large proportion of the urban population scraped a living in what has
come to be known as the 'informal sector'. The informal sector was first
documented in the early 1970s (Hart 1973), and interest in it soon grew
as a result of research by the International Labour Organisation (ILO).
This research suggested that the informal sector was a dynamic and
productive sector of the economy which could contribute much to economic development if allowed to do so (ILO 1972). The implications of
this analysis were that governments should encourage and facilitate the
informal sector, and should nurture income-earning opportunities in
whatever form these might arise, rather than relying on costly, capital-
intensive industries which create few jobs.

Such ideas were opposed by many, particularly urban planners and
administrators, who tended to see informal sector activities as illegal,
unauthorised, dangerous to health, and unfair competition to 'legitimate' businesses. A commonly held view was that, since much of the
informal sector is in services, this does not form a viable economic base
for the city, despite the fact that services now account for the great
majority of jobs in most western cities. Others using a Marxist analysis,
saw the informal sector as exploited out-workers of the capitalist system
(Scott 1979). More recently, questions have been raised concerning some
of the generalised assumptions about the informal sector (Amis 1989:
383) and about the distribution of the benefits of informal sector activities. The debate over the informal sector has been well documented
elsewhere (Bromley and Gerry 1979; Moser 1977; Turnham *et al.* 1990).
Suffice it to say here that the concept of the informal sector has had a
profound influence on the thinking about the urban economy.

Out of this has emerged a rather more realistic analysis of the role of
the city in the national economy. The interdependent nature of so much
commercial and industrial activity, in which physical proximity is often
crucial, means that the city provides the natural locus for economic
growth. Even if there were the powers and the resources to decentralise
industry and economic activities away from the city, there would be a
real risk of 'killing the goose that lays the golden egg'.[2] Increasingly, the
city is being seen once more as the 'engine of economic growth'. That
being so, the role of the planner/urban manager may be regarded as one
of promoting urban economic development and attracting new investment to the city, rather than one of trying to prevent further development.

Box 3.5   Promoting economic development in the City of Birmingham

In many cities, municipal authorities are adopting a more proactive role in promoting development, in contrast with the more traditional urban planning approach of trying to control and limit development. The City of Birmingham, UK, for example, has been a leading exponent of this new approach to urban development. In common with many other industrial cities in Britain, Birmingham suffered from substantial economic decline during the 1970s and 1980s as its traditional industries faced strong competition from abroad. The City Council therefore adopted a number of strategies to promote development in the city:

1   The construction of a highly successful National Exhibition Centre on a site next to the airport, which was itself upgraded to international standards, and the subsequent construction of an International Convention Centre, Symphony Hall and Indoor Arena in the city centre; these facilities, which rival anything elsewhere in Britain, are all designed to attract new business to the city.
2   The use of public and private sector resources to reclaim derelict industrial land and to make it available for new uses; one example is the establishment of a partnership between private companies and the City Council to develop Heartlands, a 1,200 ha area of land, much of which had been derelict; this process involved assembling land, providing new infrastructure, improving the local environment, making available sites of different sizes for industrial, commercial and residential development, providing skills training, and attracting new businesses.
3   The strategic use of public funds, for example in essential infrastructure and environmental improvements, in order to lever private sector finance for a variety of types of development; similarly, the strategic use of public funds as seed money to generate private sector finance for new businesses trying to establish themselves.
4   The adoption of an innovative approach to promoting the improvement of the older, privately owned terraced housing stock by a technique known as 'enveloping' which uses public funds to rehabilitate the external shell, thereby encouraging private resources to be used on internal improvements, and preventing the unnecessary deterioration and loss of housing assets.
5   Establishing a Development Department to bring together the functions of urban planning, estates management and local economic development, with a clear aim of greater responsiveness to development opportunities; advisory services for small businesses, building consultancy services, access to financial resources, and simplified planning regulations in certain zones are all part of an attempt to attract investment and encourage development in the city.

The dominance of housing and the vision of spontaneous settlements

The recognition of the informal sector had its parallels in the housing field, through the work of Charles Abrams and John Turner in particular (Abrams 1964; 1966; J F C Turner 1969). During the 1950s and 1960s, the provision of an adequate supply of housing had been the dominant preoccupation for urban planners and managers.[3] The huge numbers of people migrating to the city required shelter, and the conventional view, inherited from Britain and other developed countries, was that it was responsibility of the public authorities to meet that need. City planners devoted much attention to calculating the housing deficiencies and estimating the costs of constructing sufficient housing.

Because of the size of the task, national housing authorities were established in many countries to construct public housing (Stren 1990: 37), but the scale of such provision invariably fell far short of the need. The reality was that the resources required were simply not available, nor were they likely to be available (Wakely 1988; 1989: 196). In addition, because of the high costs of constructing completed housing, what little was provided proved to be far too costly to be affordable by the poor without massive public subsidy. In order to make the limited resources go further, and to make housing more affordable, various technological and organisational solutions (the latter often referred to as aided self-help) were tried. These included prefabrication, which reduced labour costs (hardly an appropriate solution in most developing countries where labour is plentiful); core houses, in which the public authority constructed only a minimal part of the dwelling and left the occupiers to construct the rest; sites-and-services, in which the occupiers were given a serviced plot, some technical advice and building materials loans with which to construct their own houses to a standard plan; and housing co-operatives, where the work of construction was shared between the members. Yet still the need for housing far outpaced the available provision, and the poor rarely seemed to benefit at all (Stren 1990: 41; Choguill 1985).

The studies by John Turner in Latin America in the late 1960s had identified how low-income communities managed to provide shelter for themselves. He noted that, not only did they provide themselves with shelter, but also what they provided served their needs much better, and much more cheaply, than what the public authorities provided (J F C Turner 1969). For Turner, cities are built by people not by planners. The implication of this analysis was that public authorities not only should recognise such informal settlements in their planning, and provide them with essential services, but also should see dweller-construction and control as the best way of providing housing (J F C Turner and Fichter 1972; J F C Turner 1976).

Just as in the debate on the informal sector, there were opposing views. Traditionally, urban planners had seen such 'informal settlement' as illegal slums, lacking proper services or layout, and damaging both to the health of the occupants and to the appearance of the city.

Plate 10   Sites-and-services are the principal housing strategy in Zimbabwe, but the large plot sizes and the minimum house size of four rooms raise questions about how the needs of low-income groups are to be met, and about the sustainability of this policy.

Thus, the policy was to remove such settlements wherever possible, either by rehousing the residents elsewhere, or simply by destroying them. Such actions did nothing to increase the stock of available housing – indeed, it reduced it. It also ignored the fact that the residents of such settlements often preferred what they had provided for themselves to what the city authorities offered, particularly on the grounds of location and cost. Many who were resettled chose to return to their former settlements.

On the other side, the Marxist analysis identified informal sector housing as one aspect of the exploitative economic system, which allowed the poor no alternative access to adequate shelter (Drakakis-Smith 1981: 67). Far from the dwellers being in control, it was argued, they were often 'little more than tenants of land-occupation schemes organised by powerful interests (Burgess 1978; Amis and Lloyd 1990). Thus, to recognise such settlements as the principal means of housing provision would be to perpetuate the unequal class-relations in society. This would simply serve the interests of capital by keeping down the costs of labour (Drakakis-Smith 1981: 146).

Nevertheless, Turner's analysis had a major impact on the thinking about urban housing. Donor agencies in particular found that it offered a way of assisting in the shelter sector at a realistic cost, through upgrading of existing settlements and the development of sites-and-service schemes. Some governments had already recognised the folly of wholesale clearance of informal settlements and had started to improve them. In Jakarta, for instance, the Kampung Improvement Programme (KIP) had been initiated by the city government as early as 1969, well before donor agencies expressed interest (Devas 1980: 10). In Lusaka, substantial resources and innovatory management were devoted to the early slum upgrading programme (Pasteur 1979). In other places, progress was slower. Planners, bureaucrats and politicians continued to be concerned with 'proper standards' (whether or not these could be achieved), with the fact that such settlements were 'illegal' or were not in conformity with the plan, and with the effect on the 'public image' of the city. Bulldozing 'slums' was still widely practised throughout the 1970s, particularly in capital cities and in locations visible to the international visitor. Such repressive approaches to the informal housing and spontaneous settlements have become much less common today, but are by no means extinct.

Plate 11   In Jakarta, the Kampung Improvement Programme (KIP) has provided essential services to around half of the city's population; however, the installation of infrastructure into areas already built up meant that houses had to be cut back in order to create space.

Interestingly, this shift in attitude in the developing countries had parallels in both Britain and the USA. During the 1950s and 1960s, urban authorities in these countries had invested a great deal of resources in clearing and redeveloping the old slum housing. Whilst such a policy was highly popular at first, it became progressively less so. This was partly because of dissatisfaction with the type of housing provided by the public authorities (often high-rise, ghetto estates, lacking proper facilities), and partly because of regret at the destruction of established communities and attractive, old buildings (Anderson 1964; McKie 1971). Gradually, the policy swung in favour of renovation and conservation of the older housing stock.

One other element of the housing scene which has received insufficient attention until recently is the private rental sector. For a very large proportion of low-income groups in most cities renting is the first, and often the only, option. The provision of rental accommodation is also one way in which those who are slightly better off can finance their own housing. Yet the rental sector has received little attention from planners, urban managers or researchers. Development control codes often seek to prevent the construction of rental units, or to set unrealisticly high standards. Rent control policies, intended to protect tenants, have generally had the effect of reducing the supply of rental accommodation, and discouraging maintenance of the stock (Gilbert 1989; Tipple and Willis 1989). Whether or not the private rental sector offers a satisfactory solution to the needs of the poor remains a hotly debated issue (Gilbert and Varley 1990; Aina 1990). Nevertheless, this sector deserves more attention.

The recognition of access to land as a key issue

The arguments about informal housing have moved on. Baross has pointed out that a particular advantage of 'informal' settlements for low-income households lies in the sequencing of development. This sequencing (occupation–building–servicing–planning) matches the priorities of the low-income groups, whereas sequencing of publicly provided schemes (planning–servicing–building–occupation) does not (Baross 1990). The critical constraint for people trying to provide their own shelter is access to land. Thus, the issue is not about house construction, nor even the provision of services, but about obtaining land. This recognition has led to an increasing interest in, and research into, the processes of urban land development, and the mechanisms by which the poor obtain access to land (Angel *et al.* 1983; Payne 1989; Hosaka 1988; Baross and van der Linden 1990; Amis 1990).

In the past, the poor have been able to obtain access to land in a variety of ways. In much of Africa communal land was allocated by traditional chiefs in accordance with need. In Latin America and South Asia, squatting on publicly owned (and privately owned) land, and invasions of land have been common. In many parts of the world, one of the main ways in which people have obtained access to land has been through informal, private subdivisions, particularly of fringe land. This process of subdivision is often illegal, in the sense that it contravenes planning or building codes (notably minimum plot size regulations), but such controls are rarely effective. For some, including the World Bank, this process of private subdivision is regarded as the key to urban development and housing strategies in the future (Doebele 1987; World Bank and UNCHS 1989).

Whatever the mechanisms, though, it appears that it has become progressively more difficult for the poor to obtain land (Baross and van der Linden 1990: 2). It may well be that some of the earlier notions about 'informal' housing processes were naïve. But there does appear to have been a marked trend worldwide towards greater commercial articulation of urban land. It is clear that many of the 'no cost' (or minimal cost) options are no longer open. Thus, in many parts of Africa, traditional land allocations have effectively become market transactions (Devas 1989c: 210; van Westen 1990: 98; Amis and Lloyd 1990); occupations of public and private land, and 'unauthorised settlements', are increasingly organised by 'land grabbers' and illegal subdividers, usually supported by politicians (P Ward 1990; Siddiqui and Khan 1990); and private subdivisions of land are now largely controlled by commercial property developers (Steinberg 1990; Angel and Pornchockchai 1990).

Plate 12   Pirate subdivision of fringe urban land, as here in Karachi, Pakistan, can result in some very unsatisfactory patterns of development; note the various stages of plot development shown in this picture.

Structure planning and action planning

In the realm of urban planning itself, dissatisfaction with traditional, rigid and inappropriate master plans led to two rather different responses: Structure Planning and Action Planning. In Britain, the Planning Advisory Group had reported in 1965 on the weaknesses of the Development Plans prescribed by the 1947 Act. The Group considered these plans to be too detailed, too rigid and too limited in scope to provide effective tools for guiding development (Amos 1986: 141). As a result, in 1968 a system of Structure Plans was introduced. These plans were intended to provide a broader, strategic framework for subsequent local plans, and were to take account of the regional context, and of transportation, housing and environmental issues (Ministry of Housing and Local Government 1970: 4).

The introduction of Structure Plans coincided with the emergence of a 'systems' view of planning. Drawing on the principles of cybernetics, this approach sought to model urban systems and to identify optimum patterns of development. These ideas, developed particularly in the United States, seemed to offer new hope of the planner's ability to handle urban problems (McLoughlin 1969: 17). This approach was facilitated by the arrival of computer simulation techniques which permitted large quantities of data to be handled and a large range of alternatives to be tested. Computer simulation was used in particular to develop large-scale regional land-use and transportation models, and such models influenced the preparation of a number of the structure plans in Britain.

However, the experience of structure planning in Britain was, on the whole, not a particularly happy one. The 'possibilities offered by computer-driven models proved to be something of a mirage. Vast quantities of data were amassed, elaborate models constructed, and numerous options proposed and tested. The process took a very long time: some structure plans did not appear until fifteen years after the legislation. Yet the results of all this effort often seemed little better than guesswork. Somehow, the basic aims seemed to have been submerged by the weight of technology and data. Meanwhile, responsibilities for planning were divided between levels of government: counties for structure planning, districts for local planning and plan implementation. This led to inevitable and irreconcilable conflicts, and to the marginalisation of the structure planning function. In addition, the statutory limitation of structure planning to land use issues meant that, as new concerns emerged such as economic decline, social deprivation and the need for urban regeneration, the structure planners seemed to have little of practical use to offer.

All this is not to say that strategic planning is irrelevant – far from it. But the way in which structure planning was implemented in Britain does illustrate some of the potential pitfalls. Few developing countries sought to follow the particular British model of structure plans. One which did was Malaysia, and it appears that they have encountered many of these same problems (G B Lee 1991) – see Box 3.6.

Box 3.6 Structure planning in Malaysia

Malaysia's Town and Country Planning Act 1976 introduced a system of structure planning. This Act was modelled very closely on the equivalent British legislation of 1971, including much of the procedure for preparation and approval of structure plans. As in Britain, the aim was to introduce a framework of strategic planning and policies to guide the social, economic and physical development of urban areas. According to the Act, structure plans consist of written statements accompanied by diagrams and illus-

Box 3.6   Structure planning in Malaysia (*continued*)

trations, and provide the basis for the preparation of detailed local plans. In Malaysia, structure planning replaced the previous system of map-based plans, prepared under the Town Board Enactment, which had come to be seen as rigid and unable to cope with the rapid pace of urban development.

The first structure plan to be prepared was for Kuala Lumpur and this was approved in 1984. In the decade following the Act, only two other structure plans were completed and approved, with a further eleven in course of preparation. Goh Ban Lee (1991: 86–8) describes the structure planning process in Penang Island as involving four phases:

1   establishing the machinery under the State Planning Committee for preparing the plan and establishing terms of reference for the project
2   preparing a report of survey on matters likely to affect the development of the area
3   preparing the draft structure plan itself
4   exhibition of the draft plan for public objections before approval by the State Planning Committee.

The structure planning system in Malaysia has considerable advantages over the previous system: it is much more comprehensive in terms of its consideration of the various factors which influence development; it is much more flexible to allow for changing circumstances; it is much better able to respond to community needs and aspirations; and it distinguishes between the broad goals and strategies on the one hand and the detailed physical development involved in local plans on the other.

However, it has also revealed serious shortcomings. The process of plan preparation has taken far too long, with the risk that plans are out of date before they are approved. The delay in preparation has been due partly to a shortage of skilled planning staff, but also to a tendency to be too comprehensive, to collect too many data, and to involve too many committee stages. The legislation itself imposes heavy obligations in terms of survey, often in areas where information is not readily available, and of time-consuming procedures which if not carried out precisely as prescribed could render the plan null and void.

Whilst it is clear that there is a need in Malaysia for some form of development strategy planning for the urban areas, and that the present system of structure planning represents a considerable improvement over what was there before, there must be questions about the appropriateness to Malaysia's current situation of the model of structure planning imported virtually wholesale from Britain.

(Material taken from G B Lee 1991; G B Lee and Siew 1991.)

Many of those concerned with urban planning practice in the developing world saw the problems of the master planning approach more in terms of its failure to deliver results on the ground (Koenigsberger 1964; Safier 1974). They identified the problem as being, in particular, the amount of time and effort required to produce a master plan, and the apparent irrelevance of most such plans to the real needs of the citizens. They advocated instead an 'Action Planning' approach which would identify the key urban problems and situations which were amenable to immediate action, and to identify those interventions which were within the resources and capacity of the authorities to carry out (Safier 1983; Mumtaz 1983). They developed a simplified series of steps:

1 **reconnaissance**: rapid appraisal of the dominant features of the area under consideration, identifying the strategic issues and problems
2 **guiding concept**: the principles to be applied in approaching the issues and problems identified, and the framework to be used for public sector and joint public/private/community initiatives on infrastructure, transport, housing, services, etc.
3 **action programme**: selection of a series of interconnected development strategies concerned with investment, land use and other resource use, designed to tackle the identified problems and to make best use of scarce resources
4 **role casting**: specification of the roles of the various agencies to be responsible for implementation of the components of the action programme, including detailed planning, financing, controlling, legalising, etc.
5 **monitoring and feedback**: an institutional arrangement for gathering information on the progress of implementation, on the problems encountered and on public responses, for feedback into the process of plan and programme revision.

(For further elaboration of the components of action planning, see Safier 1974 and Baross 1991).

The action planning approach has undoubtedly had some effect in shifting the emphasis of urban planning practice in the developing world away from the master planning model and towards a recognition of the urgency of the tasks involved. The approach fitted well with the requirements of donor agencies, who wanted to be able to divide up the task of urban improvement into manageable and fundable projects. One obvious problem with the action planning approach, though, is precisely its primary concern with action, to the possible detriment of an adequate strategic planning framework with which to guide the more specific action plans. The risk is, as with any 'projects approach', that action planning may end up as a series of disconnected interventions which fail to deal with the underlying problems. The somewhat negative experience of structure planning in Britain should not detract from the fundamental need for a proper strategic framework within which detailed plans and 'action plans' can be prepared, and for that framework to be concerned with the broader social, economic and regional considerations rather than merely with local land-use control. In a number of cases, such as Calcutta and Jakarta, the rapid preparation of a strategic planning framework provided an essential first stage in a metropolitan planning exercise, and provided the basis for specific action plans, notably in the realm of infrastructure development.

Infrastructure development

The critical needs for water, sanitation and transportation in the rapidly growing cities of the world has meant that infrastructure development has always been a key concern for urban planners and managers. But as well as its intrinsic importance, the provision of urban infrastructure also plays a crucial, instrumental role in determining the pattern of land development. As Courtney (1978) suggests, infrastructure development may be far more effective than any master plan or any system of land-use regulation in determining where development will take place. According to Linn, 'Extension of public services throughout the city is the most effective policy instrument for expanding the supply of urban housing' (Linn 1983: 183). Yet, all too often, while the planners continued to work on their master plans, the crucial decisions were being taken by public works engineers, through their programmes of infrastructure development. More recently, planners have come to acknowledge the need not only to be involved with the planning of new infrastructure, but also to use the provision of infrastructure as one of the key means for influencing the pattern of land development. Such an approach, under the title of Guided Land Development, was, for instance, adopted in the Metropolitan Development Plan for Greater Jakarta (Devas 1983; Marulanda and Steinberg 1991); it has also been adopted for the development of Kathmandu (C B Shrestha and Malla 1991: 14).

Once again, the donor agencies have often been the main advocates of such an approach, since it fitted well with their interests in identifying fundable infrastructure projects. Such projects are particularly amenable to the application of standard techniques of project evaluation. However, in the absence of a proper strategic planning framework, project evaluation techniques can be used to justify almost anything, and their use has tended to reinforce the power of the project engineer and the donor agency. Clearly, though, involvement in the programming of infrastructure investment provides a way for planners both to influence the decision-making process, and to operationalise their development plans. Calcutta's Metropolitan Planning Organisation (subsequently the Calcutta Metropolitan Development Authority) was one of the first examples of such an approach (Sivaramakrishnan and Green 1986: 155); Manila's Capital Investment Folio is another example (see Box 3.5). Nor is it simply a matter of infrastructure programming: increasingly it is seen that planners and urban managers need to be involved in the whole municipal budgeting process, in order to be able to influence the patterns of service delivery, operation and maintenance, as well as the pattern of investment.

Box 3.7   Manila's Capital Investment Folio (CIF)

The CIF was developed during the 1980s as a way of co-ordinating infrastructure investment decisions with the physical planning process for Metro Manila. The multiplicity of agencies involved in the city's development – government departments, state enterprises and local governments, as well as the Metro Manila Commission itself – had made co-ordination difficult: each agency had tended to pursue its own investment plans with little regard for the metropolitan-wide planning strategy. This situation also created uncertainty for service agencies about future development patterns, about demand levels, and about the provision of complementary infrastructure.

Originally conceived simply as a 'shopping list' of infrastructure projects, the CIF has evolved into a prioritised, five-year rolling capital expenditure programme which is integrated into the annual budgeting process of the agencies concerned. It has provided a forum for discussion between all the agencies and local governments involved in the metropolitan region about future expenditure plans. The main features of the CIF are

1   a regional development plan for Metro Manila, including policies, targets and strategies, recognised by all the major agencies
2   identification of all the proposed public sector projects and programmes in the region according to location, anticipated timing and intended beneficiaries
3   identification of likely financial resources
4   an evaluation procedure to establish priorities between projects
5   preparation of a five-year investment programme which is rolled forward each year as the first year enters the annual capital budgets of the implementing agencies and local governments concerned.

The uncertain economic situation of the 1980s necessitated the incorporation of alternative projections of financial resources into the evaluation process. It also required a more thorough screening of projects, including consideration of whether ongoing projects should be cut back or deferred to make way for higher priority projects. The evaluation process does not seek to duplicate project appraisal already undertaken by the agencies concerned or by funders, but rather to prioritise all projects against a common set of criteria and according to varying assumptions about future resource availability. The criteria include socio-political acceptability, government budgetary requirements, debt service requirements, economic profitability and institutional capacity.

The CIF process also involves the development of sectoral strategies which cover policies, institutional measures and opportunities for private sector investment as well as specifying the public sector investment programmes. These sectoral strategies, like the CIF itself, are developed in conjunction with the agencies concerned. This is important since the Metro Manila Commission has no power to determine the investment decisions of other government agencies.

The CIF has provided a framework for co-ordinating infrastructure

> **Box 3.7   Manila's Capital Investment Folio (CIF)** (*continued*)
> investment decisions in relation to the physical development plan, and
> thereby of influencing the pattern of physical development of the metro-
> politan area.
> (Based on material from Nathaniel von Einsiedel, former Project Director,
> Metro Manila Commission)

Institution building

In parallel with this growing awareness of the key role of infrastructure
development, there arose an increasing concern with the inadequacies
of the existing institutions of urban government. During the 1950s and
1960s, colonial-style institutions continued to dominate the scene, with
municipal authorities generally having primary responsibility for urban
development. But during the late 1960s and the 1970s, many new institutions were formed: national housing authorities, water and sewerage
undertakings, urban development corporations and so on. In some
countries, particularly in Africa, governments established national
land-use and planning authorities to control urban land development
(Franklin 1979: 18).

There were a number of reasons for the mushrooming of these new
institutions. The first was the general tendency towards centralisation,
at the expense of local government, as newly independent regimes
sought to consolidate their power at national level. The second was the
belief that existing institutions like local authorities lacked the capacity –
technical, managerial and financial – to manage the complex process of
urban development. Local authorities also often lacked the range of
functions and powers, as well as the territorial jurisdictions, required for
comprehensive urban management. And third, donor agencies often
insisted on the establishment of separate, specialist organisations to
manage the particular sector or project with which the donor agency
was concerned. During the 1970s and early 1980s, donor agencies put
considerable resources of technical assistance and training into building
up these new institutions, often alongside existing institutions.

One particular institutional approach adopted in a number of cities
was the establishment of a metropolitan development authority (Sivaramakrishnan and Green 1986: 8). The justification for this, apart from any
shortcomings in the capacity of existing local authorities, was that in
most cases the metropolitan area covered a number of existing local
authorities, and hence there was a need for one metropolitan-wide authority to co-ordinate development. Whilst such organisations took various forms in different countries, a common characteristic was their
much wider powers and greater financial resources compared to existing

local authorities. As a result, they were able to undertake relatively large-scale urban infrastructure investment (Menezes 1985). Such organisations were often strongly supported by donor agencies, who saw them as effective vehicles for channelling investment resources.

During the 1980s there has been a growing disenchantment with this approach. Institutions tended to proliferate, as new ones were created but old ones were not disbanded (Bolaffi 1989: 13). The results were overlapping responsibilities, confusions of authority, lack of co-ordination and the growth of empires of vested interests. In some cases, the metropolitan development authorities had little or no leverage over any of the 'kaleidoscope of organisations' which they were supposed to be co-ordinating (Amos 1989a: 205). Metropolitan authorities also had a habit of constructing new infrastructure and then handing it over to municipal councils which had no capacity to operate or maintain it. In addition, these metropolitan institutions generally lacked any adequate mechanism for popular participation. However weak and corrupted the old systems of local government may have become, they usually provided some avenue for the public to make its views known and to influence decisions. This is not generally the case with the parastatal organisations, whose lines of accountability are to the central (or state) government. There is, therefore, a real risk that such organisations are insensitive to the needs and aspirations of the local community.

For all these reasons, the late 1980s saw a re-emergence in a number of countries, and in the thinking of the donor agencies, of the role of local government (Stren 1990: 48). It is too early to say how far this approach will be pursued, but it is clear that it can be effective only if steps are taken to deal with the various institutional capacity problems – finance, technical and managerial skills, internal organisation – which led to the establishment of alternative institutions in the first place.

Another model which appears to be receiving greater attention recently is that of the non-governmental organisation (NGO), or in American usage, the private voluntary organisation (PVO). Traditionally, most governments have been suspicious of NGOs, regarding them as a potential political threat, although in many cases they have relied on them to provide certain services, particularly to the poor. By contrast, donors have often found NGOs to be a useful way of targeting assistance on particular groups such as the poor. They are also likely to be more innovative and cost effective than government agencies (Rodwin 1987: 27). Depending on the particular national situation, NGOs often have better networks within poor communities, may be more representative of the interests of those communities, and may be better motivated, than governmental agencies. On the other hand, NGOs too can be elitist, paternalistic, unaccountable and concerned primarily with their own vested interests. Clearly, NGOs cannot be a substitute for democratic local government, but within an overall system, there should be a significant role for a variety of NGOs as 'competitors' to governmental agencies and as 'goads' to those agencies. These are issues to which we will return in later chapters.

The urban management model

Along with the concern about institutional reform went a concern about the approach to management itself. The colonial inheritance of public administration in most countries had been one of a rigid bureaucracy, the main purpose of which was to preserve public order. Tasks were divided up so as to suit the colonial authorities and to ensure control by colonial administrators. In most countries, administrative systems remained much the same after independence, except that they soon became inflated with large numbers of inadequately skilled, inadequately supervised, under-paid and under-motivated officials (Amos 1989a: 207). As a result, the ability to deliver routine public services, which had been relatively good in a number of municipal councils around the time of independence, tended to decline.

The traditional patterns of administration, with powerful departments, rigid hierarchies, and an emphasis on bureaucratic control, were not well suited to the tasks of managing urban development (Sivaramakrishnan and Green 1986: 62). During the late 1960s and the 1970s, new ideas about public sector management had emerged in Europe and North America. Drawing on the models of private sector businesses, a new emphasis was placed on corporate management, with clearly defined organisational goals, objectives and strategies, and with a corporate management team to ensure co-ordination between departments in achieving those organisational goals. The 'corporate approach' became an important feature of local authority management in Britain during the 1970s (J Stewart 1988). Following the reorganisation of local government in Britain in 1974, most local authorities restructured their administrations under a Chief Executive, and established a central Policy and Resources Committee of elected members to determine council strategy and policy. Within that corporate approach, the planner was often seen as playing a key role as a member of the local authority's management team.

During the 1980s, financial stringency and a changing political climate meant a retreat from some of the grander ideas of municipal management in many developed countries. A greater emphasis has been placed on cost-effectiveness, efficiency and 'value for money' in the provision of local services. Once again, many of the models adopted have been borrowed from the private sector. One such model is the decentralisation of resource and service management. Under such a model, responsibilities for management are assigned to self-accounting 'cost centres' which are required to maximise service performance within their given resources in a quasi-commercial (or even a fully commercial) manner. Another model is the separation of 'client' and 'contractor' roles of local government such that the standard of service required is specified by the client department and the service is provided on a contractual basis by a 'service unit' or direct labour organisation within the authority. This permits greater transparency of decisions about service levels and costs. It also permits the opening up of service provision to competition with private sector contractors on the basis of service specifications drawn up and monitored by the client department. In an extreme version of this model, the local authority would cease to provide any services directly but would simply contract private operators through competitive tender to supply all services on a specified basis.

In all this, the watchwords are increased efficiency (obtaining greater output from fewer resources), transparency (being able to identify clearly what is being provided by whom, to whom, and at what cost), and accountability (the processes by which decision-makers and managers are called to account for the performance of the services for which they are responsible).

In the developing world, such ideas seem not to have penetrated very far. There are, of course, examples of organisations which have adopted a corporate approach to management, and which are actively pursuing greater cost-effectiveness in service delivery, but these examples are mainly among the newer organisations such as urban development corporations and single purpose agencies. By-and-large, local government structures still tend to be highly compartmentalised and hierarchical, and concerned primarily with bureaucratic control. Donor agencies, such as the World Bank, have long been concerned with cost recovery, and this has led to an interest in organisational management and efficiency at both national and local levels, but the results so far have been limited. More recently, international concerns with accountability and 'good government' have begun to find responses in a number of developing countries, but in most cases there remains a long way to go.

One thing that has begun to emerge is a recognition of the nature of the relationship between planning and management. As we noted in Chapter 2, planning can no longer be seen as an activity separate from management, but should be regarded as an integral part of it, concerned as much with the delivery of urban services as with plan preparation. Plan implementation has to be achieved through influence on both the private sector and the political process, and through promotion, guidance and facilitation of private sector development, rather than through the mere preparation of plan documents and application of negative land-use controls. All this calls for new systems of management and decision-making, and for effective procedures for monitoring and feedback on performance (Sivaramakrishnan and Green 1986: 60–2).

There are, of course, substantial obstacles to achieving improved urban management. One is the acute lack of management skills within the public sector in most developing countries. Another is the resistance of various interest groups such as civil servants and politicians to new approaches and more transparent and accountable processes. The former may perceive improved management as a threat to their comfortable positions or to their power; the latter may see an increasingly 'technocratic' management as eroding their scope for patronage and influence. There are also valid questions about how such 'technocratic' approaches to management, and particularly the more market-oriented models, can be reconciled with the legitimate role of political participation, and with the need to be responsive to the community, particularly the poor.

Concern for the poor and for the community

A key issue in the discussion about urban planning and management concerns the impact of these activities on the urban poor. Whether the debate is about the urban economy, about shelter, or about service provision, a central question is how the position of the urban poor can be improved. A related question is how the local community can influence the decisions which affect their community and their living environment.

The late 1960s and the 1970s saw a disenchantment with traditional theories of economic growth, with their implication that economic growth would benefit everyone. The reality was that, in most cases, economic growth had widened the gaps between rich and poor. Moreover, such had been the failure in many countries of the benefits of growth to 'trickle-down' to the poor, that the poor often found themselves worse off than before, at least in relative terms. The gap between rich and poor is particularly apparent in cities like Rio de Janiero, Manila, Jakarta and Lagos, where palatial houses, luxury cars and opulent lifestyles contrast starkly with cardboard shacks and beggars in the streets.

In the early 1970s, development theorists and aid agencies began to search for strategies for achieving 'growth with equity' (Chenery *et al.* 1974). Clearly, governments of developing countries did not have the resources to establish comprehensive welfare systems, while wholesale redistribution of income was seen as jeopardising economic growth – as well as being virtually impossible to implement. One strategy which was advocated was the 'Basic Needs' approach under which resources would be redirected towards ensuring that everyone has access to a minimum level of essential services. Governments in many developing countries made at least some shift in policy towards a basic needs approach, with greater emphases on primary education, primary health care, support for small-scale agriculture, and income-generating activities. In the urban sector, the basic needs approach involved an emphasis on the provision of minimum levels of water and sanitation, through public standpipes and pit latrines, and on the upgrading of informal settlements.

Those on the radical left saw the failure of economic growth to benefit the poor as an inevitable consequence of capitalism. For them, the basic needs approach was a mere palliative, which obliged the poor to accept an inferior level of services. Others saw that the need was not so much to invent new programmes to serve the poor, which in any case were likely to be commandeered by the better off, but to reorient the routine programmes of government agencies so as to improve access by the poor (Batley and Devas 1988: 178).

Much of the policy towards the urban poor had, traditionally, been paternalistic and 'top-down', in which the public sector agencies con-

Plate 13 Economic growth has not ensured satisfactory living conditions for all: squatters living alongside the railway tracks in Jakarta.

tinued to have sole responsibility for the provision of services to the poor. Such a welfarist approach had been evident in most of the 'aided self-help' housing projects of the 1960s and 1970s. Although sites-and-services projects all required substantial amounts of individual or community self-help in house construction and, in some cases, in infrastructure development, the key decisions invariably lay outside the control of the 'beneficiaries'. Similarly, the process of 'participation' in most settlement upgrading projects has been a top-down form of consultation, co-option and mobilisation (Devas 1980; Moser 1989a). One of the more celebrated examples of participation and self-help was the Hyderabad Urban Community Development Programme in India, but even here it seems that, as the project increased in scale, it shifted from being one led by local communities to one led by technical experts (Thomson 1989: 172). Although the 1976 Habitat Conference in Vancouver marked a clear shift in national and international human settlements policy in favour of the urban poor, the approach was still very much a top-down one.

In recent years, the value of top-down forms of 'participation' has increasingly been questioned, especially where it means that the poor have to contribute resources of time, effort and money in order to obtain services which the rest of society obtains without direct contribution. Unless the process of participation leads to empowerment of the poor, and an effective shift in resources to those things which the poor need, it is argued, then it is a waste of their time and effort. In recent years, there has been much talk of 'enabling' – a process by which the local community (or individuals) are enabled to realise their own goals in a manner which is satisfactory to them (Moser 1989a; Rondinelli and Cheema 1988). It may be contrasted with the 'disabling' approach of much governmental intervention which is paternalistic, bureaucratic, lacking in choice, and which reduces the capacity of the recipients to help themselves. 'Enabling' is clearly an attractive concept, but there seems to be little consensus about its precise meaning, let alone about how exactly it is to be achieved.

One particular aspect of the broader distributional and participation questions which has begun to receive greater attention in recent years is the gender issue (Moser 1989b; Rakodi 1991b). Conventional planning and management approaches have tended to regard women as 'invisible', despite the fact that in many cities, a very large proportion of households are headed by women. Increasingly, it has been recognised that women have interests and priorities which are distinctly different from those of men, particularly in relation to the planning of the living and working environment. Women generally bear much of the burden of inadequate urban services, and may be particularly vulnerable to negative controls on informal sector activities. In addition, the conventional assumption that women have 'free time' in which to participate in 'self-help' projects is extremely dubious (Moser 1989a: 88).

Clearly, the whole question of the impact of programmes on the urban poor and on women, and of how the community can influence the decisions which affect them, is an integral part of the wider political context. Politics is not, as some would have it, merely about the role of 'elected members' or 'politicians'. It is about the whole process by which decisions are reached – about who decides what and how. For many planners and administrators, 'politics' is viewed as an obstacle to good governance and as an arrangement by which the 'politicians interfere' with sound administrative processes in order to further their personal and political ends.[4] Whilst there may often be a large element of truth in that, such an analysis assumes that administrative decisions are somehow neutral and 'technically correct'. Yet urban planning and management is fundamentally about the allocation of resources between competing claimants – something which is essentially political in nature. Furthermore, planners and managers are themselves active participants in the decision-making process, often with their own vested interests and agenda. These are some of the issues which will be discussed further by Richard Batley in Chapter 7 and Carole Rakodi in Chapter 8.

Resurgence of the market mechanism and the role of the private sector

Probably the dominant feature of political landscape worldwide during the 1980s, as we noted in Chapter 1, has been the shift to the right. The 'neo-classical counter-revolution' (Killick 1986; Todaro 1989: 82), with its emphasis on market mechanisms and the private sector, has had a profound effect on the thinking of both governments and donor agencies, and has affected capitalist and socialist economies alike. 'Deregulation' is firmly on the political agenda in many parts of the developing world. Government regulation, it is argued, has tended to restrain the dynamism of the private sector and to divert resources from productive activities into 'rent-seeking', thereby reducing economic growth (Kreuger 1974; Lal 1985).

For much of the developing world, the vast majority of economic activities take place within the private market, and most development is carried out by the private sector. Except in a few command economies, the role of the state is essentially a negative one of regulating the private sector in the public interest. However laudable its aims, such regulation has frequently not improved situations in practice, and in many cases has made things worse. Nowhere is this more true than the urban land market, where government interventions of all sorts have tended to make it more difficult for the poor to obtain land for housing (Payne 1989: 14; Baross and van der Linden 1990: 13). This has led donor agencies and governments to examine more carefully how private land markets operate, and how it might be possible to work with, and influence, the operation of land markets, rather than seeking to suppress them. One method is through the provision of infrastructure, as discussed earlier; another is through land taxation systems (Shoup 1978; Devas 1983; Doebele 1987; Siddiqui and Khan 1990).

In terms of urban development, the debate is not whether the private sector should do everything or the public sector should do everything. Rather it is about how governments can use their (limited) resources most effectively to bring about a desired outcome. By providing the right framework, and making a strategic use of their resources, government agencies may be able to lever substantial resources from the private sector. There are many examples of this in the developed world (for example, urban regeneration in Baltimore, USA, and in Birmingham, UK – see Box 3.5, p. 79), but relatively few in the developing world; Kingston, Jamaica may be one (Knight 1989: 37). There is, however, an important question about the balance between public and private interests. For example, the London Docklands scheme is sometimes hailed as an example of how substantial private investment can be levered by modest public investment; the reality, though, is that the relaxing of planning controls on extremely valuable land close to the City of London has resulted in a monumental speculative development, with little or no concession to the wider public interest. This is not so much levering private resources to achieve a public benefit, as simply giving away public assets to private developers. When it rides on the back of a massive speculative property boom, a collapse in commercial property prices threatens the whole endeavour and results in private sector appeals to be baled out by additional public sector inputs, as was seen in London in 1992.

In the area of service provision too the role of the private sector has re-emerged. Over the years, the public sector has tended to displace private sector provision of services. But poor management, lack of competition, and corruption have all contributed to reducing the quality of the services provided by the public sector in most developing countries. In recent years, there has been a strong trend towards the privatisation of state-owned industries, and the contracting out of public services to private sector suppliers. Other models, too, are being adopted, such as joint ventures, public/private co-operation agreements, and the re-estab-lishment of public sector agencies as commercial undertakings (Roth 1987).

Whilst countries such as Britain and the USA have gone a long way down this road, the presumption that governments should provide public services continues in most developing countries. One exception is public transport, which in most developing countries has long been dominated by the private sector (Roth 1987). The private sector/free market ideology is now firmly established within donor agencies such as the World Bank, USAID and ODA, and such agencies can be expected to use their leverage to encourage developing countries to follow suit.

However, the dangers of the private sector/free market approach are real. Quite apart from the wider ideological questions, there are a number of practical questions. First, in many countries, government agencies are providing services simply because no private business is willing or able to provide them. Merely advocating private provision of services does not mean that private enterprises will find it profitable to provide them. Second, many public services are natural monopolies, while others tend towards monopoly control in developing countries because of the small size of the market and the lack of access to capital. Whilst there is no guarantee that a public sector monopoly will produce a socially desirable outcome, the risks involved in allowing free rein to a private monopolist – who is not accountable to the public in any way – would seem to be even greater. Third, for the urban planner/manager, there is also the problem of how to achieve a co-ordinated provision of public services when each agency is pursuing its own private goals without accountability to any public authority. Given these problems, any policy of privatising public services will still require some frame-work of public sector regulation to ensure that the public interest is served.

Thus the argument is not about whether or not there should be regu-lation, but about what form that regulation should take and how it should be applied. It is also about how the public sector can use its influence to promote the sort of developments and services it wants, rather than doing everything itself, and how it can 'enable' the private sector, the community and individuals to provide the services which society requires (Brooke 1989). There is much ground still to be explored here.

Increasing environmental awareness

The last of the themes which we shall consider in this section concerns the environment. The rapid growth in awareness of environmental issues during the latter half of the 1980s would appear to be at odds with the notions of the supremacy of markets and of the private sector. Environmental consciousness has been growing within the affluent 'north' for some time. As long ago as 1970, the British Government established a Department of the Environment, although that turned out to be no more than a renaming of the old Ministry of Housing and Local Government, with minimal interest in environmental issues. But during the 1980s, awareness of global interdependence and the fragility of the world's ecological system has grown considerably. Nor has this new consciousness been confined to the developed nations. A growing concern has been expressed worldwide about such problems as the destruction of the rain forests, desertification, the dumping of toxic waste, atmospheric pollution around major cities, global warming, and the consequent risks of flooding in many parts of the world. Whilst many of these problems have been caused by excessive levels of consumption by the rich, the problems affect everyone, and the primary victims are often the poor.

Quite apart from the environmental problems caused by affluence, it has become increasingly apparent that the pattern of urban growth in the poorer countries of the world has created some very serious environmental problems which require urgent attention. These include:

1   the pollution of water supplies: by disposal of sewage, solid waste and toxic waste into water supplies or in close proximity to ground water sources; by salt-water penetration of ground-water sources close to the sea as a result of excessive ground-water extraction; by development on aquifer recharge zones; and so on
2   construction of housing on dangerous and ecologically fragile zones such as steep hillsides, canal and river banks, and natural drainage zones
3   the destruction of vegetation and forests, both for urban development and for fuelwood, thereby worsening problems of soil erosion and increasing risks of flooding
4   dangerous levels of atmospheric pollution in many cities, due particularly to vehicle and industrial emissions
5   the uncontrolled dumping of vast quantities of domestic and industrial waste, some of which may be toxic.

Increased attention is now being given to these issues in many quarters.[5] However, action to tackle these problems in the rapidly growing cities of the world has hardly begun. Developing country governments clearly lack the resources to tackle these vast problems directly, while regulatory controls pose dilemmas both about effectiveness of enforcement and about unintended consequences of intervention. At the same time, it is not enough to assume that the mechanisms of the free market or private initiatives will solve the problems. Once again, the question is how governments can use their limited resources, both financial and managerial, in the most strategic ways in order to bring about the greatest beneficial impact on the growing environmental problems.

The new realism

If there is a common characteristic within the approaches currently being advocated in relation to urban planning and management, that characteristic is probably a new realism:

1 realism about urban population growth, recognising that it is neither possible, nor in most cases desirable, to prevent cities from growing; thus urban population growth must be planned for and accommodated

2 recognition that the form of cities is determined largely by the decisions of individuals and organisations, rather than by governments, and that the private sector will continue to play a dominant role in city development

3 recognition of the limitations on the abilities of governments to intervene effectively in the urban system; in the past, government interventions have, for a variety of reasons, produced unintended and often undesirable results; a more realistic approach distinguishes between those aspects where government intervention is both essential and can be implemented effectively, and those aspects which are best left to the market

4 realism about the resource constraints which governments face, at both national and local level, particularly those in countries which are debt-laden and undergoing 'structural adjustment'

5 realism about what people, especially the poor, can afford to pay for improved urban services and shelter

6 from the above two, realism about the standards of services which can be adopted (the issue of affordability), how these should be priced (the issue of cost recovery), and how they should be allocated between competing claimants, so that all may benefit rather than just a limited group (the issues of equity and replicability)

7 recognition that the planning process cannot be a tidy, linear sequence of survey–plan–action; rather, these stages need to be pursued concurrently and iteratively; plans need to be flexible and incremental, rather than rigid, end-state blueprints; this requires an effective system of monitoring and feedback

8 realism about the limited capacity of institutions to implement plans and programmes, in terms of technical skills, management capacity, institutional efficiency, and inter-agency conflict

9 realism about the limited ability of planning authorities to enforce regulatory systems of development control, due to limited administrative capacity and political will, weaknesses of the legal system and problems of corruption; hence the need to identify alternative ways of influencing the pattern of land development, for example, through infrastructure development

10 recognition of the importance of incrementalism, whether in housing construction (enabling people to build gradually over time as their resources permit), in urban projects (building steadily on proven performance, rather than introducing radical and untried

approaches on a massive scale) or in institution building (regular review and incremental reform, rather than wholesale overthrowing of existing institutions)

11 realism about the nature of political agendas and political processes, recognising why plans are so often not implemented and seeing 'politics' not as an obstacle to the implementation of a plan or a programme, but as a framework within which an 'implementable' plan or programme must be developed.

Some may see this 'new realism' as mere pragmatism, lacking the vision of the founding fathers of planning. Some may see it as no more than the current conventional wisdom of the World Bank and other donor agencies, heavily influenced by the thinking of the 'new right'. But it does seek to go further than the more simplistic calls to 'roll back the frontiers of the public sector' and to leave market forces to sort out the mess. Rather, the aim is to develop an approach which can actually bring about perceptible improvements in living conditions in the cities of the developing world, particularly for the poor. If it is to do that, the approaches have to be realistic in terms of the conditions, the resources and the constraints which apply in the real-life context of the world's fast growing cities.

Notes

1. Readers may justifiably question my earlier analysis which traced the origins of British town planning to the Victorian reformers, rather than to the great civic builders of earlier generations. However, while the great architects like Wren and Nash did have a profound effect on ideas about the form of cities, the present *system* of town planning in Britain derives much more directly from the building by-laws of the second half of the nineteenth century.
2. In reality, planners – whatever they may imagine – rarely have the power to move industry and commerce around. Turner quotes an example of planners in one South American country who imagined that, merely by zoning their plans an appropriate colour, they could achieve industrial relocation (A Turner 1989: 4).
3. It is interesting that housing has also been by far the dominant theme in the literature on urban development until quite recently.
4. This struggle between the politician and the administrator was brilliantly satirised in the BBC Television series *Yes, Minister*.
5. For example, the International Institute for Environment and Development recently launched a journal specifically concerned with urban environmental issues under the title: *Environment and Urbanisation*.

CHAPTER 4

Urban management intervention in land markets

Michael Mattingly

There are two kinds of mechanisms for distributing resources within a society: markets and governments. Because land is a basic resource for urban development, urban government needs an ability to manage to some degree the ownership and use of land and the taxes and fees which may be drawn from it. In undertaking the interventions which management demands, most developing countries' governments have had too little regard for urban land markets. Land-use controls have been applied with little or no concern for market side-effects. Where governments have been endowed with large quantities of public land and have specified use and ownership as terms of their allocation, this stewardship has suffered from a failure to understand how allocated land can be subject to market forces.

The purpose of this chapter is to show how government management of urban land is intertwined with the operations of urban land markets, such that these markets must be better understood if government actions are to be more successful.

Urban management and land markets

Management

Effective urban management is critical to achieving the proper functioning of urban areas in the developing world so that these areas can play their roles in the social and economic development of their people. Land is only one of several resources which must be managed, and there is more to managing land than simply planning what will happen to it. Management is also concerned, even if sometimes only in a general way, with the development of land, with the operation of activities which use the land, with maintaining land for its continued use, and with finding the resources for its development, use, and maintenance.

Responsibilities for management first need to be focused and accepted. In most cases, there has been no single manager of urban areas and no single manager of urban land. In the future more responsibility is likely to be taken by local authorities, although all levels of government lack adequate resources. Priorities for attention need to be decided. But this necessitates a hard look at what urban management by local government is likely to be able to do. A number of possibilities can be eliminated when the operations of urban land markets are taken into account.

Land markets

An urban land market is the set of activities by which, through exchanges of value, rights to land are transferred. Different theories attempting to explain land markets do not so much conflict as they have different focuses and therefore have different comments to make about market activities. Neo-classical economics is concerned with supply and demand and the transaction prices which result from their interaction. It is interested in the efficiency with which the market functions, and seeks to identify barriers to the smooth interplay of supply and demand. Marxist theory talks of the social relations which are the source of land values. It is most concerned with who creates these values, how they are created, who enjoys these values, and how. It is often used to examine the fairness of market results. While the former can tell about the creation of land prices and something of the economic costs and benefits, the latter can help identify who gets the costs and benefits, including social costs and benefits. Both can be concerned with who uses the land: neo-classical economic theory, by focusing on the efficiency of market operations which can be identified with particular social or economic groups; Marxist theory by identifying who obtains the various benefits of market exchanges. Yet Marxist theory has little interest in the particular use to which a piece of urban land is put. Neo-classical economics sees use as a consequence of factors of market demand, location, and physical qualities and worries over the efficiency of systems for producing goods and services as a consequence of land use arrangements.

The view taken here is that understanding the urban land market means understanding matters from both these approaches: the interplay of supply and demand and the economic cost and benefits, as well as the roles of the social agents in the production of land prices and the social costs and benefits involved. The reasons for this are that the weaknesses of policy which can be traced to land rights transactions clearly connect with all of these matters. Differences in the natures and objectives of policies will determine that certain matters will be of special concern with regard to any one policy, and for that a particular body of theory may be more useful.

Even so, reference to the land market is a convention of convenience, for it is obvious that this market is fragmented in various ways which are probably interconnected. According to the interests of the observer, the market may be broken down in various ways: for example, into major land uses, into income groups, or into areas within a city or town. Studies of residential land markets in the less developed countries have identified growing informal markets operating alongside those which have been seen as regular. Also, there are reasons to distinguish the market for raw land from that for land to be used a second time for urban purposes.

The market and its divisions into specific sub-markets are not well represented by the available theories. Economists point out, for instance, how each parcel of land is different from another, and therefore does not fit well into classical models of supply and demand inter-relationships. Marxist analysis to explain a particular urban sub-market requires information of a kind and of a detail which it is not practical to obtain. Nevertheless, these theories and combinations of them identify the elements of what can be called market activity, and mark important matters which may affect or be affected by the interventions of urban management.

Management interventions in markets

Urban management practice includes many acts of, or attempts at, intervention in land markets, some of them unintentional. Planned land-use patterns, density regulations, the timing and location of new roads and water pipes, taxes based on land values: all these and more comprise the substance of a long tradition of urban growth management. To these in recent times have been added others, most notably, programmes to make renters and squatters into owners. Yet the logic and possibilities for success of many such urban land market interventions are subject to question. This seems especially true in developing countries where traditional land planning practices, poor data sources, rapid urban growth, and fast-changing political and economic conditions create a distinctive setting.

There is need to appreciate the importance of urban land as a marketable commodity in less developed countries. The special characteristics of these countries heighten the basic competition among would-be users of space – the families seeking houses, the entrepreneurs wanting places for factories and shops, and so on. To begin with, rapid urbanisation steadily increases the numbers needing space and therefore engaged in the competition for land. But land also offers a relatively safe haven for capital in economies which can fluctuate wildly. Moreover, urban land is a more attractive investment where alternatives in manufacturing or service industry are both very few and subject to great risks. So investors enter the competition, and do so with more funds. To this already large and growing demand is added the speculators, whose prospects are greatly increased by the promise of a demand which is not only growing, but usually growing rapidly. The original speculative investment may be recovered in a matter of two or three years, especially where inflation is rapid, after which it is all profit and no risk.

Meanwhile, supply does not keep pace. A major constraint is the shortage of services. This is typically a consequence of limited government financial resources and the relatively weak claim which service provisions can make upon them. These are again special characteristics of the less developed countries. So are the confusions over ownership of undeveloped land arising from traditional systems of land tenure and the poorly developed legal and administrative mechanisms for land transfer.

In few parts of the developing world has government action through the urban land market been effective. Rarely have public authorities managed to increase the supply of urban land for avowed target groups, matched supplies of services and transport to demand at particular locations, or channelled unearned profits from landowners to resource-starved government agencies. Rarely have they avoided contributing to these unearned profits when buying lands for public purposes, or con-tributing to personal fortunes when allocating public lands.

There are examples to the contrary: urban land readjustment and the tax on land value increases in Taiwan, land development in Ismailia, Egypt, and land sharing in Bangkok. But these are not examples of what is generally done. These cases were so peculiar that there has not been substantial repetition of their experiences. They establish what might be if more of the world were similar to their special circumstances, rather than what is possible in many cases. And prominent in these circum-stances were unique market conditions.

Certainly the poor record of urban land management in developing countries cannot be wholly explained as inattention to market oper-ations. There are other technical areas fraught with problems, such as unexpected population growth and inattention to costs. There are common factors of national economy, such as the decline of many national productive systems which has reduced government funds for everything from development control administration to public land acquisition. Proposals are thwarted for political reasons because of the power bases which arise from the economic or social value of land. Urban administrators and technicians have fortunately become more aware of economic, administrative and political factors. Nevertheless, things being what they are, each of these other factors in some way bears upon the land market.

It is not just that strategies of direct intervention too often produce results different from those wanted, or no results at all, because of faulty assumptions as to how, when and where urban land changes hands. There are market side-effects to a multitude of other governmental actions which create or intensify problems of urban development or interfere with land market interventions. National programmes promot-ing large-scale industries will increase land demand in certain large cities; rural development schemes will do the same in towns which serve the farmers. Transport improvements between or within certain cities may increase the attractiveness of those cities to bidders for commercial and residential land. Corporate taxes or import restrictions may make less appealing some of the chief alternatives to investing in urban land. Too frequently these side-effects upon the urban markets seem to catch urban decisions makers by surprise.

Then there are the hidden agendas which deflect intervention. Ad-ministrators recognise opportunities for personal gain in the transactions which they carry out. Individuals with power may be guided in their decision-making by a sense of whose lands will most gain in value from particular public investments. Though seemingly unsophisticated in many instances, their awareness of market effects too often seems more lively than that of the planning and management professionals, especially those imported as consultants into unfamiliar situations.

Evidence from widely distributed experiences leads to the conclusion that urban land management pays too little attention to urban land markets, understands them poorly, and suffers greatly as a result (see Angel *et al.* 1983; Baross and van der Linden 1990). If urban government is to be an important voice in urban affairs in developing countries, and if it is to increase the effectiveness of its actions, it must recognise how failure to adequately understand land markets has weakened management efforts in the past. This failure is examined here with respect to common policies affecting urban land.

Land markets and common policies affecting land

The purposes of urban land policies are, in general terms, to affect the ownership of land, its price and its use, and to utilise land values as a basis for obtaining public funds. These aspects are interconnected. Ownership affects the choice of use and investment in land. Use potential affects the price of land and who can afford the rights to it. These interrelationships are exploited by policies which obtain revenue from land values.

Policies to affect ownership

Policies to determine ownership are usually directed at the needs for land of both governments and the poor. Sometimes, these are essentially the same, for currently much of government market intervention has the ultimate objective of improving access to land for low-income households.

Land for the poor
Efforts to improve the housing conditions of low-income families through land policies have encountered some unexpected market effects. An initial surprise was that schemes for housing the poor could not easily be delivered to their intended beneficiaries. Corruption and favouritism were blamed, then the political necessity of satisfying middle income groups which are a pivotal support of governments in power. These explanations reflected market forces which were not properly accounted for in the formulation of strategies – forces which determined who benefited from government intervention. Then the concept of affordability took shape, recognising how some of the basic mismatches of supply and demand blocked low income families from access to housing intended for them. This was followed by programmes aiming

106

to give legal tenure to households who have purchased rights to illegally developed housing areas or who have claimed these rights as squatters.

Difficulties arise from failing to understand adequately the linkages and overlappings of markets sought by middle- and low-income populations. Where middle-income households are demanding more land than is supplied, they can move into the low-cost housing part of the market, adding to the demand there. This will push up prices for those parcels to which they are attracted. Moreover, by taking these parcels out of the low cost market, they will reduce supplies there, causing an overall increase in competition among those demanding low cost plots. The result may be a general rise in the prices of low cost plots, or higher densities of residential accommodation among the poorest (so that the amount of land purchased per dwelling unit is reduced), or both.

Plate 14   Where there is a shortage of serviced land for housing, plots intended for low-income groups inevitably tend to filter upwards to middle- and even upper-income groups, especially where, as here in Lusaka, plots are quite large.

There is an alternative to paying high prices or to accepting a smaller plot. This is to obtain land through informal markets, where there is an additional supply at prices which may be lower because of illegalities or uncertainties which cloud the land rights. Van der Linden (1986: 5) observes that the World Bank now goes for slum upgrading projects because land costs tend to be cheaper where land has been illegally occupied. Informal markets for middle income households also seem to exist (Varley 1989).

If not enough is known about formal land markets, even less is understood about informal markets. Although illegality clouds rights to lands which have been squatted upon or developed without proper authorisation, the rights can nevertheless be traded in informal markets. The questions raised about policies to improve tenure reflect the possibility that clouded rights may protect some of the poor from being outbid by higher income groups who do not wish to accept the risks attached to land traded in informal markets (UNCHS undated). In this or other ways not yet clearly identified, informal markets provide the poor with what they can afford, offering them lower prices for accepting greater risk, just as happens with the use of cheaper building materials and methods.

Informal land markets are widespread and they are thriving. Examination of land delivery systems reveals that most arrangements for obtaining land for housing by the poor fall outside the formal land market. Even so, there are situations where informal markets serve the middle-income and possibly even the high-income groups. In some cases the informal market, although small, may be the only real urban land market, such as in Tanzania, where the allocation of nationalised land is the only formal mechanism of distribution.

Investigations are providing surprising information about informal markets. To some of the poor with no alternatives, the informal market may provide enough security of claim to cause them to invest in their housing, even though these claims are not recognised as collateral for loans from housing finance institutions. Ramirez *et al.* (1991) report that government programmes to install infrastructure have encouraged illegal occupants to upgrade the manner in which they use land in barrios of Caracas. It is possible that some informal markets have been operating long enough or widely enough such that they have established confidence in their transactions which approaches that of the formal markets

Existing accounts of the relationship between formal and informal markets do not tell enough about their interactions. Demand satisfied in one will obviously reduce demand in the other. The ingenuity of entrepreneurs at generating land to feed the informal market increases the sum of supply traded in both markets. This may lower the cost of formal market land for which the poor would otherwise compete: those lands of marginal interest to middle-income buyers, those lower priced plots which the richer of the poor might afford, and those lands which the poor might rent at densities high enough to make them affordable.

Land for government

Strategies to improve tenure for low-income groups have usually involved ownership of land by government. This is because public land has been invaded by squatters, because squatters must be relocated to public land, or because land must be purchased as an intermediate step toward transfer of improved rights to users. But governments have additional critical needs for land which must be met. Day-to-day functions require roads, schools, health facilities, recreation and open spaces, administration offices, and a variety of other public facilities, all of which require land.

In most cases where there have been quantities of land in public ownership, nearly all of these have been disbursed with a lavishness which, on the face of it, ignored market values. Public land has also been used to build the private fortunes and to support the political futures of those in government, because of the very great value its use rights could command when they were allocated to individuals. While this was occurring, few steps were taken to replenish finite supplies of public land by buying in advance of price rises brought about by urban growth. Now high land prices ensure that governments are incapable of substantial land acquisition, and their capabilities to change land ownership are rapidly diminishing.

Policies to affect land prices

In theory, one reason for extensive government ownership is to change market supplies and thereby affect price rises. Holland and Sweden are often cited (see Lichfield and Darin-Drabkin 1980) as having succeeded for a time in slowing down the rate of growth in land prices with long-term programmes of public land purchasing. Their successes have not been paralleled in the developing countries. One wonders if there has been much potential for their replication in circumstances where scarcity attracted so many buyers who wished to protect themselves against inflation or to speculate on rising land prices. The history of frequent changes in governments and in their policies which typifies many developing countries may have served to support hopes for higher prices even when policies were actually reducing pressure on supplies.

Strategies like those of Holland and Sweden have been ill suited to the high land prices and inflation typical of market conditions in less developed nations, and the financial poverty of governments there. If anything, interventions of this sort in the land market have contributed to rises in market prices. The Delhi Development Authority (DDA) had the exceptional opportunity of carrying out large-scale land purchases, mainly because it started with low-priced lands purchased in the early 1960s and was well financed from the beginning. But rather than use its land resources to increase supplies when demand pressed prices upward, the DDA supported high prices by releasing limited amounts of its reserves in strategic sales aimed at profitable sectors of the land markets, in order to maximise its own revenues. Although the DDA appears to have lost sight of its primary purposes for entering the market, this remains one of the few substantial public land management episodes which demonstrates competent intervention and manipulation of urban land markets (Sarin 1983; Misra 1986).

Nationalisation

Some governments have seen nationalisation as the simplest response: replace the market with government allocation of land. More often than not this has failed to produce the desired effects on land prices. Land nationalisation has been followed by the reappearance of old markets outside the legal framework. This is evidence that market pressures have not been adequately accommodated by the strategies or practices of government land allocation programmes. Once land is released by government, even on leasehold, the right to use it becomes a marketable commodity. Even illegal rights to government land taken over by squatters are traded. This appears to have happened extensively in Tanzania (Lusagga-Kironde 1989) and probably in Nigeria. Ironically, critics of Nigeria's 1978 Land Use Decree point out that it has been successful in transferring the use of land from peasants on the urban periphery to the urban elite, probably at prices below that which a normal market exchange would have demanded. There is evidence that nationalisation of certain classes of urban land in Iran have achieved moderate success in improving access to land for lower-income groups (Majedi-Ardekhani 1990). However, as a side-effect, nationalisation seems to have supported very high prices in the remaining formal and informal markets where land is obtained by those not eligible to obtain state land.

Price freezing
Price freezing is a strategy which sees little application to urban land in less developed countries. This is not surprising when considered in relation to market conditions. To begin with, there has been need for good knowledge, which governments rarely possess, of current price levels for parcels of lands with particular qualities. But the biggest drawback must surely have come from the enormous pressures which governments feel from politically powerful landowning classes attracted as investors and speculators to urban land markets by rapidly rising land prices. Given that the strategies of so many middle- and low-income households for material advancement depend upon appreciation of the market price of their lands (and buildings), few governments in developing countries would have had adequate political support to achieve acceptance of price freezing as a socially legitimate action, even if there had been the administrative capacity to enforce such a policy.

Policies to increase supplies

To alter price trends requires good knowledge of the factors shaping supply and demand. Little policy intervention has been aimed at demand except futile (and probably misguided) attempts to slow urban population growth. Meanwhile, minimum plot size standards and coverage regulations have had the unintended effect of increasing the demand for land.

Most attention has been given to increasing land supplies. India's Land Ceiling Act and that of Sri Lanka are of this kind. Their failures arise from their inability to cope with the tremendous importance of land as a marketable commodity. The size of profits from land have been so great as to inspire ingenious strategies for evasion by landowners and to fatally undermine the administrative and political determination to make such policies work. Moreover, in India this policy failed to anticipate the way in which it would cause transactions on large land parcels to become frozen because of legal battles and insufficient public funds to complete purchases. As a result, market supplies have been reduced rather than increased (Misra 1986).

A number of factors have been accused of causing bottlenecks in the supply of land to the urban market. UNCHS (1989c) has concluded that inadequate public services provision is a major reason that usable sites are kept out of the market. Extensions of public services are held back by the difficulties of obtaining funding. Even so, there are practices and standards which limit the areas which can be serviced with the moneys made available. These practices require certain levels of quality (for example requiring sewerage or water pipe connections to every residential plot) and of land use. Land-use standards may specify intensities of plot use and even establish typical shapes for land parcels, thereby determining the unit cost of servicing a plot. The practice of installing services shows little concern to use these factors to fight rising land prices. More importantly, little is known of the actual potential to enlarge supplies to a degree which would dampen price rises. The overwhelming concern of service programmes and of changes in standards is not to fall further behind need. The scale to which current levels of provisiion must be increased in order to reduce market price rises is never calculated.

It should not be forgotten that servicing land in itself raises its price. This of course is a reflection of its increased ability to satisfy a demand. Yet, what is so often missing is a good sense of the price rise which will accompany each increased level of service provision, such that a particular market demand can be targeted with a greater supply. This is not simply a matter of ensuring that the service installation costs to be recovered do not push beyond affordable levels when added to raw land costs. Almost always the quality of services provided has been attractive to an unsatisfied demand with greater resources than the targeted demand. The unexpectedly greater number of bidders and their greater capacities to pay have fostered price rises, and much of the land serviced has found its way into the hands of others than those for whom it was intended.

The UNCHS has also concluded that uncertainty about claims to land and inadequate legal registration of plots renders many urban land markets inefficient (1989c). Efforts are being made to improve the registration of plots. Since the early 1980s, the World Bank has financed urban projects with land registration components. In the absence of adequate information about plot boundaries and their legal ownership, market transactions are slow and costly. Obtaining or creating this information can itself be a costly business. A study in Malawi showed cadastral survey costs alone could be five times the value of the plot (World Bank 1985c). Often at issue is the degree of survey and mapping which is necessary for legal recording of a land parcel. Conventional practices rely upon recognised professionals who may be in very short supply. Similarly, confusion about ownership rights slows market trading, raising costs and keeping some land off the market. Transitions from traditional land tenure, and the presence of multiple ownership or absentee ownership, especially by foreigners, characterise such situations.

Policies to establish and register ownership can fail to appreciate that, where market demand for land is very great, market pressures will bypass these institutional requirements of the formal market. Thus another kind of market is created to ease transactions blocked by such circumstances, and the overall land supply is effectively increased. Costs have been avoided, but they reappear as risks arising from claims to land which are uncertain and/or not acknowledged by the formal legal system. As a consequence, in these informal markets land prices tend to be lower to a degree which is not just an expression of the greater supply of marketable land which they provide. Obviously, the two markets are linked by the freedom of some buyers to transact in both formal and informal markets. This may mean that price rises in the formal market are slowed by the ability of the informal market to bypass ownership and registration bottlenecks.

Taxes on vacant land are sometimes imposed as penalties to bring about development of sites held off the market, usually for speculative purposes. It is both a strategy to augment market supplies and a way to bring about changes in use which will utilise land already serviced. Though often discussed, it is not often practised, and even more rarely is it made effective. A major fault is to set taxation rates at levels which are of little consequence in relation to the actual land value rises which are enjoyed each year. Even the practice of steadily increasing the tax rate from one year to the next has no bite if the initial rate is too small or if annual increases are less than the rise in land values.

Plate 15 Strategically located land is often held off the market for speculative reasons: this piece of 'agricultural land' in the middle of Jakarta is locally known as the 'Golden Triangle' because it is surrounded on all three sides by highways lined with prestigious office developments.

Meanwhile, land-use controls can create bottlenecks in the flow of land supplies to markets, resulting in higher land prices. Controls may try to limit the total area of a city given to a particular use and thus limit the amount of land which owners can legitimately offer for sale for each use. The effects of this may bear more heavily upon certain sub-markets than others, for example land with access to work opportunities or to good services.

Policies to affect use

Urban managers attempt to determine the uses of land in order to improve the health and safety of the general public or to achieve policies of urban planning. Some of the means – like vacant land taxation mentioned earlier – force changes from undeveloped or rural land to built-upon urban land. Others, such as land-use regulatory controls, have the capacity to determine the locations of specific uses or to fix the intensity with which land is used.

Regulatory control of land use is a common enough activity, but according to some accounts has achieved only marginal effects in many developing countries (see for example McAuslan 1985; Rivkin 1978; Courtney 1978; Wigglesworth 1982). A fundamental reason why land-use controls do not have teeth in these cases is that they are not backed by sufficient political will and public support. Another is that a number of market factors are working against government efforts to determine the uses of urban land. For one, market activity can be so great as to overwhelm even a reasonable degree of government determination to regulate land use. The fast-growing, unsatisfied demand for land in cities like São Paulo and Manila cannot be matched by the existing administrative and enforcement apparatus. Critics point out the inappropriateness of procedures inherited from colonial rulers or copied from western industrialised nations where urban growth rates are slower and where public institutions are more developed (see for example McAuslan 1985; Koenigsberger 1975).

Yet another possibility is that controls are wielded as tools to implement strategies which are impossible because they ignore market realities. The standards and other requirements they contain often demand that humans behave in ways they cannot if they are to survive. The poor majority in so many places cannot afford the minimum plot sizes or the restrictions on plot coverage which the regulations demand. Although this has been known for some time, urban managers and their political masters are very slow to move to standards which the market can accommodate. This may be evidence that it is more than the relatively simple relationships of affordability which are not understood. Perhaps not enough attention is given to covert political and personal motivations of decision-makers which are tied to land values.

Attention should be given to the market operations of entrepreneurs who build houses, offices, shops and factories for profit. It has been observed that a developer may need only to forgo the expense of a business lunch to favour a development control officer with a gift equal to an entire month's salary. These are market forces at play. A system will not work which does not fit with the relatively enormous stakes to be won in so many urban areas. Yet where development control does have bite, it can be so slow and cumbersome as to frustrate would be builders, business people and industrialists. Not only is time money when large loans are involved or attractive alternative investments are at hand, but also delays can destructively change the timing of a market strategy.

Nevertheless, there are circumstances in the less developed countries where land-use controls are effective. These may be in more authoritarian cultures or states, or occur when urban growth rates are lower. They may concentrate upon the activities of certain social or economic groups in a country. Nearly all administrations attempting land-use controls seem to impose some policy measures upon middle- and high-income housing and upon erection of the larger shops, offices and factories. There are very few places (Seoul and Delhi are two) where greenbelts are maintained or other policies implemented which limit outward growth, and where it is therefore likely that a city-wide shortage of land has resulted. However, it is common practice to require particular uses in designated zones, thereby limiting the supplies of land available for particular purposes, and to do this irrespective of the market demand. When plans are implemented which underestimate demand, or choose not to match it for strategic reasons, the shortages will raise prices. It is no wonder that the poor then seek to enlarge the supply somewhat by breaking the law.

Land-use controls remain in place, although they may be weak or unevenly applied. This may be explained in part at least in terms of who creates transaction prices and who enjoys the benefits of them. For example, controls which call for low densities may increase the prices fetched by landowners simply by increasing the land consumed by each house, in effect enlarging demand against a fixed supply. At the same time, it may serve the interests of the landowning elite if controls are badly enforced upon those unable to afford the minimum standards, so that the latter are still able to exert effective demand in the market. Moreover, when controls are seeking to restrict urban expansion, illegal residential development of land may allow some landowners to sell in the informal markets of the poor, at the same time that enforcement of controls elsewhere maintains high land values in the legal markets. A similar result may be had by illegally constructing to higher densities than would be permitted.

Probably the strongest of public actions currently affecting the uses of urban land are those expenditures to build roads, service systems, schools and other facilities. Planned public expenditures cannot decide specific uses for individual land parcels as might land-use controls, but the presence or promise of the facilities they create is a major factor in making land usable for urban purposes and enhancing its value. Typically, lack of co-ordination between planning bodies and the various agencies responsible for each investment has meant that these actions are carried out unconscious of their potential for guiding the land market toward planned objectives. In practice, planning recognises and makes greatest use of transport improvements – roads usually, but occasionally mass transport as in São Paulo and Curitiba, Brazil. The possibilities have not yet been demonstrated of the guided land development concept proposed for Jakarta. This intended to work at a local scale using differing levels of infrastructure provision to create differing land values, leading to correspondingly different uses of the land (Marulanda and Steinberg 1991). Something along its lines may have been implemented independently in Gaborone and Francistown, Botswana, where infrastructure has been used to create planned land development patterns (Viking 1990). Site and service schemes, slum upgrading projects and their like are actions of this kind, so they can have profound effects on the land market. Too often governments find the effects confusing. Canny individuals of all income levels discover ways to profit from the price rises. Those households genuinely seeking residency have to fight tempting offers, greedy landlords, and maybe the tax collector in order to stay, and the project officials frequently seem puzzled that the ultimate beneficiaries are not those originally intended.

Plate 16 Serviced plot development in Gaborone by the city's Self-Help Housing Agency: Botswana has been one of the few countries to undertake a programme of land preparation and service provision on a scale which comes anywhere near to matching the need for urban housing land; however, densities remain very low with consequences for service costs and transport.

115

Though potentially the most influential approaches of those yet discussed, market intervention by means of public capital expenditures is usually that least influenced by the overall urban development planning processes. Preparation of the Capital Investment Folio for Manila is one positive attempt to integrate these processes (UNCHS 1989a). But there has been disappointingly little progress on this elsewhere since the close association of planning and capital programming in Calcutta in the 1960s (Sivaramakrishnan and Green 1986). Even so, there is little evidence that any of these capital programming efforts, new and old, are informed by analysis of their comprehensive effects on the urban land markets.

Policies to obtain revenues

There is no difficulty facing urban managers which is more persistent or pervasive than the shortage of financial resources to carry out tasks. Because urban land acts as a repository of capital value, it is a favoured source of the financial means with which to conduct government.

The most direct and obvious interventions in land markets to improve the wealth of governments are straightforward entrepreneurial ventures. In these, governments might speculate on future land price rises, increase the value of their land holdings by investing in improvements, and the like. But the occasions are very rare indeed when this is consciously done.

There are examples of exceptions scattered over the globe. The local housing authority in Maiduguri, Nigeria, built shops for rent on one of its last bits of land in order to finance its continued operation. In Dhaka, Bangladesh, anticipating price rises which its public works would bring to a vacant area, the government purchased land adjoining the route of a planned major road, so that it could profit by selling commercial plots along the road frontage. Two housing development authorities operated successfully for many years in Ismailia, Egypt, using the funds generated from their land banks. They followed similar strategies of setting out plots, installing water pipes, drains, footpaths and roads, and selling land at prices which the markets could bear. The sums generated were then used to pay costs and then to develop new lands. It was even possible to cross-subsidise in favour of the lowest income groups (Sims 1982). Public authorities in Curitiba, Brazil, were less skilful with land they obtained around the stations at the extremities of the mass transportation corridors which they created. They misjudged demand and prices, with the result that there was a poor take-up of the commercial plots which they set out. Instead, small traders operated from cheaper plots outside the station compound. And, it must be remembered that the Delhi Development Authority so successfully accumulated wealth from its land dealings that it seemingly abandoned its public welfare objectives.

What is surprising is how little attention has been paid to these lessons of experience, both the good and the bad. Now that enablement of the market and of private and public partnership endeavours are popular strategies, one might expect to find local government, or at least an arm of central government, acting as a leading land developer in any community which is experiencing growth. That this is not so is in part because these organisations are not equipped with the proper skills for financing and marketing land development. It was only a decade ago that British urban planning, so rich in staff resources, was heavily criticised for this weakness (McKee 1981).

A fundamental opportunity has been generally ignored which could now be yielding substantial funds. This was the chance to establish rents and sales prices for state lands in and around urban areas which truly reflected market values, and continued to do so as these values rose. Governments throughout the developing world have consistently given away rights to land for payments representing only small fractions of their market values. The funds lost could today be financing all manner of real development achievements in the cities and towns concerned.

In highly charged land markets, rights to plots allocated one day have been sold the next at many times the cost to the allottees. These have included sites for offices, shops, industries, and middle- and high-cost housing, where questions of subsidy for social equity reasons did not arise. Even where a subsidy was intended – whether to attract a manufacturing firm or to make housing affordable to low-income families – authorities have acted with a poor sense of the real market value of the land they were doling out. No accurate balance could be drawn between the aims of the subsidisation policies and the true value of the land so disposed of.

Because the value attributed to land reflects – among other things – the beneficial effects of government actions and the wealth accruing to possession of the land, the market price of land is commonly taken as a fair basis for taxation. However, it is not unusual for land valuations in the less developed countries to fail to relate to market prices. One result is that additional revenues are not obtained. Indeed, real revenues are declining in many cases, and intentions to share tax burdens equitably are not achieved. A major reason is that the urban land markets involved are changing so rapidly that the administrative machinery and procedures to revise valuations and update property registers are totally overwhelmed.

Land markets and prospects for land management

Better urban land management requires a better understanding of land markets. This in turn requires resources of time, money and staff to be devoted to studying urban land markets. Priorities for such research must reflect the government's priorities for policy and action.

Priorities for land management policy

On the agenda of urban management concerns, several involving land market interventions are consistently near the top. The next section

117

examines how the prospects for such interventions depend upon an understanding of selective market features.

Improving access to housing land for the poor
Some steps to enlarge the land supply bottleneck which the poor encounter seem less promising than others. UNCHS (1984b: 33–5) has suggested that the supply of land can be increased for housing low income and other disadvantaged groups by:

- appropriating vacant public lands
- acquiring land for them through the private market, at a price based on the present productive income from the land
- trading land or the development right to land for land in alternative locations
- freezing land prices in specific locations
- pre-empting the sale of land when the value declared by its owner for purposes of sale or taxation is below its market value
- appropriating land in lieu of taxes on inherited land
- appropriating land at lower than market value through the use of development gains taxes
- nationalising land without compensation.

The experiences illustrated in earlier pages of this chapter suggest that these approaches have fared poorly when put into the real market context of developing countries today, where land is a commodity which is a principal source of wealth and power, and thus an object of political action. Few of them have been given more than superficial political support, if that. Much less have they been backed by money or consistent enforcement adequate to achieve significant impact on land supplies. Unless policy-makers are content with marginal benefits from the odd conjunction of market and political forces, these strategies do not offer much hope for meeting the needs of urban managers in general. In most countries, vacant public lands are now few because they have not been replaced as government – and squatters – have used them. New acquisitions on any substantial scale are beyond the means of public authorities. Trading development rights depends upon effective land-use control, a sophisticated administrative process, and good knowledge of land markets. Even then, it may do no more than shift the geographic location of land for the poor, rather than enlarge the supply. Freezing land prices, pre-empting its sale, appropriating land in lieu of taxes, and appropriating land as part of development gains taxes, all must be founded upon a high level of enduring political commitment to extract benefits from landowners for the advantage of the low income. Commitment of this kind has been witnessed in developing countries only occasionally, and there is little reason to believe future prospects are substantially different. If these approaches offer little promise, then how much less is the chance that nationalisation without compensation will occur short of revolution?

More recently, it has been suggested that the land bottleneck is a matter of insufficient land at appropriate locations which low-income households can afford (UNCHS 1989c). With this in mind, the means have been sought to develop urban fringe areas which are affordable to poor households and which have acceptable access to jobs and services. This is a call for intervention in the market to produce what may be impossible. When access to jobs and services is adequate, market prices reflect this with levels which the poor cannot afford – which is why the poor lack this degree of access in the first place. In any event, there are few promising strategies for wider and faster servicing of raw land in order to catch up with demand, especially strategies which will not burden the poor beyond their means with the actual costs of services installation. One possibility may be demonstrated by the community-based systems of providing services in Sri Lanka. Here an increase in the supply of housing land has been possible without large-scale government direct intervention and without the problems for government of cost recovery. In part this is as a result of community groups using their own labour, combined with government funds and technical advice, to plan and install basic service system improvements (UNCHS 1992).

Easing the legal strictures on the minimum size of a piece of land which may be traded should not be overlooked. The markets in fact deal with units of land area defined by the functions which buyers and sellers ascribe to them. Therefore, housing plots are usually traded, not housing land. The amount of land on the market suitable for residential use will provide a varying number of housing plots depending upon the sizes of plots traded. Allowing plot sizes to decrease below current norms will increase the supply of plots generated by a given quantity of land. So will increasing the allowable plot coverage and reducing the maximum plot sizes permitted.

It is ironic that, with the worsening shortage of public land, governments throughout the Third World have been focusing on strategies to improve tenure held by low income occupants of residential land (Angel 1983b; Baross 1983; UNCHS 1989c). Virtually all of these strategies depend upon public ownership of the land at some point. Bangkok's land sharing – affecting a very small amount of land – is an exception. Yet for years it has been known that new opportunities for illegal occupation of public lands are disappearing (see Angel *et al.* 1983). In the future then, if tenure is to be improved, this will usually require the purchase of private lands which have been rented or occupied illegally. However, now that urban land markets have become more consolidated and ordered, with the consequence that everyone knows that land is valuable, government cannot expect to purchase on a large scale the rights it wishes to transfer – inevitably at below market prices – to renters or squatters.

There are some who advocate as a strategic option for land development that informal settlements be incorporated into formal systems of land management (UNCHS 1989c: iv). This could do more harm than good if taken too far. Consider the programmes to improve land tenure conditions. If middle-income buyers do penetrate the markets of the poor when security of tenure is increased, they may have a knock-on impact which pushes the poorest of the poor into even worse conditions. At the same time, some of the poor may choose to liquidate the greater capital value which tenure gives them in the formal market, and then return to the informal market confident that they can replace what they have sold, while retaining a profit. Thus it is necessary to deal with middle-income land shortages in order to improve conditions in the markets – both formal and informal – which serve the poor.

Plate 17   Although the opportunities are shrinking, low-income groups are still able to benefit from marginal land; in this case, a low-income community which had been dispossessed from land in central Bangkok was able, with the help of an NGO, to negotiate some compensation with which to buy this parcel of swampy land with poor access on which to re-establish itself.

Cheap land is disappearing at the same time as actions are taken to regularise land in informal markets. Governments may have opportunities to prolong the existence of the supply of cheap land. They can keep land out of the formal market by keeping it in public ownership. But in the future, it is likely that private landowners will supply the informal markets with most of the affordable parcels: those which defy land-use plans, minimum plot size restrictions, plot coverage requirements, or other density specifications. Support for these informal markets or at least tolerant acceptance may be the best government response to many such situations in order that they can serve the poor. Support requires a very good understanding of the systems by which the poor obtain cheap land. For example, adding to service networks will make sites attractive to middle- and high-income bidders, and thus may not be effective in serving the poor until these higher income demands are satisfied.

In general, it will be important for urban managers to learn more about who gains and who pays as a result of policies directed at improving the access of the poor to land. This will reduce the occasions when managers advocate policies which in the end make the situation worse. Negotiation – a political process – may be more significant for increasing supply for the poor in the future, but urban managers and planners will have to know the land market to be clever in negotiations. They must know the costs and benefits.

Ensuring affordable land for government activities

Urgent issues surround the public ownership of land. Old and new varieties of this form of intervention are the basis for many current strategies for dealing with urban growth, including those just discussed of giving tenure to squatters and directly augmenting market supplies of land for the poor. Growing cities and towns produce needs for new government actions in addition to programmes to improve the lives of those already there. There is a backlog of needed recreation facilities, schools, clinics and community centres which require land. A number of popular strategies are underpinned by the assumption that government is rich enough to purchase rights to substantial areas of well located urban land. Yet it seems that the time when this is possible is drawing quickly to a close. Land values have risen before the very noses of governments who have been powerless to stop them and unwilling to buy now to save later. The old supplies of public land have been used up, or are about to be, by committed projects. In Jakarta, planning of schools and the like can no longer be implemented because there is too little money with which to purchase sites in a market of sky-rocketing prices. These circumstances can be found in countless neighbourhoods throughout the developing world.

Urban land prices will remain high, even if there is occasionally some decline in their levels as has been noted in Latin America (Fitzwilliam Memorandum 1991). Purchases of land on a large scale will be beyond the budgets and political will of governments hard pressed to respond to urgent short-term needs for services. Fundamental social and economic development programmes, such as those extending or deepening education and health care will be inhibited without properly sized plots at good locations. Consequently, governments may be unable to provide basic services for new urban populations.

Some approaches offer a small degree of hope. Government does not have to purchase land in order to affect its ownership. A number of strategies strike bargains with private landowners to achieve public objectives. Among these are development and redevelopment schemes involving cross subsidies which make a percentage of parcels affordable to low-income families. Enforcement of subdivision regulations or the granting of permissions to build may be used to extract land for public purposes from private landowners. There are reports of practices akin to the British concept of planning gain. Land for government sponsored housing has been obtained from developers in São Paulo in exchange for permission to build to greater heights or densities (Namur 1989). D'Souza (1987: 4) has proposed manipulation of development rights in Bombay to improve high-density housing for the poor in the very centre of the city. These are strategies formulated with a better understanding of land markets than has been evident in the past. For those who would copy them, they raise issues about the markets where they would be applied. Developers must see substantial profit to horse-trade with government. There must be stability in the markets for the offices or housing units they wish to build such that they can lower their profit margins with confidence. But in the urban areas of developing countries where the poor are often the majority, it is unlikely that the scale of land needed for public uses and for the poor can be matched by the relatively few opportunities for negotiating public gain from land development schemes for the middle- and high-income housing and for formal commerce and industry.

Urban land readjustment – sometimes called land pooling – is attracting much attention as a means of changing and reordering land-use arrangements, especially in areas of transition on the urban fringe (see Box 4.1). It does not require government to actually purchase land, but allows it to govern temporarily land rights so as to reorganise them. It works precisely because it fits closely to land market dynamics and manipulates them to the advantage of public interests. In a land readjustment scheme, the improvements undertaken by government must raise land values in the scheme to a degree which allows the original owners to be given back parcels of substantially greater total economic worth than the larger parcels which they initially contributed to the scheme. It is this factor which motivates the participation of landowners in an agreement which allows government to extract some land for itself to cover its costs and even to provide for needs elsewhere. The difficulties of making this strategy work well in countries other than Japan, South Korea and Taiwan no doubt arise from market aspects which are not adequately understood or appreciated. Prominent among these is the need for a demand for the plots after completion of the scheme which is elastic enough to allow trading at substantially higher prices. For such to be the case on any substantial scale, it may be necessary for incomes to be growing rapidly, as has been the case in the three nations where urban land readjustment has been most effective.

Box 4.1   Land readjustment[1]

Land readjustment (or land pooling or land consolidation as it is also known) is a mechanism for facilitating the orderly development and servicing of fringe urban land which is currently held by many owners of small parcels. It is a technique which has been used extensively in Japan, South Korea and Taiwan, and is increasingly being adopted in a number of Asian countries including Indonesia and India.

Land readjustment can operate in a number of different ways, and may be undertaken by the municipal government, by some other government agency, or as a voluntary arrangement between land owners. It generally involves the following features:

Box 4.1   Land readjustment (*continued*)

1   agreement between the owners of all plots of undeveloped land in a particular area to pool their land holdings to permit the scheme to proceed
2   careful measurement of all plots and plot characteristics before the temporary surrender of ownership rights to the implementing agency
3   demarcating a new layout of plots suitable for urban development, and the reservation of land for roads and other services
4   surrendering of a proportion of new plots to the implementing agency in order to finance the provision of an agreed level of infrastructural services
5   reallocation of the remaining plots to the original owners in proportion to the relative size and quality of their original holdings.

Land readjustment offers considerable benefits. Landowners benefit from receiving serviced plots suitable for development or sale. Whilst these may be smaller and possibly not in exactly the same position, they are considerably more valuable than their original holding. As far as the implementing agency is concerned, the scheme is self-financing, since the sale of surrendered plots meets the costs of the new infrastructure. As far as the community is concerned, serviced land has been made available for development in an orderly manner without creating a tax burden.

Land readjustment does, however, necessitate quite a sophisticated system of cadastral survey, and the capacity to reach agreement between all landowners in an area. The scope for conflict is obviously considerable, and the time required for negotiation can be substantial. Nor can it be relied upon as a mechanism to provide low-cost land to house the poor: the main beneficiaries are the existing landowners, who may choose to hold on to the serviced plots for speculative purposes rather than to develop them. Meanwhile, the implementing agency has a vested interest in limiting the number of schemes it carries out in order to keep up the prices of the serviced plots which it has to sell. Thus, the experience of land readjustment in South Korea has been that it has served mainly the upper- and middle-income groups (I-J Kim *et al.* 1982: 165).

Nevertheless, the mechanism does offer one possible approach to the provision of serviced land for urban development. In Indonesia, some thirty land readjustment projects have been carried out during the 1980s, despite the absence of a really adequate legal framework (Archer 1987: 8). (For further material on land readjustment, see Doebele 1982; Archer 1987, 1991.)

But there is a more fundamental question which arises from these accounts of strategies of negotiation with landowners: by withdrawing a degree of its intervention as part of the bargain, will government be giving up more than it is gaining? Obviously it may be accepting costs elsewhere – decreased road access, overloaded drains – which have to be compared to the benefits gained. Bargaining with land-use policies in these ways seems to imply that the original aims of the restrictions are of no real consequence. This suggests that some of its reasons for intervention in the market with land-use controls were not important ones after all.

Regarding the remaining supplies of vacant state-owned land, the pressing need is that they be used more frugally and wisely than in the past. They should be administered with greater respect for their market values. This would mean less generous allocations to low priority purposes and less wasteful employment of space. Old practices are harder to depart from where their results are in the public view and invite comparisons. Despite the public resistance such comparisons engender, a growing number of changes in land allocations policies – Nigerian Federal and State governments are cases in point – suggest a trend toward smaller plot sizes for all uses.

To extract government revenue from land and its improvements
Those same high and rising market prices of urban land, which are the source of so many management problems, can conversely be a source for their solution. The prospects are good, if among other things, urban managers have better market data.

Annual land and property taxation will continue to be seen as the likely source of major additions to funds for local governments. Problems abound which can hinder the establishment of effective systems of urban land and property taxation, but efforts can be made at least to ensure the land value assessments for tax purposes move in line with changes in real market values.

In many cases, taxation will not be possible until land registration is greatly improved. Some administrations, locked into the benefits – sometimes illicit – of traditional systems, may resist such reforms. But the benefits, in terms not only of increased tax revenues but also of the easing of land market transactions, can be considerable.

It is often argued that profits which fall to landowners as prices rise are not earned by them, but rather derive from the provision of services by government and the development of the urban economy by the collective efforts of all its members. Consequently, some governments have policies which claim a portion of this land value increase. Taiwan has been notable in this regard, setting up a workable system for identifying realistic prices used for purchase and resale of land, a system which depends upon good knowledge of market values. Over the years, however, the percentage of land value increase which is taken as tax has steadily declined in response to a mixture of market and political pressures. One consideration has been that tax levels must not cut profit so much that land needed for urban growth is withheld from the market.

Where governments continue to own rights to land, there are important opportunities to use these to generate substantial financial resources. When the need for funds to manage urban areas is so urgent, there can be few justifications for leasing or selling public lands to high- and middle-income households or commercial and industrial entrepreneurs at prices below those which the market will support. Where conditions of leases already permit, reviews can bring rents as close as possible to market levels. Public authorities can also anticipate the value rises which their own capital expenditures will produce – especially road construction and commercial redevelopment – and manage their own land or secure agreements with private land developer partners to produce revenue streams for public use. A wide range of possibilities are there, limited only by the imaginations of public officials who have not yet learned to think as property developers. And, as property developers, they will have to monitor closely the sub-markets and become familiar with commercial prospects and the intricacies of property transactions.

It may not be necessary for government to have land rights of its own in order to generate income from land development. Partnership agreements to provide commercial developers with up-front financing or public facilities, combined with relaxations of land-use control measures can be employed to obtain a share of the profits from the development of lands which initially are privately owned. Moreover, increased taxes can be expected from any enhanced property values which result.

To implement physical development strategies
Giving more attention to the activities of urban land markets will enhance the prospects for implementing physical development planning as part of urban management. Land-use proposals have to be narrowed down to those which can be made politically feasible. Part of the argument in support of them will have to be built upon knowledge of who gains and who loses in the land markets as a result of land-use proposals. It is pointless to pursue strategies which encounter market pressures and reactions which consistently overwhelm the available means and commitments to carry them out, as has been happening in so many instances. At the same time, if plans merely follow what the market dictates there is no point to planning. The need is for realistic assessment of market intervention possibilities, a factor commonly absent from the technical considerations of planners in the developing world, and elsewhere, for that matter.

This may require in the first instance a different element in the training of urban managers and planners. In place of some investigations of the methods of planning, they will need to study land market principles and the methods for understanding market operations. Second, it may require that managers and planners reorient themselves to more modest ambitions with respect to arrangements of urban land uses. Some of these ambitions may have been bred by the experiences of countries where the land market was a less formidable adversary because landowners held a smaller share of political power, or different factors prevailed. But in all quarters of the globe there has been a tradition of unhealthy disrespect for land markets among urban planners who have been able to rationalise their failures in other terms.

The lessons of experience have shown that land-use controls can all too easily intervene in land markets to the detriment of a number of social and economic – as well as physical – development policies. At the same time, market factors usually work to greatly weaken the force of land-use controls. It may be time in many developing countries to reduce these controls to manageable levels, concentrating efforts upon major environmental threats to health and safety, and on the critical actions of land development, such as the probable location and timing of infrastructure construction. The controls which remain need to be applied with far greater sensitivity to their likely market effects.

All the same, it is obvious that the full potential of planned public capital expenditures has not been harnessed to shape the physical development of towns and cities using market forces. More experimentation with service facility installation can be expected which aims to influence land values and uses, as has been proposed in the guided land development strategy for Jakarta (Marulanda and Steinberg 1991). Urban authorities can become more skilled at managing capital expenditure programmes as tools to implement physical development strategies, guiding the property development of commercial firms and individuals to planned locations at planned times. Yet, strategies to influence land use through public investments are based upon somewhat crude calculations of causes and effects in the land market. Because of their latent power, there is much more to be obtained here through a better understanding of the market. Given the failings of land-use controls and the declining fortunes of public land purchasing, this form of intervention merits much more investigation and experimental application.

More private and public partnership schemes for urban development and redevelopment, especially of commercial areas are being initiated in developing countries, with public investments in service infrastructure and sometimes in land. Examples are provided by urban development authorities in both Malaysia and Jamaica. Often government's leading role in these is advantageous if it has more skill and experience at land development than the private entrepreneur and/or if it takes financial risks which private entrepreneurs will not. Clearly, the success of such ventures will depend upon good working knowledge of both land and property markets. These are dangerous areas for market interventions, for the sums of public moneys involved tend to be very large and the social costs are often high. In ignorance of true market conditions, urban managers can be lulled into a state of false confidence by the assumptions of full cost recovery which usually underlie these proposals and by the expectations of an increased tax base from enhanced land and property values.

Land market knowledge for urban management

Empirical evidence is not available to establish whether it is the weaknesses of existing theory or the failure to carry out analysis utilising this theory which has so badly informed the formulation of policy. Local governments are groping in the dark. Without up-to-date and reasonably accurate knowledge of what is happening and sensible theories or models to tie together what is known, it is difficult if not impossible to plan for and promote urban development. Yet the whole picture will never be clear. The information obtainable is always less than that which is wanted; theories with which to explain what is observed are incomplete and sometimes conflicting. Nevertheless, urban managers must try to understand the land market if they are to intervene in it.

Plate 18 Disconnected pattern of fringe urban development in Yogyakarta, Indonesia: urban managers need to have a much better understanding about the processes of land development if they are to influence them.

A sizeable collection of studies specific to particular cities now exists. Payne (1989) has noted that they present at least three distinct approaches: a slice through a city's land markets at a particular time, as typified by the work of Gilbert and Ward (1985) in Latin America; a more dynamic picture of processes of land development, such as done by Durand-Lasserve (1987) and Struyk *et al.* (1990); and those which identify political-economy aspects in studies of the operations of land markets, as reported by Angel and others (1987) and Baross and van der Linden (1990).

A number of studies of the last kind have now been undertaken as part of a programme supported by the World Bank and UNCHS (Habitat). Dowall has set out the steps of these operations-focused studies (UNCHS 1989b; Dowall 1991). It is argued that the most important use of this kind of study is to determine if the market is performing efficiently. In the shape of that carried out in Bangkok, it calls for collection and analysis of data which will:

1 determine if the price of land increases faster than the rate of inflation, indicating that the land market is constrained

127

2   identify variations in the increase of land values across the urban area
3   determine the amount of serviced land government has been providing
4   identify where residential land conversion is taking place
5   determine the current pace of land conversion for residential development
6   estimate the current and five-year supply of land for residential development
7   determine if there is an adequate supply of land for future housing demand
8   determine if housing prices and affordability has changed over the past five years
9   identify the segments of the population not being served by the formal private sector, and if segments of the supply can be shifted to meet the housing needs of low- and middle-income households
10 determine if there are specific public policies or actions which are constraining the land market.

The list of tasks is very extensive, and calls for a land economist, a land planner, a statistician, data analysts, research assistants, a computer, records of infrastructure development, zonal tabulations of rates and patterns of land conversions, land values by parcels, and so on. It is estimated to take, for a city the size of Bangkok, between six and twelve months and require between five and ten person years of staff time (UNCHS 1989b). This raises concern about the scale of resources required to mount a study of such scope and to maintain it as an established urban management function. In some circumstances, a more appropriate approach may be the relatively simple land value studies advocated by the UNCHS in another publication (undated) or of that used in Ismailia, Egypt, demanding much more limited information and fewer resources (Davidson and Payne 1983).

No matter how extensive, this kind of study may be incomplete in other ways. In terms of the actual purposes which will be served by the study of a particular city or town, the steps suggested by Dowall may tell both more and less than is wanted. They focus upon supply, demand and market efficiency, and thus examine the land market as it is defined by neo-classical economics. This leaves out many of the considerations which past failures have shown to be crucial, such as who pays costs for whose benefits and what are the roles of the various social agents involved.

It is logical that the general and specific purposes of a study should determine what it looks for and, therefore, what information it seeks. In terms of general urban management purposes, effective intervention in the urban land market seems to require knowledge of the market's operation sufficient to achieve three things: first, to identify how, when, where, and how much to intervene in order to get the desired result; second, to judge whether a chosen strategy can achieve the desired result with efficiency relative to alternative strategies; and third, to be able to decide on changes in the nature of an intervention as its effects are revealed. To satisfy these requirements, studies need to inform about both the face of a market:

- how much land of what kind is wanted
- where and how much is offered
- the prices involved

and the social and economic relations behind that market:

- what critical factors, local and at a larger scale, are determining supply and demand
- who is selling and who is buying
- why they value land as they do.

The motives of policy interventions themselves need to be understood. All of these factors are very much related in their particulars to place and history. Altogether this may mean examining:

1 macro-level influences on land markets: physical events such as catastrophes, social events such as urbanisation, economic events such as changes in investment opportunities for capital
2 past patterns of spatial development which set the physical location and nature of new conversions from raw land to urban and from one urban use to another
3 the legal and social traditions of property relations which include attitudes to law and to land planning
4 the economic and social sectors involved in land transactions and the ways they operate and relate, including

- land developers, both households and firms
- landowners
- land users
- intermediaries: real estate agents and land brokers
- credit institutions.

It is necessary to emphasise that the dynamic nature of land markets requires a continuous flow of information to those who seek to influence its actions. Consequently, to have lasting value, market studies must be sustainable and the approaches, institutional structures, and financial and human resources utilised must be sustainable. It is not at all certain that some of the large-scale efforts currently held up as models can in fact be carried out again in the foreseeable future, much less on a regular basis, in view of the extraordinary national and international resources they have employed. Yet some key elements within them need to be maintained in order to improve decision-making. Closer examination of the experiences will reveal which are these key elements.

Doebele (1983) has noted that there are times when market conditions are especially fluid and consequently there is more opportunity for intervention. Concerned primarily with changing tenure, he identifies three 'moments of transition' in particular: when land is converted from agricultural into urban land; when important urban services are installed at a site; and when building construction begins. He calls for research to understand what happens at these special times so that strategies can be designed to take advantage of the room for manoeuvre which they provide. Perhaps there are a host of such moments, each relating to certain governmental objectives and to certain qualities of land. Urban managers obviously could perform better if they learned to recognise the signs of these critical moments in the land market and to seize the opportunities they provide.

The scale of resources to mount and maintain an extensive investigation seems unlikely to be forthcoming in many cases, given other claims and given the threat to vested interests which some may perceive in a high-profile study. Yet, only a sketch of the market may not provide any of the key answers required for intelligent policies and actions. There is need then in a given set of circumstances to identify clearly the purposes of a study and the corresponding elements of the market to be investigated. It may be most important to know the effects of the policies proposed and the effects of the trends which shape urban growth problems and opportunities. Of concern here is effective intervention, rather than an effective market. Clearly a strategy is required for the very act of obtaining understanding of markets.

Knowledge of the politics of intervention
Central to this discussion is the difficulty of fitting government development operations to the urban land market so that interventions are successful. The better the knowledge of the market, the more accurate and powerful will be the intervention based upon it. However, no amount of familiarity with market activities and their mechanisms, and no amount of research and study, will overcome the fact that intervention is ultimately a political action. Urban land is a basic resource for production and existence. Any attempt to alter the kind of use, the right of use, and the price of land will change the manner in which its benefits are distributed. Thus these interventions have the potential to change private incomes, wealth, and economic power, and so they will be resisted strongly by those who will lose out, while being pushed by those who recognise the chance to gain. Urban land management will not achieve any significant objectives without the political thrust to make things happen and to overcome opposing forces.

It should be no surprise to those undertaking planning that their efforts in pursuit of public benefits are resisted, deflected, and thwarted. A market intervention which is smooth, enduring, and unaltered by resistance must necessarily affect no one or only the weakest, and therefore must be insignificant in terms of the development objectives of today. Yet so many government strategies for urban land are put forward as if they were unbiased public actions whose impersonal rationality will automatically win adequate and enduring political support. Hopefully, a better sense of market realities will help dispel some of these whimsical notions and put more rigour and practicality into proposals.

Conclusion

Urban growth management must concern itself with land, a basic resource for social, economic, as well as physical development. Public development policies seek changes in prices, ownership and use of land from that which the market mechanism produces. Interventions are made in the market to achieve these changes alongside other interventions by public authorities aimed at altogether different ends.

In the developing countries, the record of planned interventions is generally one of unwanted effects and surprises for those who attempt to manage urban growth. This record can be explained to a large extent by the indifference shown to urban land markets, ignorance of the features and operations of those markets, and even unawareness that the effects observed are occurring as a consequence of government actions. Strategies affecting land too often seem to be formulated with little or no reference to the market.

This has produced particularly disappointing results in terms of efforts to improve access to land for the poor and implementation of physical development plans. Moreover, it has allowed badly needed resources of revenues and land to slip needlessly out of the grasp of public authorities.

Therefore, acquiring knowledge of land markets must be given a prominent place on most urban management agendas in the developing world. In addition to basic information about supply and demand, attention must be given to the relationships between formal and informal markets and to the dynamics of politics surrounding intervention. There are few models on which to base studies of urban land markets in the unique conditions of developing countries. This points up the need to experiment with approaches geared to very specific management objectives and which make the best use of limited resources.

Note

1. Box 4.1 compiled by Nick Devas.

CHAPTER 5

Planning and managing urban services

Jim Amos

The nature of urban services

Although the term 'urban services' suggests a group of activities which are necessary for the efficient performance of the key economic operations of an urban settlement, it is far from easy to distinguish these services from other key functions. Water supply and drainage, roads and electricity supply are often referred to as urban infrastructure services. However, providing and maintaining the supply of electricity and water requires major industrial undertakings which employ large numbers of staff and which are expected to be at least self-financing. They are, therefore, in their own right important economic activities and could thus be regarded as key functions.

In the case of services such as education and health, similarly large numbers of staff are employed in large-scale operations, financed either by the state or by private/commercial organisations. These activities are without question important social services, but their scale and cost make them also important economic functions. Furthermore, although some of the more sophisticated elements of these services are located in the urban settlements, the services themselves are not essentially urban.

To take this line of reasoning one stage further, should banking and financial services be regarded as urban services? In the sense that they facilitate and sustain commercial activities they are certainly services but, on the other hand, financial services are themselves an important key economic activity.

The question of definition is rendered even more complex by the fact that many of these activities either directly or indirectly service each other. Education services provide medical staff who use water provided by means of capital investment obtained through financial services whose staff use medical services and on and on without conclusion.

There is, therefore, a network of interdependence between agencies, which means that any consideration of the planning and management of urban services cannot be confined to a specific group of activities with common characteristics. Rather, the task must be seen as monitoring the whole range of activities which are components of the socio-economic character of an urban settlement. The task must also include taking action to ensure that the operations of any one service do not adversely affect the achievement and maintenance of adequate standards in other sectors.

Monitoring for effective management does, however, depend upon a framework against which the levels of provision and performance of various providers of services can be assessed. Great care must be exercised in devising a framework to ensure that it is neither inhibiting nor misdirecting. On the one hand it must avoid the tendency, found in many town planning strategies, of being overly definitive and excessively concerned with land use. On the other hand, it must also avoid being excessively prescriptive about the nature of the economic system.

That is not to say that physical development plans or economic programmes are unnecessary or that they should not be definitive or detailed. In fact, the reverse is the case: both physical and economic programmes are essential, but where the management of services by interdependent organisations is concerned, the objective should be the design and implementation of complementary programmes of service provision.

The feasibility of these complementary programmes is dependent in part upon there being an overall coherence of policies, in the various sectors of government so that there is a general compatibility between different programmes which is supportive of inter-agency complementarity. The extent to which this coherence of policies is achieved varies from country to country and depends upon the extent and effectiveness of systems of strategic planning. This topic lies outside the scope of this chapter, but it should be borne in mind that, where there is found to be a chronic condition of dysfunction and/or counter-productive activities, the systems of strategic decision making should be reviewed and evaluated.

Nevertheless where complementary programmes are feasible two service issues have to be addressed by management. The first is who should take an overview of the network of interdependencies and how should interventions be made to secure complementarity? The second issue is how should individual services be managed to optimise efficiency? The way these issues are dealt with varies, both according to the nature of service in question and in relation to the situation requiring attention. Both of these matters will be discussed in following sections.

The urban planning context

The effective planning and management of individual urban services can be achieved only on the basis of reliable information and forecasts about the general urban situation within which the services will operate. Both public and private sector service managers need to know about population growth, changes in the economic and social structure and the distribution and intensity of major urban activities.

In the current climate of rapid urbanisation there is a pressing need for urban service development on a large scale to make good existing short-falls; to promote economic development, to improve lifestyles and to protect and improve public health.

Plate 19   Failure to provide basic infrastructure such as drainage in advance of development can have disastrous consequences for residents.

In theory at least, the plans prepared by town planning agencies should lay down a strategy for growth and provide the basis for co-ordinated physical development. However, in practice, there are many settlements which have no such plans or have plans which are inad-equate in several respects. The most basic flaw in many plans is that they are either so out of date that they no longer provide for current and future growth or that they have been deliberately designed on the sup-position that urban growth can be prevented. In these cases the remedy is self-evident: plans should be made realistic in terms of growth and should be continuously reviewed and updated. But this alone will do little to facilitate the effective and co-ordinated provision of infrastruc-ture services.

The need for services arises when land is converted from one use to another. The major forces bringing about this conversion are commercial developers and entrepreneurs, state agencies, and new settlers, all of whom make demands which overload existing services and which generate demands for services in new areas.

Quite apart from failing to make appropriate and sufficient land allo-

134

cations, town plans fail because, in their preparation, too little regard is paid to the motivation and resources of the various urbanising forces. Consequently entrepreneurial developers develop land where there is the highest profit potential and public agencies develop land to suit their own operational priorities without regard to approved town plans. This means that service providers have no confidence in the town planning system and are, of necessity, forced to follow demand – a process which inevitably entails a time lag in service provision and may give rise to uneconomic servicing systems.

It would, however, be over-simple to argue that such a defect in the planning system can be overcome by rigorous enforcement of an approved plan. In many instances cultural values regarding rights in land and freedom of the individual make rigorous enforcement socially and politically unacceptable, quite apart from the lack of confidence in plans because of past experience. Realism about what land is likely to be developed and the purpose to which it will be put can be acquired only by a close association between the planning agency and the various agencies generating urban development. These may be divided into three categories.

The first category is government agencies, other than infrastructure agencies. By their nature these bodies have to prepare budgets and programmes for their own operations. These budgets and programmes are usually subject to approval by an authority, after which they are normally accessible by other public agencies. It would enhance the realism of town plans if the planning agencies regularly examined these state development budgets to identify the location and timing of proposed developments and used this information to establish the pattern of state capital investment and to enhance the effectiveness of state investment plans.

The second category is entrepreneurial developers who invest in activities and locations where they expect to be able to maximise their profits. The larger developers in this category may well have budgets and programmes similar to public sector organisations, but the smaller investors tend to be more opportunistic and less systematic. However, neither large nor small entrepreneurs will make their intentions known, since secrecy is often essential for the achievement of economic and commercial advantage. Realistic town plans for the private sector, therefore, cannot be arrived at by a process of examining private sector intentions in the manner applicable for the public sector. There are, however, two alternative means by which a degree of commercial realism can be introduced into town plans. One method is to retain in the planning service some commercial/economic expertise that can assess existing conditions and draft plans in terms of how entrepreneurs will react to them. The other method is to create fora of entrepreneurs for consultative purposes. These fora can be used to test propositions and to deduce entrepreneurial attitudes and trends. Although such methods are indirect and imperfect, they can greatly increase the capacity of a planning agency to influence private sector decisions and improve the viability of its plans.

The third category of developer is not always recognised as such, yet squatters and other informal sector housing producers take over large tracts of land and convert its use to their purposes. Such people usually have no knowledge of, or regard for, plans. They need land, they cannot afford to acquire and develop it by conventional means and they therefore take land wherever they believe that they have a good chance of not being removed. Squatting has now become such a large-scale irreversible operation that, in many developing countries, it is now formally or informally recognised as a process of urbanisation which leads to *post hoc* regularisation of tenure and the provision of infrastructure services.

Because of the irregular nature of this activity authorities have tended to adopt a passive role, only occasionally removing squatters from key sites and otherwise enduring the consequences of this unplanned and often inconveniently located urban growth. In view of the problems resulting from this adventitious form of development it is surprising and unfortunate that more authorities have not adopted the practice which prevailed for a period in Istanbul. There, through an informal political system, groups of intending squatters were advised by the planning authority of suitable locations and were provided with site layouts. By this means development occurred in convenient locations and in a form which facilitated the subsequent introduction of infrastructure services.

There are, therefore, a number of ways in which the town planning process can not only improve its own effectiveness, but also provide a valuable aid to the planners and managers of infrastructure services by indicating more reliably where and when development is likely to occur.

Physical infrastructure

Provision of physical infrastructure in the form of water and sanitation services, roads and electricity supply has been the subject of much study and experimentation in terms of planning and management for fairly obvious reasons. In urban development there is a high degree of interdependence between these services, yet very often each is separately managed by an autonomous agency. Furthermore, these services require very large-scale capital investment at the outset and significant consequential operating costs which make cost recovery difficult. The preceding discussion has shown how an improved town planning system can facilitate the co-ordination necessary to achieve efficiency and cost effectiveness, but where such an improved system does not exist service managers will themselves have to make good this deficiency.

However, once an improved information base has been obtained, service managers can prepare their own development programmes taking into account the answers to three contextual questions. First, there is the question of whether all infrastructure services are being introduced into the same area, thereby making it more attractive for real estate development than it would otherwise be; or whether there will be a larger number of partially serviced areas. Second, there is the question of whether the service development proposals reflect the land use proposals introduced in the town plan. If not there is a case for amending either the town plan or the service programmes. Third, there is the question of the adequacy of the service programmes in terms of social need. This last question is of fundamental importance to the effective management of urban services.

It is almost universal experience in developing countries that the programmes for the supply of services fall far short of the social need. The current rates of urban growth greatly exceed the resources available for service provision, with the result that there has been serious and continuous deterioration over many years. Service managers, therefore, have first to ask of the national budgetary system whether resources are distributed to best effect. The social and economic costs of poor health and bad communications can be estimated so that the costs and benefits of improved basic services can be compared with the costs of the current situation. Second, and in parallel with the first question, managers must consider whether they are using available resources to best effect.

To some extent service providers are likely to be forced into uneconomic operations as a consequence of demands from areas of unplanned and haphazard development. But there are other aspects of service provision which are more subject to their control. One such matter relates to the quality standards which the agency has adopted (UNCHS 1984c). In the case of water supply, the installation of stand-pipes tends to limit water consumption and is cheaper than supply to individual sites. In sanitation, waterborne sewerage systems are extremely expensive and in some instances pit latrines may be an acceptable cheap alternative. However, it is in circumstances such as these that the interdependence of services is of great importance. For instance the use of pit latrines may depend upon an adequate supply of piped potable water so that residents do not have to depend upon shallow wells likely to be polluted by the latrines.

It is also arguable that, if at the initial stages of a project, the design brief specified both the expenditure ceiling and the target population to be provided with basic services, then the resulting schemes would differ greatly from conventional designs and would be considerably more cost-effective. However, there are many factors militating against such an approach. Governments and consumers are reluctant to adopt standards which are inferior to those in developed countries. Professional designers are reluctant to prepare schemes which they regard as inferior to best practice. External funding agencies often insist on standards which they consider will protect their investment. And inevitably innovative schemes require substantial research and design investment and have a higher risk factor than conventional designs.

Cost recovery is another factor which affects both capital investment and operating policies and which has tended to separate service agencies from the all-purpose local administrations. In this respect it is useful to compare the supply of electricity and water. Electricity installations were usually established on a commercial basis with metered supply and charging systems intended to cover operating costs and to recover over a period the cost of capital investment. To a large extent this situation continues to be the general case and most electricity under-takings are financially self-sufficient.

By way of contrast, water supply has followed a somewhat different pattern influenced by the fallacious reasoning that water is a natural resource and, therefore, should be freely available. There is also the rather more humanitarian argument that water is such an essential of human life that the poor should not be deprived of a supply of water because of their poverty. Consequently many water supply systems were developed by local authorities or other bodies with access to public funds, thus making it possible for water charges to be subsidised. Since the managing institutions have frequently not been obliged to recover costs directly from consumers, there has been a tendency for the subsidy to increase at least in gross terms. Now, faced with the need to make major capital investments in order to meet the increased need/demand water authorities have difficulty in securing development finance. National governments do not have sufficient resources and loan agencies do not perceive conventional local authorities which supply water as a sound investment. To overcome this problem many water authorities have been established in recent years as separate entities required to apply charging systems which, in the long term, will convert them into viable commercial operations. However, it is not uncommon for strong political and consumer pressures to inhibit this transition.

There are, however, other infrastructure services where direct cost recovery is impracticable because of the nature of the service. Highways are a good example of this because it is difficult to charge users, except in the case of limited access toll roads. Sewerage systems and waste disposal are unsuitable for direct charging on the basis of intensity of use and because charging could lead to charge avoidance practices which would create health hazards. Although there are some cases where sewerage and water supply are operated by one agency which makes a combined charge, road and sanitation costs are most often met out of general taxation.

The cost recovery situation also has serious implications for the achievement of efficiency and for adequate programmes of maintenance. Efficiency cannot be effectively assessed in monopoly situations and it is almost always the case that infrastructure services are monopolistic. However, some valuable surrogate tests are now being developed and applied in various institutional development programmes. This is perhaps best illustrated where a service operates on a commercial basis in an expanding market, as is usually the case with electricity supply, since it is not too difficult to apply charging tariffs which cover capital, maintenance and operating costs. There is, of course, still no satisfactory test of efficiency.

Where there is indirect funding out of general taxation, with or without a subsidising element, there is a perpetual pressure to hold down costs so as to avoid increased taxation. This very often leads to under-funding with its serious consequential effects. Regular and effective maintenance is the item of expenditure most often cut, with the result that asset deterioration accelerates and necessitates early capital replacement which the agency cannot finance. The service agency is thus caught in a downward spiral of depreciation in an environment in which efficiency is never tested.

Standards of maintenance even in the better resourced agencies are poorer than they might be, partly because of low skill levels amongst maintenance staff, but more particularly because of poor supervision and management. This is an institutional issue which is discussed later.

Plate 20   Inadequate maintenance – of public housing in Calcutta in this case – is a common problem in the developing world, resulting in rapid deterioration of public assets.

The problems – inefficiency, cost recovery, under-funding, under-investment, inadequate maintenance and ineffective management – have resulted in a number of donor agencies insisting on packaged aid programmes. These often tie capital investment loans to the establishment of single-purpose agencies, institutional development in the fields of financial and general management, and guaranteed planned maintenance programmes. Worthwhile as these packages are for the development of the service in question, they do have the unfortunate effect of deflecting local resources from other necessary activities which are not in receipt of foreign assistance and which are thus rendered more impoverished and less effective.

One may, therefore, see that despite the unquestionable practical need to co-ordinate and extend the provision of infrastructure services, there are a number of processes at work which have the reverse effect. Fragmented organisational structures, inadequate capital funding, differentiated charging systems and poor management capability not only result in a lack of cohesion between services, but also in poor performance levels within individual services. Furthermore, in many instances the town planning system which might provide a framework for decisions on service development is too often non-existent or in disrepute.

Historically many of these services were provided by local authorities which, at that time, were financially more robust than they are at present. Consequently not only were those authorities able to provide the required services, but also they were able to secure the necessary co-ordination. However, it would be difficult to revert to the local authority system because urban areas have grown beyond the boundaries of the administrative units in many instances; because the operational boundaries of some service agencies now extend even beyond the urban area; because local authorities are often seriously under-resourced and their governmental/managerial capacity is inadequate for the enhanced role.

The difficulties in service provision now being encountered suggest that conventional institutional environments no longer allow the installation and maintenance of services on a scale commensurate with the need. New thinking is, therefore, needed in three fields. First, cost-effectiveness has to be achieved in respect of general management, the design and adoption of low-cost schemes and the achievement of financial self-sufficiency. Second, provision must keep pace with need and this will require both the opportunity to raise funds for large-scale capital works, together with the technical and administrative capacity to plan for future growth. Third, there must be complementarity in the provision of various services through the co-ordination of capital provision and through a more effective method of development planning.

Social infrastructure

Social infrastructure comprising education and health services, recreational and cultural facilities such as places of worship and assembly has some characteristics in common with physical infrastructure, but it is sufficiently different to merit separate consideration. The common characteristics are that they are both composed of a number of discrete activities with markedly different funding systems. The essential differences between the two types of infrastructures is that whereas the physical infrastructure meets generalised impersonal basic needs of a community for undifferentiated services such as water, sanitation, power and mobility, the social infrastructure meets the individual and personal needs present in a community. There is, therefore, a much broader range of potential components and consequently a much greater variety of demand and provision.

Even in the case of education, although the requirement is almost universal, the demand is segmented between state, commercial, religious, linguistic, economic and cultural groupings. The mix of population in any given area is, therefore, likely to determine what educational facilities are required. Social structure will similarly shape the demand for other social facilities eliminating the need for some and placing great emphasis on the need for others.

Furthermore, demand will vary over time. Fluctuations in age structure will generate shifts in the size of the demand for service for young persons, the mature and the elderly. Furthermore, changes in demand and fashion will occur much more rapidly than it is practicable to change the physical fabric of a human settlement. This presents particular problems for the adequate and appropriate supply of social facilities.

In the first place, it is possible to make advance provision only in the most general and imprecise terms. Whereas one can forecast with certainty that most building sites will require access and basic utility services, it is not possible to forecast with any degree of certainty whether one large school or several smaller schools will be required, each catering for needs of a particular group within the area. Furthermore, fashions change rapidly, particularly in the field of leisure and recreation. Hence provision has to follow demand rather than anticipate it as discussed in respect of physical infrastructure.

In some respects this demand-led development represents a state of cost-effectiveness, since inaccurate forecasts cannot result in unnecessary provision and because much of the funding for these facilities will come from commercial organisations, philanthropic bodies and voluntary activities. However, in respect of land provision the situation is more difficult.

In most urban situations land is a scarce commodity and land within serviced areas has a high value. Consequently the development agency, whether it be a state organisation or an entrepreneur, will wish to put all the serviced land under its control to a remunerative use as quickly as possible. However, if the supply of social facilities is to follow demand there is an implied necessity to keep some land undeveloped to accommodate the facilities as they are required. This represents to the developer a capital investment which yields no return. The possibility of recouping this loss by charging a higher price for the deferred disposal is strictly limited, since the ultimate probable uses are not such as would be able to countenance high land costs. Furthermore, some social facilities, such as sports fields and playgrounds, are never likely to generate an income which could cover land costs. Over and above these financial considerations is the fact that land left vacant within a developed area may become subject to squatting or may become so neglected and derelict that it is environmentally offensive. The prohibition or removal of squatting is operationally difficult and usually politically unpopular, since the authority is perceived to be overbearing. This problem has yet to be solved, but there are indications that where local communities have a desire to keep land open for a particular purpose they can be more effective than larger authorities in ensuring its preservation.

Social infrastructure provision can, therefore, become a serious land management problem. In principle it would be reasonable to expect the community, in the form of the local authority, to hold and maintain such land until it is required on the basis that it is being reserved for the benefit of the community. However, many local authorities are not sufficiently well financed to be able to meet the costs of such a land banking operation and those who could perform this role might be too easily tempted to indulge in land speculation to the detriment of social infrastructure provision.

A much more serious situation regarding the provision of social infrastructure occurs in the fields of education and health services where, unlike physical infrastructure, operating costs are a much greater financial burden than the capital development costs. The building of schools and medical centres has a great emotional appeal and is widely regarded as an admirable activity. As a consequence there are various situations which tend to encourage the construction of these facilities without sufficient regard to the subsequent operating costs. These situations range from international aid gifts of buildings for schools, clinics and hospitals, through political posturing about improving services, to central government encouragement of community self-help by undertaking to provide teachers and nurses if the communities construct schools and clinics.

The effect of these inducements to erect social facility accommodation is twofold. In the first place the owning authorities seldom have sufficient funds to employ the appropriate staff and to meet the cost of consumables, equipment, building operation and maintenance. In the second place, even if there are sufficient financial resources, there is seldom a sufficient cadre of qualified persons to staff the facility effectively. While there may be some merit in the contention that something is better than nothing, there is a lower limit below which the benefits do not justify the expenditure. The employment of semi-literate persons as teachers in Ethiopia, clinics without any medical supplies in Tanzania and a hospital which remained unused for several years in Trinidad, all illustrate the hazards of excessive expenditure on capital projects.

This type of situation also illustrates the need for improved methods of financial planning. Conventional one-year budgets for both capital and recurrent expenditure hide from decision-makers the consequences of their own decisions. Capital programmes ought to extend over several years so as to ensure that construction finance will be available when design work is concluded and that it will continue to be available through the successive years of construction. Recurrent expenditure budgets also ought to extend over several years so that the operating costs arising from the product of the current capital programme can be anticipated and accommodated.

These requirements, which imply a financial time horizon of about five years, should provide an adequate safeguard against serious over-commitment or equally serious underspends. There is, of course, the hazard that it is difficult to anticipate the financial situation five years hence. However, an examination of expenditure over a sequence of past years almost always indicates there have only been incremental changes year on year. It is, therefore, not overly difficult to make five-year forecasts which can be refined as the programme is rolled forward on an annual basis.

Such a system of financial planning should, however, depend on a kind of strategic investment planning which is entirely different from that of the conventional town planning process, although both need to be constructed on the same basic information about people. Trends in population structure, migration and employment should be used so far as they or surrogate information are available to provide the basis for complementarity between social infrastructure development programmes and town plans. No matter how crudely it has to be done it is important that this basis is used to ensure not only that town plans make the necessary land reservations, but also that those plans do not contain proposals that are demonstrably unaffordable.

There is, therefore, a substantial adventitious factor in the provision of social infrastructure for, although certain basic provision of education and medical services will be necessary, it is impractical to discover in advance the precise form which that provision should take. Also, in the case of cultural and leisure facilities, it is not even certain that some of these will be required at all, or, if required, that they will continue to be needed for a significant period of time.

There does, however, have to be some arrangement which will ensure that there are opportunities to meet the demand for facilities as it arises and this means some physical and administrative space must be preserved. Physical space can take the form of land reservations or buildings, which can be used for various purposes to suit fluctuations in demand, or provision for intensification of land use to accommodate new activities or facilities. Administrative space is necessary in the form of tenure arrangements that allow occupancy of accommodation to change hands smoothly and expeditiously when the demand for new activities supersedes the demand for existing facilities. It also means a flexibility in regulatory systems so that they do not unnecessarily inhibit transitions.

Entrepreneurial infrastructure

Entrepreneurial infrastructure is a contrived term which is used here to describe services and facilities which make possible the wide range of economic transactions which constitute and determine the commercial vitality of an urban area. It includes banking and financial services; legal and other professional services; maintenance and repair services necessary for the support of commerce and industry; private house building and other economic activities.

In a command economy many of these services are likely to be state operated and may, therefore, be subject to the same type of planning processes as have been discussed in relation to physical infrastructure. However, in a market economy, there is an underlying presumption that these services will be self-regulating through the processes of the market. In practice, though, markets are never perfect and there are occasions when the outcomes of the market processes fail to satisfy community objectives.

There are, therefore, good reasons why urban managers should monitor the provision of entrepreneurial infrastructure and why they should intervene where serious distortions of provision occur. Direct intervention, by which a public authority provides and operates an entrepreneurial service, have seldom been successful because public servants lack entrepreneurial talents, bureaucratic systems are too ponderous and, once having entered the system of service provision, it is difficult to withdraw. Intervention through financial inducement can be more effective, more flexible and less hazardous. Common examples of financial intervention are cheap loans for house building, and subsidised rents for community buildings and sports grounds. Other inducements may be the provision of high quality physical infrastructure specially suited to the needs of particularly desirable types of commerce and industry. Repressive interventions may in some cases be achieved through taxation or by bureaucratic regulatory obstruction.

Market intervention is, however, a highly sophisticated and sensitive operation. Urban managers should, therefore, embark upon intervention only after they have fully satisfied themselves that it is necessary and that the chosen method will be effective. In reality the expertise on such matters lies in the private sector and this means that urban managers ought to develop a strong pattern of relationships with that sector. This is a further dimension of the liaison already discussed in respect of town plans and the identification of trends in capital investment. Once in operation the liaison system itself can be used to inform, persuade and induce the private sector to act in certain ways and thus obviate the need to actively intervene.

It should, however, be emphasised that credit benefits should be geared to ensure that they are also enjoyed by small borrowers. The Grameen Bank in Bangladesh is a good example of this arrangement. It makes small loans available only to low-income borrowers and management costs are held down by working through self-managing loan groups.

Since entrepreneurial service provision is essentially a private sector activity, it rests with the private sector to manage its operational and maintenance activities and, except for some aspects of environmental maintenance which are discussed in the following paragraph, it is not a problem for urban managers.

Environmental management

Environmental management differs from other services discussed in this chapter in two respects. In relative terms it is less dependent on capital investment and has high levels of recurrent expenditure. It is also different in that it is more concerned with the way things are done than with what is done.

In urban management there are three major constituents of environmental programmes. They are the management of waste material, the control of pollution and the maintenance and appearance of public areas. All three are labour intensive and all three are concerned with qualitative standards. Although the management and maintenance of plant and equipment is not unimportant, the key management issues are concerned with standards, processes and personnel, each of which affects the other two.

The setting of standards in respect of waste, pollution or public areas has to be based on what is achievable. This means that account must be taken of what powers exist for the enforcement of standards; what financial resources are available for the operation of waste collection and disposal services; what systems and procedures are most cost-effective; what personnel are required and what managerial supervisory and technical skills they should have. Standards which are set too high will mean that targets will not be achieved. As a consequence there is loss of public confidence and the motivation of the labour force deteriorates. Yet standards which are set too low result in lost opportunities and an underuse of resources.

In waste management and the maintenance of public areas the setting of standards is a domestic issue in that the responsible organisation can determine what it can afford to do. However, in the case of pollution control, the situation is very different. In the case of atmospheric and water pollution the detrimental effects can spread beyond local and national boundaries and consequently controls ought to be applied over extensive areas. Furthermore, because pollution is most effectively controlled at source, there is a general presumption that the originators of the pollution should introduce their own remedies at their own cost. This means that standards must be set at levels which the polluters can afford and this inevitably creates a state of tension and potential conflict. Polluters will argue that they cannot afford improvements because it would make their operations uneconomic and will assert that the required standards are impracticable. To counter these objections the environmental agency must be able to be authoritative, either by reference to national standards which have been recognised as practical and affordable, or by having at its command high quality specialist expertise. Since such expertise is costly it is necessary to establish national standards and/or a national specialist service which can assist local environmental managers.

There are, however, national and international aspects of the principle that the polluting agency must bear the cost of the remedy. In the case of products designed for national in-country markets, national standards have to be enforced uniformly if some producers are not to enjoy an unfair advantage over their competitors as a consequence of some localities not enforcing pollution controls. Logically the same principles should apply to products for international markets, but in practice there are several difficulties. No single developing country can afford to adopt high environmental standards unilaterally because of competition from other countries. If, however, developed countries which are more environmentally conscious were to ban the import of products of Third World countries with bad pollution records, that would further impoverish these countries and thus diminish their ability to improve production methods. There is, therefore, a case for applying elsewhere the kind of international pollution control mechanisms which are now being put into effect in the European Community. Community members jointly agree to conform to certain standards and members states which do not enforce these standards are liable to prosecution and to the imposition of penalties.

In waste management and maintenance of public areas large numbers of workers with limited skills have to be deployed over extensive areas in relatively small groups. The effectiveness of the services in these areas, therefore, depends upon the quality of processes and organisational control. Operational research and work study are, therefore, of prime importance in ensuring that systems of work allocation and the logistics of decentralisation are efficient. This must be matched with skill training for the work force, coupled with special development programmes for supervisors and incentive bonus schemes to encourage high performance standards.

However, it should not be assumed that improved methods and skill development are necessarily best achieved through local authority direct labour operations. The fact that the task of waste management can be precisely defined and that performance can be measured without serious difficulties means that the local authority can delegate the operation to other entities. One form of delegation is to put out the work to a private contractor, and this can be a useful way of assessing efficiency and cost-effectiveness, although there is a risk that cost cutting may lower standards. Alternatively, local communities may be encouraged to assume responsibility for waste disposal. In such cases community self-help can reduce costs and community self-interest can result in high standards, but these benefits can be achieved only where there is high community motivation. As a consequence, standards may vary from area to area and because of the voluntary nature of these arrangements the local authority may have difficulty in enforcing minimum standards in some areas. There are also some urban centres in which the local authority plays no active part in waste management because semi-informal scavenging has made the operation into a profitable commercial activity. One should, therefore, not automatically regard waste management as being a local authority responsibility.

Institutional considerations

The foregoing review of some of the problems of planning and managing urban services reveals that, although urban settlements are complex systems of interacting groups and agencies which sustain and depend upon each other, the mechanisms for ensuring effective and beneficial interaction are far from being comprehensive. But that is not to imply that comprehensiveness is a desirable objective in urban management. Experience has shown that there is a point beyond which the number of activities makes the achievement of coherence more costly than the benefits. And there is also the philosophical question of who should have the power to achieve that co-ordination.

The more practical and immediate question is at what point do the disbenefits take the benefits of co-ordination beyond the optimal situation. Almost certainly that point will vary according to the nature of the society in which co-ordination is being attempted. It would, therefore, be unrewarding to attempt to look for absolute criteria. However, what may be more useful is to consider some of the existing co-ordinating mechanisms and some of the activities where lack of coherence appears to be disadvantageous, and to ask how the mechanisms might be improved and the disadvantages be reduced.

Plate 21 Inadequate systems of waste disposal have consequences for other public services and infrastructure, as in the case of this drainage channel in Manila.

The role of development plans

Development plans are a fairly obvious co-ordinating mechanism with which to commence this exploration. A major concern is how to make these plans more realistic. The master planning approach to development plans has often been criticised for being both inflexible and inappropriate. As originally conceived they would not have merited such criticism, but current practice has certainly imposed this character upon them in many instances. If practice is not to impose the same shortcomings on any new type of plan it is important to identify how this situation has come about. Legislation almost invariably makes some provision for revising plans, but these provisions may not have been exploited due to lack of skilled staff, or due to inordinate procedural delays, or due to a political or administrative environment which is hostile to change or reluctant to open up a planning debate.

There is also the possibility that planning methodologies were adopted from a developed country, when the need for a dynamic plan derived from an iterative process had not been recognised. Additionally, the principal staff may have been trained in a way and at a time when plans were not dynamic. Where this occurs it is not merely the plan which is inappropriate, but also the processes for its preparation and review. In such circumstances it may be that professional staff are not willing to change the system, either because of their own sense of uncertainty, or because change may be rejected or misdirected at a political level. Consequently in revising legislation a balance has to be made between technical needs and capability on the one hand, and social and political aspirations on the other.

Hence the question must be asked that if plans and processes are seen to be inappropriate, why have they not been changed? Is it that suitable alternatives are not available or not known? Or that the required skills and resources cannot be obtained? Or that despite, or because of, the inadequacies of the existing system people are too comfortable with the status quo?

Appropriate development control

The problems of inappropriateness and inflexibility extend from plans into the control systems. The rigorous separation of land uses is an imported practice which tends to be out of accord with socio-economic systems in which places of work and residence are frequently combined. Similarly, planning and building codes may require standards which are beyond the reach of low-income groups and which fail to take account of modern construction methods, or the need for intensive land use.

Changes in the substance of regulations should and must flow from the review of the planning process, but complexity of regulations is a separate matter. Excessive complexity can be debilitating in several respects. Not only does it make for incomprehensibility, but also it imposes a demand for skilled staff which may not be available, or which if available, could be put to better use. Furthermore, many such regulations do not improve the quality of development and may also become a vehicle for corruption.

There is, therefore, a strong case in favour of reducing both the number and the complexity of development controls: but there is a question as to how these controls should be reduced and what form they should take. Land-use separation could be replaced with user performance criteria which allow any area of land to be put to any use, provided that it does not constitute a nuisance to adjoining and other land users. Controls would be based on limitation of noise, dust, fumes, overshadowing, traffic generation and possibly site cover. Standards could be different for different areas, but for each location would be precise, measurable and enforceable. However, such criteria would require skilled staff for their application. Alternatively, regulations could be reduced to a few essential and simple rules which could be easily applied, albeit with limited flexibility. How should the choice be made, and how should it be implemented?

Making better use of available resources

A further shortcoming in relation to plans is the problem of resource allocation and availability in relation to the plans for physical development. Plans may be prepared for political kudos with little regard for resource availability, and there is at least one strange case of a development plan adopting an unrealistically low population forecast because there would not be resources sufficient to meet the needs of the probable future population (D'Souza 1989).

Resource availability is too often seen as an external factor undermining sound physical planning, whereas physical planning ought to be seen as part of a much more extensive planning system. In reality it is unrealistic to attempt to sustain an effective system of physical planning which does not take full account of resource constraints within a broader system of urban management.

In this connection, it may be useful to consider the resource implications of the various common perceptions of the urban planning process. First, there is an elitist role which presumes an ideal or near ideal scheme of urban activities which can be embodied in fixed end-state plans. It presumes that the intrinsic quality of such plans will have such appeal that most agencies and people will be prepared to conform and that those who are not will be prevented from taking dissenting action. This role implies the prescription of resource allocations in accordance with the plans.

Second, there is the facilitatory role which sees the planning process as providing a framework within which all agencies and bodies can achieve their own purposes. Such plans may be seen either as directionless or as the summation of the achievable objectives present in the community. In either case effectiveness depends upon a thorough knowledge of how different bodies obtain and deploy resources.

Third, there is the caretaker role which depends to some degree on the idea of an ideal scheme, but which recognises that while parts of that scheme will be realised by agencies pursuing their own interests other parts which are equally essential will be provided only if the planning agency has the resources to provide them.

Fourth, there is the managerial role which attempts to manage and steer the resource deployment of various bodies to achieve the optimum derivable benefit. Like the facilitatory role it depends on a thorough knowledge of how other bodies manage resources.

Each one of these perceptions has highly important resource implications. The elitist role implies a prescription of resource allocation, which makes it clear that it would be foolhardy to attempt to perform an effective physical planning operation without being wholly conversant with resource availability and management. In reality planning is an amalgam of all these perceptions and all require a synthesis of resource allocating mechanisms with land development mechanisms.

The synthesis of physical and resource planning raises institutional issues referred to later, but in addition to this there are issues of process. How can one-year governmental budgetary processes be reconciled with longer-term investment planning? Should development plans be reviewed on an annual basis? Should annual budgets be presented on a sectoral or a spatial basis or both? What should be the sanctioning process for synthesised financial/physical plans?

Financial resources

Apart from being seen as the means of development, capital investment must also be seen as both initiating and competing with operating costs. A balance between recurrent operational costs and capital investment must, therefore, always be maintained. Yet the income or revenue of local government and other agencies providing urban services is seldom sufficient to meet all these costs. As a consequence they are not in a position either to enlarge their services to meet the needs of a growing population, or to maintain their existing capital investment. Where development is carried out by agencies which are not also responsible for operation and maintenance, this problem can also lead to serious institutional tensions. If planning is to take proper account of resource considerations it must, therefore, seek forms and methods of development which keep both development and maintenance costs as low as possible.

In terms of financing development, aid agencies have done much in recent years to make cost recovery an essential requirement of development projects. However, where urban services cannot be financed by user charges and have to be financed out of general taxation, difficulties arise because of restrictive taxation ceilings, which suggest that local taxation needs radical reform (for a further discussion of local taxation and its reform, see Box 6.2, p. 170). Such reform is preferable to the alternative of encouraging local authorities to raise income from commercial sources. The profitability of such commercial ventures can be severely restricted as a result of price controls and/or national-level trading taxes. Furthermore, few public servants have the entrepreneurial skills necessary to manage commercial activities effectively.

Finance also affects how reasonable levels of operation and maintenance can be ensured. Foreign assistance programmes should extend the practice of including a maintenance period as part of a capital development project. Or they could make assistance conditional upon the beneficiary demonstrating its maintenance and operating capability. In either instance institutional and human resource development is very likely to be necessary.

Land management

There is also as great a need to relate planning to land administration, since this is a factor which significantly affects the selection of areas to be developed and serviced. But how can planning be made more effective where powerful land markets dominate? In Britain planning has become sufficiently established to substantially influence relative values in land. A similar situation could be brought about in countries which have a sufficiency of skilled staff and strong political support. However, other mechanisms are necessary for good land management and development in societies where such human resources are scarce or where, due to national or communal ownership of land, there is no formal land market. There are many instances where beneficial urban development has been inhibited because there is no security for investment in buildings or services. Some aid and funding agencies are advocating economic restructuring which is intended to promote private enterprise, including a market in land. But this is not necessarily the only way or the appropriate way. Urban settlements are not peculiar to western societies with market economies, yet directed and undirected pressures are pushing urban management in the direction of western land tenure systems. Some small successes have been achieved with adoptions of traditional tenure systems in community self-help schemes, but much further work is needed in this field.

In terms of land management, development authorities have played a valuable role in managing the development of extensive areas. They have gone some way towards recovering infrastructure costs through land disposal and have used pricing mechanisms to achieve cross-subsidisation in aid of lower income groups. However, their methods have been devised for the development of rural or vacant land. Experiments in squatter upgrading, the community urban improvement project in Hyderabad and various urban renewal programmes in Europe all suggest new institutional arrangements to deal with the task of rehabilitating or renewing the outworn fabric of older areas.

Institutional structures for urban development

The mention of development agencies raises the question of institutional structure. The need to take cognizance of financial and land management requirements, political objectives and other environmental considerations requires that planning should be an intrinsic part of the overall urban management process. But such an involvement raises certain institutional problems. First, in many governmental structures co-ordination at a national level is confined largely to finance and broad policy, but the introduction of development co-ordination does not fit easily into these structures. Neither finance nor policy departments are geared to handle spatial development management. Yet if this is made the responsibility of a special department, then the department tends to be ignored if its powers are limited, or resented and opposed if it has the powers necessary for effectiveness. One may, therefore, conclude that development planning agencies must develop policy and financial skills to the point where they command the respect of the bodies currently operating in these fields.

This situation is sometimes further aggravated by a second problem, where physical planning is treated solely as a local government function. The ministry for local government may have only an administrative oversight of local authorities and have no planning expertise. Co-ordination then depends upon an interplay between local physical planning, national macro-economic planning and national sectoral programmes, and communication can become byzantine and ineffectual. To overcome these problems urban planning competence should be established at national level; intermediate agencies are needed to interpret national policy and programmes to local government and to aggregate and articulate local issues at national level. It is, therefore, to be regretted that in some countries provincial/regional government is being dismantled, since this diminishes the opportunity to realistically plan and manage urban areas in the context of their hinterlands.

Management skills and training

Many of the management problems referred to in this chapter stem from the fact that not only are the tasks of urban management growing in scale and complexity, but also professional understanding of the development process is growing and deepening. There is, therefore, an urgent need for skill upgrading. In terms of quantity, more urban managers and planners are needed to cope with both scale and complexity. In terms of skill, task knowledge requirements need to be redefined and many staff need to be trained up or retrained to perform new roles. However, training in developed countries should be limited because it is expensive and may not be geared to local circumstances. Wherever possible in-country training centres should be created which are sufficiently well resourced to be able to form an authoritative diagnostic view of human resource development needs and to convert that appraisal into an effective training for operational planning.

One may, therefore, conclude that there appear to be many areas in which improvements could be effected, but the extent of the costs and the benefits will only be discovered from experience. Hence the essential benefit of any institutional development programme must be the capacity to learn from experience and to respond to changing circumstances.

CHAPTER 6

The institutional framework for planning, and the role of local government

Kenneth Davey

Sooner or later all discussion of urban planning turns to institutional issues. One can define goals for urban planning and management in terms of improved living conditions, equitable access to land, shelter and basic services, the protection of environmental quality, efficient use of resources and so on, but who are the planners and managers? Are they capable of acting strategically, equitably, efficiently? Or, rather, does the institutional framework within which they operate permit them to do so? And if not, how can it be improved?

The urban planning task

Discussion in earlier chapters suggests that government has two basic planning tasks if urban growth is to be 'managed', that is regulated or guided to avoid environmental deterioration and intolerable levels of personal deprivation. The first is regulatory. Much of the evidence casts doubt on the efficacy of the traditional armoury of physical planning controls – zoning restrictions, floor space indices, construction standards, etc. But planners cannot be allowed to abdicate completely. Some controls on plot layout and density, and some reservation of public space are unavoidable if basic services are to be provided sooner or later. Even if one despairs of the ability of planned and serviced development to keep ahead of demand for land and shelter, even if one recognises the efficiencies or inevitability of unplanned development or downright squatting, there remain tracts of land which ought to be preserved from urban use, either because they are unserviceable or because settlement would have irreparable environmental consequences, water catchment areas being the most obvious. And increased emphasis is being placed on other forms of regulation associated with environmental protection – enforcing treatment of effluents, controlling emission of smoke and gases, restricting traffic.

Second, the expansion of infrastructure has to be planned and executed. This may be largely reactive – catching up with pre-emptive development, formal or informal. But the speed and economy with which basic services can be provided may be facilitated by infrastructural investment which anticipates settlement and guides it into directions most readily served. In this respect transportation, water supplies and sanitation are the crucial investments – both in terms of their impact on the location and scale of land development, and of the economies to be achieved by optimising locations. (Sanitation may not have a significant impact on location, but location has a major effect upon the ability to develop sanitation.) And even purely reactive investment ought to be informed by some capacity to think 'globally' about the match between overall needs and resources, ie about affordable standards and equitable distribution of whatever services could be provided uniformly.

A few observations can be made about the way these tasks are performed. City government may seek to anticipate and direct urban settlement by advance planning and servicing – illustrated by the operations of the Karachi Development Authority (Sivaramakrishnan and Green 1986), and investment in Ibadan by the Western Nigeria Housing Corporation (Mabogunje 1989). The highly planned expansion of Curitiba has been achieved largely by a combination of disciplined development control, planned extensions of utilities and lavish provision of public transport along selected corridors. Alternatively public intervention may be largely reactive – a 'mopping up operation' devoted to servicing areas of unplanned settlement such as Jakarta's Kampung Improvement Programme (Devas 1980), the incorporation of gecekondus into Turkish municipalities and Bombay's 1 million houses scheme. The two approaches may, of course, go side by side in the same city, often distinguished by the incomes of their clientele – planned estates for the middle class, upgraded slums for the poor.

Public interventions have traditionally been self-contained in character: government regulates, the general public complies; government provides services, the general public consumes them. At least, this has been the self-image of governmental operations, even if it has not corresponded with the reality. But even governments are recognising that their resources of authority, money and personnel are insufficient to regulate development and provide services at current rates of urban growth and are being forced to adopt a more participative/voluntarist approach. Neighbourhoods clear land for access and services by agreement; they contribute to infrastructural provision through some cost-sharing agreement rather than through imposed taxes or charges. Bargaining replaces the imposition of legal restraints or obligations; making individuals comply becomes a function of communal pressure rather than law enforcement. Similarly public sector finance may need to stimulate private sector investment in urban infrastructure, through tax concessions, through key investments which make private sector development viable, or through the location of a public sector facility which increases demand for private sector housing or commercial development.

The pace of urbanisation and the paucity of public sector resources demand a capacity for strategic management – a nose for the critical interventions which will stimulate the most widespread and most beneficial public responses, an understanding of the key linkages between sectoral investments, a flexible ability to respond to rates of growth which can neither be forecast nor regulated with any precision.

The municipal role

Who plans and manages a city? The usual normative assumption is that municipal government does so. Greek ideals of the self-governing city, Victorian concepts of civic improvement and American 'home rule' traditions have spread worldwide over the last century to endow most countries with the trappings of municipal administration and an assumption that it is the instrument by which citizens manage and foster their own living environment. This assumption has become increasingly questionable since the early 1960s, but it has been revived recently by national programmes of 'decentralisation' and a host of donor interventions. The latter includes 65 World Bank projects with some element of 'municipal strengthening'. The underlying rationale is the belief that enhanced participation by local rather than central government in urban management will:

1 improve the efficiency of urban investment through the involvement of local knowledge and choice
2 improve the execution of urban investment through the local accountability of management
3 increase the recovery of costs of urban infrastructure from its beneficiaries through local taxes and charges.

In practice there are enormous variations between countries and between cities in the extent to which municipal government does effectively plan and manage urban growth. In some its role might be regarded as peripheral at best. But there are cases where municipal government is indeed in the driving seat. In Curitiba city government has had a powerful influence on the city's ordered development (Wilheim 1989). Local government has been described as playing a 'paramount role in the management of the urban economy' in Zimbabwe (Wekwete 1989). The dynamic and strategic role of the Metropolitan Municipality in Istanbul's development during Dalan's mayoralty can also be cited (Davey 1989b). It is worth examining such examples to see what institutional characteristics are critical to the effectiveness of municipal government in the urban planning and management roles. What features does municipal government need for this purpose?

Size and territorial jurisdiction

The first dimension relates to size and territorial jurisdiction. Is a municipality big enough to employ the staff, plant and other resources to execute essential urban functions? Do its borders permit it to plan and manage expansion of the urban settlement, or to cope with tasks such as

Plate 22   City Hall, Bulawayo: in Zimbabwe, local government has long
played a major role in the urban planning process.

waste disposal, public transportation or flood control? If these conditions are absent, what mechanisms can help to mitigate the weaknesses of the structure?

There are many contrasts. In countries like Turkey and Zimbabwe it
has been legally and politically possible for municipalities to expand
their boundaries to incorporate areas of peri-urban growth. In Zimbabwe, as in Kenya or Tanzania, a single municipal council is normally
responsible for the whole built up town and its immediate environs.
Indeed in Kenya there have been frequent and major extensions of
municipal boundaries during the 1970s and 1980s to take in areas of peri-
urban settlement. In Turkey, also, municipal boundaries have been
readily expanded to incorporate and service unplanned settlements, and
a powerful upper tier metropolitan authority has been created for the
larger conurbations.

In contrast Calcutta or Manila exemplify urban settlements fragmented between a large number of municipal administrations which are
severely constrained in any strategic planning role as a result (Sivaramakrishnan and Green 1986). The world's largest metropolis, Mexico
City, comprises the Federal District and seventeen municipalities in the
surrounding State of Mexico. Some countries have managed to maintain
substantial economies of scale in municipal organisation; only a handful
of Indonesian authorities fall below 100,000 and Nigeria's reorganisation
in 1976 was based upon a minimum population size of 150,000 per
jurisdiction. But historical identities and political pressure often defy
such approaches. France has 33,000 communes with populations below

2,000; Turkey has created 200 new municipalities with populations below 5,000 since 1984. Both small size and geographical fragmentation are major constraints upon the capacity of municipal government for effective management of urban growth and services.

These constraints can, of course, be overcome by a variety of institutional arrangements. These are discussed later in the chapter.

The range of functions

The second issue is the range of functions entrusted to municipal government. How far does local government possess the regulatory powers and manage the infrastructure which influence the pattern of urban growth and determine the conditions of urban life? In particular, how far does it control or influence those functions which need some integration in their direction if a strategic approach is to be taken?

The functions of municipal government vary enormously, even within a single country. There are Indian States where local authorities do little beyond refuse collection and street lighting; state line departments and utility corporations exercise physical planning powers and manage most urban services, albeit in frequent isolation from each other. But Bombay Metropolitan Corporation runs hospitals, water supplies, schools, electricity distribution and the bus service in addition to the normal run of roads, drains, refuse collection and markets.

Is there an optimal range of municipal functions, a 'critical mass' of tasks essential to effective urban management? Clearly much depends upon the factors of geographical coherence and size already mentioned. Experience suggests, however, that for a municipality to play the lead role in managing a growing urban settlement, it needs responsibility for, or at least heavy leverage over land use planning and development control, transportation, housing development, water supplies and sewerage, and drainage. These are the functions which need to 'hang together'. Municipal responsibility for social services such as education and curative medicine may increase the responsiveness of such services. But it is not crucial to overall planning since the community political process tends to generate schools, clinics and so on regardless of the location of functional responsibility. Nor does their development require the expensive network development that characterises roads, water, sewers and drains and calls for integrated investment. But social services do have heavy operating costs, which can be a serious drain on municipal budgets unless supported by unusually buoyant local taxes like Bombay and Karachi's octroi or a generous and reliable grant system as in Indonesia (Devas 1989b).

One further point needs to be made on functional responsibilities. It is often the practice to divorce responsibility for capital investment from operation and maintenance. Government or its parastatals build, while municipalities are supposed to operate and maintain. This is not a recipe for success. Agencies which do not have to maintain an investment may cut corners and neglect the maintenance costs and implications of their design choices; cheaper constructions may be more expensive to heat or

157

light and require more frequent repair, for example. Municipalities may be unwilling, or even unable to maintain infrastructure which they have not chosen or designed.

Executive capacity

The third dimension is that of executive capacity. This depends on several factors. One, clearly, is the ability to employ professional and technical staff, related in turn to the general skilled personnel supply, the competitive nature of municipal salaries and career prospects, and the satisfactions or frustrations arising from the local authority's range of tasks and its general working environment. The biggest disincentive to municipal employment is exclusion from capital investment. Skilled and ambitious professionals like to create and design, not just to maintain. Involvement in capital investment brings job satisfaction as well as the less creditable rewards of contract supervision. Good leadership and a challenging development programme will often attract quality staff despite unfavourable terms of service.

There are a number of different bases for municipal employment:

1 employment by individual local authorities but on career terms (ie with security of tenure and salary progression)
2 employment by individual local authorities but on short-term contract (often tied to the term of office of the chief executive)
3 secondment from a unified local government service, ie central cadre of officials appointed by central or state government specifically for deployment in municipalities
4 secondment from the national (or state) civil service.

These systems may run in parallel so that a local authority may have staff employed upon two or more of these bases. There is no ideal system. Each has its merits and demerits (UN 1966). Appointment by the individual local authority enhances a sense of identification with it; appointment on career terms offers greater security and immunity from political pressure, but short-term contracts allow municipal leadership to introduce managers or planners who share its ambitions and values. Secondment from national or unified services offers greater career progression and security, but detracts from a sense of loyalty to the local authority and its leadership. One feature of importance to the effectiveness of all systems is the chance of career mobility – training and promotion prospects either within the authority or outside which are open to all employees regardless of their initial qualifications and basis of employment. Stagnation tends to be a frequent vice of municipal employment.

Another ingredient of executive capacity is the internal management structure and processes of municipal government. How can these promote the values and behaviour which the planning and management tasks demand – a strategic approach but combined with responsiveness, concerns for equity but also efficiency?

Organisation theory has tended to develop in industrial rather than public service contexts and to be subject to changing fashion. But the recent interest in organisational culture and the models of 'loose/tight' management ascribed by Peters and Waterman (1982) to 'excellent' business firms – tight central prescription of objectives, targets and standards, but a high degree of delegation in respect of detailed implementation – seem highly appropriate to municipal government facing rapid growth. A strong sense of strategic direction is desirable to guide settlement and integrate investment in areas most economically serviced, and to attract economic activity and employment. But service managers need delegated authority to develop and operate infrastructure speedily and to negotiate with private enterprises and community groups with whom deals have to be made and partnerships struck.

Unfortunately municipal government has tended to reverse the loose/tight model: it has been unable to determine or enforce strategic policy, while retaining over-centralised control of implementation. All expenditures exceeding \$12 require the approval of the Municipal Committee in Turkey; in many systems all expenditures and hiring even casual labourers need the mayor's consent.

Ostensibly the greatest need is for corporate planning machinery within a municipality which can integrate physical and financial planning, and give strategic direction to land use planning, development control and infrastructural investment. Such machinery needs both intellectual skills and political authority to make its strategy stick – the ear and confidence of the decision makers. Examples exist. In Curitiba the corporate planning agency (IPPUC) has played a crucial role in determining both physical planning and transportation strategies, and formulating investment projects, the right hand of a mayor, Jaime Lerner, with a planner's vision and a politician's flair (see Box 6.1).

Box 6.1   Curitiba: a planner's city

Curitiba, capital of Paraná State in south-central Brazil, is a fast growing city of 1.4 million people. It is a visibly orderly, well-planned city with an efficient network of public services.

Curitiba's orderly development is closely associated with a professional planner, Jaime Lerner, who has served three terms as mayor. In his first term he created the Institute of Planning and Research (IPPUC), which is a cross between a think tank and a planning department. IPPUC has played a leading role under successive municipal administrations in promoting a strategic approach to the city's development.

The core of the physical strategy has been, since 1970, the location of commercial and industrial development along four corridors radiating outwards from the central area. The corridors have been developed along major routes, largely based on existing roads, which contain a divided roadway for high speed traffic, inner lanes for slower two-way traffic streets and a central lane for an express bus system. This public transportation system has stations every 400 m, providing links to suburban and

---

Box 6.1   Curitiba: a planner's city (*continued*)

peripheral routes and attraction points for commercial investment. Today there are fifteen terminals and an integrated bus network of express, inter-district, feeder and student buses. The city manages the system, including the fare structure, although it is operated by private bus companies. Traffic system performance is helped by computerised traffic lights. In another attempt to improve traffic circulation, a bicycle network is being developed (Lerner 1991).

Prior to implementation, the Municipality purchased undeveloped land along the routes, which has enabled it to provide lower-income housing areas near to public transport (Lerner 1991). Implementation of the strategy has been assisted by rigorous application of zoning laws, and an agreement with the State Government by which all development and repair of utilities is subject to coordination and approval by IPPUC. The same instruments are now being adapted to a modification of the strategy through creation of nine secondary centres for high-density commercial development. Strict enforcement of zoning laws has been accompanied by incentives to compliance, and in particular a computerised supply of information about the legal requirements for planning consent, and a fast track system for approving conforming plans.

Equally business-like approaches have been adopted to the improvement of the few squatter settlements and the organisation of low-cost food supplies to poor households.

Curitiba's high standards of public service are abetted by a buoyant local economy, and the ability of the city administration to tap this through taxation of services and a share of value added tax on production. Paraná has been largely populated by recent migrants; it has the vigour of youth and a businesslike culture which encourage purposeful administration. These conditions are not easily replicated, but some of the practical steps taken to implement strategic management of urban growth are of wider relevance.

But more often than not municipalities lack such a focus for reconciling physical and financial planning. The isolation of town planning within engineering departments of the Zimbabwean municipalities has been described by Wekwete (1989). Associated with this problem is the undeveloped nature of financial planning models. Much attention has been paid to techniques of physical planning, cadastral survey, capitalised accounting, programme budgeting or project appraisal; by contrast very little effort has gone into designing, testing and disseminating far more relevant methods of medium-term financial planning including such processes as unit costing, revenue forecasting and estimating recurrent expenditure growth in the light of capital investment and population increases. Even where the skills and processes are in place, there may be no commitment by political leaders or service departments to accept the directions and disciplines which the strategy and the plans require.

In practice an effective municipal response to urban growth may stem not from strategic planning but from the political process. In cities like Ankara or Mexico City the unplanned settlements, the gecekondu and the ejidal land invasions, have turned into orderly, serviced neighbourhoods, by pressurising the municipality and the utility enterprises into the extension of services (Gilbert 1990; P Ward 1990). The process is harsh, messy and unsightly in its early stages, and conceivably more expensive in public sector investment costs than planned expansion. From the settlers' point of view it may be highly efficient, the initial hassle and privations being offset by a lower overall and ultimate cost of obtaining shelter and services, and a slower accumulation of commitment which coincides with a household's advancement in the urban economy.

Plate 23   Political recognition of the rights of squatters on publicly owned land in Quezon city, Metro Manila, following the fall of the Marcos regime, enabled households to start replacing temporary houses with permanent ones; note the continued cultivation of crops in the foreground on land awaiting development.

Just why some municipal systems respond more readily to pre-emptive development has not been analysed in organisational terms although the political process and payrolls have been frequently described (Gilbert and Ward 1985). It is probable that concentration of political and executive authority is the key. An elected 'strong mayor' is both more accessible to community pressure and better able to direct an integrated response by municipal departments and enterprises than the traditional British government-by-committee or the appointed city

161

manager. The 'strong mayor' usually carries more weight, also, with the non-municipal bodies like state electricity corporations, and can negotiate deals with private enterprise or community organisations more effectively because of his or her ability to deliver the municipal side of the bargain. But every rule has its exception; a single political executive can become the focus of antagonisms which frustrate the possibility of cooperation with external agencies. Moreover a 'strong mayor' system does not fit well with a weak incumbent; a concentration of authority compounds ineptitude as well as leadership.

These last paragraphs have touched on the 'tight' aspects of the loose/tight model, the central direction. In large cities particularly, responsiveness may well depend upon access of the public to officials at neighbourhood as well as city hall levels and their command of at least limited resources. This raises the issue of decentralisation within municipalities, both political and administrative. This has been subject to much recent experiment. Creating a two-tier structure and hiving off routine operation and maintenance of services to the lower tier has been one approach, illustrated by the zonal municipalities in Karachi or the district municipalities in Istanbul. Calcutta's Borough Committees represent a less radical solution, bringing together ward councillors and local branch officers of city departments in a consultative mechanism without creating new bodies corporate. Bombay has had a similar pattern of zonal organisation for many years, and has gone further in budgetary delegation, with expenditure allocations disaggregated to the fourth level of management. In some large Latin American cities area offices operate under the immediate supervision of a 'Delegate', ie a direct representative of the Mayor.

Parallel developments in Britain have seen compulsory delegation of budget management to individual schools, and widespread delegation of resource management to area levels in fields like social services and rental housing. Until recently these have been restricted experiments. They are now being duplicated in response to government policy aimed at diluting the power of 'town halls'. (It has to be remembered that British local authorities are relatively large in average size.) Just how successful these reforms will be in bringing management of local services closer to the consumer or the local community remains to be seen. One of the main challenges has been the need to place the geographical disaggregation of service budgets on a uniform and objective basis – a highly desirable trend in the long run, although problematic in the transitional phase since local authorities have to distinguish historical favouritism from 'special needs'.

Financial resources

Another critical dimension is the financial resources of municipal government. The importance of the financial base to the planning capacity of a municipality is generally understood, but the nature of the problem is less well recognised. Two aspects of the revenue base are critical. One is its buoyancy – the response of the municipality's revenues to the pressures of inflation, increasing population and economic growth which fuel demands on its budget. The second is the political sensitivity of the revenues – the degree of political cost involved in determining tariffs, assessing liability and enforcing payment. Many systems of municipal government are faced with an unhappy conjunction; they are the most politically exposed level of government, and their basic revenue sources – property taxes and user charges – are the least buoyant and the most politically costly to exploit. Whereas the yield of levies like income, excise and value added taxes expand automatically with prices, the property tax base increases only after a revaluation or a specific increase in tariff. User charges also require specific tariff revisions to respond to cost inflation. Such increases are particularly sensitive because of the direct methods of payment of these levies.

When municipalities do play a leading role in urban development, their financing usually departs from this model, with substantial access to taxation of income or expenditure as well as property, whether through a local tax, surcharging or revenue sharing. Taking the examples already cited of municipal authorities which have played such a role, those in Zimbabwe combine property taxation with more buoyant and less sensitive levies on electricity consumption and motor vehicle licencing. Curitiba is financed principally by a sales tax on services and a significant proportion of value added tax. Turkish authorities receive substantial shares of national revenues, and have a mixed portfolio of local taxes including taxes on energy consumption and telecommunications, as well as property.

Much international assistance has gone into the provision of loan finance to municipal capital investment, and the development of regular credit channels through municipal development funds or banks. These have been generally successful in accelerating the pace of capital investment and in spreading donor assistance over a wide range of towns of varying size. In another respect the interventions have been less successful. It has generally been assumed that the municipal funds or banks will be careful to assess the viability of the projects they finance and the credit worthiness of their borrowers, and will stimulate careful project appraisal and improved cost recovery to ensure repayment of their own lending. In practice this rarely occurs, because most governmental lending to municipalities is secured at source by deducting debt service from grants or revenue shares payable to municipalities. The lending institution is simply not at risk from a non viable project or municipality. If it has any incentive it is to lend as much as possible, both in order to disburse the credit available from the external donor, and to cover its own overheads from 'spread'. Capital investment credit needs to be accompanied by far more rigorous appraisal of debt service capacity – not by some statutory formula, but by examining the real internal viability of a revenue generating project or by projecting the growth of recurrent revenues and expenditures in the case of an investment which does not generate revenue (Davey 1988).

Box 6.2 (at the end of this chapter) considers in more detail the question of mobilising financial resources for urban development.

The nature of central government control

The effectiveness of municipal administration is also conditioned by the nature of central and state government control. This extent varies widely from the high degree of constitutional autonomy enjoyed by Brazilian municipalities (Davey 1989a), to the dependence of their Mexican counterparts on state executives and congresses for determination of user charges, zoning restrictions, tax rates, in fact every decision which places restraints or obligations on their citizens (World Bank 1991). There are no fewer than 185 clauses in the Kenya Local Government Act conferring powers of intervention on the minister. Much depends also on the way the controls are exercised; they can be an instrument of support and positive guidance, of sabotaging a rival political machine, or of patronage in a competitive political game. What is at stake however is the self-confidence of the municipality.

The problems of local government usually start in central government – in Britain as much as elsewhere. The armoury of central controls in most municipal legislation assumes that the central government will act with greater wisdom or moral rectitude than the municipality, an expectation often sadly disappointed. And so reform has to start in central government with the development of more responsive and supportive attitudes, and greater skill and sensitivity on the part of the bureaucracy involved. Here donor intervention can be important; partnership with a donor agency in a municipal development programme can make service in the ministry of local government more glamorous and provide support in battles with resource ministries unsympathetic to devolution. But the partnership has to be properly directed. All too often donor support has been given to ministries concerned with the physical aspects of urban development and has ignored the ministries of the interior or local government which have legal control over the processes crucial to municipal effectiveness – revenue sources, staffing systems, budgeting and accounting structures, etc.

Motivation and culture

Which brings us to the final factor – the motivation and culture of municipal government. Papers submitted to the 1989 international workshop on urban planning referred to the preoccupation of municipalities with short-term expediency, to venality in the enforcement of planning disciplines, and to reluctance to bear the political costs of policies required to safeguard the urban environment. Does a municipal administration, restricted as in Mexico to a three-year term and debarred from re-election, have the incentive or opportunity to plan strategically?

One could easily jump to the conclusion that the political dynamics of municipal government are incompatible with the strategic approach to urban planning and management. This ignores a number of uncomfortable facts. One is the relative success of some municipal administrations in this role. Another is the failure of central governments to effect an improvement when they supersede elected bodies, Calcutta and Nairobi being notable examples. The pressures of land speculation, the competition for construction contracts, the urgency of getting a licence do not go away with abolition of municipal elections; they simply transfer their attention from mayors to ministers, and from one set of bureaucrats to another; but the process is less open to public view.

What is important is to acknowledge the significance of the political cost–benefit ratio in urban government. To manage a growing city effectively involves a myriad of politically expensive decisions – enforcing planning regulations and reservations, increasing water charges, collecting property taxes, curbing nuisances, restricting street parking. These costs are acceptable only if their benefits – better services and an improved environment – can be delivered in the perception of the electorates. One can expect a municipal administration to have the self-confidence to manage urban growth effectively only if it has the functional mandate, the discretion, the buoyant revenue bases and the skills to achieve visible improvement within its electoral life.

Institutional alternatives

What happens if constraints such as territorial fragmentation frustrate any hope of improving municipal capability in urban planning and management to a significant extent? Are there alternative loci of responsibility?

There are several models. The first, a variation on the municipal theme, has already been touched on, namely the two-tier system. In this an elected upper-tier metropolitan authority is responsible for strategic planning and for tasks such as bulk water supply, transportation, waste disposal and flood control which appear to require conurbation-wide management. This is the Turkish model to which reference has been made (Davey 1989b).

One weakness of two-tier systems is the separation of plan formulation from execution, where physical and investment planning policies and rules are formulated by the upper tier but application (particularly through development control) rests with the lower tier of municipalities. The latter are often reluctant to exercise development control within rules set externally, partly because of loss of room for political manoeuvre, partly because two sets of planners rarely agree. Lower-tier authorities may also oppose and seek to frustrate strategies which restrict particular types of growth, for example of heavy industry or major shopping complexes, within their own boundaries and direct these elsewhere within the metropolitan area.

The greatest obstacle to creating an elected metropolitan tier is political jealousy. An elected authority representing several million people can easily be regarded as too big for its boots by central government, or the constituent municipalities, or both. One does not have to look much further than this to explain the demise of the Greater London Council and the Metropolitan County Councils in Britain. Indirect election may soften the hostility of the lower tier, as in Istanbul or Toronto. It may, however, weaken the capacity of the upper tier to make strategic rather than compromise decisions, for example on location of waste disposal sites, as members will see themselves as delegates from particular localities rather than responsible for the metropolis as a whole. Greater Toronto is often held up as a model of a metropolitan council which has been successful because it was created by the constituent municipalities themselves out of perceived need for co-ordination, rather than imposed by national legislation (Feldman 1981). Metropolitan Istanbul was relatively successful in imposing a strategic vision under Dalan's leadership because it was so superior in power and resources that it could buy the co-operation of the districts.

A second model is joint action by municipalities setting up an association or a special purpose authority to execute functions on their behalf. The preponderance of small communes in France is partially offset by the existence of nearly 2,000 'syndicats' maintaining roads, water supplies and social and educational services on behalf of member communes which pay a compulsory contribution to their cost. Over 11,500 syndicats provide a single service; water supplies, schools, electricity, gas or flood control (World Bank 1986). Joint action is common in western Europe, but less so in the Third World where state intervention has been all too ready to substitute for inter-municipal co-operation. There are examples: some Brazilian associations of neighbouring municipalities share professional services and road maintenance units; in Turkey the Union of Municipalities of the Sea of Marmara provides a variety of services to its 130 members including equipment purchase, insurance and training; municipalities combine for waste disposal in three Mexican conurbations. The examples are all too few and do not extend beyond individual services to strategic planning.

A third model is for municipalities to contract out service provision to commercial concessionaires or to a core municipal authority which can provide economies of scale. A classic example of the first approach is the franchising of two large but competing water supply companies by the great majority of French communes, and of the second the contracting of services like refuse collection and fire protection to the County Authority by the majority of suburban municipalities in Los Angeles (World Bank 1986). In the case of franchising, the concessionaire normally recovers costs directly from the consumer, within regulations and tariffs approved by the municipality, whereas 'contracting out' remains a charge on the municipal budget.

Franchising and contracting out have considerable potential advantages in so far as they exploit economies of scale and the incentives to efficiency and productivity produced by competition. Moreover, separating direct delivery of a service from its regulation can enhance the ability of a municipality to set and enforce standards which might be compromised when the functions are combined 'in house'. But potential advantages do depend upon genuine competition – upon the existence of alternative suppliers who do compete and do not 'ring' – and upon the municipality exercising an objective and incorrupt choice between them. They depend also upon municipal capacity to formulate, monitor and enforce contracts with clear specifications, performance standards and non-compliance penalties including termination, although these capacities can be supplemented externally, eg by guidance from municipal associations or professional institutes (Walsh 1991).

A fourth model is the creation by central or state government of a parastatal authority to undertake strategic planning and conurbation-wide services, or to plan and service new settlements. The Metro Manila Commission or the development authorities in cities like Calcutta, Delhi, Karachi and Lahore are examples (Sivaramakrishnan and Green 1986). This is more common in Asia than in Africa, where municipal jurisdictions have been less fragmented, or Latin America where municipal governments have generally resisted such encroachments on their authority; metropolitan planning authorities have been largely ineffective in Brazil, for example (Davey 1989a).

Appointed metropolitan authorities have had some success in providing planned initial services for large tracts of publicly owned land, or a conduit for external and central government investment funds to other executing agencies including municipalities. They are subject to the same dangers as elected metropolitan bodies, and municipal bodies will be reluctant to implement the land use plans and development control rules they formulate. They tend to be compromised by their own financial base. Not being elected, they usually cannot tax; without taxes they are dependent upon someone else to maintain the things they construct (unless these can be totally financed by user charges). If, as is so often the case, they are capitalised (with cash or land) and then required to earn their keep commercially, investment becomes driven by rates of return, usually to the neglect of lower income groups. This bias can be aggravated by their lack of electoral accountability.

The final institutional option in urban planning and the management of urban services is direct execution by central and state government ministries. Direct intervention by central government ministries has the potential of applying superior resources of revenue and professional manpower to urban needs, reinforced by international aid. This can be highly effective if provided in support of local institutions. Problems arise where central government operations are basically competitive rather than supportive. According to Mabogunje, Nigerian Town Planning Authorities have been paralysed by their divorce from local government, 'tied to a separate ministerial stable' (Mabogunje 1989). This is a frequent problem with ministries of public works or urban development, driven by appetite for the design and construction game, and unconcerned with the implementation of their plans or the maintenance of their projects. Perhaps the ultimate in predetermined irresponsibility is the Turkish Iller Bank, effectively a construction agency which can build what it likes and recover what costs it likes from the national revenue shares it channels to the municipalities (Davey 1989b).

The separation of planning and construction on the one hand from operation and maintenance on the other is a frequent weakness of central/state government interventions. Another is the fact that central/state government agencies tend to work in considerable isolation from each other. Strategic planning and integrated development are difficult to achieve within a central government framework, because instruments of co-ordination at central level are remote and weak, and locally based planners or administrators have little power over the operations of line ministries which behave like feudal warlords, particularly with capital investment funds in their armouries. Responsiveness is compromised because the access of local people to decision-making is highly differentiated; it is only big political patrons or powerful business interests who can bring pressure to bear on ministers. Their local representatives, who may be more widely accessible, do not have independent powers to respond.

Plate 24   Whatever institutional arrangements are adopted, the need for co-ordination is critical; here (in south Jakarta) drivers are presented with a hazardous road layout as a result of problems of co-ordinating infrastructure works.

The possibilities of reform

What are the possibilities and priorities for improving the institutional framework for urban planning and management?

There is great variety in the institutional patterns of urban government, much of it due to particular historical and geographical circumstances. But certain features stand out as characteristics of the more effective governments in growing cities:

1   responsibility for a hard core of functions including roads and public transport, preventive health, water supply and sanitation, land-use and development control, and housing development

2   responsibility for both capital construction and operation and main-
    tenance of infrastructure and services
3   access to buoyant taxes on income or expenditure, whether by direct
    levy, surcharging or revenue sharing
4   regular accountability to the electorate
5   a clear focus of executive authority.

These suggest targets for reform where such conditions do not already
exist. Also important is some form of strategy to overcome the weakness
of small municipalities and the fragmentation of urban areas between
local jurisdictions.

Such reforms would, however, constitute major institutional change
for which opportunity may not readily arise. Other possible improvements are more procedural and may be easier to achieve. Examples
include:

1   improved budgeting and financial planning based on realistic rev-
    enue estimation, and use of demand projections, standards and unit
    costing to provide for recurrent costs of expanding basic services
2   decentralisation of budget management to operational levels, com-
    bined with mechanisms of neighbourhood consultation between
    local representatives and service branch managers
3   conditions of service and training which provide for career advance-
    ment at all levels of municipal service
4   regular annual revisions of user charge tariffs which will keep abreast
    of cost inflation and be more politically acceptable than infrequent
    but substantial rises
5   improved and more sensitive procedures in daily transactions with
    the general public.

Postscript

It is not difficult to suggest necessary conditions for effective urban
planning and management. History demonstrates that they are not sufficient conditions. So much seems to depend upon apparent accidents of
leadership or upon the wider culture of the city. Birmingham's development in the late nineteenth century is inseparable from the drive and
vision of Joseph Chamberlain, but why did Birmingham wait till the
1880s, thirty years after Leeds or Manchester, to embrace 'civic improvement' (Briggs 1963)? Curitiba's ordered development is clearly a product
of Lerner's leadership; but was that leadership a 'lucky break' for Curitiba or a response to public expectations born of a prosperous business
culture? Perhaps we are back to the chicken and the egg.

Whilst these questions are unanswerable, experience does suggest
that the opportunities for reform occur in unpredictable ways. Ideas can
be developed, changes promoted, plans made, people trained, but no
progress is apparently made. Then without warning some apparently
accidental event – a crisis like a water shortage, a riot, a major fire or
perhaps a change of minister, mayor or permanent secretary – suddenly

opens the way for change. Such opportunities may be shortlived or the enthusiasms ephemeral. What counts is that the ground has been prepared and that there are positive proposals and committed apostles to follow them through. External assistance may also help at such juncture, but it has to be quick and flexible in its response if it is to catch the favourable wind.

Box 6.2 Mobilising financial resources for urban development[1]

Inadequate financial resources remains one of the key constraints on the provision of satisfactory urban services in almost every developing country. Resources are inadequate because

1. the taxes assigned to local government are often unsuitable for various reasons, being low yielding, inelastic, costly to collect and inequitable in their incidence
2. charges for services are not properly related to the costs of those services, and are not revised in line with inflation
3. revenue collection systems are inefficient and ineffective
4. the grants from central or state level on which municipalities depend do not match their financial needs, and are often erratic in their payment
5. suitable loan finance is not available for capital investment
6. budgeting systems are inadequate as tools for policy implementation or effective financial management.

The most common form of urban local tax is the property tax (see Table 6.1). In many places it provides the bulk of local own revenues. Property tax has many positive features (ease of identification, ease of assignment to the correct local government and a crude equity). But it suffers from a serious lack of buoyancy: revenues fall behind population growth and inflation because property registers are not updated and properties are not revalued regularly. Also, the high visibility of the property tax which, unlike a sales tax or income tax, cannot easily be disguised, makes it politically sensitive. The shortage of skilled valuers often presents a serious problem. Nevertheless, successful efforts have been made in a number of places (Manila, Delhi, Jakarta) to improve the performance of the property tax, and the potential of the tax remains considerable.

Other fairly common local taxes are those on entertainments (cinemas, theatres, hotels, restaurants, etc.) and motor vehicles. Revenues from these can be elastic if levied *ad valorem*, they are relatively easy to administer, and the burdens are at least roughly related to ability to pay. Taxes on utilities like electricity and telephones are becoming increasingly common, and have the advantage of being very easy and cheap to administer, as well as falling mainly on high-income groups; however, their non-neutrality (that is, their differential impact on prices) can be an issue, especially for the pricing policies of state electricity and telephone companies. A local tax on motor fuel is similarly easy to implement, falls mainly on the rich and, in addition, may have a beneficial effect on the environment by discouraging private car use. It probably represents one of the most fruitful possibili-

Box 6.2   Mobilising financial resources for urban development (*continued*)

Table 6.1   Sources of finance for local government (percentage shares)

	Calcutta 1981–5	Karachi 1984/5	Dhaka 1982/3	Seoul 1985	Thailand 1985	Indonesia 1983/4	Malaysia 1987	Brazil 1988	Kenya 1988	Zimbabwe 1986
Property taxes[a]	34	27	34	33	10	4	64	4	31	8
Property transfer taxes[b]	0	1	3	15	3	0	0	0	0	0
Motor vehicle taxes	0	0	0	7	20	7	0	0	0	0
Professions/business taxes[c]	3	0	1	3	17	0	0	0	0	0
Electricity taxes	0	0	0	0	0	0	0	0	0	0
Entertainment taxes	0	1	2	0	0	1	0	0	0	0
Octroi-type taxes[d]	26	61	0	0	0	0	0	0	0	0
Fuel taxes[e]	0	0	0	0	0	0	0	0	0	0
Other local taxes[f]	0	1	0	15	14	3	0	11	12	2
Sub-total: local taxes	63	91	40	73	64	14	64	15	43	10
Non-tax revenues[g]	8	6	35	25	14	7	28	18	55	49
Total local own revenues	71	98	75	98	78	21	92	33	98	59
Subsidies/grants	29	2	25	2	22	79	8	67	2	41
Total revenues	100	100	100	100	100	100	100	100	100	100

Notes:
[a] Includes rates for water, conservancy, etc.
[b] Betterment tax in the case of Karachi; Land development tax in the case of Thailand
[c] For Thailand: surcharge on sales tax
[d] Octroi is a shared tax in some cases (eg Calcutta)
[e] A shared tax in the case of Thailand
[f] For Brazil: mainly share of value added tax; for Kenya: mainly crop cesses
[g] For Zimbabwe: largely profits from manufacture and sale of beer.

Definitions and data sources:
Calcutta: all Urban Local Bodies in Calcutta Metropolitan Area: average for 1981–5: Bannerjee 1989: Table 2; Sivaramakrishnan and Green 1986: Table 10.4
Karachi: includes KMC, KDA, KWSB, Military Lands. Cantonments: Bengali *et al.* 1989: Table 2
Dhaka: World Bank 1985a: 21 and 24
Indonesia: all local governments (Provinces plus Dati II); Devas 1989b
Thailand: all local authorities: Poshyananda 1987
Malaysia:a   sample of 38 local governments (Mailis): Malaysia: Ministry of Housing 1988: 103
Seoul: General Account only: D-H Kim 1989: Tables 7 and 8
Brazil: all municipal governments: IMF 1990
Kenya: all local governments: IMF 1990
Zimbabwe: all local governments: IMF 1990

Box 6.2   Mobilising financial resources for urban development (*continued*)

ties for raising additional local revenue, if only the central government can be persuaded to allow local governments to share in this field.

Many developed countries levy local taxes on personal incomes and business profits or turnover, and in some cases on sales. Where these taxes can be levied as surcharges on national taxes, they are relatively cheap and easy to administer. But in most developing countries, the large share of informal sector activities and the difficulty of assessing incomes, profits and turnover, often renders such taxes impractical at the local level. In addition, there are often problems of assigning the revenues to the right local governments since businesses operate across local government boundaries. However, local governments in a number of countries do levy taxes on trades and professions, and the patente or business licence is the main revenue source for many cities in Francophone Africa. In South Asia, octroi (a tax on goods entering a local jurisdiction) remains the most important source of revenue for many municipalities, providing over 60% of revenue for Karachi and over 50% for municipalities in Nepal (Bengali *et al.* 1989; Nepal: Legislative Study Team 1987). This source has proved to be highly elastic, since it is levied on the value of goods, but its distorting effect on internal trade means it has a negative effect on economic development.

In many countries, local governments are left with a variety of small and unsatisfactory taxes – on radios, dogs, non-motorised vehicles, certain types of local produce and so on. Many of these are expensive to collect, inequitable in their incidence, distorting on the economy, and often create more nuisance than revenue. Abolition of such taxes would seem to be called for. In addition, a number of countries in Africa still retain some form of poll tax, although often now incorporating some graduation in relation to income.[2]

Municipal governments generally provide many services for which charges can and should be levied. Ideally, charges should be related to the costs of serving the particular consumer (the principle of marginal cost pricing). In this way, scarce resources can be rationed, wastage avoided, and resources generated to expand the service. There are, of course, services where charging, or at least full cost recovery charging, is inappropriate: where services are pure 'public goods', where exclusion of non-payers is difficult or expensive, or where there are large public benefits, such as waste disposal and primary health services.

It is often argued that essential services such as water supply or health services need to be heavily subsidised, or provided free of charge, so that the poor can benefit. However, the usual consequence of such a policy is that the services concerned are inadequately funded, so that supply lags far behind demand and quality deteriorates. The main beneficiaries of such a policy are often the rich, since they are the ones who are most likely to have access to the subsidised services. Meanwhile, the poor are often forced to pay far more for services from private suppliers: water from private vendors is a common example. There may be some scope for cross-subsidisation within a service such as water supply. However, experience suggests that, in the developing country situation, where effective means-testing is rarely practical, subsidies have to be accompanied by some sort of

Box 6.2   Mobilising financial resources for urban development (*continued*)

product differentiation: provision of water from public stand-pipes, which the rich are unlikely to use, would be one example.

In practice, municipal governments in the developing world often have no clear policy about charging for their public services. They may also lack proper information about the costs of those services on which to base their

Plate 25   Inadequate water supply systems mean that the poor have to pay far more to buy their water from vendors than do those who are connected to the mains supply; these vendors in Jakarta are queuing to refill their containers at one of the few public standpipes.

charges. As a result, services may be subsidised unintentionally. This can be a major drain on financial resources. (For a more detailed discussion of pricing policies, see Meier 1983.)

For most local taxes and charges, there is considerable scope for improving the performance of revenue collection and administration, in terms of both effectiveness (the proportion of the tax potential which is actually collected), and efficiency (the proportion of the tax yield remaining after deduction of collection costs). Improving performance requires:

1   a proper estimation of the potential yield of the local tax/charge, so that performance of revenue collection can be measured
2   regular revision of tax and charge rates, where appropriate
3   proper tax registers, regularly updated through field inspection and alternative sources of information, with unified registers where there are multiple levies

---

Box 6.2   Mobilising financial resources for urban development (*continued*)

4   assessment systems which are both simple to use and minimise the scope for collusion between taxpayer and assessor
5   collection systems which facilitate payment, such as automatic surcharges on bills, payroll deductions, the use of accessible payment points such as banks and post offices, etc.
6   effective and prompt enforcement procedures against defaulters
7   records systems which facilitate cross-checking, with effective systems for both routine and random checking, and disciplinary action where fraud is revealed
8   regular reporting on performance, with systems for follow-up
9   improved personnel management to achieve greater staff productivity and performance.

Grant systems can be used to reward local governments for improving the performance of their local revenue collection. This is being done in Sri Lanka, for example. Grant systems also need to be carefully designed to distribute resources equitably between local governments (and between levels of government) in a way which reflects both their needs and their local revenue potential. However, the limitations of data mean that, for most countries, grant allocation formulae need be kept relatively simple. This also aids comprehension and hence acceptability of the allocation formulae. Equally important is that grant allocations should be announced well in advance, and should be paid in full and on time, thereby facilitating municipal budgeting and financial management.

Municipal governments need an accessible source of loan finance to enable them to fund capital expenditures, particularly for infrastructure. Many countries (Philippines, Indonesia, Sri Lanka, for example) have established Municipal Loans Funds, usually as a means of channelling donor finance. Loans should not be subsidised, since this erodes the funds available and benefits those local governments which can afford to borrow most; rather, funds should be allowed to revolve. Safeguards are also required to ensure that borrowing municipalities do not become over-committed.

Finally, mention should be made of one other potential source of finance for cities: the rising value of urban land. Municipal governments face a huge burden of investing in infrastructure to match the needs of their growing populations. It has often been argued that landowners who benefit from the increased value of their land as a result of the conversion of land from agricultural to urban uses or as a result of the provision of infrastructure, should contribute to the costs of new infrastructure from their 'windfall' gains. At one extreme, taxation of the full increase in value (or 'betterment') has generally proved unworkable, although Taiwan's Land Value Increment Tax is perhaps the nearest example (R C T Lee 1982). Where there is an effective system of capital gains taxation, that can be used, although such systems are rarely effective in developing countries. At the other extreme, a simple system of charging land developers for the additional costs of urban infrastructure arising from their projects would seem to be a minimum requirement. In between are the various forms of Valorisation Charge, quite widely used in Latin America, notably in Colombia, which recover the costs of new urban infrastructure from the adjoining property owners in proportion to the increase in the value of

---

Box 6.2   Mobilising financial resources for urban development (*continued*)

their property which results (Macon and Mañon 1977). Land readjustment schemes, where a proportion of the land being developed is surrendered to the municipallity to finance the new infrastructure is another possible method (Doebele 1982).

The permutations are numerous, and the appropriate solution will vary according to a particular country's situation and traditions. Many such schemes encounter problems of administrative complexity which inhibit implementation. In addition, there may be problems of perceived unfairness, especially where owners of existing houses, rather than owners of undeveloped or about-to-be developed land, are faced with large tax bills which they may be able to meet only by selling up. Nevertheless, the rapid increase in land values which accompanies urban development remains a significant potential resource to finance essential urban infrastructure. (For a fuller discussion of municipal finance issues, see Davey 1983; Bahl and Linn 1992.)

Notes

1. Box 6.2 compiled by Nick Devas.
2. Interestingly, an attempt to introduce a local poll tax in Britain in 1990 proved so unpopular that it was quickly abandoned and led to the downfall of its main proponent, the prime minister, Mrs Thatcher.

CHAPTER 7

Political control of urban planning and management

Richard Batley

The politics of urban planning and management

Public administration is a political act, most obviously because it involves governmental discretion in the distribution of resources. If, as this book suggests, it should have more than a regulatory role and be involved also in the promotion of development, it is required more clearly to take sides in transforming, rather than simply maintaining, the status quo. The question is then whether planning and urban management, as a part of the official process of decision-making, can do more than reflect the existing balance of political interests. Can they be agents of change? If they operate outside their time and context, they risk marginalisation from all reality; if they operate within it, their transforming role is in question.

The governmental role in the management of urban resources is inescapable but it may be more or less extensive. Two sorts of roles might be identified. First, there is government's direct allocative role. At the most obvious level, tangible resources (water, roads, houses) are allocated, but urban management is often also about the allocation of intangibles – for example, permissions (to build or to undertake an activity), definitions of land use, penalties and controls, and taxes which may not only raise resources for other activities but also be used to distribute penalties and incentives. In all of these, government differentially distributes scarce 'resources' between sections of the population; incidentally, these are often resources (and therefore scarcities) which government has itself created. Second, government also intervenes in other distributive systems, principally that of the market but also that of customary rights. To say 'intervenes' in the market may be inappropriate given that the market and public allocation systems are so closely intertwined; most clearly in developing countries, government is often the instrument through which market relations are extended and traditional systems displaced, for example by establishing private over communal landownership and, historically, by using taxes to push self-sufficient people into the labour market. Government also intentionally or unintentionally influences the relations between people involved in market transactions: for example, by supervising and restricting contracts between owners and tenants, limiting or protecting land title, and regulating food markets. Of course the influence may also work in the other direction: the market may enter public administration, perhaps in the form of corruption, and traditional power relations may enter formal politics and administration for example as clientelism.

Plate 26   The process of land development involves conflicting interests: here in north Jakarta, squatters have been forced off the land behind the fence which is scheduled for commercial development; some have re-erected temporary shacks this side of the fence.

Urban management and planning are political not only in the sense that they produce *outcomes* from which some gain and others lose but also in the sense that they are *political processes* for conciliating interests which cannot all be equally satisfied. Techniques may be developed for understanding problems, possible solutions and their costs and benefits but there is no technically correct judgement about how much resource to put into the solution and about which demands are legitimate or to be favoured. It is not only through party politics that alternative interests are brought into the making of decisions: planners and managers, as well as politicians, make political judgements. Cullingworth (1973) puts it as follows:

> Planning should be conceived, therefore, not as the identification of problems and their resolution, but as a process of balancing conflicting claims on scarce resources, of deciding who is to benefit and who is to bear the costs of planning decisions, and of achieving compromises between conflicting interests. (Cullingworth 1973: 156)

The question is then whose voice is heard in that process. On the one hand, the process cannot include everybody all the time: organisations, professions and procedures, after all, exist to mark limits, to maintain entry barriers and to define appropriate behaviour. They are, therefore, bound to be biased and somewhat exclusive, as McAuslan argues for planning law in Chapter 9. On the other hand, the very recognition of management and planning as political as well as technical processes delegitimises claims to exclusive competence by professionals and elites and therefore legitimises wide participation. If some voices can be heard, why not others? The tension between inevitable bias and the expectation of inclusiveness makes this, like any sphere of political decision-making, a conflictual business.

If urban management is a political and not just a technical process, it has to correspond to the particular politics of the society in which it is lodged. The adoption of practices developed in other societies with other political systems and interests is likely to mean that those practices will be either overridden and ignored or 'colonised' with other meanings. Procedures can be imposed but not the way that they are understood or used. It is commonly recognised, not least in this book but also in many of the conference papers on which it draws (von Einsiedel 1989; Mabogunje 1989; Wekwete 1989; Wilheim 1989; Ahmed 1989; D'Souza 1989; and so on), that town plans are made but frequently not implemented or are used to serve very narrow interests.

Urban management is therefore political in the sense that it decides distributive outcomes and that in the process of decision-making it includes some interests and subordinates others. This political perspective raises three questions which will be pursued in this chapter:

1   How far are current prescriptions for planning and management adapted to local political circumstances?
2   How might the 'politics of urban management' be analysed in order to identify opportunities for change?
3   Can the processes of planning and management be made more inclusive of hitherto excluded interests?

In the following sections we first examine the 'new convention' in urban planning and management and ask whether it is politically sensitive and feasible. Second, we consider whether particular political and economic conditions generate their own appropriate forms of government intervention. Third, we propose a framework for the analysis of political processes and outcomes in urban policy. Fourth, this framework is then explored and illustrated in a series of detailed sections. Lastly, we consider 'what is to be done' to make the politics of urban management more inclusive.

The new convention

A new convention about the role of government in urban development can be identified, not least from the contributions to the conference on which this book is based. Some aid agencies – particularly the World Bank – are powerful propagators of this convention not only in the field of urban development but also more generally. However, it is clearly part of a more general mood against state direction shared on both Right and Left. One question is whether this constitutes an attempt to apply a generalised convention, derived from the situation of more developed countries, to the different conditions of developing countries (Batley and Devas 1988). Is it sensitive to different political conditions? Is it politically and managerially feasible?

At the outset, it should be made clear that what is defined here as the 'new convention' is not the same as the 'new realism' advocated in Chapter 3. They have links but the 'new realism' is largely about a realistic recognition of the limits on state action. The convention identified here is about what is then suggested or implied is the appropriate role of government, and specifically of urban planners and managers. My argument is that, paradoxically, the role that is proposed may be more complex and sensitive (managerially and politically) than ever before.

The common critical denominator in this new convention is the rejection of governmental monopoly in the definition and solution of social and economic problems. In the particular case of urban development, it rejects technically derived, end-state master plans and limits government's role as direct provider to those spheres (such as infrastructural provision and land agglomeration) in which the market and self-help are ineffective. Urban planning and management become processes not products – that is, rather than being focused on the production of ineffectual plans and other inaccessible goods (houses, etc.), they are concerned with the processes of negotiating with and enabling alternative possible providers in the private or the public sectors. They work within the framework of broad policy objectives but are required to adjust flexibly or incrementally to what is possible rather than to impose preconceived outcomes. The roles of public officials are then more analytic, political and managerial than technical: they have to understand the motivation of and interrelation between actors, negotiate between them and decide where judicious intervention is required to induce change. In this way, public officials are expected to straddle the divide between working with the powers-that-be and bringing about change in favour of the needs of the poor or the majority. They also have to try to co-ordinate, harmonise or decide between the investment plans and development objectives of public and private actors in different sectors.

On the whole, the appropriate level for this activity is taken to be local: community-based, 'bottom-up' planning and action by local government with local groups and enterprises are favoured. Four main interlinked reasons for this localism are commonly given or assumed: first, this is the level at which practical services operate and can therefore be co-ordinated; second, it is 'closer to the people' and has a more direct relationship than the centre to the recipients of governmental action; third, it is likely to be more responsive to and aware of local needs and opportunities; and fourth, local government's commitment is likely to be more continuous and permanent than that of a distant agency.

The new convention proposes generalised methods for achieving outcomes which are relevant to specific localities. Decentralisation, negotiation, action planning, participation, enablement and analysis are all methods through which specific local interests, needs and opportunities are to be brought into account. In that sense this approach recognises urban planning and management as political processes. What is in doubt is whether the methods being proposed are appropriate to the situation of developing countries.[1] The negotiated, bottom-up participatory style may be appropriate in a western context of pluralist democracy but less so in a context of elite dominance, popular exclusion from policy formation, and political vulnerability of public officials. The new convention demands skills of both analysis and mediation between sectors and interests. Besides the question whether such skills are widely available, there is the fundamental question whether officials can openly engage in such mediatory politics without threatening politicians and exposing themselves to charges of bias or corruption. In an exclusive political system, is it possible to serve both the poor and the powerful?

In brief, while the new convention does seek to provide a framework for a form of urban management which is more responsive to local demands and in that sense more relevant, the question is whether its very political openness may make it unrealisable.

Several authors recognise the problem and try to resolve it with the participation of external aid agencies and consultants. K Watts (1989) stresses the need for external agents to remain accountable to national governments and to work 'with the most important power sources' but argues that it is possible to guide them into an understanding of the 'political imperative' of urban reform, in other words to demonstrate to them that it is in their own interests. Walton (1989) argues that it may be necessary for external agencies to apply pressure to bring about the positive political setting within which 'people-led' planning will be tolerated. Besides any ethical question which this may raise with regard to national sovereignty, there is the practical possibility that if powerful external agencies impose practices which are not politically or managerially appropriate these practices risk being short-lived, bypassed or reinterpreted.

An alternative may be not so much to seek to bring about change as to support 'positive' tendencies. McAuslan (1989), writing about planning law, emphasises the need to work within particular national cultures and practices, but points out that these are neither static nor monolithic; it is therefore possible to find opportunities for incremental movement towards principles such as equity, participation, flexibility and efficiency. M Lee (1989) describes USAID's support for an Indian housing finance organisation selected because it was already attuned to the aid agency's objectives. The German technical aid agency, GTZ, has worked in Nepal over long periods to support the development of local institutions through which communities and politicians can define their own priorities (Matthaeus 1989). This long-term commitment and working with local organisations to develop their own approaches is similar to the style of the UNICEF urban community development and basic services programmes.

In this section some doubts have been expressed about whether the 'new convention' assumes conditions which are not typical of many developing countries: the acceptance that alternative claims are legitimate and that they can be openly conciliated and selectively 'enabled' by professionals and administrators as well as politicians. However, it would be false to imply that there is a choice between this and a technically neutral form of management. As we argued in the first section, urban planning and management are necessarily political acts and conciliation and selective enabling have always gone on, though under cover of neutrality. The question is whether urban administration by officials can be more openly and inclusively political.

Political economy and urban administration

In the previous section, we considered whether the new convention assumed the existence of pluralist and liberal assumptions which permit an enabling or negotiating role on the part of officials and which tolerate or encourage redistributive demands. In this section, we shall consider whether particular political and economic conditions generate their own, appropriate forms of urban administration (a word we shall use for policy-making, planning and implementation).

A first and fundamental question is whether the political conditions exist for *any* sort of effective public sector intervention. Urban administration is often advocated on rational technical grounds as a means of achieving orderly city growth or on welfarist grounds as a means of achieving redistribution to the poor. This section suggests that effective administration (rather than mere ideology) occurs not for these technical or benevolent reasons but in response to more fundamental and less altruistic pressures. A clearly documented case is the influence of colonial interests in maintaining exclusivity in the spatial arrangement and administration of towns (King 1990; Lufadeju 1989; Wekwete 1989; Mabogunje 1989). Another is modern town planning in Britain: this did not emerge at the time of most rapid urban growth when, in a technical sense, it was most appropriate but only after the emergence of social forces which had an interest in the imposition of a new order. Insanitary conditions affected and offended large sections of the upper and rising middle classes as well as the poor who lived among them; more particularly, large-scale manufacturers recognised the need to bring about improvements in their infrastructure and conditions of their workforce on a town-wide scale (Briggs 1963). Without elaborating the point, it serves to raise the question whether and which powerful interests in favour of urban administration are likely to occur in less industrialised countries where large-scale enterprise is scarce or uncommitted to any particular location. In a society of small entrepreneurs and where large sections of the population remain outside the realm of mass production, consumption and formal politics, it is difficult to see from where the demand (or necessity) would come for generalised and systematic public sector management (Mabogunje 1989).

One answer might be: from the public sector managers themselves. Three sorts of motivation might be suggested. First, in some governmental cities, public officials are in sufficient numbers and sufficiently organised to form a demand block with shared interests as *recipients* of effective policies. This shades into a second position, which depends less on the idea of public officials as a demand group within the wider political process and more on the managerial interest of bureaucrats and politicians. Public choice theorists (Niskanen 1971) argue that the managers have an interest in the extension of state activities as a vehicle for maximising their own claim on resources as 'rent seekers': as planning regulations and state provision increase, their monopoly control is extended. In that case, the effectiveness of plans and services is less important than the legitimation that these activities give to careers and salaries and the control of budgets and staffs. Third, there is the view that bureaucracies and professions may be the agents of institutional inertia: practices built up historically 'sediment' (Benson 1980) in organisations and roles which have an interest in their own persistence. For example, the impetus to conserve inherited forms of colonial administration may be strong in the absence of powerful pressures for change from outside the 'public service'. There is every reason, in particular, why public officials and politicians would be keen to preserve the 'statist' forms of service provision and regulatory planning which the 'new convention' seeks to demolish.

Forms of urban administration are likely to be adopted from practices in more developed countries. The question is then what are the social origins of these practices and how relevant are they to the conditions of different developing countries. We shall suggest that the more interventionist or statist approach to administration was appropriate to a certain period of development in the 'advanced' capitalist countries, that these conditions have changed and that new administrative approaches are developing in response. The danger is in the assumption that the changing practices of advanced capitalist countries are appropriate and exportable elsewhere.

Stoker (1989) has used 'regulation' theory to explain recent changes in the role of local government in advanced western countries. Briefly, the argument is that patterns of public sector intervention and regulation grew up to support the form of economic organisation which was predominant in western countries between the 1930s and 1970s. Mass production in the leading sectors based on large-scale plants and routine assembly line operations generated a mass workforce and standardised patterns of production. These 'Fordist' (ie typical of the Ford Motor Company) conditions of production and consumption were sustained by the extension of the state's role in collective provision; moreover state organisation itself was influenced by the dominant Fordist organisational form (large scale, centralised, hierarchical and standardised).

This was the era in which local government was developed as the primary agent of mass collective provision in housing, social services, public health, education, transport and physical infrastructure; comprehensive development planning assumed this degree of public sector control. Many of these British or western practices were then exported as 'good practice' to the rest of the world.

Since the 1970s, the 'post-Fordist' economy has begun to emerge out of changed technical conditions of production and more discriminating consumer demand in a wealthier market; it is associated with shorter runs of more specialist production, higher market segmentation and more flexible forms of organisation. This represents a threat to the traditional form and content of state intervention: public sector provision becomes less necessary and bureaucratic uniformity less appropriate. Likewise, it might be argued that the shift from blueprint planning, the weakening of regulatory planning, and its replacement by experiments in action and market-led planning reflect the transition from the conditions of Fordism towards those of flexible production and more differentiated markets.

This is not a deterministic approach. It identifies the technological, productive and social conditions which are generating change, but different responses are possible:

> Individual nation states are finding their own route to post-Fordism by a process of trial-and-error. The choice is made in the context of the economic and political legacy of the country and in response to the balance of current social interests. (Stoker 1989: 147)

The response of the British government has been to favour the marketisation of public services and the weakening of local government's providing role, but in several other west European countries it has been to decentralise government and reduce controls on local public services (Batley and Stoker 1991). Thus, as in the Fordist era, different western countries have found different ways of responding.

This argues that planning and management practices should be appropriate to the particular history and political economy of individual countries, although it also identifies generalisable characteristics of western economies. It throws into question the transfer of practices: and raises the specific question whether the new convention is a derivative of post-Fordist conditions rather than those of the developing countries to which it is to be applied. If Britain is an emerging post-Fordist society, others such as Korea or Turkey have moved very rapidly into mass production, labour organisation and consumption, and there are others where pre-industrial conditions prevail. This is not to suggest that there are stages of development through which all countries must progress; changes in processes of production are on a world scale, capital is mobile and the most advanced forms of production can locate in Korea or India as well as Japan (N Harris 1984). Present-day industrialising countries face distinct technological, consumer and labour market conditions. However, it may be that some elements of standardised service provision and regulatory planning *are* appropriate to those countries or regions which are experiencing a transition to large-scale production and consumption; some level of standardised public service provision may have to be constructed (at least for those in the large-scale sector) before more flexible forms of provision and consumption can emerge. The Ankara 1990 master plan (Altaban and Güvenç 1990) might be not only effective but also appropriate to the need for mass collective provision.

In some countries, 'pre-Fordist' conditions may persist. Mabogunje (1989) suggests that a clientelistic form of neighbourhood planning may be appropriate where, as in Nigeria, economies are principally based on localised small-scale production. He argues that the master planning tradition was appropriate to the development and maintenance of capitalist conditions of production (providing a land market, ordering space, managing socialised costs of production) and that it therefore assumes and protects social segregation on a class-residential basis. In his view, such planning has failed and town planning agencies have consequently been marginalised because they are inappropriate to a society such as Nigeria with a large informal sector and wide kinship relations leading to the bridging of class divisions. He argues that planning and implementation should work with the patronage power of local leaders instead of seeking to bypass it. This sort of localised or 'bottom-up' planning may have much less egalitarian or democratic implications than the new convention supposes. It may nevertheless have more popular support and be more accessible to more people than a purportedly fairer but alien system.

This section has suggested that there are constraints on the transferability of administrative systems. This is a matter of particular relevance to external agencies seeking to bring about changes, and to internal practitioners seeking to adopt the most 'modern' practice. There is a danger that in the absence of any real internal demand for effective administration, adopted practices become merely a further vehicle for the extension of the interests of the administrators themselves (politicians and managers) and of external agencies.

Practices have to relate to the particular political and economic context, but within these limits choices can be made and the limits can perhaps be extended. We will return to this question of 'room for manoeuvre' in the last section of this chapter.

A framework for analysis

All this implies the need for greater political sensitivity in planning and management – the need for methods to be appropriate to the context, for intervention to be based on an understanding of the constellation of interests which are likely to support or obstruct them, for appraisal of impacts on different groups, and for adjustment to changing demands and realities. Planners, managers and activists need to carry out some level of political analysis if they are to intervene appropriately, build alliances and avoid the worst distortions of their policies. This section proposes a framework for analysis which will then be explored in more detail:

1 Systems of urban planning and management are likely to be established at national level, but the politics which operate through and within them require analysis by location and by sector: regions and towns have their own political economies and influential elites; different policy sectors bring different interests and organisations into play. The first step in the analysis is to describe the socio-economic interests which are present and likely to be affected.
2 The next level of analysis identifies where power is located in the structure of government. This examines the organisational arrangements for the allocation of responsibility and discretion between public and private sectors, levels of government, departments, politicians and officials, domestic and external agencies.
3 The analysis can then address the question about which interests identified in the first step have influence in the formal processes of decision-making identified in the second step.
4 More important than the formal arrangements may be the informal procedures of policy formation and implementation, especially in the absence of effective democracy. Informal networks and social connections may be important influences on leading actors.
5 Having looked at the identity, location and influence of powerful interests, the analysis should turn to the effect of procedures of implementation on the relatively powerless, those who are the objects rather than the subjects of urban administration. Do forms and reforms of administration have the effect of extending or limiting their access and influence?
6 This leads to the question of popular organisation and how far it creates a basis for wider participation and pressure or for elite domination. This question will be taken up in Chapter 8.

The following sections are intended to illustrate these analytic categories rather than to exhaustively explore them.

Politics at the level of location and sector

Nation states and national economies are not monolithic. The organisational framework of urban administration may be in common throughout a nation but it will encounter quite different constellations of interests and demands in different localities and in different sectors of public action. Planners and managers need to understand not only how local circumstances may require different policies but also how local actors may constrain or permit policy implementation.

As Rondinelli (1983) points out, towns differ in their origins, their economic role and their potential for development. For example, the comparative advantages of rural market towns clearly differ from those of towns based on mineral resources, defensive functions, government administration, industry, domestic commerce or foreign trade. If planning is to be a more developmental activity, at the very least planners have to understand these different economic bases before they can intervene discriminatingly to develop them. This is more than a technical matter for professional analysis. All of these alternative urban functions are represented by people in organisations who have to be consulted, informed, responded to or resisted. Planners and managers (as well as local politicians) are therefore drawn into political processes of negotiation which will vary from place to place, both in terms of the actors with whom they negotiate and the outcomes which emerge. This, as Hardoy and Satterthwaite (1989a: 270) suggest, is one argument for urban local government: that the diversity of towns requires some means of bringing local interests directly into the process of decision-making, rather than just as objects of professional analysis and official decision.

Urban administration therefore operates in a varying political environment of major and minor actors. If we were to consider only those actors who can be defined in mainly economic terms, the key variables might be: the nature of the main activities or principal functions of the town, the structure and location of ownership of enterprises and land, and, especially for small market towns, the structure of surrounding rural landownership. The effects of these variables are in terms of their definition of dominant interests, their influence on forms of popular organisation, the nature of demands for urban planning and services, and the channels of demand. Together these factors will powerfully influence the implementation of policy if not always its formulation (which may often take no account of any local interest).

For example, the urban manager in New Delhi or Brasilia operates in an environment dominated by public sector agencies and enterprises. These are not only the major economic activities and employers but also important landowners; they generate a basis of wider social organisation in large trade unions, professional associations and residential areas defined on the basis of official status; moreover, all these interests have access to influence through their participation in the machinery of government. This is a *relatively* predictable world, where housing allocation can be adjusted to bureaucratic categories, rush hours may be adjusted by changing office times, and even master plans *may* be fulfilled.

In Bombay or São Paulo, on the other hand, where urban managers operate in a financial, commercial and industrial environment, most of the powerful actors are outside government; some of the most powerful are large firms with international connections and (in Brazil) foreign ownership; trade unions may be powerful in the leading sectors but popular organisation will be generally more heterogeneous and fragmented especially among the employees of small firms; land is largely in the hands of a myriad of private owners. This is clearly an environment in which the official apparatus has less control but also one where it may be subject to less direct pressure because more demands can be satisfied (or not) by the market rather than politically or administratively. Single company towns, cantonment towns and market towns present the urban administrator with yet other political environments, demands and possibilities.

Political actors vary not only by location but also by policy sector. Urban planners and managers are directly or indirectly concerned with a wide range of governmental activity from the regulation of land use, to the promotion of economic development, to the location, installation and maintenance of social and infrastructural services. They are thus continually being brought into touch not only with the different traditions of other departments but also their established relationships with private actors. These sectoral universes may often be contradictory between each other. As Unikel (1982) notes for Mexican regional policy,

> the multiplicity of interests represented within the public sector makes the adoption of any single coherent political line impossible beyond mere self-defence against popular pressure. (Unikel 1982: 272)

The problem is not peculiar to developing countries. Berg (1989) notes the fragmentation of the Netherlands system of public administration. Lodden (1991) describes the role of the Norwegian Ministry of Local Government as advocate on behalf of local authorities which need to deal with the different ministries of central government, each with its own agenda. The co-ordinating role of urban planning requires it to straddle those contradictions and thus to understand and negotiate between the interests which operate in different sectors.

This may be a question not only of which interests are active in different sectors but also of what *sort* of politics operate. Saunders (1979) and Offe (1976), writing about the advanced capitalist countries, have suggested that different forms of politics operate in the spheres of production and consumption; in the former, a corporatist partnership between the state, big business and organised labour restricts participation, while the field of consumption (for example of collective services) allows wider expression of demands and more open, pluralist politics. Grindle (1980) writing about developing countries, differentiates between the politics associated with collective benefits (for example water supply, public transport or squatter upgrading) which arouse collective popular demands, and those associated with divisible benefits (for example housing) which lead to individual and therefore more controllable demands.

Sensitivity to the politics of localities and sectors is important to urban administrators if they are to avoid the failures which result from the attempt to impose technically derived and uniform policies. Interventions can be better made if there is some understanding of the interests which will support or prevent them. Other actors can be identified and their motives assessed, opposition can be anticipated, alliances built and strategies developed for including those who have a weak voice in the political process.

Organisational power and discretion

Formal organisational arrangements of government provide an important arena within which interests have to be active if they are to be effective. There are other, informal arenas which may operate in parallel with or, in extreme cases of breakdown, as substitutes for formal government. However, any analysis of urban politics has to take account of the formally institutionalised relations between levels and agencies of government, between politicians and officials, between government and citizens, and between national and external agencies. Among the many possible questions these relations can raise, there are two fundamental points: where are functions located and with what degree of discretion can they be performed?

The functions of urban administration are local in their application but not necessarily locally controlled. Key functions would be: the installation of basic infrastructure (water, sewerage, roads, electricity) and basic services (refuse disposal, health and sanitation, and education); the supporting and co-ordinating role of town planning particularly with regard to land management; and the economic development role of allocating permissions and incentives for investment. It would be rare for all of these functions to be wholly controlled at one level of government. Indeed, it has been common experience in developing countries for 'local' functions to be appropriated by higher levels of government; parastatal agencies have often been created particularly to take over infrastructural functions frequently at the instigation of aid organisations. External aid agencies have also become important actors in their own right, supporting the development of specialist agencies and semi-autonomous projects. Functions may be split not only 'vertically' (giving separate agencies responsibility for entire functions) but also 'horizontally', typically separating the central activities of policy-making, plan-making and strategy from local responsibility for implementation and maintenance. Such 'functional fragmentation' (Walsh 1969) is a clear impediment to the co-ordinating role of urban administration which faces not only organisational and professional divisions but also divided lines of political responsibility.

Even when a responsibility is formally allocated to an agency its ability to exercise discretion may be limited. Many of its decisions, not only about policy and planning but also about the details of implementation and maintenance, may be effectively controlled by other levels of the political and administrative apparatus. Page and Goldsmith (1987) writing about European local government identify the following types of constraints imposed from the centre: legal requirements, non-legal influence, mandating of services and financial dependence. Common legal constraints would be local supervision or tutelage by central officials such as district commissioners in Africa or collectors in India, or the control by central and state tribunals of accounts of local budgetary decisions in Brazil. Requirements for local decisions to conform to national and sectoral plans may be a matter either of legal obligation or of non-legal expectation; similarly central and state advice and technical expertise may be offered on a nominally voluntary but, in practice, compulsory basis. Services may be mandated from higher to lower levels of government or from government to private bodies, in which case the implementer becomes an agent of others' decisions about standards and levels of service controlled by detailed regulations. Such requirements and expectations may be enforced through financial dependence and the conditional allocation of grants and loans to conform with central or aid agency requirements. Another tacit form of control may be the appointment by higher levels of government of local executives and senior staff: for example municipal commissioners in India or the Unified Local Government Service in Botswana.

Besides these administrative procedures, discretion may also be limited (or extended) through more overtly political channels. Political executive power at the local level may be formally located with, for example, the mayor in Latin America or the council in Anglophone Africa but be constrained in several ways. At the local level, executive power may be limited by accountability to a legislature and ultimately an electorate: whether, how and how far these do constitute limits will be matters of great variation. Party discipline may operate both locally and nationally to set the policy agenda and put limits on executive decision. Central political leaders may exert more direct forms of personal control over local politicians through, for example, patronage and the promise of higher office. On the other hand, some of these instruments of political control may also act in the other direction as instruments of *access* to influence on policy decisions beyond the local level. Local political actors may be able to bypass some of the formal limits on their discretion by using party structures, personal links and their own political careers to bring benefits to their localities. Mayors of big cities in Latin America have commonly held high state or national office and maintain influence at those levels.

Any analysis of the power structure of urban administration must therefore take into account the location not only of responsibilities but also of discretion and influence. Local politicians and officials may often have the responsibility but not the power to deliver effective plans, services, development and maintenance. External (aid) agencies, as well as central governments, may have a particular propensity to live this double life: urging 'bottom-up' planning, for example, while imposing their own administrative routines, financial terms, project frameworks, conditionality and penalties.

Functional fragmentation, compounded by the dispersal of discretionary power between levels of government and external agencies, must represent a particular problem for the classical approach to (master) planning which assumes that planners have both control and the support of politicians. Far from having control, the position of planning is likely to be one of institutional weakness, easily overridden by other professions, departments, private bodies or the courts, and controlling none of the instruments of discretionary power (finance, land, spending power, legal control).

One response would be to try to locate planning nearer to the centre of discretionary power, for example in the chief executive's office as Wekwete (1989) proposes; but this assumes that responsibilities and discretion are more concentrated than we have indicated. Another possibility, as Lufadeju (1989) suggests, is to award planners the control of investment funds so that they have leverage over other agencies. An example exists in the Town Planning and Valuation Department of the Indian State of Gujarat which manages both land pooling arrangements and expenditure on some investment programmes (Batley 1990).

Another response to planning's weak organisational position is the one suggested by the 'new convention': to play down the concept of planning as regulator and controller and to see it more as analyst, enabler and 'political' broker between the array of power sources. The question we have already raised is whether this infringes the boundaries between the roles of politicians and officials.

This last question raises profound issues to do with the division of discretion and control between politicians and officials. At the heart of it is the Weberian dilemma: the need for organisational arrangements which guarantee the technical efficiency of the bureaucracy and at the same time its political accountability. This involves an

> invariably tense system of checks and balances which requires the close interdependence yet relative autonomy of both the political and the administrative elements in the state system. (Brett 1988: 10)

The commonplace, particularly in developing countries, is of failure to maintain this delicate balance, resulting either in the political subversion of professional judgement or in unaccountable bureaucracy or both. Official corruption and 'political interference' are common complaints in the field of planning whether in Manila (von Einsiedel 1989), Bombay (D'Souza 1989) or São Paulo (Bolaffi 1989). In such situations a more proactive and transparently partisan (on behalf of the poor or of business investors) role for urban planners, and administrators generally, might further tip the balance against accountability and towards corruption. An alternative might be to fully acknowledge the political nature of urban administration and to let politicians do it more directly, as is being tried in Greater Calcutta (Blore 1989) or as in Mabogunje's (1989) proposed clientelistic neighbourhood planning. The price that has to be paid for this overt politicisation of planning, as Mabogunje recognises, is that it becomes an instrument of political and personal favouritism.

The new planning assumes that relations between officials and politicians are securely based on agreed boundaries from which some flexibility and limited discretion can be allowed. Organisational analysis is required to know whether these conditions exist in specific cases. In their absence, it may be better to spend time and energy in constructing professional competence, bureaucratic efficiency and political account-ability rather than in trying to supersede them.

Interests in organisations

Synthesising the two previous sections, we have to establish how certain of the interests present and concerned with particular policy areas have influence within the formal organisational apparatus. The urban administrator faces a world of different and often contradictory demands and expectations from groups with different levels of resources with which to advance their claims. Important among these resources is their influence within centres of functional responsibility and discretion. In a highly fragmented system of urban government – with functions and discretionary power spread between levels of government, professional departments, politicians and officials, and external agencies – the urban administrator has to co-ordinate and build alliances not only between agencies but also effectively between the social interests which have influence within them. Adding further to the complexity of the life of the 'analytic planner' and the 'enabling manager' is the fact that their control over some of these agencies and their associated interests will be greater than others. In particular, local planners, managers and politicians will have least influence on interests which operate through central government and external organisations. This, however, is the point of the analytic, negotiating and enabling approach: to understand the relative power of groups and organisations so as to selectively intervene, support and construct alliances. Some forces may set limits on policy implementation while others may enable it.

We might identify three sorts or levels of interest which may have some presence within the organisational apparatus. There are first, the direct participants (the operators and possibly the beneficiaries), second, those who contribute direct inputs into the system or who establish the terms on which it operates (for example the contractors, the creditors, high-level policy-makers and intermediaries), and third, those who have a more indirect but often profound influence without being directly involved in the organisation (for example, landowners).

The conference papers on which this book draws identified as control-ling interests most often those who were direct participants or made direct inputs: national and local politicians, political parties, professions, private consultants, foreign aid agencies and national governments. These were often seen as disruptive to effective planning: whether through political interference and short-term perspectives in Manila or Bombay (von Einsiedel 1989; D'Souza 1989), political instability in Kara-chi (Ahmed 1989), the anti-strategic, pro-design orientation of engineers in Bombay and Zimbabwe (D'Souza 1989; Wekwete 1989) and of private consultants in Brazil (Bolaffi 1989), the 'patrimonial appropriation of government by professions, parties and politicians' in Brazil (Wilheim 1989), and the fragmented pressures of aid agencies. Some writers go on

Plate 27   Landowners and developers often have considerable power to
influence decision-making processes, as symbolised by this
imposing entrance to a new private housing estate in Bangkok.

to identify the profound influence of interests external to government:
colonialists and their inheritors in favour of protected land use in Africa
(Lufadeju 1989; Wekwete 1989), landowners against land-use controls in
Bombay and São Paulo (D'Souza 1989; Bolaffi 1989), and 'the conditions
for capitalism' in Nigeria (Mabogunje 1989).

Fagence (1977: 141–2) writing particularly, but not only, about the
direct participants in the British planning process identified the following groups: elected representatives, public servants, the public (*en masse*,
as interest groups and as individuals), 'external' agencies (other public
and professional bodies) and expert consultants. Such categories will
always contain different and shifting interests (between professions and
sections of the public for example) but our earlier analysis suggested a
particular tendency to fragmentation and a less coherent and uncertain
distribution of functions and discretion in the situation of developing
countries.

Angel (1983a) identifies the variety of different motives of the participants (engineers, 'housers', community builders, politicians, international funders and slum dwellers) in the relatively simple activity of
providing infrastructure to slums. There is also the likelihood of the
direct participation in decisions at local level of central (or regional)
politicians and officials with an implicit detachment of local decision-
making from local interests. Foreign aid agencies and creditors are likely
to play an important part in determining urban policy and the terms and

conditions of implementation, again with a consequent detachment from local pressures and instead a subjection to demands (ideological and material) originating in the donor country. The weakness of local political autonomy and the possibly unclear boundaries between politicians and officials are likely to give the participation of 'elected representatives' in the planning process a distinct significance. They may be there less as representatives of an area interest and more as claimants for particular interests. The weakness of formal representative processes may itself promote another set of participants in the management or urban development: intermediaries who act as fixers, patrons or brokers between the official world and sections of the public. Politically sponsored organisers of land invasions are just one such example (Gilbert and Ward 1982).

Benson (1980) has offered a general framework for analysing the groups

> whose vested interests are 'structured' into the sector's administrative organisation. The operation of this sector tends to 'serve' those interests which are built into its structure. (Benson 1980: 18)

Rather than identifying particular interests, which will vary from policy sector to policy sector and from place to place, he identifies the sort of role which interests may play within an administrative structure as demand groups, support groups, administrative groups, provider groups or co-ordinating groups. The particular interests which occupy these group roles run beyond official participants to those who are external to the official machine but whose needs and values are so privileged as to be effectively taken for granted.

Demand groups include the recipients of services or programmes but also all of those who may gain from its incidental output of opportunities (contractors, developers and intermediaries or brokers, for example). **Support groups** provide essential financial and other resources and political commitment to the organisations in the policy sector: for example creditors, legislators, aid agencies or lobbyists who may support a particular programme. Even more fundamentally, in less stable countries the support of the police and military may be crucial. **Administrative groups** are the elites who control the major organisations of a policy area and who are concerned to defend, maintain and extend their spheres of control. **Provider groups** include the professions, the bureaucracy and other occupations engaged in the delivery of services or conduct of programmes: contractors and consultants may become sufficiently entrenched to form part of this group. Their perception of problems and feasible solutions, advice to administrators and politicians and defence of 'standards' help to define not only policy and operational practices but also professional dominance and job opportunities. **Co-ordinating groups** are those which operate at the 'apex' in budgetary, auditing or cross-sectoral planning organisations to try to rationalise functions, reduce inefficiencies and effectively to suppress the partisan aspirations of other groups; unfortunately, as Benson (1980) points out, they are not above a partisan desire to extend their own role which may lead to the technocratic inefficiencies of centralisation and burdensome data collection.

This section has emphasised that in order to be effective interests have to have some involvement in the formal structures of urban planning and management, which assumes that the formal structures are themselves effective. The direct participants, the planners and managers at all levels of government, are themselves obviously in a ready position to assert influence, not only as neutral instruments of politicians but also according to their own interests, values and perceptions in their administrative, provider and co-ordinator roles. As Weber warned, in the absence of the rule of law and effective political accountability, the servants may become masters. In the context of developing countries, the planners and managers are likely to be divided among themselves (given the fragmentation of government) and to include powerful central government and foreign interests divorced from real local accountability. The beneficiaries, on the other hand, while being part of the organisational system as a demand group, are only one part and often relatively inarticulate and disorganised. Other non-official interests (landowners, contractors, developers, financiers, commercial and industrial entrepreneurs) may gain some access to the official machine as demanders, suppliers and providers but may well be in a competitive situation which will weaken their influence except where common interests arise. Three ways of maximising their influence individually present themselves: to gain some restricted official status, for example as 'recognised and short-listed contractors (Batley 1981); to gain political office as direct representatives of their own interest; or to engage in informal networks of influence and social connections with leading officials and politicians.

Informal networks

Grindle (1980) argues that political activity is likely to focus on policy implementation rather than policy formulation in developing countries. This is partly because the closed political regimes which are common will seek to exclude the wide representation of demands at the stage of policy formulation; parties, where they exist, will function more as channels of clientelistic distribution than as instruments for channelling demands upwards. It is also because people who will be affected by policy may have little opportunity to obtain information and little capacity to organise and articulate their views at the national level. Only when policies are applied and plans implemented at local level does their significance become apparent to affected groups. By then it is formally too late to influence policy. Typically, as we saw earlier, implementing agencies (including local government) will have little formal discretion to adjust policy to local realities.

So political demands may focus precisely at the point that their expression is illegitimate – where policy and plans should be implemented rather than made. The necessary adjustments to local circumstances may therefore be experienced as crises of rule-breaking (squatting for example), corruption, or 'interference' by 'irresponsible' local politicians who bypass the rules that higher level politicians and officials expect them loyally to defend. Long bureaucratic hierarchies between formal policy-making and implementation make crisis almost routine (Schaffer 1969). This may mean that the formal retention of discretionary power at the centre breaks down in informal practice.

The alternative to such critical challenges is the operation of networks of influence between 'insiders' and selected 'outsiders' (Schaffer 1980) whose views are taken into account in the continuous process of making, refining, detailing, interpreting and changing policy. Saunders (1979), writing about British urban politics, draws a distinction between those groups (for example squatters) who challenge policy head on and who are 'defined out' of real influence on the system, and those (for example, business interests) who achieve influence by regular interaction

> with political leaders who generally believe what they believe, think what they think and want what they want ... opinions, suggestions and modes of thought pass almost imperceptibly, like osmosis, from businessmen to politicians, and from politicians to businessmen. (Saunders 1979: 324)

Widening our concern to include not only politicians but also officials, we shall consider what may be the channels of this more imperceptible influence on the makers and implementers of policy.

Six types of influence networks will be briefly identified, based on recruitment, professionalism, dependency, social proximity, physical proximity and client relationships. Some of these may act to consolidate the position of certain groups within the power structure, while others may broaden the linkage of 'insiders' with groups which have little other influence.

The recruitment process does not determine all future social values and connections but will probably condition them. It may operate on a basis which is expressly designed to maintain privileged social connections and the dominance of clientelistic leaders, by favouring the entry of those with particular family, ethnic, regional or religious backgrounds. It may seek to break such privilege by, as in India, setting up quota or reserved access system for 'backward' groups, intended not only to give access to the particular entrant but also to bring another range of interests and connections into the decision-making system. It will usually, however, be claimed that recruitment works on a neutral merit basis; but even this principle will build up a non-neutral service in the sense that it consolidates the power of the 'technocracy' and its connections to other educated and professional sections of the population.

Contingent on the recruitment process, the shared socialisation of professional groups can act as a mechanism of highly selective contact. Some professions (for example town planners and senior administrative classes) are almost exclusively of the public sector and may build a very introverted identity which may nevertheless run across levels of government and embrace foreign advisers. Others (for example engineers) straddle the public/private sector divide and may in that sense be more inclusive, responsive for example to the views of private contractors. The 'watertightness' of professions may be particularly strong in the case of the career public services of Anglophone Africa or Asia as opposed to the more transient services of Latin America.

'Organisational dependency' on other bodies for support (creditors, politicians, aid agencies, police and military) and for joint implementation (other government departments, private contractors and consultants) may develop into personal loyalties and shared assumptions about what is reasonable. Conditions may not need to be imposed because they are understood; team identities may grow up through long periods of working together with foreign agents as Meikle (1989) shows in the Iraqi case and Matthaeus (1989) in Nepal. Common understanding, supported sometimes by common professional backgrounds, may thus give certain nominally external interests direct influence on those who have formal responsibility and discretion.

'Social proximity' concerns the social relations which urban administrators maintain once in office. On the one hand, there are the residential locations and social life associated with their income group, occupation and official status, and, on the other hand, kinship, ethnic, caste, religious or regional associations which may link them to wider social groups. The latter may be weak or absent in western, class-based societies. Saunders (1979: 309–24) recounts the informal interaction between business people and politicians in social clubs and voluntary committees in a London borough. Lomnitz (1971: quoted in Roberts 1978) describes the clubs, coffee drinking and sport that sustain links between the Chilean urban upper class. Particularly in Africa, the exclusivity of class and official status may be breached by links through kinship, ethnic and regional connections (Lloyd 1979: 193). This possibility, however, needs to be qualified by a considerable literature which indicates that such associations are more likely to be used as instruments of elite dominance and mobilisation than as bases of lower-class influence (Sandbrook 1982); they are anyway less important to the social life of urban dwellers than particularistic linkages (Peil 1977: 302); cross-class linkages are breaking down in a situation of increasing social polarisation in which the urban elite has been able to protect itself partly through its political connections (Amis 1990: 6).

Special residential areas and administrative cities are two ways in which physical barriers may limit contact with wider social groups. In some cases, such as Brasilia, housing types may even maintain divisions between administrative categories. More generally, policy-makers and implementers are simply physically nearer to the experience of some sections of the population by the location of their offices, homes, travel to work and leisure. This may not only generate greater sensitivity to middle- or upper-class problems (protective zoning, commuting routes, shopping centres) and restrict contact with poorer communities, but also contribute to the application of upper-class perceptions of normality to the situation of poorer areas – the concern to give the city a 'respectable face' (Peattie 1979), or to protect its international image (Amis 1990) and to resist invasion by migrants. At a wider level, there is the possibility of a greater sensitivity to the demands of the populations of big and capital cities arising from the location there of senior officials and politicians (Lipton 1977).

One form of informal, influence network which may include poorer sections of the population is the relationship which may grow up between the providers and recipients (or clients of service). As Bailey (1977) pointed out, bureaucratic impersonality may be breached by frequent contact and growing empathy with clients. The interests of clients may thus be carried into the organisation, leading perhaps to adjustments of policy and implementation practice. Three qualifications should however be made. First, such empathy may include any client of any service and not only the poor; it is only in a narrow range of urban services (squatter upgrading, sites and services, community development, health) that particular contact may be made with the poor. Second, the officials who have direct contact are likely to be at the bottom of the organisational hierarchy with little discretion to modify practice except at the margins. Third, given the incapacity of such officials to make major adjustments in policy, it is very likely that their empathy remains at the level of personal or group favouritism or clientelism.

This brief survey suggests that informal networks are likely to grow up between those who are already part of or closely linked to the formal structure of power. Rather than widely extending the range of influences, it seems that they are more likely to 'particularise' the interests which do have influence. For example, all private contractors may have a potential place but only some will be able to exploit informal networks to gain personal connections.

The experience of the controlled

This chapter has been principally concerned with the question of who controls urban planning and management, and through what formal and informal organisational arrangements. There is also the question of how the procedures of urban administration may have the effect of controlling the relatively powerless and affecting their access to influence and to government outputs. Once again, because we are dealing with everywhere but nowhere ('Erewhon'), we shall outline a sequence of considerations and possibilities.

Town planning is explicitly concerned with control and regulation as well as with the more positive sounding functions of co-ordination, integration and promotion (for example of economic development or of the position of the poor). Indeed the positive and negative are necessary to each other: co-ordination and promotion imply that somebody else is being ordered and demoted. Less explicitly than in planning, public services also have a controlling role, excluding as well as selecting beneficiaries, privileging some users or applicants over others, hearing some demands but ignoring others, obliging people to pursue their claims in certain ordered ways.

Bureaucratic routine and technical rationality are frequently criticised as complex and exclusive. The criticism may often be justified but there is another side to the argument. The absence of routine forms of delivery and systematic regulation is the more common experience of the poor. They are exposed to unregulated and often rapacious forms of market supply (water-carriers, money-lenders, illicit land developers) or periodic harassment and clientelistic favouritism from the political authorities (amnesties, temporary permission, tolerated but illicit electricity connections, extension of services on special appeal). The regulation of distribution is important to the poor because it can represent escape from uncertain (and often high) prices, political manipulation and exploitation. A public bureaucracy which is effective and technically competent is, in this sense, fundamental to the principle of citizenship: that citizens receive services 'as of right' and are treated 'without regard to person', systematically according to rules rather than wilfully and unpredictably.

However, while these are necessary they are not sufficient conditions for inclusive citizenship. First and foremost, as has already been indicated, if public bureaucracies are not themselves to become self-serving, they must be politically accountable:

> effective public provision cannot be expected in societies where the basic conditions of pluralist democracy are absent. Bureaucrats will inevitably fail without effective political surveillance. (Brett 1988: 10)

Second, effective public bureaucracy assumes certain conditions in its environment: that there is sufficient stability for the rules and procedures to have some durability, adequate supply to at least hold the promise of meeting demand and sufficient social homogeneity to suit standardised solutions. Third, it assumes certain capacities in its clientele: that applicants understand bureaucracy, its rules and procedures, that they are competent to deal with bureaucratic requirements, and that their need is not so grave that they cannot tolerate the delays of 'due process' (Schaffer 1969).

It is quite apparent that these conditions are in short supply, particularly in developing countries. The very virtues of bureaucracy – impersonality, standardised procedures and products, fairness – may break down in situations of dire scarcity, acute need, extreme local diversity and incomprehension of the rules of the game. The political and administrative centralism and hierarchy, which were described earlier in this chapter, aggravate the situation by removing discretionary power from the point that it could make adaptations to local circumstances and clients' capacities. Urban plans and service distribution procedures are imposed from the centre; the plans and procedures cannot cope with the diversity and volume of local demands, and every situation becomes a crisis demanding reference to the top – or else there is breakdown and free for all. Officials may then shelter behind rules and professional standards as a way of fending off demand and responsibility. Even those programmes which are designed to help the poor (upgrading or sites and service schemes) are frequently unrelated to local priorities or so complex in their selection rules that they can be most easily understood and manipulated by the non-poor (Nientied and van der Linden 1988).

In such situations, even the best intentioned government programmes may represent forms of control from the point of view of the 'beneficiaries'. Either they have to accept and adjust to the rigid application of the administration's rationality, even if it does not correspond to their needs and capacities; or they have to appeal to the patronage of politicians and officials, accepting their own subordination.

Patron-clientelism is particularly likely to occur, as Grindle (1980) suggests, where politics focuses on the attempt to extract advantage at the implementation stage. Local politicians with few formal responsibilities may resort to the 'irresponsible' distortion of the rules in order to build their constituencies. The client or client group may offer political support in return for building permits, slum upgrading, housing, plots, the convenient routing of utilities and roads, the avoidance of demolition or removal. As Amis (1989: 387) notes, the authorisation of the informal sector and squatter settlements provides particular opportunities for political patronage and administrative pay-offs. However, the effect may be more inclusive for some than bureaucratically rational distribution: for example, the clientelistic distribution of services to squatter areas in Caracas was found to be more inclusive of poorer communities than a formal programme of upgrading which was slower moving and focused on technically selected areas (Batley 1981). Through patron-clientelism, the elite makes direct links with poorer sectors of the public, in what might otherwise be politically exclusive systems. However, there is a price to pay in the political subjugation of the client population; the relationship is inherently unequal.

The influence of reforms on control

Attempts to overcome these problems of failed, distorted or manipulative access also have political implications. Three types of reforms, each of them trying to reach client requirements more effectively, might be indicated: administrative reform, non-state solutions, political reform. In finding problems with each of these, the intention is not to rule them out but to indicate possible political effects on the population.

Administrative reforms may take several and to some extent contradictory forms. In common, however, these may be seen as ways of maintaining the pre-eminence of state action while enhancing the roles of officials over politicians. On the one hand, there is the centralist solution, which seeks to overcome political distortions and local managerial deficiencies by imposing centrally conceived plans and programmes, bypassing the normal local problems so as to 'get things done'. Aid programmes working through central government, with the leverage of cash and with short time frames for achievement, may have had a particular propensity to encourage solutions through special agencies (development authorities) and special funding and administrative arrangements. On the other hand, there is the localist but still managerial solution: the devolution of functions and discretion to local managers and planners, leading to the more effective 'targeting' of need groups and the more sensitive identification of their 'basic needs'. Much current aid thinking is along these lines; indeed, the 'new convention' identified earlier is part of this tendency. Unlike the centralist solution, at least it strengthens local institutions and enhances the social and physical proximity between the administrators and the administered, through formal and informal networks.

Plate 28   Much aid funding is now channelled through municipal government, as here with a World Bank funded project in the Philippines, with the aim of making projects more sensitive to the needs of the local community.

Both types of administrative reform increase the predominance of the planner and manager, unless localised administration is accompanied by political decentralisation. The consequence for the recipient population *may* be the strengthening of official definitions of needs, problems and solutions but without any corresponding increase in the capacity of the 'target groups' to articulate their demands. Local interests are still seen as clients rather than masters (through politicians) of the bureaucracy (White 1987: 177).

Non-state solutions, one way or the other, seek to make supply more responsive to demand rather than officially defined 'need'. Most clearly the resort to the private entrepreneurial sector seeks to make competing suppliers responsive to the consumer. In this view, even planning should be 'market led' on the understanding that market developers understand consumer needs (Brindley *et al.* 1989). Alternatively recognising the necessary inequity in the operation of the open individualistic market and often the simple lack of private entrepreneurs in weaker economies, co-operatives and other forms of social ownership may be encouraged as collective operators 'subject to market forces, yet outside the state' (Brett 1988). Outside the formal market as well as outside the state are two other forms of operation: non-governmental voluntary organisations (NGOs) and self-help through individual or group action. These may claim to avoid the necessity for demands to be made, let alone needs analysed: self-helpers find their own solutions while NGOs may frequently *claim* an unmediated contact or empathy with the poor.

There are many claims about these forms of provision which we shall not address. The point to be made is that none really does avoid state action, each requires some level of state support and intervention. 'Market led' planning in Britain has been turned on its head; instead of leading, the market has to be 'levered-in' by state subsidy (Brindley *et al.* 1989). As regards co-operatives and voluntary agencies, 'in most cases success will probably only occur where they are also given substantial degrees of support by state or aid agencies' (Brett 1988: 10). Conyers and Kaul (1990) find that successful community projects depend, among other factors, on supportive national or local government. Moreover, public administration may still be drawn back in to provide for those who do *not* gain access to the market, or to co-operatives and self-help groups, or where these forms of provision fail. Do private entrepreneurs exist or do they have to be encouraged? Can they reach low-income markets at affordable prices? Who can help themselves? Is self-help an illusion? In parts of Africa, private renting appears now to be taking the place of publicly provided and self-built housing (Amis 1989).

From the point of view of the administered population, the ironical result of 'state withdrawal' from planning, regulation and provision may be that while the majority of the population lose their 'as of right' claim, the state continues to support private providers and their clienteles. A British example is London's Docklands, where the population felt politically disenfranchised by the removal of local government's responsibility for the area and its substitution by a development corporation practising 'leverage' or 'market-led' planning (Batley 1989). Their aspirations and demands were effectively depoliticised and removed from the public arena because there was no longer a forum in which they could be heard nor a body which appealed for their support.

Political reform may have the opposite objective, of creating fora and increasing the responsiveness of public administration to the public, either directly or through political representatives. We have already examined the possibility that a less regulatory and more enabling, negotiated and participatory form of planning assumes the conditions of pluralist democracy and of confidence between politicians and officials. Political reforms in the sphere of urban development are more limited in the conditions they hope to bring about.

The first type of reform – political decentralisation – devolves function and discretionary powers to regional and local government, that is to locally accountable politicians. However, 'decentralisation' in practice often amounts to no more than administrative deconcentration (Mawhood 1983), that is the allocation of functions to local levels of administration, which may in fact be a way of strengthening the presence of central government at local level. An example of real though limited political decentralisation is the allocation to the municipal bodies of Greater Calcutta of responsibility for deciding priorities for urban development (Blore 1989; Werlin 1987).

The second type of political reform aims to increase the direct participation (unmediated by politicians) of the affected population, usually in specific planning exercises or projects. The concept and practices of participation will be discussed fully in Chapter 7; here we wish briefly to relate them to the question of control. Like 'decentralisation', 'participation' is a term which shades from administrative into overtly political meanings. These shades of meaning have been described by several writers in similar terms since Arnstein's 'ladder of participation' (Arnstein 1969; Holnsteiner 1977; Uphoff *et al*. 1979; Paul 1987; Moser 1989a). In the case of the World Bank's experience of development projects, Paul (1987: v) identifies a scale from participation in the more administrative sense of sharing project costs, improving project efficiency and increasing project effectiveness, through the building of beneficiary capacity to (political) empowerment. As Moser (1989a: 84) points out these are not necessarily discrete categories: participation as an administrative means can develop into participation as a political end. However, the evidence is clear that governmentally conceived urban development projects usually treat 'participation' as a means to the achievement of administrative goals rather than as a method of increasing control by the community (Paul 1987: 15–16).

So, while at the rhetorical level 'decentralisation' and 'participation' may be about the transfer of control, in practice programmes which bear these names are very often about ways (raising cash, contributing labour, etc.) of implementing centrally and officially conceived plans and policies (Moser 1989a: 85). Even if political decentralisation and participation are genuinely achieved we should not be too innocently sanguine about the effects on the client population. Several sceptical qualifications should be made.

Given the natural reluctance of central elites to lose power and also the necessity to retain national integration, it is very likely that the award of greater local autonomy with one hand will be accompanied by its withdrawal with another. I have already indicated several ways in which a government may allocate formal powers yet retain control: through party mechanisms, financial allocations and requirements to confirm with higher level plans. Party control may be what makes the Calcutta decentralisation tolerable (Blore 1989). Indeed, the whole point of raising political participation at the local level may be not to generate local political autonomy but to create local structures for mobilising the population behind the regime's political ideology. Such a case is the Peruvian programme under a military regime for settlement improvement through state promoted neighbourhood organisation (Michl 1973) although it has to be added that independent organisations did never-theless emerge (Batley 1981; Skinner 1983). Furthermore, power allo-cated to the local government or community level will itself not be universally shared: 'empowerment' is never universal. Access and influence will probably be extended to local elites rather than to the powerless as the section on politics at the local level indicated; it is possible, as national governments often argue, that the exclusion and control of the weak will even be increased (Werlin 1989).

It should be concluded that the effects of these reforms depend not only on governmental motives and constraints but also on the capacity of sections of the population to organise to take advantage of opportuni-ties. Earlier we saw that informal networks are more likely to link already influential groups to the power structure. Organisations which involve the poor may have little lasting political effect on behalf of the poor. Work-based organisation is likely to be weak given that 'most workers are employed in small or medium sized enterprises and are rarely unionised' (Roberts 1978: 154) and that the self-employed are usually in competition. The main basis of independent organisation is the neighbourhood but the purpose of such organisation, at least in Latin America, is often only to deal with the authorities in the hope of gaining security and services:

> Mobilisation over urban services tends to encourage vertical structures of dependence between local community and central authorities. . . . In this way, demand-making on urban government often becomes a means of extending government control over localities at relatively little cost. (Roberts 1978: 154–5)

Amis (1989: 387) and Sandbrook (1982: 205) present a similar argument for Africa. Lastly, as we saw earlier, organisations which involve the poor – ethnic associations (Kasfir 1976; Sandbrook 1982: 198), trade unions (Sandbrook 1982: 202–3; Amis 1989: 387), political parties (Roberts 1978: 152–3) – are commonly a basis for mobilisation and patronage on behalf of elites.

Political reform addresses many of the factors identified earlier in this chapter as weakening the effectiveness and inclusiveness of urban plan-ning: centralised discretion, fragmented functions, the dominance of self-serving 'insider' interests, the political exclusivity of policy forma-tion, rigidly standardised implementation unrelated to local diversity, rule-breaking by clientelistic local politicians without real responsi-bilities. Decentralisation and political participation are difficult to achieve, however, precisely because they may address the problem: that is the problem of control by central elites, including politicians, adminis-trators, professionals and linked non-official interests. It could only be in situations of extreme crisis or extreme sophistication that such elites might willingly accept that power-sharing is to their own advantage: 'to expand their power, governments must share it. If they do not allow participation, they cannot expect cooperation' (Werlin 1987). The prob-lem for the elite is that the conditions demanded by the new planning – decentralisation, participation, analytic and enabling officials – have no natural limits. More demand may be uncovered than can be satisfied and even more profoundly:

> Many authorities ... fear that once they allow a community to participate in the execution of a project, the people will resort to 'undemocratic' methods if they do not have their way, and will start demanding participation in other spheres of life, in particular in political affairs. (UNCHS 1984a: 8)

Participation in particular experimental projects may, nevertheless, be seen by the authorities as more containable than a more generalised and long-term decentralisation to political representatives capable of building-up their own following.

What is to be done?

The framework for analysis used in this chapter serves several possible functions. First, it has been a basis for setting out the different ways in which politics is part of the process of planning and management. Second, it provides a framework for the planner, manager or activist who needs to assess the interests and power relations of other actors so as to engage in politically feasible action: master planners, perhaps even more than enablers/negotiators, need to be (but usually are not) political analysts because they have to anticipate rather than react to the postures of other actors. Third, it provides a set of considerations for deciding what forms of urban administration are politically appropriate.

One of the main arguments of this chapter is that there is no single right form of planning and management. These have to be evolved in particular contexts and each has to be built on the existence of certain conditions. Models transferred from current preoccupations in the west are likely to become tools of technocratic mystification and to change their meanings in other contexts. The 'enabling and supporting' approach assumes the existence of multiple and inclusive providers and a relationship of trust and accountability between politicians and officials. Master planning and 'top down' state provision *may* be appropriate to societies which are building mass production and consumption economies, but they assume a capacity for political control and managerial co-ordination.

This chapter has identified conditions which stand in the way of any sort of systematic, responsive and effective planning. The boundaries between political and official discretion may often be unclear making it difficult and even dangerous for professionals and administrators to take initiative. Power may be fragmented vertically between sectors and agencies making control, co-ordination and even prediction difficult. At the same time discretionary power, if not responsibility, may be highly concentrated (though fragmented) at the level of central government, making responsiveness to local diversity impossible. Rule-bound systems, confronting diversity and local influence networks, collapse into rule-breaking systems. Politics comes to focus covertly on the implementation process rather than overtly on policy- and plan-making.

These conditions cannot be dealt with by proposing new planning techniques. Broader institutional changes need to be made within which planning (of any sort) can play a role as an open and informed forum for the balancing of conflicting interests. Such changes cannot easily be made but they can be proposed as objectives.

The political decentralisation to local government of power as well as responsibility for urban functions can have several beneficial effects: allowing greater control and co-ordination of grouped functions, a more direct relation between fund-raising and expenditure, openness to local demands and diversities. Where policy- and plan-making are closer to the scene of implementation, there is a greater likelihood that they will be open to formal politics and influence networks. It should not be expected, however, that local political processes will be more benevolent than central ones. They will probably be exclusive and manipulative though on a less grand scale and with more scope for inclusion than is likely in centralised systems.

Within this framework of decentralised power, urban planning and management can be built up as matters of technical competence in the service of political representatives. Locally accountable bureaucracies have the potential to combine the virtues of local responsiveness with systematic administration. In most developing countries, however, it is necessary to establish the 'relative autonomy' of the official and political roles: the official needs to have space for technical judgement, a sphere of discretion subject to political accountability but not subject to particularistic political interference. If there is to be a style of action planning which involves the very political acts of negotiating, selectively intervening and enabling, then the boundaries of professional and political competence need to be clearly demarcated. The official's role is not to do the deals but to prepare the ground, maximising and appraising the information and options available to politicians.

This is not only a technical matter: if planning is a forum for the balancing of conflicting interests, then planners may play a role in broadening access to the forum. They may function as the bearers and seekers of information between levels of government, across sectors and from citizen to politician, maximising participation in the planning and policy-making process to the extent which is politically feasible. This means, particularly, reaching out to the groups which are excluded from the formal structures and informal networks. It may not always be possible to encourage their direct representation but indirect methods are available. For example, the physical and social proximity between officials and the poor can be developed by locating offices in poor neighbourhoods. Service agencies (in education, health, community development) which are directly exposed to clients can be brought into the decision-making process.

Most fundamentally, accountable bureaucracies and responsive politics require informed and demanding publics. Without pressure from below, too much depends on goodwill from above.

Note

1. The editors have pointed out to me that some of the approaches within my 'new convention', and particularly action planning (Koenigsberger) have been developed specifically in recognition of problems of planning in rapidly urbanising countries. I may overstress the question of transfer but the fact that methods are developed (by westerners) in developing countries does not mean that they are necessarily appropriate. I should stress that I am not so much discussing the social and technical merits of these approaches but their political acceptability as tools of official action.

CHAPTER 8

Planning for whom?

Carole Rakodi

Planners have little understanding about how the poor survive. As a result, urban plans and policies generally have little relevance to the situation which the poor face and may well make it far worse. Possibly the most pervasive outcome of a planning system geared to ensuring orderly development is the constraint it places on the supply of serviced land and housing. The inability of land and service delivery agencies both to keep pace with the demand and to satisfy planning standards renders most of the attempts by the poor to gain access to land, housing and even infrastructure illegal. This further reduces their access to other officially provided services and facilities. However, in addition, urban experience worldwide contains examples of projects, notably those involving redevelopment of slum areas or resettlement to official housing areas, which have so far worsened the living situation for residents that they have abandoned the new areas. Redevelopment in central Lagos, rehousing of favela residents in multi-storey flats in Brazil, and relocation of squatters in Karachi and Manila to distant sites and services schemes are well-known examples from the 1950s and 1960s (Ahmed 1989; von Einsiedel 1989).

In order to avoid such mistakes in future and evolve a management system which is responsive to the needs of the poor majority, planners and policy-makers must first understand what life is like for the poor. The first part of this chapter describes the situation in which poor urban dwellers typically live. However, 'the poor' cannot be treated as a homogeneous mass and attention will be drawn to differentiating factors, notably gender and sector of employment. Second, it is necessary to analyse what characteristics of planning systems and policies have rendered them inappropriate. In the third part of the chapter, attempts to make planning and policy more responsive are evaluated. Finally, the implications of this experience for the development of an urban management system which enables and empowers poor people rather than constrains and oppresses them are assessed.

The situation of the poor

Even if dramatic reductions in migration are achieved cities will continue to grow rapidly. The numbers of poor families will be added to, above all, by new households formed from among the urban population itself. This general statement need not blind us to the continued and changing significance of migration in the survival strategies of the poor (see below), but emphasises the need to accommodate and absorb urban growth. In this section, the most significant elements in urban people's lives are discussed in turn: economic activity, household survival strategies, and access to housing, infrastructure and services.

Economic opportunities in the wage sector

In establishing themselves in urban life, the primary concern of poor people, whether migrants or school leavers, is to earn an income. Although households engage in a variety of other activities to maintain themselves, in urban areas with their predominantly cash economy, monetary income is crucial. Most workers aspire to a wage job in the formal sector, because this generally, although not always, implies a level of prosperity and security which is greater than alternative means of maintaining themselves. In the 1950s and late 1960s, it was assumed that as development proceeded, accompanied by urbanisation and economic transformation, the great majority of urban workers would gain access to a formal sector family wage. By the 1960s, it was clear that in the great majority of cases, the urban labour force was growing much faster than the demand for wage labour and that, with the exception of a minority of skilled workers, the wages paid were far from sufficient to support a family.

This is not to say that wage employment is unimportant – it is much the most important source of work and income in most middle- and some lower-income countries. These include the NICs, as might be expected, other middle-income countries such as Zimbabwe and Malaysia and some lower-income countries, such as Zambia. Acquiring the skills needed to obtain access to wage jobs is, therefore, for most poor households, a major element in their strategies. If parents do not themselves possess the necessary skills, great importance is attached to providing opportunities for as many as possible of their children to acquire the skills and formal educational qualifications which are necessary, but not sufficient, to obtain formal sector employment. Access to schools, both in terms of physical proximity and cost, is, therefore, important to poor families, as well as access to the industrial and commercial areas of cities where wage employment is available.

However, it is clear that the aspirations of many are frustrated. In part this is due to the structural economic constraints which have inhibited the growth of formal sector manufacturing and services, including worsening terms of trade, the debt crisis, reliance on (capital intensive) foreign investment, obstacles to the development of both import substitution and export oriented manufacturing, and the greater attraction of investment overseas or in property for domestic capital. In many countries, cities have not realised their potential as a major engine of economic growth (N Harris 1989), both because of national economic problems and because the facilities provided are insufficient to provide an urban environment conducive to profitable investment and efficient operation.

Even where formal sector manufacturing and services are reasonably well developed, however, there are insufficient jobs to accommodate the whole urban labour force. Particular categories of workers are excluded, or confined to the least stable and least well paid jobs and sectors. Typically, these are the least well educated, with low levels of literacy and lacking skills. They may be migrants, although theree is evidence from some countries that migrants are both better educated on average and obtain disproportionately greater access to wage jobs than urban born people, depending on the selectiveness of the migration process and the distribution of educational facilities (S Green 1978). The disadvantaged in employment terms are likely to be young, especially in those countries which have introduced universal primary education and expanded secondary education relatively recently, at a rate exceeding the growth in wage employment. Above all, they are likely to be women. Almost universally, the participation rate by women in the wage labour force is lower than that of men, both because of their lower educational levels and because of social norms about the type of work which women should do. Where they are wage workers, they are often in unskilled and poorly paid occupations, especially domestic service and construction work (Fawcett *et al.* 1984; Rodgers 1989).

However, this situation is neither universal nor unchanging. Changes in technology and the global organisation of production, in particular the investment strategies of multinational corporations, have led to the development in selected countries of electrical and electronic assembly industries, textiles and clothing, and so on, which have provided growing numbers of jobs, often for young women (Ariffin 1984; Hong 1984; Jones 1984). In countries such as Malaysia, where there is little tradition of wage work for women, this has led to changes in economic activity rates and tensions as new work patterns come into conflict with social norms.

Casual workers are often the poorest and most vulnerable (Harriss 1989) and constitute a large proportion of the labour force. The increasing prevalence of subcontracting has also led to casualisation of previously secure jobs. This occurs especially where governments fail to enforce workers' rights in their attempts to attract the foreign investment which is supposedly going to enable them to enter the export market and solve their debt repayment problems.

Further components of the Structural Adjustment medicine of the 1980s have been retrenchment and wage freezes, in both the public and the private sectors. Job security has, in many countries, been threatened and wages have failed to keep pace with the cost of living. The latter has increased as a result of inflation, reduced subsidies, and increased food prices which have been introduced to encourage agricultural production and have benefited those rural producers able to respond. The result has been widespread erosion of urban living standards, not only among the poor, but also among middle-income groups. Deterioration in food consumption patterrns and increased malnutrition were detected among poor urban families in the 1980s (Cornia *et al.* 1987; Elson 1988).

Analysis of individual employment and earnings is still of significance in assessing the impact of changing economic structures on employment conditions and wage incomes overall, and the extent to which these have differential impact on segments of the labour force distinguished by level of skills, gender or sector of employment (UN 1980; Anker and Hein 1986). However, for the purpose of understanding the situation of the poor, emphasis has shifted to analysis of the role of informal sector economic activity, household income and subsistence.

Informal sector economic activities

The 'informal sector' is a common shorthand term for small-scale, unenumerated, sometimes illegal, economic activity. The limitations of its descriptive nature and the dualism it implies have long been recognised (Gerry and Bromley 1977; Moser 1978). Nevertheless, the obvious importance of the manufacturing and service activities subsumed under this heading in absorbing urban workers (as much as 60 per cent of the labour force in some countries: J Harriss 1989) and enabling people to survive, has led to its continued use. Policy statements in which governments pin great hopes on fostering the informal sector as a means of solving urban unemployment problems proliferate. This is despite the increasing evidence that the potential of this sector is often limited by its relationships with large-scale formal sector enterprises, by the stagnation in demand for its products and services during general economic recession, and by many government economic and urban development policies.

Early ideas about the ease of entry to informal sector activities by the poor (ILO 1972) have given way to a more differentiated picture. Access to such activities may, depending on circumstances, be related to the possession of skills, access to contacts, availability of capital, etc. The means by which, for example, credit and supplies are obtained for processing or sale, or a rickshaw is hired, may impose constraints on autonomy in business decision-making and profitability. In addition, contacts may be required to provide introductions to suppliers, merchants or owners. Those with no skills, contacts or capital, less time or restricted freedom of movement, tend to be confined to the less lucrative types of economic activity (Heyzer 1981; Bujra 1986).

Nelson (1977), for example, notes that in a low-income area in Nairobi, men are less restricted than women in their choice of informal sector activity: men keep the general stores and butcheries, sell charcoal and provide services such as tailoring; women tend to be sellers of fruit and vegetables, brew beer or provide sexual services. The economic activities which are socially acceptable for women are, therefore, exten-

Plate 29   Informal, roadside industry in Zimbabwe.

sions of their reproductive activities and where economic activity outside the home is frowned upon, women's chances of success in business
may be lessened, even if they devise strategies to increase its social
acceptability. Lessinger (1990), for example, describes the limitations on
the activities of Madras women market traders, despite the stratagems
they have devised to maintain respectability.

The restrictions on women's economic activity do, however, vary
widely from country to country, and, in some cases, the growth of the
parallel economy may provide opportunities. MacGaffey's (1988) work
in Zaïre, for example, suggests that women have been able to exploit
opportunities in real estate, transport, trade and smuggling, as the informal has overtaken the formal economy in scale; this is because in the
second economy they do not require a knowledge of French, educational qualifications, official (male) approval, formal sector credit or
their husband's permission.

Both formal and informal sector economic activities are concerned
with earning cash incomes. Traditionally, this type of work has received
most attention from analysts and policy makers, has been considered of
higher status than unpaid work, and has been analysed in terms of
enterprises and individual workers. In part, this emphasis is inevitable
within an economy organised on capitalist lines, in which production in
the workplace generates the profits for reinvestment which drive the
system. Typically, in such an economy, the workplace is separated from
the home. The latter is merely the site of reproduction, aided by the
collective provision of certain services, such as education, health and
utilities. As a result, reproductive activity has been ignored and under-
valued in economic analysis and 'work' often defined to exclude that

211

which is carried out within the household and which is essential both to household survival and to the wider reproduction of the labour force (UN 1980; Buvinić 1983; Moser 1987a).

Household survival strategies

Poverty has been attributed to low wages and the 'marginality' of informal sector activities, and its multidimensional character not always recognised. It is related to lack of assets, indebtedness, dependence, vulnerability, physical weakness or disability, as well as low incomes (Chambers 1989). Poverty, therefore, is related to household characteristics, and the survival strategies of the poor are essentially based on the household.

The most usual definition of a household is, perhaps,

> a person [or] ... group of two or more persons who make common provision for food or other essentials for living. The persons may pool their incomes and to a greater or less extent, have a common budget; they may be related or unrelated. (UN 1976: 139)

However, the household concept is problematic, both in definitional and analytical terms (Rakodi 1991a). It is, of course, a slippery concept. Not only does the above definition not capture the great variety of living arrangements within, let alone between, cities and countries, but also household composition changes over time, as households gain or lose individual members. In analytical terms, the household is neither the only decision-making entity to which an individual belongs nor necessarily always unified. People are members of wider family, neighbourhood and other social networks, providing them with responsibilities, rights and resources. Most analysis of urban households has assumed them to be units, for housing or planning purposes. Such a unified concept has been attractive, Bruce (1989) suggests, because it is simpler to consider the behaviour of and address policies to households as units: analysing the behaviour of more than one actor in a household, perhaps with differing economic and personal interests, requires new and more complex methodologies. It has been easier for policy-makers to assume that benefits directed at the household benefit all its members, ignoring intra-household inequalities and conflicts.

However, the interests, behaviour and contributions of household members may vary considerably. Inequality, especially between men and women, in assets, income and social norms and obligations, is widespread, although the precise forms and extent of these inequalities vary widely. Many analysts agree that income pooling and sharing of information within the household cannot be assumed, either because of patterns of social organisation or because of internal conflict (eg Folbre 1986; Bruce 1989). While vulnerable household members, especially women, may seek additional income-earning opportunities and autonomy in their decisions over the use of their earnings, the household is still the basic living unit. Policy formulation must take account of household composition, the volume and sources of household resources and the relative contributions of household members to expenses and decision-making.

Households, Evers (1989) suggests, may be regarded as labour pooling units, which flexibly supply different forms of labour (wage labour in the formal and informal sectors, own account work, household work for production and reproduction) in order to maximise income and security (see also Moser 1987a). The work undertaken may take the form of subsistence production or service activities. Productive activities may be undertaken both for the reproduction of the family and for sale, including, for example, cooked food production (Tinker and Cohen 1985), sewing, urban food production (Rakodi 1988; Yeung 1988), scavenging, or house construction. Service activities such as cooking, cleaning, washing and child care may, likewise, be undertaken for the household or for others. Evers (1989) estimates that in Jakarta such subsistence production accounts on average for 18 per cent of total monthly household expenditure, and its relative contribution is greater the lower the monetary income of a household, while in Bangkok, 24 per cent of household labour time is used, on average, for household production (Evers and Korff 1986).

The concept of a livelihood system is particularly useful here (Grown and Sebstad 1989). This refers to

the mix of individual and household survival strategies, developed over a given period of time, that seeks to mobilise available resources and opportunities. Resources can be physical assets such as property, human assets such as time and skills, social assets, and collective assets, ... [such as public sector services]. Opportunities include kin and friendship networks, institutional mechanisms, organizational and group membership, and partnership relations. The mix of livelihood strategies thus includes labor market involvement; savings, accumulation and investment; borrowing; innovation and adaption of different technologies for production; social networking; changes in consumption patterns; and income, labor and asset pooling. (Grown and Sebstad 1989: 941)

Households and individuals adjust this mix according to their own circumstances (age, life cycle, educational level, tasks) and the changing context in which they live.

The concept of a livelihoods system allows the goals which characterise different poverty groups (survival, security and growth) to be distinguished. The poorest households aim to survive by generating sufficient income or other means of satisfying their basic needs, and rarely have the scope to also engage in 'enterprise'; nor may the less poor, to any great extent, as they diversify their activities to spread risks. This emphasis on coping with crisis and risk also typifies the literature on rural poverty, major features of which are recognition of the import-

213

ance of diversification of household activities and of the trade-off made by households between current consumption and investment to provide future security. However, those who have achieved a basic level of security may be able to engage in more risky but also potentially more profitable economic enterprises, which, if successful, lead to income growth (Grown and Sebstad 1989: 941).

The strategies open to households may be divided, for the sake of convenience, into individual, household and community strategies, although these are related, and certain decisions reflect a mixture of considerations (Rakodi 1991a). Individual strategies are likely to refer in particular to income-earning activities. Thus one important decision is whether to participate in the labour force and in what way, having weighed the potential and the constraints on so doing. Migration decisions are also significant elements in individual-cum-household strategies. Early migration research viewed migration decisions as individual, and focused on the migration decisions of men, influenced by the colonial concern with male migration. Subsequently, the importance of household and family decision-making in individual migration movements was acknowledged, and, even more recently, it has been recognised that women are not always passive migrants, following their husbands to urban areas, and that women's migration decisions should be studied in their own right (Fawcett *et al.* 1984). Changes in migration patterns, such as the continued and even increased importance of circular migration which has been recorded in countries such as Indonesia following the reduced effective distance between village of origin and major city, are both influences on and products of household strategies.

Households have working resources, which they use directly (domestic work) and in the wider economy, to acquire goods and services needed for reproduction. These may be acquired through purchase, use of state provided services, saving, inheritance and mutual help, the combination of means of access depending on circumstances (Mingione 1983). Household composition may itself be part of a household strategy, for example, the decision by women-headed households to live together, freeing one woman for participation in income earning activity by the availability of the other (perhaps a sister or mother) to undertake reproductive tasks; or the acceptance by adult children of the need to live with and support a widowed parent.

Bridging the gap between household and wider strategies are the ties with primary social networks, including families, friends and neighbours. Kinship networks have traditionally been relied on to assist survival, but the extent to which such obligations have been honoured has differed from place to place and group to group. In Africa, support by kin has proved to have limits in the face of disaster (war, famine) or the economic crisis of the 1980s (Iliffe 1987). Kinship networks may provide assistance with accommodation on first arrival in town, subsistence while seeking work, help in job search, cash in time of need, and so on, but also constitute a drain on resources limited in the urban context by the fixed nature of wages. Kinship networks are, of course, not purely urban, and urban–rural relationships, particularly with respect to rights to rural land and flows of goods, money and investment between urban and rural areas may be elements in urban household survival strategies. Over time, as kinship obligations are alternately honoured or evaded, the obligations which are accepted may change, while at the same time, urban networks of fictive kin may be developed to supplement true kin. Networks of friends and neighbours may also develop co-operative relationships within which goods and services are shared and circulate (Finquelievich 1987); the co-operative arrangements which provide soup kitchens and crèches in some Latin American cities are an example.

Household management and decision-making is, therefore, an important area of study, incorporating the management of material resources (income, cash and property), and the study of the actions taken by household members to develop and maintain patterns of sociability. The latter may be important in providing information, social life and mutual support (Sharma 1986). A logical extension of household management is community management, in which household members may take an active role, especially to secure access to housing and related services.

Access to housing

From the household's point of view, access to housing can be seen in terms of demand and supply. Demand reflects household needs, availability of income and capital, decision-making with respect to resources of labour and finance, and trade-offs made between expenditure on housing and other household needs and wants. In meeting its needs, the household has a choice between consuming housing produced by another agent or producing its own housing. Evidence is growing that the typical response to overwhelming housing need is to rent, especially where opportunities for squatting are non-existent or reduced. Gaining access to a plot, even in illegal subdivisions, far from being 'spontaneous', requires a complex and deliberate strategy of obtaining access to contacts, information, finance, skilled labour and materials (Coquery 1990).

In examining a household's access to housing, therefore, it is necessary to analyse its past housing history, who has made past housing decisions (see Chant 1987) and what has determined these decisions. These determinants may be internal to the household, related to its changing composition and dynamics, and the resources available to it. Alternatively, they may be external, including the operation of land and housing markets, legal entitlements, bureaucratic procedures, eligibility criteria, housing finance systems and building and town planning regulations. Such regulations influence the suitability of housing available through official channels for low-income households, through, for example, the imposition of standards of construction, requirements for speed in building or restrictions on the use of residential property for business activities. They also influence the arrangement of land uses, which in turn has implications for access to facilities and income-earning opportunities, as well as conditions for the efficient operation of public

215

transport. A household's satisfaction with its current housing conditions and its aspirations should be assessed, although care will be needed in evaluating the extent to which preferences reflect a realistic and knowledgeable view of the alternatives available and their cost in relation to household resources.

Using the concept of housing strategies, rather than merely analysing current housing conditions, implies that housing decisions vary over time in relation not only to changing economic and housing market conditions and policy provisions, but also to changing household circumstances. Thus Volbeda (1989) stresses the significance of stage in the household life cycle in relation to housing decisions. The poorest, it is suggested, including young adults, single elderly women and female-headed households, compete for sub-let rooms, while young families compete for illegal land and begin to build their own houses. Later, households are able to consolidate their shelter, and may build additional rooms for rent to supplement the income needed to support a growing family. How soon the children leave home depends on the availability of both income-earning opportunities and appropriate housing, as well as social and cultural norms. The household may then diminish in size, its housing strategy depending on its sources of income and support, as well as the location and circumstances of the children.

As with decisions on economic survival, in evaluating housing alternatives and reaching housing decisions, members of the household may take individual decisions (eg to leave home and rent a room), or the household may act as a unit. This does not imply either equality of contributions or that members of the household have an equal say in decision-making. While the household head and perhaps his wife may make resources available for housing, the extent to which this is so needs investigation, in the context of different practices on income pooling. In particular, the extent to which the income of other household members, such as relatives or grown-up children, is made available for housing, needs to be based on local empirical assessment. Little information is available on which household members in different countries and income groups make housing-related decisions (Chant 1987). The relationship between a household and its accommodation may be two-way: while the needs of, and resources available to, a household influence its housing choices, the availability of housing may also influence household composition.

Finally, a household may employ wider strategies in its quest for adequate housing, utilising informal groups of kin or friends in the search for accommodation, the accumulation of financial resources for construction or purchase, and the construction process itself (Evers and Korff 1986). The extent to which inter-household transfers of labour or cash are available for housing varies from country to country. In Zambia, for example, although hired labour is widely used, relatives may assist in building. However, cash contributions from members of other households are relatively rare. A household may also join a formal group, such as a mutual help building group or a co-operative, in the context of a particular housing programme.

Infrastructure and services availability

Access to services and infrastructure is primarily determined by government provision, unless these have been privatised. In the former case, formal eligibility criteria may be as, or more, significant than ability to pay. However, access is not only externally determined: household strategies may differ and influence the extent to which they take advantage of what provisions there are. Thus households may adopt the role of passive recipients, taking advantage of what is available, but not taking any positive action to influence the services and infrastructure to which they have access. Alternatively, individual households may take action to improve their position, by moving to a better serviced house or more favourable location, or by evading the formal eligibility criteria by the use of contacts, kin or bribes. Lastly, residents may take collective action to demand services or infrastructure, by community organisation or bringing political pressure to bear; this will be discussed later in this chapter.

Plate 30   Inadequacies of essential services place particular burdens on the poor, and especially on women.

Characteristics of the urban planning and policy process

Urban planning has traditionally been concerned with the allocation of land for various uses, the control of development and the installation of infrastructure. Public sector investment has concentrated on the provision of utilities and services, and the development of industrial estates or housing schemes. However, in most urban areas private sector investment is at least as important. This includes industrial or commercial development, the building of residential estates for sale to upper- and middle-income urban households, and investment in rental housing, as well as construction by households or small-scale enterprises. Because of the limited resources available to the public sector, direct investment has had limited impact, while unauthorised development has resulted from the failure of official supplies of serviced land and housing to meet demand. Urban planning and policy-making has often been based on the use of official statistics, thus biasing its policies in favour of the formal sector and against unenumerated economic activities.

Such a bias is reinforced by the origins and inheritance of town planning, which developed as a fusion of public health regulations and a belief that improving the physical conditions of urban life would solve social problems. Single-use zoning, which separated industrial uses from residential, and advocated the suburbs as the appropriate location for the latter, aimed at improving the physical environment, given the dirty and noisy industrial technologies of nineteenth-century Europe. Town planning, therefore, reinforced the separation of home and workplace which had already arisen as a result of industrial organisation, and which had transformed the family from a joint production unit into a reproductive unit devoted to caring for men and children whose work and training took them elsewhere. Residential environments were planned, largely by men, with this type of social and economic organisation in mind (Women and Geography Study Group 1984; Little et al. 1988). When town planning ideas were exported to the colonies, they reflected the economic and social organisation of nineteenth- and twentieth-century Europe, rather than urban patterns based on the mixed land uses of pre-industrial cities (Rakodi 1991b; D'Souza 1989).

The daily workload of household members at home, especially women, including home-based enterprise and reproductive activities, is rarely taken into account in the design of houses, physical infrastructure or residential areas (Strassman 1987; McCallum and Benjamin 1985; Singh and Kelles-Viitanen 1987). Thus the internal environment of the house is often poorly designed or dangerous and home-based enterprises may be prohibited. The design of physical infrastructure, especially sanitation arrangements, deters its use or exacerbates maintenance problems. The layout of housing may inhibit rather than facilitate mutual interaction and assistance with child care (Schlyter 1988). Further, the social facilities to which household members need access (clinics, schools and day care facilities) may be inappropriately located. An unrecognised productive activity is agriculture, including the keeping of livestock, which is widespread in (but not confined to) low density cities.[1] However, not only is this often penalised by the slashing of crops, but also land-use allocation and provision of water supply rarely consider the benefits of encouraging the use of land for food production on a permanent or temporary basis (Sachs 1986; Lee-Smith *et al*. 1987; Rakodi 1988; Yeung 1988; Harpham *et al*. 1988).

Services, including utilities and public transport, often fail to meet the needs of the poor. Utilities may not reflect the priorities of poor households, may be provided in a form which is culturally unacceptable, may be too costly, and may present difficulties in obtaining access. Women's needs may differ from men's, because they use local supplies and facilities more intensively and have different social constraints on their actions. For example, they may give higher priority to sanitation because they may be more aware of the health benefits and because privacy may be more important to them (Rakodi 1991b).

Transport systems also often do not meet the needs of the poor. Although public transport policy increasingly considers the needs of poor people, especially in the encouragement of paratransit, implementation is not always very successful because of the inherited urban form, shortages of foreign exchange for vehicles and spare parts, and poor management. Poor women, whose travel needs differ from those of men because of their multiple responsibilities to earn income, take children to health facilities and so on, are particularly disadvantaged. However, none of the standard public transport literature on Third World cities appears to consider the needs of men and women separately, although it is well known in the west that the travel demand and trip patterns of women differ from those of men.

Access to electricity and other energy sources is determined primarily by income, but also by whether households live in serviced areas. The energy needs of poor households, and especially the continued reliance on many of woodfuel, are rarely taken into account in urban policy (L R Brown and Jacobson 1987; Lee-Smith *et al*. 1987).

Urban policy and planning has, therefore, been influenced by its historical origins, its colonial history, its professional concerns with order and standards, its association with government and its domination by men. Urban policy is a function of central and local government to varying degrees and so its content and outcomes critically depend on the interests represented in the state at these levels. Although these vary from time to time and place to place, they are, in most cases, the interests of the formal economic sector, incorporating large-scale domestic enterprises and foreign investment, and those classes with economic and political power (the landowning elites, the national and bureaucratic bourgeoisies and often the military). A town planning system which evolved to meet the needs of colonial administrators, settlers and economic enterprises has been perpetuated because it serves the ongoing interests of the dominant classes. The re-orientation of urban policy to meet the needs of the poor depends, for example, on the extent to which ruling political elites depend on support from the poor for legitimacy and electoral victory, and adhere to populist or socialist ideology. It also depends on the extent to which large-scale economic enterprises recognise the adverse impacts on productivity of poor living conditions, and the degree of autonomy given to the local state for decision making and revenue generation.

A further source of discrimination lies in the legislation and regulations associated with planning. Land law is probably the most crucial, but planning and public health regulations and eligibility criteria for access to public programmes may also discriminate against poor households in general or against women and female-headed households in particular (McAuslan 1985; Moser 1987a; Schlyter 1988). The poor's experience of urban development is thus shaped both by the strategies adopted at a household level and by the way in which they are affected by or can affect planning, investment and management decisions made at the neighbourhood or city level. This last issue will be taken up in the next section, in which the attempts to make planning and policy more responsive to the needs of poor urban residents, and the outcomes of these attempts, are explored.

Responsive planning: the question of participation

In recent years, there have been a variety of attempts to make urban planning and policy more reponsive. These have been stimulated, among other things, by studies of informal sector economic activity and unauthorised residential neighbourhoods, which have increased awareness both of the adverse circumstances in which the urban poor live and of their resourcefulness. In addition, many evaluations of infrastructure provision, housing, serviced plot and other programmes have shown that these have not fulfilled their objectives of improving access by and the living conditions of the poor. Meanwhile, the limits on resources available to the public sector to solve urban problems have become increasingly obvious.

Traditionally, the urban plan preparation system, at least in ex-British colonies, incorporated requirements for public exhibition of, or at least access to, draft plans. This provided an opportunity for objections which then might or might not be taken into account in final plan preparation. In India, for example, no attempt is made to explain the plans when these are made available for public scrutiny and so the only effect is to generate opposition from landowners affected by proposed reservations of land for amenity purposes (D'Souza 1989).

In Britain this token consultation gave way in the 1970s to a more wide-ranging consultation of residents during the process of plan preparation in the 1970s, partly in order to obtain views, information and ideas and partly to defuse potential opposition to plan proposals. Even here, the difficulty of obtaining residents' views on strategic or policy issues was recognised. Similar procedures did not penetrate widely to developing countries. One major obstacle was the lower level of literacy of their populations. Other difficulties included communications and transport restrictions, the relative dearth of organised interest groups representing a variety of views, and the more centralised and *ad hoc* nature of the urban policy formulation and plan preparation processes.

These obstacles were said to make such a process of 'participation' in the formal policy formulation and plan preparation process inappropriate in most cases. As a result, 'In most situations urban residents are objects for policies, they are not active participants in policy formulation' (Wekwete 1989: 31).

In some cases, however, participation occurred either by means of the political process or by special arrangements made during the planning and implementation of specific development projects. In some cases, poor urban residents had sufficient political clout to influence policy and investment decisions. This occurred in situations as diverse as the multiparty democracies which have operated at different times in a variety of Latin American countries and in the one-party states of Tanzania or Zambia.

In the former, poor residents were able to trade their votes for particular benefits, for example, the regularisation of an unauthorised housing area, or the provision of infrastructure and services. This demand/response style of urban management depended on communities being able to organise themselves, a process in which women often played a significant role in mobilising for community facilities and services, although rarely as leaders (Moser 1987b). It may also make communities vulnerable to co-option (Gilbert and Ward 1984a; 1984b). Once the immediate needs of selected communities have been met, their leaders recognised and perhaps rewarded, further demands for legislative change or infrastructure provision may be defused. In addition, allocation of resources by means of *ad hoc* responses to those areas with the loudest voice frequently detracts from more generall policy-making processes, in which the needs of different areas are balanced in order to achieve a rational city-wide distribution of resources. In one-party states, such as Tanzania and Zambia, the need of governments for populist political support led to the development of local level party organisation. This served as a channel for demands for recognition of illegal housing areas and for the provision of basic services in these areas, a process which in Zambia was implemented with the assistance of the party organisation (Rakodi and Schlyter 1981).

In an attempt to make urban development projects more appropriate to the needs of the urban poor, participatory procedures have been incorporated. These reflect a variety of approaches, a variety of understandings of what is meant by participation and a variety of outcomes. Participation is an umbrella term, incorporating a number of meanings and activities. Initially it is possible to distinguish between participation as a means and as an end. Participation as a means may have a variety of aims. It may be intended as a way of sharing project costs by mobilising residents' cash or labour to supplement public sector inputs. It may be seen as a way to improve project efficiency and increase effectiveness, by prior consultation, leading to a better information base for planning and design, defusing potential opposition and gaining the support of residents. It may also be intended to build beneficiary capacity, to increase the self-reliance of both households and the community and to increase commitment to the upkeep of community facilities and infrastructure. Participation as an end aims to achieve empowerment, or the right to a say in decision-making. While participation at the outset is a precondition for empowerment, participation during implementation and maintenance is more common and is usually aimed at improving effectiveness and mobilising support and resources (Rakodi 1990a; Rakodi and Schlyter 1981; Skinner 1983; Coit 1986; Moser 1989a).

'Participation' is generally coupled with the term 'community'. Just as in discussing the household we noted that it is misleading to treat it as an undifferentiated income pooling unit, so it is incorrect to see the community as a homogenous group with interests in common. Such an approach may ignore the different interests and access to power of people differentiated by economic resources, political allegiance, religious affiliation, tenure or gender (Rakodi and Schlyter 1981; Moser 1989a). The emergence and role of community leaders has been discussed by P M Ward and Chant (1987). Moser emphasises, in particular, the tendency of services and housing projects to give a say to house-owwners while excluding tenants from project design and benefits. In addition, such projects, she asserts, fail to recognise explicitly the roles of women as contributors to household income in households headed by men, as supporters of households headed by women, and as organisers of community groups. These failures may result in the exclusion of some households from project benefits, or in inappropriate project designs which, for example, mistakenly assume that residents have ample free time to devote to the process of participation and contributions of labour to community activities or house construction. Ignorance of the lifestyles of residents may also lead to the adoption of inappropriate mechanisms for consultation and participation during implementation and maintenance.

Moser (1989a) then proceeds to review a variety of participatory approaches adopted in urban projects initiated and implemented by the World Bank, central and local government, international grant-making agencies and small NGOs. She shows that in projects in Lusaka, El Salvador and Kenya,

> the role of the World Bank was to provide the loan for an agreed project with the consultants involved in project design and the implementing agency largely determining the objectives of community participation within the project. However, the fact that over time the extent of community participation in World Bank projects has increased suggests that the Bank can and does play an important advocacy role in withholding loans from projects lacking participatory components, while supporting those which do. At the same time, however, the Bank's particular concern with the project cycle and cost recovery tends to reduce its capacity to think innovatively about incorporating community participation, particularly in the decision making and design stages of projects. (Moser 1989a: 105–6; see also Rakodi and Schlyter 1981)

Governments may, for political and bureaucratic reasons, be reluctant to involve residents fully in decision-making, while being happy to mobilise resources from them during project implementation, as demonstrated by projects in Lusaka and Nairobi. However, in other circum-

Plate 31   Project designs which involve the community in construction works
(in this case in an upgrading project in Lusaka) tend to assume that
people – especially women – have ample free time.

stances, governments are prepared to hand over greater responsibility
and power to local communities to run their own projects. Examples are
quoted in Lima and Nicaragua (Moser 1989a; see also UN 1986).

Moser's review of UNICEF-supported projects in Hyderabad, India
and Karachi concludes that the organisation's

> capacity to introduce community participation into project design and to
> ensure its implementation in practice is largely determined by local political,
> economic and cultural factors, with the shift from paternal welfarism to more
> empowering community based projects often difficult to accomplish in many

223

parts of the world. It is also important to recognise that because their [UNICEF's] target group is women and children this does not mean that their projects .F?&. . empower women. In practice they are far more likely simply to rely on the unpaid, voluntary participation of women for project efficiency, which in assuming women have 'free time' often results in complications for women in terms of their reproductive and productive responsibilities. (Moser 1989a: 114)

Finally, brief evaluations of two NGO projects highlight the participatory manner in which such projects can be structured and organised. Participation and the development of local organisation in such projects may be a more important goal than efficiency, implying significant demands on project staff, an open-ended project time scale, modest size and less emphasis on cost recovery (Moser 1989a). All of these are characteristics which inhibit replicability and the implementation of such projects on a larger scale.

The positive qualities of NGOs are often that they are flexible and able to respond rapidly, attentive to local needs, in a position to innovate, experiment and promote the use of local resources, and have dedicated and highly motivated staff. However, they may also be ill-prepared, insufficiently knowledgeable, lack an overall strategy, refuse to co-operate with each other or government agencies and fail to follow up the initial 'fire-fighting' project (Schneider 1988). Increasingly governments are seeing them as potential partners. Thus in the Philippines, for example, they are being tapped by some government agencies to serve as financial conduits, to assist in the monitoring of government projects and to serve as discussants of policy at all levels (von Einsiedel 1989). They may provide parallel resources to the state, co-produce with the state or pressure the state to provide better facilities. As their numbers proliferate and their scope expands, there is a danger that the state will try to control them (Annis 1987), if indeed its perception of them as a threat has not inhibited their development from the outset.

Segments of the NGO community are moving beyond the fostering of small-scale self-reliant local development to re-examine strategic issues related to sustainability, breadth of impact and recurrent cost recovery. As a result, they are moving towards a strategy in which the focus is on facilitating wider sustainable changes. This implies involvement with the public and private organisations which control resources and determine the policies which bear on local development. Their aims may be to encourage the widespread adoption of approaches seen to work in NGO projects, or to remove policy obstacles to achieving development which is oriented towards the needs of the poor. Their role is a catalytic one, and their strategy to form networks or coalitions and to increase their professional expertise (Korten 1987).

Critical factors affecting community participation thus include the political position of the national government, financial issues, internal organisational matters and characteristics of the community structure. Governments may resist the devolution of real power by paying lip-service to participation, but not provide the political or financial support to make it successful. Empowering participation may therefore be more feasible in projects which are local, small scale, and concerned with housing and social services rather than wider economic and social issues. Many, especially NGO, projects have successfully incorporated capacity building without government commitment, but if a project or community organisation is too successful in moving from capacity building to empowerment, government may become hostile and repressive towards it, as has occurred at times in El Salvador and the Philippines.

Financial and related issues which influence the scope for participation include the rigidity of project design, funding and scheduling, rights of access to land, and the funding of professional and local community workers. The funding and status of the latter is also a crucial internal organisational factor. At the community level, a number of contradictions affect the scope for participation, for example:

> the degree of community homogeneity required in order to develop effective local level organisation, and the economic, political and social heterogeneity which actually exists in communities ... the collective solidarity necessary as the basis for community level organisation and the intense individualism generated by the survival strategies of low income populations. (Moser 1989a: 127)

A spatial area organises itself as a community only if residents have interests in common, particularly the establishment or regularisation of land rights, and even this may conceal differences of interest between owners and tenants. Meanwhile the outcome of participation also depends on the community organisation with which the project agency elects to work, and whether and how residents are incorporated.

Potential contradictions in and limitations of the process of community participation are clearly revealed by this review. However, it provides a starting-point from which to explore the characteristics of an urban management process which could, in future, be more responsive to the needs of poor and disadvantaged urban residents.

Urban management: who controls and who participates?

The authors in this volume are advocating both changes in the approach to planning and a greater awareness of its political nature and distributional effects. Planning ahead for the allocation of land in order to guide new development is appropriate and necessitates a degree of control over the built environment. However, we have recognised that land-use planning comprises only one element in a more action-oriented approach to planning, focusing on project investment to develop or improve areas for various uses and groups. This approach implies that planners need to take people's needs and views into account in decision-making and to consider the impact of policies and programmes on them. In addition, we have recognised the need for planning to be closely linked with management, which aims to ensure that the components of an urban system operate efficiently and equitably. The daily functioning of a city should facilitate economic activity of all kinds, and enable residents to meet their basic needs for access to shelter, utilities and services, and income-generating opportunities. Attention therefore needs to be paid both to the political and institutional frameworks for decision-making at city and local levels, and to the extent to which land, service and housing delivery systems and regulations facilitate or impede the livelihood strategies of poor households.

In considering future directions for responsive planning and management, we need to refer to three elements: first, to some of the issues which need to be tackled, second, to principles on which appropriate approaches might be based, and third, to the processes and institutions by which they might be developed and implemented. Issues which have emerged from the discussion in this chapter include the situation of the poor and the elements of their livelihood strategies which have been insufficiently considered in conventional approaches to planning. In particular, appropriate approaches to planning for economic activity, domestic production, housing, services and infrastructure will be briefly discussed below.

Issues to be tackled

Livelihood and survival

Planning is concerned with promoting a viable work-residence relationship. However, in practice this has typically been based on the separation, often by considerable distances, of home and work. This has led to transport problems and to discrimination against home or locally based enterprise. In particular the needs of women to reconcile work and income-earning opportunities with reproductive tasks has been ignored. Much economic activity is not incompatible with residential uses, although regulations might need to be changed to allow economic activities on residential plots and to allocate sites for small-scale enterprises within residential areas.

With respect to the particular needs of women, Khoo *et al.* (1984) suggest disaggregating low-income women into groups identified by age, marital status, economic activity and family responsibilities. This would facilitate the design of land-use patterns and efficient and responsive services. Such policies should apply to housing, the location of employment centres, public transport provision and the provision and location of child care facilities. Programmes to assist households with their economic strategies, such as credit and technical assistance programmes for small-scale enterprises, or support for women's activities, have not always achieved their objectives, but some pointers can be drawn from experience about the type of programmes and design features which are more likely to be successful (Bromley 1984; Harper 1984; Ashe 1985; Buvinić 1986).

Programmes should be based on an analysis of the internal and external constraints on small and micro-enterprises (UNCHS 1986a). Internal constraints which may be addressed are deficiencies in technical or management skills, lack of capital, or inadequate premises. External constraints include problems in obtaining raw materials or equipment, lack of access to institutional credit, excessive competition and inadequate services, especially electricity supply. While credit may often be a high priority for small enterprises, it is not always the main constraint. For some businesses in some cities shortages of raw materials or equipment, monopoly of supply by one or more large companies, or failure to identify a market niche which is not oversubscribed, may be more significant problems.

Whatever constraint is being tackled, appropriate programme design is vital. With respect to credit, for example, critical features seem to include simple and quick application procedures; initial access to very small loans with automatic eligibility for successive loans following prompt repayment; and the availablity of loans for both fixeed and working capital. In addition, group loan guarantees and repayment schedules which suit the needs of particular enterprises may be appropriate. Training in management skills, including elementary bookkeeping, should generally not require the entrepreneur to be absent from his or her business for more than a short period, while technical and vocational skills training should be accompanied by basic management training. More appropriate than management training in any formal sense may be advice with respect to assessing the feasibility of a business idea, market research or marketing (Harper 1984; Ashe 1985; Hurley 1990). Sites and services and upgrading projects may be designed in such a way as to maximise their employment generation potential, for example in the production of building materials, house construction and service provision and maintenance (UNCHS 1986a; 1989f).

A further productive activity which has potential both as a diet and as an income supplement for poor households is urban agriculture. It may be located on the urban periphery, within the built-up area on temporarily unused or specially allocated land, or on residential plots, and may be pursued on an individual or co-operative basis. It has been established in the Indian context that 6 sq m of space can potentially produce all the vegetable needs for a family of four for a year (Yeung 1988: 81). An alternative estimate suggests that a 200 sq m garden would provide one-fifth of the food intake of a family of five. To provide such gardens for one-quarter of São Paulo's population would use less than one-seventh of the empty land inside the São Paulo municipio (Sachs 1986: 8). In Buenos Aires, it was estimated that a successful garden could save between 10 and 30 per cent of the cost of an appropriate diet for a family (Gutman 1986: 23).

Opportunities for urban agriculture are fewer where land markets are characterised by speculation, extensive private ownership and spiralling prices; thus cultivation is likely to be less common in large, densely settled urban areas. However, the space needs of urban agriculture vary with climate, access to water for irrigation, soil and intensity of cultivation. Programmes to increase productivity may include extension services, promotion of intensive production and recycling of human, food and garden waste, and improved water supply (Wade 1986a; 1986b).

While further investigation is needed of the environmental and health implications of urban cultivation and livestock rearing, and the real costs of programmes to increase agricultural production, the potential benefits to poor households seem to justify allocation of land for cultivation or use of temporarily vacant land.

Shelter

The key shelter problems faced by the poor include access to land, the cost and financing of housing, eligibility requirements, access to information, procedures and regulations, lack of skills, time and self-confidence and unsuitable housing designs. Legislative change may be needed, especially with regard to rights to land. Access to land may be improved by introducing new forms of tenure, simplifying the bureaucratic and legal processes, and making regulations more appropriate, for example by allowing incremental house construction. The criteria for qualifying for credit and the terms on which loans are given often discriminate against low-income households; generally greater flexibility is called for, taking into account regular income transfers and income from informal sector activities and accepting non-traditional collateral, including group guarantees (Moser 1987a; Boleat 1987). Reducing the downpayment required, simplifying transaction procedures, establishing branches of financial institutions in low-income areas with hours suited to low-income clients, requiring joint husband and wife decisions on taking out a loan and allowing flexible repayment schedules may all help.

Poor households often lack information about the availability of land, housing, construction materials and credit. Bureaucratic procedures also assume literacy. Means of giving information should be appropriate, application procedures and forms simplified and restrictions on plot use avoided (Hosken 1987). A wide choice of building materials should be permitted (with beneficial impacts on the cost of construction and readiness to attempt building) and training opportunities provided in construction and maintenance, especially for women (INSTRAW 1987). Houses and their surroundings should be designed in consultation with users, both men and women: in supporting household strategies, designers need to know how people use space, especially in the tasks of caring for children, maintaining households and generating income, and these patterns of activity should be taken into account in the layout and servicing of residential areas (Rakodi 1991b).

Public transport and urban services

An efficient public transport system is required, in which total supply is adequate to meet demand, and patterns of supply match needs. The need for movement can be reduced by shortening the distance between homes and workplaces. Planning should take into account what people need from services – their priorities and difficulties in obtaining access. Thus, with respect to utilities, women's priorities may differ from men's because they use local supplies and facilities more intensively and have different social constraints on their actions. In the design and siting of communal taps, latrines and refuse collection systems, the views of local residents, especially women, are crucial. Training of residents, including women, may be a way of solving maintenance problems at the local level. Successful involvement of women in infrastructure design and installation has occurred in, for example, Colombo (Wanathamulla) (INSTRAW 1987) and Baldia, Karachi (B Turner and Maskrey 1988).

Energy

An explicit energy policy is needed for cities, which takes into account the needs of the poor in addition to the wider cost and environmental implications. Where electricity or gas can be made available, these need to be supported by the development of cheap appliances and education in the use of the new fuel. If there is no alternative to woodfuel, at least in the short term, increased production should be promoted, as well as more efficient utilisation, for example, by the development and dissemination of improved wood and charcoal stoves.

Planning for residential areas and for city-wide infrastructure and services should, therefore, be based on an understanding of how the poor survive and of the different needs of women and men. Sectoral, spatial and environmental concerns should be integrated. Pilot residential area development, upgrading or renewal schemes can be used:

1 to assesss the need and potential for local economic activity and to test programmes of technical assistance
2 to devise appropriate designs for water supply and sanitation and mechanisms for cost recovery and subsidy where relevant
3 to assess alternative forms of residential layout and tenure
4 to provide opportunities for experiments with locally organised child care, health programmes, training and credit.

Principles for appropriate planning and management

So far in this final section, we have briefly discussed some of the issues with which urban programmes must deal in order to meet the needs of poor residents. However, as already stressed, urban planning and management are not purely technical activities, and the process of policy formulation and implementation of programmes and projects is as important as, if not more important than the content of policies. As a prelude to a more critical discussion, we can list some of the principles upon which planning and management must be based in order to ensure that the approaches it adopts are, indeed, responsive to the needs of those so frequently disadvantaged under past and present systems:

1 Given the limited resources of central and local government in developing countries, planning should be realistic about what official policies and institutions can hope to achieve; it should mobilise the resources of the private sector, as well as households and communi-

ties, to assist in the production and management of the urban built environment; it should, therefore, be enabling.

2   In order to ensure that policies and programmes are appropriate to the needs of poor people, the planning process should be consultative and decision-makers should be accountable to the urban majority and not just to the politically powerful.

3   In order to ensure sustainability, especially the ongoing operation and maintenance of services and facilities, decision-making and implementation should be consultative; residents should be involved in decisions regarding design and operation, as well as – in some cases – in implementation and maintenance.

4   If communities are to take on such responsibilities, they must be equipped with appropriate knowledge and skills, as well as resources on the basis of which they can take decisions: the planning process should be participatory and empowering.

Processes and institutions for responsive planning and management

Participation, as we have already noted, is often little more than co-option and manipulation unless it leads to empowerment and the reallocation of resources. In practice, the most common forms of participation are mobilisation and consultation. Mobilisation within the implementation stage has a long history, but is particularly associated with the 'efficiency' approach to development now prevalent among the international agencies. Mobilisation of the supposed free time and under-utilised cash resources of urban residents is intended to compensate for reduced government resources (Moser 1989b). In some cases, these resources may indeed be released and result in improved project effectiveness and effiiciency; in others the supposed potential is built on misconceptions of the nature of the struggle for survival in which the poor are engaged.

Consultation may occur at the design and decision-making stage and most urban managers would see it as an essential element in planning. It embraces the collection of background information, as well as informing residents of proposals and obtaining their views. The former improves the information base on which plans and policies are based, with the result that they be more realistic and feasible. Much more effort should go into informing people about proposals and decisions, it is argued, because 'By and large, the community will ignore bureaucratic rules it can neither understand nor see the need for' (A Turner 1989: 23). The nature of the consultation process must necessarily be very different at strategic and local levels, or where existing and new areas are under discussion. It is easiest to consult residents in existing areas where improvements are intended and action plans being prepared (Knight 1989). However, with respect to new development and at the city-wide level, this is more problematic. It may be possible through the political process, if elected councillors are representative and they consult and

Plate 32   A community meeting in Lusaka to discuss the proposed upgrading of their area.

involve their constituents. Otherwise, planners and managers can provide a framework for the poor to articulate their demands and a channel to transmit these to the decision makers: a risky strategy in certain political situations (Devas 1989a).

A further stage is to include residents in the decision-making process, although the extent to which they take decisions will depend on a variety of factors, including the nature of the political system and the level of government planning and action which is being considered. In a multi-party system, service provision may be used to reward sup-porters, buy votes or strengthen support for the political party; it is, therefore, likely to be inequitable and to adopt a short-term perspective. Planners concerned with equity cannot challenge powerful interests in society directly: in grossly inequitable systems, participation is unlikely to result in redistribution. There may, however, be scope for taking measures which benefit the poor without directly challenging the rich, and for disseminating information so that the incidence, causes and implications of inequities are more widely understood. Leverage may be exerted by building alliances with NGOs and community organisations.

At the local level, rather than attempting to benefit poor residents by the introduction of top-down welfare programmes, residents may be involved in local groups working around their interests. The type of project funding and tightly scheduled implementation favoured by in-ternational agencies does not suit this mode of working. Instead, flexible systems of financing are needed, which allow financial inputs to match the capacity of the community to manage itself. The development of such community capacity is a long-term, open-ended and unpredictable process. Funding also needs, therefore, to be long term and to give equal priority to funding community development work and infrastructure installation. Parallel with this is a need to increase the value and status placed on community workers' skills and knowledge and to recognise the need for continued and repeated dialogue with a community as its leadership changes. Funding also needs to be responsive to the differing rates and degrees of uptake over time and between residential areas; it needs to start small and rely on a demonstration effect to create conditions for the spread of programmes. The establishment of an extension service to provide technical advice may complement a revolving community fund, enabling the development of capacity for community management and providing incentives for repayment (Moser 1989a).

It may be possible to increase the capacity for locally determined and self-managed programmes at community level through the existing administrative system, using locally elected representatives and development committees, or existing community organisations. There is also a role for NGOs, which have been shown to have advantages over mainstream bureaucracies in this type of work because of their ideology, the nature of their organisation and their relatively small scale. NGOs can reach low-income people and operate in a flexible, open-ended way. Although their small-scale limits the reach of their projects, this has certain advantages from the point of view of governments: small-scale projects, even if they empower residents, do not pose a threat to the government's power or legitimacy and, if unsuccessful, can be ended more easily than programmes which become established and carry with them the vested interests of civil servants and their bureaucracies (Moser 1989b).

In considering what form self-reliant community development might take in a clientelistic political system in Nigeria, (Mabogunje 1989) recommends acceptance of the political system which at least ensures the access of poor people to resources, even though it is potentially exploitative and repressive. The neighbourhood clientelistic political structure should, he argues, be formalised in local neighbourhood councils and allocated a functional role in the administration of services and collection of revenue.

In many political systems, NGOs and planners are faced with dilemmas with respect to their role. If their 'prime client' (the national or city government) is open to the needs of poor urban residents, then planners and NGOs can transmit the information necessary for appropriate decisions. However, decision-makers may be interested neither in community needs nor, indeed, in planning urban development. Should planners jeopardise their limited influence over the management of urban growth and infrastructure provision by adopting an advocacy role? This ultimately must be an individual decision: in repressive political systems, planners may feel that they cannot take the risk. Elsewhere, rather than a futile battle with decision-makers, planners may be better advised to await a moment when some room for manoeuvre opens up as a result of political change or the possibility of an alliance with other groups.

Planners must also be perceptive about what type of participation is desirable in different situations. Community level organisation may be inappropriate for large-scale operations, some technical decisions, long-term maintenance of major infrastructure or regular gathering of revenue (Amos 1989b; A Turner 1989; Rakodi 1990b). Accountability via the system of political representation at city level is more suitable for resource allocation in which the interests of different areas need to be balanced. Even within communities, residents may prefer that certain services are delivered by outside agencies without their direct participation, providing that the agencies can be held to account by consumer behaviour or by elected representatives.

It may also be the case that the really poor and disorganised may lose out in a participative management style, if they lack the energy and understanding to take advantage of unfamiliar and time-consuming opportunities for participation. For such households, a more paternalistic management style for welfare services may be necessary, at least temporarily, and special efforts may be needed to enable them to take advantage of opportunities to improve their living conditions. However, when staff and resources are limited, a trade-off must be made between the very intensive inputs the very poor may require and the less intensive inputs needed to produce similar results in a less poor and better organised community.

The scope for an enabling approach, in which developing the capacity of local residents to manage their own affairs at household and community level, varies with political circumstances and with the level of resource allocation and decision-making. Opinions also differ on the appropriate role for public authorities in such a process: those on the left of the political spectrum advocate a proactive role, while those on the right would hold that enabling is best achieved by withdrawing the deadening hand of the state, thereby releasing individual initiative. Enabling people to help themselves is, however, ultimately limited, as it does not necessarily imply redistribution of the resources which individuals and communities need.

Empowerment is a stronger term which implies the capacity of oppressed groups,

> to increase their own self-reliance and internal strength. This is identified as the right to determine choices in life and to influence the direction of change, through the ability to gain control over crucial material and non-material resources. (Moser 1989b: 1,815)

Well-known examples of approaches which result in empowerment are the Self Employed Women's Association in Ahmedabad and the Working Women's Forum in Madras, which combine credit and training programmes to enable women to generate income with support for women who are challenging their subordination by society or the state (J Brown 1981: 337–8; Brydon and Chant 1989: 222–3; Hurley 1990: 108–

11). Again, however, advocates of empowerment may be making quite different assumptions about the reasons for and means of achieving this. Those on the political left advocate empowerment of the oppressed in order that society may be restructured in their interests, but traditionally through centralist politics. Those on the right, however, equate empowerment with choice, which implies individual 'freedom'. Politics, it is suggested, is disempowering, because it tends to be captured by the elite for its own advantage.

The extreme reaction by new right economists to this view of politics and society has been to roll back the state, privatise services wherever possible and give individuals and households the opportunity to maximise choice, downgrading the role of communities. However, while there is much evidence of the inefficiency and ineffectiveness of over-extended bureaucracies, the poor are vulnerable in a market situation, while their poverty means that their power to exercise such choice is limited. There is currently, therefore, a quest for an alternative organisation for society, in which tasks are appropriately divided between the public sector, NGOs, the private sector, and individuals and households.

The need to devise appropriate frameworks and relationships applies to urban management, which seeks to ensure that cities provide viable locations for economic activity and meet the needs of their residents for housing and access to work and services. This implies that land, infrastructure and buildings need to be made available for large as well as small-scale manufacturing, commerce as well as industry, pedestrians and cyclists as well as motor vehicles, low as well as high-income groups and women as well as men. To fulfil this task, an appropriate division of labour needs to be achieved between:

1 the public sector: national government, city-wide administration and special agencies
2 the social/community sector: community organisation and NGOs
3 the private sector: large and small-scale enterprises
4 individuals and households.

In ensuring a public sector which is accountable and responsive to the needs of the poor, a system of representative national and local government is needed. This in turn can act to ensure both that conditions are created in which private enterprise can flourish and that the necessary curbs exist to ensure the social and environmental accountability of the private sector.

However, formal systems of electoral representation and large-scale administrative systems have limitations. It is also important, therefore, to recognise and assess the role of the social/community sector and its relationships with the public and private sectors (Annis 1987; Korten 1987). Garilão (1987) suggests that as indigenous NGOs mature, founded on stable resource bases, local leadership, increasing expertise and the forging of alliances with other NGOs, these not-for-profit organisations may become a distinct sector in society. Such a sector substitutes neither for individual and household livelihood strategies, nor for the role of bureaucracies in the planning and delivery of land and services where appropriate. However, it can act as an intermediary between these two sets of actors and as a catalyst for action and change.

Note

1. In Kenya 31 per cent of urban households had access to urban land for farming (varying from 22 per cent in Nairobi to 59 per cent in Kitui), and 17 per cent kept livestock. In half of these cases, households were using their backyards as gardens, although the poorest had insufficient space for cultivation around their houses. Over half the farmers did not own the land they were cultivating. Instead, cultivation rights to public land had, in most cases, been granted by the municipal authorities. Most of the produce was consumed by the households concerned, 40 per cent of whom said that they would starve if they stopped producing food. A minority of cultivators produced a surplus for sale. In urban Kenya, the average size of an urban garden was 484 sq m, varying from 99 sq m in Nairobi to 1,349 sq m in Kisumu. However, the productivity of Nairobi gardens was greatest, although half the cultivators claimed that their production was restricted by lack of water for irrigation (Lee-Smith *et al*. 1987). A survey of cultivators conducted in 1988 found that two-thirds were women and 47 per cent had no other source of income (Lado 1990).

    Evidence from Zambia is similar: in the 1970s, the proportion of households in low- and lower-middle income areas who cultivated urban gardens varied from 25 per cent to 80 per cent, depending on the density of the settlement, availability of land and suitability of local soils. Many households had both small on-plot gardens of 25–30 sq m and larger rainy season gardens on unused land within walking distance. Large, poor households were more likely to grow some of their own food. Most households produced for their own consumption rather than sale. A nutrition survey in 1977 estimated that home-produced food saved 10–15 per cent of low-income household food budgets during the harvesting season (Ledogar and Lungu 1978). Sanyal (1981) suggested that the survival of the poorest households would be jeopardised without access to land for cultivation and that home-produced food provided an important supplement to the diets of middle-income families.

CHAPTER 9

The role of law in urban planning

Patrick McAuslan

Law in urban development: an overview

Law has profound implications for urban development. It defines the system of urban government, it establishes the system of urban planning and regulation of land development, and it delimits the powers of the urban planners and managers. But law, contrary to the commonly held view, is not a neutral instrument. In this chapter I shall examine the way in which the law is a reflection of the society and the system of which it is a part, and the ways in which the law, its use and abuse, influence the urban development process. From this, I shall then set out some principles to guide the reform of urban law.

In the mid-1960s, most western legal scholars tended to see law as a neutral body of norms, above the struggle for resources or power, policing the struggle, providing remedies where the struggle erupted into conflict, or where people alleged that they had been injured in the struggle. In the early 1990s, largely as a result of the input of other social sciences into legal scholarship and of the work of those lawyers – both academic and in practice – interested in the role of law in development and social change, we know better (Ghai *et al.* 1987). The use of law, of certain legal techniques, the decision to subject certain activities to a regime of legal control while leaving others free of such control, the implementation of law, the legal culture of a society, all are value-laden, part of the social struggles within society. Law is a weapon in the struggle over resources, often a very powerful weapon, so that those who control the making and the implementation of law have or may have a head-start on the control of society's resources. So questions about the role of law in urban development cannot just be answered by reference to specific topics which legislation may deal with – finance for housing, control of the development of land, provision of potable water – since the questions inevitably raise issues about power and resources: who controls the development process? To what ends is the process being used? Who gains and who loses from any particular decision to enact and/or enforce or not enforce any law?

The understanding that we now have of the possible impact of law on society also requires us to 'tread carefully' before proposing or implementing any particular legal reform, and to consider a range of general matters before doing so. The world is littered with examples of legal reforms and experiments which proceeded without proper consideration of all their implications or which were naïvely based on the assumption that one sector of the population would benefit – for example, the urban poor – whereas a little thought would have shown that the particular legal regime being introduced would be more likely to benefit a different sector of the population.

Thus, behind any existing urban law, or any proposal for a new urban law lie political and policy issues and not just technical issues. If these fundamental questions are not addressed, however inconvenient it may be to address them, then any proposal for a new legal regime is largely valueless and risks misleading those to whom it is addressed. Furthermore, these fundamental questions must be faced before specific topics are reformed or legislated upon, because until they are, it is difficult to know what is the purpose of any legal input into the development process. These points may seem rather obvious to some people, rather subversive to others. They can be best illustrated by a couple of examples with which I am familiar.

Zimbabwe

In 1981 a UN team went to Zimbabwe to advise on that country's urban and regional planning system, and to suggest what reforms might be necessary in the light of the transition to Independence. My brief was to survey and report on the legal framework for urban and regional planning.

In 1976 Zimbabwe, or Rhodesia as it was then, had enacted a Town and Country Planning Act which was modelled on the English reforms introduced in 1968. In England, the purpose of the reforms of 1968 had been to introduce a more flexible policy-orientated approach to planning in anticipation of rapid public-sector led economic growth, an approach which in turn fed into the system of development control, so that that too became more policy orientated and wide-ranging in its consideration of individual planning applications. In Rhodesia, however, the new planning system had been designed to fit into the existing planning and development control system rather than replace it. The existing system was rigid, based on strict zoning policed by a Town Planning Court, which could, after a formal hearing, sanction departures from permitted uses in zones. In England then, the law and the system of planning were moving in the direction of greater recognition of the policy and political content of planning; in Zimbabwe the system was being maintained as a legalistic one in which policy was non-existent and law uppermost, despite changes in the law which superficially might appear to be designed to alter that.

Why was the Zimbabwean system as it was? While using the legal language of English town planning law, and the legal institution of a court, presided over by a judge applying 'sound town planning principles' – a phrase used frequently – the Zimbabwean system was in reality a key tool in the creation and maintenance of a system of urban separate development – racial segregation. This was done not by the crude methods used in South Africa – for officially Rhodesia had been committed to multi-racial development – but by policies of zoning standards, open spaces between zones and strict control of variations of uses within zones. Residential zones were low density, medium density and high density, which corresponded to European, Coloured and Asian, and African areas, which were separated by open spaces, parks and so on. The language of the judgments of the Town Planning Court never, or rarely, referred to racial issues but concentrated instead on 'sound town planning principles' which were in reality taken to mean the maintenance of existing property values. The fundamental principle of the old Rhodesian planning system had been the maintenance of existing property values and this in turn had necessitated rigid zoning and strict judicial control of variations within zones. The importance of judicial control was twofold: first, it helped disguise the policy implications behind the implementation of the system – decisions of the court could more easily be presented as value-neutral than decisions of a minister; and second, it erected a system of precedent which bolstered both the status quo – the maintenance of existing property values – and itself contributed to the mystification of the policy implications.

In discussing possible reforms to make the policy-making aspects more explicit, the then Director of Physical Planning – who had served in Rhodesia for many years – stated that the Court, which has existed since 1945, had always been completely free from any political interference. Exactly; planning had apparently been a kind of technical legal exercise in which policy was almost a dirty word; it was sound town planning principles applied to each case on its merits in a series of 'judgments' which 'were to become highly respected' which had produced the segregated urban areas which existed in that country; any 'political' tampering with such a system would, by implication, lead to it not being highly respected (by whom?) any more. Legal reforms were quickly perceived as policy reforms designed to loosen up the urban structure and, it was assumed, contribute to a slump in urban property values, which the planning system existed to maintain. This was not acceptable to those who operated and benefited from the system.

Nigeria[1]

The case I want to consider in Nigeria concerns the type of planning law which that country has. This was a law originally enacted in 1946, which had survived numerous changes in the constitutional position of the country. The only significant change which had occurred in the law was the grafting on to it in many states of an urban development authority or board, whose members were appointed by the State Government and which was given the planning and development control duties under the law. Over the years, much criticism had been directed at the law; it was elitist, authoritarian, allowed for no public participation, and had not been adapted to the needs of a rapidly urbanising Nigeria. A relatively short spell of working in the Kano Urban Development Board (KUDB) showed me fairly clearly why the law had never been revised, despite all these criticisms and, over the years, specific proposals for reform. The reason was that the law accorded perfectly well with the views and attitudes of the ruling elite, both civil and military, which in this respect was not too different from those of colonial officials. Planning was not about participation, or about altering, in any significant way, the urban structure inherited from the colonial power with its low-density Government Residential Areas and its Sabon Garis for 'foreigners'. There was a very clear appreciation, on the part of the authorities, that planning was about power over land and that this was too important to be handed over to bodies over whom governments might not have complete control.

This analysis received confirmation from the Land Use Act, passed as a military Decree in 1978, which endeavoured to bring about a measure of land reform by limiting the amount of land any one person could hold and converting all freehold land into rights of occupancy held by the State (James 1987; Omotola 1982). The structure of power in the Act was the same centralised, non-participative structure as existed in the town planning legislation; the State Governor was given control of all urban land, and the power to grant rights of occupancy to such land, the only check on his power being a Land Use and Allocation Committee appointed by the Governor to advise him on any matters connected with his management of urban land in the State. Had there been the political desire either then or after the re-establishment of civilian rule in 1979 to bring about a more open or democratic approach to urban land management, that law would have been the obvious means to accomplish such a transformation; instead it further concentrated power in the ruling elite's hands.

Should the law be involved in urban development?

The case for law

A vital issue which must be considered first is whether there is a case for law to be involved in urban development at all. The arguments against can be put at two levels. The cynical level was put to me by a planning consultant in Dodoma, Tanzania. 'Why bother?' he said, 'Does it really matter whether the agency [in the instant case the Capital Development Authority] obeys the law or not? Wouldn't everything go on as "normal" if they didn't bother?' It would be hypocritical to pretend that this sort of attitude is unique; it is widespread among officials and consultants not least because it is grounded in reality. In Dodoma itself, the Capital Development Authority (CDA) in response to recommendations from its master plan consultants had 'banned' all development in certain parts of the town from early 1974, pending the completion of the master plan. There was no legal authority for such a ban yet it was enforced and observed by many potential developers of houses who left them half finished, roofless and decaying as a result. No legal challenge was mounted to the ban.

Similarly in Kano, a master plan was published in 1966 and successive urban development authorities had attempted to implement it, yet none of the formal legal steps necessary to publicise the plan, consider objections to it, and approve it, thus giving it a legal status, and legal backing to enforcement action, had been taken. No legal challenge has been mounted to any enforcement action. As it was put to me by the Chairman of the Kano Urban Development Board (KUDB), authority and power rather than law was what counted in Kano. The KUDB had the power and the apparent authority to get its way on development issues *vis-à-vis* the average person and where it had to give way, eg to the State Government or a local notable on such issues, this was because they had more power on their side and not because they had the law on their side.

The other level of argument is in a sense an alternative development argument. This argument says in general terms that the law impedes the efforts of ordinary people to house themselves, to obtain an income, to get access to potable water, electricity and other urban services and thereby to survive and better themselves in an urban environment. Law turns homesteaders into squatters, self-build houses into 'slums' and 'nuisances' which must be demolished; petty traders into criminals and job seekers into vagrants. The less the law and lawyers have to do with uncontrolled urban settlement and the informal urban economy the more chance persons in those sectors have of survival and development. Again, my own experience gives some support to this analysis. The rapidly growing squatter settlements in Dodoma were not acknowledged in official plans for urban development other than as areas to be cleared for urban development. As it was put in one development plan for a 'new' residential area, the existing houses were not of a suitable standard and most of them would have to be demolished to make way for the new model community and the existing people would likewise have to be moved elsewhere as they would not be able to afford to live in the new community.[2] The existing houses provided shelter for a long-established community of well over 1,000 low-income residents conveniently located for work in Dodoma. In Kano, great concern was generated inside the KUDB over hawkers and their 'illegal' booths which were clearly meeting a need. The concern was how to get rid of them, not how to adopt planning strategies and policies so as to accommodate them.

What answers then can be made to these legitimate and powerful criticisms of the role of law in urban development?

A general, albeit western liberal-democratic answer is that government in accordance with law is likely to be fairer, more respected, more effective in the long run than government in defiance or in disregard for the law; the tragic example of Uganda may be recalled, where a civilian government careless of legal niceties and constitutional forms was rudely replaced by a military regime careless of human rights, liberties and life, which in turn was replaced by a succession of civilian administrations utterly unable to restore law or respect for law within the country and equally unable therefore to mount any programmes of urban or rural development. A totally new beginning ultimately became necessary. But less dramatic examples can be given. If the Kano Urban Development Board need not obey the Town and County Planning Law, why should the Kano State Government? The result: government intervention and directives to the Board to ignore the master plan which the KUDB had no way or grounds to resist. Some of the difficulties in implementing the master plan in Dodoma stemmed directly from the CDA's lack of legal backing for its plans and proposals; it was a question of who got to which minister's ear first and which minister had more clout in government and party circles – a rather unsure way to proceed with developing a new capital. The presence of law will not obviate the need for inter- and intra-bureaucratic haggling and argument, but it can provide a reference point for the arguments, and in some situations, may reinforce the power of the urban development agency and thus its authority to get its way.

Within government then, law can provide a measure of certainty and support for particular policies and programmes, and institutions whose job it is to executive them. But what of government *vis-à-vis* the people? An example would be a law that confers powers on government, and rights on the people, such as a law permitting compulsory acquisition of land subject to the payment of compensation. Governments are more likely to know their powers than people their rights, and this will result in an unequal application of the law.

The trouble with this argument is that it assumes an idyllic state of 'no law' into which law intrudes unnecessarily. There are no states with no laws, although there are certainly states where very little attention is paid to law, where such laws as there are, are more concerned with conferring powers on government than rights on people or checks on government power. But the solution to this is not to decry a legal input into urban or any other sort of development, but to argue for and propose a law which moves the machinery of government just a few steps away from its existing authoritarian stance. Of course, laws can be and often are ignored. The contrast between the official treatment of squatters in Karachi and in virtually any Indian city, reinforces that point: India is a country which, whatever its imperfections, is ruled by law and in which courts can be, and are effective in halting government action against squatters;[3] Pakistan has been for too long ruled by military force and the courts have no effective role in the control of such force (van der Linden 1982). Law then can be a handle to be used in the struggle for a more humane or reasonable government, and for more humane and reasonable administration of programmes of urban development. A neat illus-

Plate 33   Law may be used to frustrate people's attempts to improve their situation by declaring informal housing illegal; alternatively, recognition of such areas, as here, can stimulate self-help improvement.

tration of this was provided by two incidents in Dodoma. A decision was taken to move some 'squatters' so that the land could be prepared for 'development' – a road. A decision was taken to pay compensation *ex gratia*. But no procedures were followed in this; no proper efforts were made to ensure that the right people were being compensated or that those who got it understood what it was for. The squatters were not in fact moved until three years after payment of compensation, but there had been no adequate preparation of a site for them to move to. Thus the decision to pay compensation, which was admirable, was vitiated by an absence of any kind of legal or other framework for its implementation. No lawyer had been consulted on procedures and no attempt had been made to adapt what legal procedures existed to the particular circumstances of the case. A repeat performance of this was planned for another area – the Kikuyu Model Community – where homes were to be demolished and squatters moved, as they did not fit in with the plans, without any consideration being given in the plan to relocation, compensation or assistance for those displaced. By drawing attention to the various legal provisions governing these matters – contained in both town and country planning and compulsory purchase legislation – it was possible to get the plan rewritten to incorporate both the necessity to pay compensation and the likely costs thereof.

There is a second and equally important reason for placing some emphasis on a role for law in urban development. I refer to this as the repatriation of decision-making. There is a great deal written about the deleterious effect that international – usually western orientated – consultants, planners and administrators can have on national priorities in respect of urban development (Hai 1981; King 1977). I shall draw attention here to one little remarked but important side effect of foreign consultancy. The decision to use foreign planning consultants to produce a master plan for an urban area or region has the inevitable effect of passing decision-making not just on the policies and shape of the plan but on its detailed implementation over to those consultants, ignoring or bypassing the national statutory procedures for plan making, approval and implementation. Sometimes this is blatant as in Dodoma, where in the early years of the capital development programme the master planners did most of their work in Toronto, their headquarters, and provided both in the plan and in their consultancy contract that no changes could take place in the plan without their being involved. The effect of this was that when some of their more far-fetched ideas were seen to be impractical by planners on the spot, a memorandum suggesting changes would be compiled and sent to Toronto; a pause would ensue until the reply came back defending the sanctity of the plan to the last eight-lane highway. The reply would be addressed to the Director-General of CDA bypassing all normal procedures, and hinting that criticisms of the plan were motivated by malice and ignorance. The reply was accepted, and the plan left untouched – and unimplemented.[4]

In Nigeria the process of foreign take-over of the planning process was less blatant, but no less serious. In Kano State no fewer than thirteen master plans were produced for thirteen urban areas by five different nationalities of planning consultants: British, Hungarian, Yugoslavian, Danish and a mixed Indian-Egyptian-Nigerian team from the planning department of Ahmadu Bello University, Zaria. None of the plans made any reference to the existing town and country planning laws of the state. The mixed Polish-Hungarian-Indian team of planners and architects occupying the higher posts in the KUDB knew equally little of the planning laws of the state, as did the mixed Swedish-German

UN team of planners, so that administration and implementation of the plans, such as it was, proceeded in a kind of a-legal Erewhon.

In Uganda the problem was subtly different. My involvement arose out of the laudable initiative of the UNDP and Habitat to set in motion machinery, men and money to rebuild the two south-western towns of Mbarara and Masaka, destroyed in the war of liberation from Amin. UN agencies understandably had no wish to get involved in the quagmire of post-Amin Ugandan politics and administration. The solution decided upon was a development agency set up outside the regular adminis-tration, reporting direct to the President and bypassing local govern-ment, central government, boards, commissions and officials. But this too betrayed a woeful ignorance of the existing laws and administration in Uganda and a somewhat astonishing naïvety that it would be possible to isolate such an agency from politics and administration merely by making it a separate corporate body by law. The concern for action rather than talk was laudable but was the approach any different from that adopted in Dodoma?

In each case my approach and my aim was the same: to bring the existing law to the attention of the policy-makers and decision-makers, to explain and stress the importance of complying with it; to highlight its defects and strong points; where necessary, to propose the principles that should inform amendments and reforms, and then finally to draft those reforms in close association with the officials of the agency I was advising.

However deficient the planning laws – and in broad outline and many details the planning Ordinances and Acts of Tanzania, Nigeria (inher-ited by Kano State) and Uganda are exactly the same and derive from the standard Colonial Office package of the 1950s[5] – they all provided for certain basic procedures to be followed in respect of plan approval: publication of draft plan; a period for the receipt of objections and comments; a consideration of the same; submission to the relevant minister of draft plan, proposed amendments in light of comments, and comments on the comments; approval with or without amendments by the minister; publication of approval and coming into force of the plan. Nothing in the procedures was very complicated or very time consum-ing: compared to the procedures most British or North American planners have to go through to get plans approved in the UK, USA and Canada, they were amazingly straightforward.

A failure to follow the law, a belief that it was not necessary to follow the law did not arise from a desire on the part of consultants for more participation and discussion than the law required – such participation could have taken place but did not – but from a desire to keep control of the plan making and implementation process and a belief that the local law was beneath bothering about. The attitude was well summed up by a member of the Canadian planning consultant's team in Dodoma who said to me: 'In Toronto, we are told that it's planning by the bulldozer in Dodoma and all we have to worry about is getting the approval of the Director General of CDA'. The planning team knew nothing and were told nothing of the planning laws.

In both Dodoma and Kano State, the realisation on the part of officials in the agencies I was advising that there were planning laws in existence which had to be, but were not being, followed, transformed, albeit temporarily, their attitude towards laws and procedures. Whereas they had viewed my mission as being designed to give them increased power to implement their plans, they suddenly found that technically they had no power at all, and indeed were highly vulnerable to legal, or, more likely, political attacks from their opponents for their failure to observe existing laws.

In the Uganda case, government officials were wary of UN proposals because these involved bypassing normal administrative procedures which the officials were trying to re-establish, and because they appeared to strengthen the powers of the President which ran counter to the then prevailing political concern. UN officials tended to see Uganda officials as tied to British ways of doing things, procrastinating and failing to understand the urgency of action. But no one in the UN team had actually investigated the law and administration governing planning, building, land use and land tenure, local government and sewerage, that would have to be addressed before any agency could be established. I wrote a memorandum summarising the relevant laws; stating that any new agency would have to fit into an existing legal framework; drawing attention to the essential attributes such an agency would have to have; and setting out possible heads of legislation that could be drafted to implement the proposals. This memorandum was effective. The UN officials understood for the first time the complexity and interlocking nature of Uganda's land use, land tenure and local government system, the political reasons for it and thus the need to respect it; the Ugandan officials were able to point to, rely on, propose amendments to a document about their system which was concrete proof that a system did exist and had to be respected and amended rather than ignored and bypassed. Knowledge and appreciation of the law was the key to realistic negotiations and a Ugandan solution to a Ugandan problem, albeit with UN assistance.[6]

Too much law is as bad as too little

The second matter for consideration is rather the reverse of the first. There may be a tendency to become too enthusiastic about the possibilities of a legal solution to an urban problem. Virtually everywhere that I have been asked to advise or draft new laws, an existing state of affairs has been presented as requiring a legal input of some sort. In Tanzania, it was the general powers of the CDA to plan and develop Dodoma; they were considered to be deficient in some way. In Uganda, the impetus for a legal input into the urban development process came from the UN itself. In Maldives and Turks and Caicos Islands the need was presented for a new, more effective legal regime to control urban development, hitherto largely uncontrolled. In Malawi, the argument was that a new system of physical development planning working down from a national physical development plan required a brand new system of planning law. In Trinidad and Tobago the effectiveness of the system of development conntrol was seen as, in part, being caused by an absence of sufficient legal sanctions.

All these arguments had some justification, but in many cases they told only half the story. Sometimes existing laws were not being utilised satisfactorily, either through ignorance of what the law was or because the political process prevented the laws being used, so that a new law would not necessarily 'solve' the problems unless the underlying problems were tackled. In Tanzania, there was, and to some extent still is, a fairly casual attitude towards legal procedures and legal backing for the exercise of power. Thus, new laws for one agency could not displace a general administrative culture which placed a low value on law, nor overcome political and administrative scepticism about the value of the whole enterprise of moving the capital from Dar es Salaam to Dodoma.

If Tanzania provides an example of existing laws being under-used, Madras and Jamaica provide examples of the opposite – the sheer amount of law and bureaucracy overwhelming the development process so that resort is made to an outside lawyer in a desperate search for a way through the morass.

In Madras there is a plethora of laws dealing with the urban land development process, and a multitude of statutory bodies. Apart from a town and country planning law, there is urban land ceiling legislation, slums clearance legislation, housing legislation, special legislation dealing with the housing of Harijans (untouchables), the siting of nuclear power installations, rent control, land acquisition and several land taxation laws. Apart from a Madras Metropolitan Development Authority (MMDA), there is a slum clearance board, a housing corporation, a water and sewerage corporation, upwards of fifty local authorities within the area of jurisdiction of MMDA, housing finance bodies and officials charged with special duties under land ceiling and taxation legislation. The laws themselves are long and prolix; they presume an understanding of legal procedures quite beyond most people, both those to whom they are directed and those who have to implement them. The development plans required by the planning laws are similarly detailed and rigidly legalistic, or would be if they were all produced, but the process is so time consuming that it is doubtful whether they ever will be. The courts are actively involved in the urban development process, or rather considerable efforts are made to involve them actively in the process but they too are rather slow at reaching decisions. The picture is one of planners and administrators in the MMDA, the body charged with planning and overseeing development within the Madras metropolitan area, feeling themselves weighed down and unable to achieve anything by the mass of law and, as they see it, hostile judicial decisions confronting them.

The situation in Madras could be paralleled in many Indian cities and is a classic example of an excess of law and legal regulation. So concerned have the authorities been to regulate the urban development process and close every loophole against illegal development, corruption, exploitation of scarce urban resources, wrongful exercise of discretion, that the principal aim of the MMDA – to get orderly and equitable development underway in Madras and its environs – has been lost sight of. The result was that the laws were not being observed or enforced; illegal and unauthorised development was widespread – and not just by squatters; plans were not being followed – the panchayats on the outskirts of the MMDA had had no input into the plan, could not understand it, and felt no obligation to apply it; and needed development and acquisition of land was being held up by lawsuits. Furthermore, the total corpus of law was not consistent; land taxation laws and administration pointed in favour of the development of land that legal plans decreed should not be developed. This was because no increase in the rate of land taxation was allowed to local authorities thus putting them into a position where the only way they could increase their revenues was by permitting land to be developed, irrespective of what the plan said.

In these circumstances, the aim must be to reduce the legal content of the development process. Too much law which leads to a paralysis of will is as bad as too little which allows power to be abused. An important matter to realise in such a situation is that there is already a selectivity of enforcement of law; low-level officials in the front line of law and plan enforcement decide for themselves, without much reference to those higher up in the bureaucracy what laws to enforce and what to ignore. Reducing the legal content of the development process – freeing much development from the need to apply for development permission; expanding the scope of permitted development within different zones; formally delegating power to make decisions away from the centre – will in reality be doing little more than bringing the law into line with practice.

The problem of linkages

A related issue is that of linkages: the interconnectedness between different facets of the urban development and management process and the futility of trying to alter one piece of the jigsaw, while leaving the rest untouched. One of the best examples arose in Jamaica. There is considered to be a problem of lack of investment in agricultural development in Jamaica; attention focused on the difficulty small landholders had in obtaining a registered title to their land and thus having the necessary security to obtain loans for agricultural development. It was thought that some new or additional legal input or technological input such as computerised land records, into the land registry process would 'solve the problem' by speeding up the issue of title. At the same time, a major UN input into the planning and development of Kingston was in process, and one component of this was the design of a 'one stop' planning application process – that is, a system whereby all the necessary permissions and approvals needed before development could commence would be obtained at the same time at one office, presumably quicker than the current system. There was no relationship between the agricultural and urban concerns.

My involvement was on the agricultural side but a brief survey of the rural land tenure and development process made clear that an input on the lines of a quick legal or technological fix would solve nothing. The issuing of a document of registered title could not be separated from the process of land surveying or the granting of permission of parish councils – the units of local government in Jamaica – to subdivide land. Subdivision permission in turn involved the town Planning Department and its role in co-ordinating comments from ten different agencies of government on any such proposal. The methods and modalities of land surveying were in turn determined by the requirements of the Registered Title Act as to what needed to be proved before the registered title could be issued, and the practice of the Commissioner of Lands in allocating plots for smallholder agricultural development. It was clear too from my survey that first, delay in issuing registered title and its effect on the market for land affected urban land no less than rural land, and second, an unofficial market in land operated in many rural areas, with land being bought, sold and pledged but never registered because of costs and delays associated with that process. As a result, the Registry of Titles, housed in a splendid Dickensian office full of huge folios and files, stretching back to 1889, the year of enactment of the Registered Title Act, was in practice an inaccurate record of landholdings on the ground.

In these circumstances, it was clear that here was a case for a fundamental rethink of the total system of land management and development in Jamaica, and that furthermore there were officials who were aware of a deep-rooted malaise within the system so that there would be some receptivity to such a proposal. It was also clear that in practice one could not separate rural from urban land management; the same institutions – Town Planning Department, Survey Department, Registry of Titles – were involved in both sectors; the same laws applied to both sectors and the same problems afflicted both sectors. It followed that any reform, even if originating in one sector, would affect the other and would be more likely to be effective if it applied to both sectors.

The importance of surveying the existing legal scene

A thorough survey of an existing system is essential before proposing reforms. It might seem an obvious point but in the haste to introduce a reform or correct what is thought to be a deficiency in a law or its implementation, such a survey is often forgone and the 'reform' fails to achieve its aim. Until such a survey is done, it is not possible to know whether the problem is too much law, too little law, out-of-date law, ignorance of law, law at variance with practice, customs and beliefs, a reasonable law unreasonably administered, law needing wholesale reform, or law needing minor adjustments. Equally, a survey will help uncover the politics of law, the hidden agenda of the legal input.

A survey of the total system, its strengths and weaknesses, the areas where a case can be made for change, and if so what kind of change and by what kinds of mechanisms, may be the first opportunity officials have had to see how the total system is working in practice; this can have an immensely valuable educational benefit.

In addition, if there is to be reform or reorganisation, it has to be sold to the officials who will be implementing it. In practice, this means that officials will be expected to learn and apply new laws, new routines, new practices. They have to be convinced that this is a necessary and worthwhile exercise. The process of putting together a survey is part of this process of educating officials to accept change. Many of them will have had an input into the survey, will have had an opportunity to express their views about the present system, and how it needs to be changed. They will or should have an opportunity to go through the survey and so increase their awareness of the system which they are a part. Producing a survey then can both create a climate of anticipation for and acceptance of change and contribute to a more aware and informed bureaucracy.

One must, however, recognise the dangers. The longer the 'delay' in producing positive proposals for a new or a revised legal input into the urban development process, the more the possibility that impatient politicians or others will go ahead with some 'reform' that will achieve nothing in the long run to cure the underlying problem. Again, a survey of the present system and its defects will give those who at present gain or who see that in the future they may gain from the maintenance of the present system an opportunity to argue for the maintenance of the status quo – as happened in the case of Zimbabwe discussed earlier. Finally, although one aim of the survey may be public education, governments are often reluctant to disclose a critical survey to a wide audience, even within the bureaucracy itself, so change, if and when it comes, still finds many people unprepared and therefore instinctively antipathetic to it.

The question of local relevance

Obtaining a thorough overview of a national system of urban development and its legal dimension will serve to guard against the too ready application of foreign models and 'standard' planning law packages.

In Tanzania, officials in CDA were bombarded with advice to introduce North American zoning regulations and Australian principles of land management derived from the experience of the National Capital Commission in Canberra. In Kano State, the Nigerian staff of the KUDB found themselves caught in a veritable cross-fire of conflicting advice from their foreign colleagues; from Indian planners to introduce the kind of detailed zoning regulations which apply in India; and from eastern European planners to adopt a formal plan-as-law similar to that found in Poland for example. In addition, each master plan made for different urban areas of the State, by consultants of different nationalities, was predicated on the likely existence of a planning system not too dissimilar from the one the consultants knew best, ie their own.

Calcutta provides an example of the *reductio ad absurdum* of foreign models. The West Bengal Town and Country Planning Act is loosely based on the current English system and includes in its provisions on development control the time-honoured legal phrase that, in considering whether to grant planning permission, the planning authority – in this case the Calcutta Metropolitan Development Authority (CMDA) – should take account of the development plan and 'any other material considerations'. I found within CMDA a widespread belief that since the same legal phrase about what to take into account in considering planning applications appeared in both West Bengal and English legislation, the English interpretation of, and practice on the basis of, that phrase would be likely to be relevant in Calcutta. However, since the urban scene is very different between West Bengal and England, how development control should be operated in Calcutta must turn on Calcutta's needs, CMDA's capacity and the wider urban socio-political context of West Bengal, rather than on what happened or was presumed to happen in England.[7]

Trinidad and Tobago provides an example of the awful fate than can befall a country that does over-rely on English precedent. The Town and Country Planning Act in Trinidad and Tobago was enacted in 1960, and is based very closely on the English law of 1947, together with some of the amendments of the 1950s.

Part VI of the Act deals with compensation. As a result of the decision of the Privy Council in *Lopinot Limestone Ltd* v *AG of Trinidad and Tobago*,[8] this part of the law has now assumed considerable importance. The Act provides that if it is shown that, as a result of a planning decision involving a refusal of permission, the value of the interest of any person in the land to which the planning decision relates is less than it would have been if the permission had been granted, then the Minister is empowered to pay compensation to that person, or an amount equal to the difference.

The relevant section of the Act was copied almost word for word from section 20 of the English Town and Country Planning Act 1954, which was an integral part of an extremely complex reform of the law relating to compensation and betterment as it had been enacted in the English Town and Country Planning Act 1947. The full details of that reform are not relevant to the issue here; the essential point however is; and that is that compensation was not based on differences in the market value of land, depending on whether planning permission was granted or refused, but on whether a claimant has a 'claim holding' under Part VI of the Act of 1947 against the sum of £300 million provided under that Act for the loss of the development value of the land 'nationalised' by that Act. Thus, whatever the theoretical justification for providing or not providing compensation in respect of some planning decisions in England, the compensation so provided is an ever-decreasing amount with an ever-decreasing value, given the incidence of inflation. In Trinidad and Tobago, on the other hand, the transfer of the same provisions and the tying of them to market value has resulted, from the same processes of inflation, in ever-increasing amounts of compensation becoming payable in the event of a claim being successfully prosecuted.

Three conclusions can be drawn from these examples. First, difficult though it may be, one should attempt to bring to the urban legal problems a mind uncluttered by foreign models. Planning and other urban laws – housing, taxation, compulsory acquisition, title, etc. – are country-specific rather than universal and must be geared to the perceived needs, and probable future needs of the country concerned. There may be a good case for as much uniformity of commercial law as possible around the world, though the issue of who gains and who loses from such uniformity tends to be neglected, but there is no case for a similar uniformity of urban laws. This is not to say that there are not likely to be common matters to be dealt with in a town planning or land planning law, but the way they are dealt with will almost certainly need to be different.

Such considerations applied to laws that I drafted for Trinidad and Tobago in 1988 and the British Virgin Islands in 1989. While using the same basic framework for each law, I found that in virtually every clause, it was necessary to alter the Trinidad and Tobago draft to make it applicable to the British Virgin Islands. It was not just that the planning problems were different; the political and constitutional framework was different; the general body of laws was different; and the administrative system and culture was different. Above all, in the British Virgin Islands, there is an immensely strong ideology of private landownership derived from the islands' history and any law which was perceived, however misguidedly, as interfering with that ownership would stand little chance of successful implementation, indeed of enactment. So it was necessary to make plain in the body of the draft Bill that ownership was not being interfered with and the words 'control' and 'enforcement' were conspicuous by their absence. At the same time, there were clear problems arising from overseas developers with large-scale proposals for development bypassing normal channels and obtaining political approval for their schemes before planning and environmental implications had been properly considered. The need here was for mechanisms which ensured proper consideration for schemes whoever took the ultimate decision. In Trinidad and Tobago on the other hand, while there is a strong ethic of landownership, the problem of planning was perceived by the planners as being a lack of order and discipline especially among the rural population who wished, contrary to the National Physical Development Plan, to subdivide their land, build houses on the subdivision to keep the family together in accordance with traditional beliefs; such subdivisions contributed to ribbon development and increased the cost of the provision of services. Thus, the need was perceived as being for tougher enforcement powers and a way round political and legal blockages to their use. At the same time, at the political level, the problem was perceived as undue rigidity of development control and overmighty planners, and therefore the need of mechanisms to enable other points of view to have an input into the planning system. The resultant Bill provided for more powers for planners but also more inputs into the planning system by local authorities; advisory committees; participation; and formal appeal mechanisms.

Second, it follows from what I have said so far, that I am sceptical of the usefulness of checklists for either laws regulating the urban development process or the contents of such laws. Checklists would either be so general as to be banal, or else be too detailed to be of much use in specific situations. The range of political and administrative factors which have to be considered before a law is drafted or implemented is so great that each country, or each state in a federation needs to work outwards from its own specific situation to solutions which may or may not involve law, rather than work inwards from an imported law or a checklist of 'topics to be legislated on'. There may, however, be a case for a checklist of principles, and I come to that later in the chapter.

Third, however, there is one important occasion when legal transplants may be a valid solution. This is in the area of building regulations applicable to large multi-storey and/or 'international' buildings – airports, major hotels, office blocks, factories for the manufacture of heavy industrial goods, chemical plants and so on – and pollution control regulations applicable to toxic and hazardous industrial processes and waste. There is a case, on public health and safety grounds, for direct transplants of, say European or American building regulations, pollution control regulations and provisions for environmental impact assessment, with any necessary modifications to take account of specified local circumstances such as earthquakes, tropical rain, termites, in situations where there is to be a direct transplant of the type of buildings and industrial processes from the countries where those rules apply.

It is, however, not so much the content of the regulations in these technical areas as the knowledge, skill and competence of the officials enforcing them which will determine their effectiveness. Until those attributes are available, it may be better to proceed by way of requiring bonds from, and imposing strict civil liability with unlimited damages on, international contractors and employers in respect of the safety of the design, construction and operation of their major facilities, such as hotels and factories, rather than have in place a modern up to date code on such matters which cannot be applied because there is no one to apply it. There is also a case for countries which lack qualified personnel making use of UN and other consultants to assist in the monitoring and control of hazardous industrial operations, for example. Such people would be expected to apply the same judgements about the effects of toxic wastes, necessary safety measures to control hazardous activities, and protection of the environment in those countries as in more developed ones. Here too then, the message is that principles may be transplantable, procedures less so.

Bench-marks for urban law reform

The need for principles

If there is any one message in this chapter, it is that a legal input into the urban development process is a matter of politics and policy and not just technicalities. A legal input involves costs for some, benefits for others;

Plate 34 Blocks of apartments in Rio de Janeiro: there is a strong case for adopting international standards for the construction of high-rise buildings.

that is a political issue. It follows that it is necessary either to discover what principles lie behind any proposed change in the legal framework for urban development or to propose principles which should guide any such change. Without knowledge of the principles behind the legislation, what form the legislation should take is difficult if not impossible to determine. It is also important to ensure that the principles behind any legislation accord with and march alongside the principles behind the urban planning and development process.

I would suggest principles as follows: any legal input into the urban development process should aim to encourage, strengthen or introduce a system of planning, regulation and management of that process which is equitable, flexible, environmentally conscious, participative and easily manageable, simple to understand and use, efficient and administratively fair. Counsels of perfection! The principles may briefly be discussed.

Equitable

The system should aim to contribute to righting the present imbalance towards the well-off in most urban development processes. It should be made easier to acquire lawful title to land, or lawful occupation of a home, to acquire funds to build a home, to comply with any regulatory provisions governing the development or construction process and to obtain basic services and facilities such as water and power. Instead of the law being used to bolster and maintain a divided urban system between the illegal or extra-legal city of the urban poor, and the legal city of the urban well-off, it should facilitate the absorption of the urban poor into the legal city.

Flexible

The system must be such that it can accommodate change and growth, the twin characteristics of most urban development processes. A rigid plan or zoning system is doomed to failure – there are countless examples of this all over the world – and merely leads to frustration, ignoring the rules, corruption, and the waste of scarce skilled personnel trying either to prevent departures from the plan or allowing them. A flexible adaptive planning system, and a development control system which concentrates on essentials, can act as an encouragement to lawful development where a rigid system discourages lawful and encourages unlawful development.

Environmentally conscious

It is now much more widely recognised in literature, if not in practice, that development and environmental conservation can and indeed should go hand in hand. To allow or do nothing to prevent urban development in areas needed for water catchment, or where industrial pollution is likely to blight residential areas, or in ecologically fragile areas, will result in development disasters; cities or islands with inadequate clean water, leading to an epidemic of waterborne illnesses; more Bhopals;[9] loss of local livelihoods from fishing, etc. Any law therefore should facilitate the integration of environmental considerations into the development processes and require that a proper balance be drawn between conservation and development. It should be said too, that an environmentally conscious planning and development system is more likely to be an equitable one, for urban environmental disasters tend to be visited on the poor rather than the rich.

Participative and easily manageable

By participation I do not mean just the kind of participation which is now an established part of the British planning system – public meetings on plans and pressure group input into the consideration of planning applications. I am concerned with involvement, with a much greater effort to find out the needs and concerns of the urban majority and cater to them and with encouraging that majority to develop either own environment in their own ways, via local self-help schemes. Again, a flexible planning system will be of assistance here as it can more easily respond to needs and concerns fed into it from below. This too is where an easily manageable system comes in. Too many legal requirements of the contents of a plan, or too centralised a system of planning and development control both impede the development of a manageable system. In the wise words of the Attorney-General of Maldives – 'less law, more power' – provide a framework for the management of the urban development process but do not crowd out initiative and flexibility with over many rules, which will in turn need over many officials to administer them.

Simple

This follows on from 'participative and easily manageable'. Any legislation or forms to be used in connection with the urban development process should be kept as simple as possible. Complexity can in my experience result as much from administrative requirements as the supposed necessities of legal drafting, so this principle is addressed to all officials involved in the urban development process. Once again, reference to the first principle of equity is relevant here; a regulatory system applicable fairly to all must be one that can be understood and used by all.

Efficient

The notion of an efficient system embraces several impacts: the costs of the system must not be allowed to grow too large; the costs of control of development must be related to some reasonably identifiable benefit to be gained from control; control for example, of hazardous industrial processes, may increase the cost of the processes concerned but the gains in diminution of danger to life and of protection of the natural environment justify those costs being imposed on the industrialists. It is likely to be more economically efficient and certainly more equitable that the costs are borne by the polluter than the polluted since the polluter is in a better position to abate the pollution. Control of a range of minor works of construction on the other hand may have no identifiable benefit over and above providing work for the controller; it should not therefore continue. Equally, this principle would direct attention to finding the most economically effective way of achieving a particular end; there is no magic in any one particular system of regulation or management; and there should be a willingness to devise a system appropriate to the government and society concerned.

Administratively fair

This is an important procedural value which unless explicitly addressed may become submerged in the concern for efficiency and ease of management. It is a particular lawyer-like concern to create a system which ensures, as far as possible, that proper consideration is given before action is taken which is likely to have adverse consequences on people; that where hearings are provided for, they are conducted in accordance with recognised principles of administrative justice; that where compensation is due, it is paid promptly and in full; that there are proper internal checks on the planners and administrators to ensure that they carry out their duties properly; and that adequate external investigations are made of allegations that they have not. One does not have to subscribe to all the details of Indian administrative law in practice to make the point that, as a matter of principle, a system which allows as much challenge to administrative action as that does, is preferable to one that allows none. Again to come back to the first principle, it is much more likely to be the poor who will lose out in an authoritarian administrative system than the wealthy or well connected.

Applying the principles

It must be clear that while these are the basic principles which should determine any legal input into the urban development process, the content of any law will naturally differ from society to society, depending on the circumstances of that society and what its fundamental political philosophy or basic urban policies are. A government whose policies are to encourage self-help and improvement amongst the urban poor via squatter upgrading programmes will focus on different specific areas of law and planning than one whose policies are to be based on large-scale public housing programmes; and a government with little land at its disposal, for example a small island state, will naturally be more concerned with control of land than a government whose principal concern is with the allocation of land which is not in short supply but is badly distributed. But in each case, the precise content of any law and the way it is put together should have regard to the basic principles. An important point must however be discussed here. Inevitably, attempts to meet all the principles will run up against the problem that in practice there may be conflicts between them; equity may not always be reconcilable with efficiency; fair administration may not always be reconcilable with simplicity. Two examples drawn from practice illustrate the problem.

How can one draft a statute creating new institutions and duties of participation, imposing new checks on administrative action, providing new opportunities for informal developments of all kinds and not finish up with a longer more complex law than the old colonial legislation which is being replaced and which basically gave planners and administrators *carte blanche* to 'get on with things' with a minimum of checks on their activities?

My experience in drafting a new planning law for Kano State may be used to illustrate this dilemma. It was designed to replace a 1962 Town Planning Law, itself just a repeat for the Northern State of Nigeria of a 1946 law, and a 1972 Kano Urban Development Board Edict, the combined lengths of which were 114 sections and 3 schedules. My proposed draft was 96 sections and 2 schedules, but many of the sections were long and the total number of words used in the replacement legislation was not that different from that in the existing legislation. Length and complexity came about from two causes; first, increasing the types of plans that could be made, thus increasing the flexibility of the planning system and stating what the purpose of the plans were – a necessary provision as each planning consultant or planning officer had his own idea as to what he hoped to achieve by preparing a plan and these ideas rarely dovetailed. Second, a great many words were used to set up and provide the outline procedures for consultation and publicity in connection with the making and approval of plans. These procedures were unquestionably open to criticism from a 'bottom up' perspective as being too heavily weighted toward 'official' participation about officially made plans, but equally unquestionably they went far further than any planning legislation in Nigeria in the direction of open participative plan-making. All the time I was drafting, I was conscious that every additional provision I put in to sharpen up participation and reduce the possibility of the provisions being ignored made the legislation longer and more complex and so paradoxically perhaps increased the likelihood of administrators, planners and consultants being tempted to ignore it. The draft Bill was not ultimately enacted so I cannot tell whether in practice I erred on the side of complexity in this matter; I think I did but I also think that fewer legal provisions would inevitably have meant placing more reliance on the goodwill of officials, and relying on bureaucratic goodwill might not have been too sensible.

One schedule in the draft legislation was long and complex. This dealt with permitted development – that is, development permitted by the law and which did not need specific planning permission. Once again the aim was straightforward, its implementation complex and possibly devious. The aim was to free as much small-scale development and economic activity from the requirements of planning permission as possible, without at the same time negating the principle of development control. The draft Bill therefore contained the principle of development control where there was in existence a development plan (that alone freed most of the state from development control on unimpeachable grounds); the schedule contained the exceptions to development control in those areas where there was a plan and therefore development control. It is not however very easy to draft provisions exempting small-scale development from control in such a way that the informal sector is left alone but developments which might cause a nuisance or pollution are caught, or exempting residential developments of a traditional kind or a certain size but catching other residential development. The only way to do it is to spell out in some detail what is permitted and what is not. In this way developers and, more importantly, officials know what they may and may not do or control. But spelling out details adds to the length and complexity of the law. The alternative – to give a wide measure of discretion to officials – ran the risk of providing a spurious legal backing to harassment of informal urban development and economic activity.

Thus demands for more participation, for more decentralisation of power, for more protection for informal economic activity and for more controls over official power – demands in short for a more complex administrative structure – led to a more complex legislative structure which in turn gave rise to the possibility of inefficiencies.

My second example came from Trinidad and Tobago, where in my Report on the existing Town and Country Planning Act I had set out the five principles which should inform any new legislation: efficiency, equality, environmentalism, education and public participation, and employment generation. These principles had been accepted as appropriate. The legislation which was to be replaced was 40 sections long; my draft was 90 sections long and some of the sections were themselves of considerable length. Why was this? First, the terseness of the 1960 Act had not been conducive to its efficient administration. Efficiency there was in practice but this was in spite of rather than because of the Act. In some places, the Act was terse to the point where it was not clear what powers were available to officials. Second, the Act had assumed that flesh could be put on its bones by regulations and orders, but with two exceptions – a General Development Order dealing principally with development control and some regulations dealing with advertisements – no regulations had been made during the life of the Act. So powers which were probably available under the Act were not used because there was no legal framework set out for their use. This led on to a third point: there were, no doubt, some political reasons why regulations had not been made to flesh out the Act; there was little pressure for a comprehensive system of planning and a good deal of pressure for allowing people to develop land as they wished. But a factor in the lack of regulation was that the Act provided no guidance, no outline of the subject matter on which regulations might be made. Without some legislative indication of what a particular exercise of power might look like, it became impossible to draw up regulations.

I took the view that any replacement legislation had to take note of the fact that regulations might not be made for some time to come if at all, but that their drafting would be easier if there were a fairly detailed framework already set out in primary legislation, ie the draft Bill. Equally, it should be possible to implement the new legislation, to exercise powers and perform duties under the legislation without being dependent on regulations. Just as important, those outside the bureaucracy should be able to get a fuller picture of what the system of town and country planning as established by law was about; they would be better placed to do that if matters were more closely and fully spelt out in the Act, the document most non-lawyers instinctively recognise and go to when they want to find out what 'the law' is on a particular topic. Thus efficiency, equity and public education would all be served by a more lengthy piece of legislation even though simplicity and some economy had been sacrificed.

A holistic approach

Any legal input should be made only in the full knowledge of both the existing system and the likely implications of that legal input. This does not mean that any reform however small can be contemplated only after a full survey of the existing system. But it does suggest that any reform or introduction of new legal or administrative arrangements is likely to have ripple effects and these should be taken account of in the manner, style and content of any reforms. It also means that, on occasions, one might have to pause and refrain from a tinkering reform if there is prima facie evidence that there are more deep-seated problems which need to be tackled. The case of the Jamaican land tenure and registration system discussed earlier is an excellent example of that: spending money, time and energy on shoring up the existing system of title registration while refusing to acknowledge that the whole administrative and legal system of land management was failing to provide an adequate service would be counter-productive to the long-term aim of creating a viable efficient and simple system of land management for that country.

A holistic approach is easy to argue for but difficult to comply with, especially if one is being pressured to come up with some reform instantly to solve what someone with political influence but maybe not much understanding of the urban development process sees as a problem. How can one as a matter of practical politics say in such circumstances: 'Wait six months, a year, two years, until we have done a thorough survey and can come forward with a considered proposal'? In such circumstances, a tactic of damage limitation may be the best approach; better a hasty 'reform' undertaken by those who understand the system than one undertaken by those who know nothing and might therefore make matters worse not better.

But there is a possible solution to this dilemma. Urban land management and the urban development processes are, for virtually all countries, major concerns of government. Political stability, economic development, social change, health, all are greatly influenced by the way cities are developed and administered. At the root of such development and administration is land, its allocation, development and use. Land-.use planning is one tool of such a process of management as are law and taxation, but too often the different tools are left in separate compartments of the bureaucracy. They may be brought together only by the, often fortuitous, appearance of a team of outside consultants brought in to try and sort out problems that are thought to have arisen. The alternative to this is for governments to create a standing committee or commission whose function would be *inter alia* to keep under constant review national urban or human settlement policies and their implementation and to produce reports on the same, either on the basis of references to it by governments or of its own assessment of what needs review and monitoring. The commission would have its own staff, could employ consultants both national and foreign, and help to ensure that urban issues were given full and careful consideration before any specific action on such issues took place. Such a commission would be semi-official; it would not be part of government in the sense that government would be committed to accepting all its views but it would be responsive to government in the sense that it would be obliged to consider issues referred to it by government and government would be its prime funder. Some states have such a body, the embryo of such a body, or have developed an equivalent body in respect of environmental protection. It is a proposal which is worth serious consideration as a way of ensuring that the holistic approach recommended here becomes more than a pious aspiration.

Building on existing systems

There is an administrative and legal culture in every society just as there is a prevailing set of beliefs and practices about land, water, homes, taxes and other aspects of an urban existence. These beliefs, practices and culture have to be taken note of in any programme or proposal for a legal input into the urban development process. They have to be worked with rather than against, adapted to new circumstances and demands rather than abolished. It is unlikely that abolition would in practice occur even if it were decreed to occur. Such a counsel of incrementalism, of working with rather than against local beliefs and practices, may be disappointing and sound pusillanimous to those who hope for radical reform in urban development processes. It may also be pointed out that this conclusion might well conflict with some of the principles enunciated earlier; if the administrative culture is not fair, if equity has not been a feature of urban development processes, how can one base any reform both on those principles and on the existing administrative culture?

In answer to the first criticism, one has to point out that a radical reform of legal or administrative processes in urban development or any other part of the development process is a consequence of, and not a forerunner of or substitute for, radical political change. Proposing a radical, grass roots, participative land-use planning system in countries where government remains in the hands of military dictators, will achieve nothing. Indeed such a system never would be introduced even if it were recommended for introduction. Only when governments become convinced of the need for radical change, for example, towards greater equity, which can happen with military as well as civilian regimes, will radical administrative, legal and planning reforms become possible.

More problems are posed by possible conflicts between principles and practice. Here too, however, I would suggest that incrementalism is the way forward. If the application of the principle of equity looks likely to conflict with current and apparently long-standing inequitable practices, then one has to try and create a situation where, over a period, principles of equity begin to be taken account of in practice. Similarly with fair administration: to create possibilities for review of decisions; for assistance in complying with administrative procedures; and for forms to be simplified and in a language understood by the urban poor; may over time bring about a fairer administrative process and will provide handles for those who want to assist the urban poor to achieve justice. I recognise that at the end of the day, incrementalism in reform as a way of creating a fairer and more efficiently managed urban development process depends, no less than does radical reform, on a receptive government or ruling elite; absent that and any proposals for reform will fall on deaf ears, or if accepted for public relations reasons, will be largely nullified in practice.

Acceptability and implementability: a balanced law

In one sense this is an elaboration of the principles of simplicity and manageability discussed above. Leaving aside questions of political philosophy, any legal input will be acceptable to government and administration to the extent that it is easy to understand and implement. But this conclusion goes further than that in two directions. First – and law has to be balanced between the regulative and facilitative – between what is sometimes called reactive and proactive. Too often, laws regulating urban development are open to the criticism that they are essentially negative; they prevent development rather than encourage it. It is important for the general societal acceptance of such laws that, while they might control some developments, they facilitate and encourage others.

It is easier to conceptualise and draft controlling devices than facilitating devices, and easier too for bureaucrats to administer negative controls than positive assistance, but the effort to undertake the latter must be made. A few pointers may be given. Not all development needs to be controlled; as much as possible should be free of planning controls though still subject to minimal building regulation in the interests of public health and safety. Simplified systems of regulation, including land registration, may be applied to certain categories of development. Standard plans for low-cost residential development may be made available. Rather than spending money on accommodation out of the financial reach of the urban majority or on large bureaucracies to administer controls, small revolving loan funds could be made available for low cost housing and commercial development, and co-operatives encouraged to manage such funds. An important suggestion made by the Indian Task Force on urban planning may also be mentioned here: rather than large-scale programmes of compulsory land acquisition which take time and cause great resentment, more effort should be put into land readjustment and land pooling programmes to make more effective use of badly or under-used urban land while not depriving anyone of all their lands. I would suggest too that a more participative legal system – a greater involvement of local authorities, customary authorities where relevant, and people in the areas subject to large-scale redevelopment – is also likely to ensure that the needs of potential developers – large, small, public and private – will be properly considered and taken account of (Salmon 1987). The question which always needs to be asked is: is this proposal or law or regulatory measure going to impede or assist development; if it is going to impede, will it be impeding development which it is desirable to prevent or not; if it is to assist development, is it development of a kind that should be assisted to take place, and does it need the kind of assistance that is being provided for it?

The second aspect of acceptability concerns public education. The legal regulation of the development process is often presented as a restrictive, negative matter. If a government decision has been taken to have a legal regulatory framework for the development process, then that decision and its implementation needs to be explained to the public or different groups of the public in a manner apt for that particular group. Thus a manual for development outlining legal requirements and administrative practices could be produced for the formal large-scale construction and development industry; this is already the case in Singapore and Jamaica to name but two; Cayman Islands (West Indies) has something similar but rather simpler. For the more informal small-scale construction sector, simpler leaflets and guides would be sufficient. In many public or adult educational programmes the positive benefits of regulation should be stressed with emphasis laid on officials' willingness to assist persons to comply with the law. Too often the regulatory system, besides being negative, is utterly unknown to the vast majority of people until some high-handed action is taken – such as demolition of squatter settlements – or some allegedly beneficial programme is announced – such as upgrading of squatter settlements – which will have far-reaching effects on the lives of the recipients of the action. It is hardly surprising in the circumstances that a common reaction to regulation is one of hostility. There always will be a barrier to overcome in terms of the general acceptability of regulation but the barrier is made unnecessarily high by too negative and too secretive an approach to regulation. If it is to be, let it be balanced and open, so that in time it will become more acceptable and more implementable. In the final analysis implementation can be carried out only with the support of both the bureaucracy and the people at large.

I am only too conscious that some of these bench-marks – perhaps all of them – may seem naïve and divorced from reality. Reality, it will be urged, is too often corrupt and incompetent, with understaffed bureaucracies responding to venal politicians or authoritarian military, who are more intent on preserving a status quo which allows them to grow wealthy at the expense of the majority of the population than set on creating an equitable, open and fair process of urban development. Any argument which stresses the need to take account of existing governmental structures and philosophy and bases proposals for change on incrementalism will merely finish up reinforcing the status quo and giving 'reform' a bad name.

I believe that such a picture of reality is a caricature. It would be idle to deny the presence of venality, incompetence, authoritarianism or worse in many parts of the Third World; it would be equally idle to deny that such regimes are often propped up by western support, and are often opposed by many of their own people. Equally, one can point to regimes which are struggling and have over a long period struggled to bring about a juster society, despite internal and external opposition. It seems to me to be a perfectly proper position to adopt, in putting forward a broad range of ideas on the nature of a possible legal input in the urban development process, that one should try and lend strength and support to those elements within all societies which are likely to be receptive to ideas about equity, openness, fairness and efficiency. Such elements are more likely to be receptive if invited to build reforms on the basis of the better aspects of existing institutions than on throwing them away and starting again. I accept that these ideas are not likely to appeal to the venal, the incompetent or the authoritarian, and may be dismissed by the cynical and conservative administrator or consultant, but my experience is that in every bureaucracy and in every government there are persons of vision, energy, and ideals who will reach out for new ideas and approaches that might help bring about a more responsive and efficient machinery of government and the better delivery of programmes to all sectors of society. It is to these persons that the ideas in this chapter, none of them particularly revolutionary, are addressed.

A final point must be made: at the end of the day, the regulation of the urban development process is going to reflect and support a government's wider economic and social policies and strategies, and any legal input into that regulation and development process will likewise be designed to advance or at least not impede, those wider policies. An awareness of this basic and inescapable fact of politics should assist any discussion of or proposal for any legal input; it will prevent too great a reliance being placed on law alone as a mechanism to bring about fundamental change in the urban development process. It will direct attention to the need to take full account of the political and societal context of that process and any possible changes to it, and of the fact that law is only one of the mechanisms which are available for use in the management and regulation of the process of urban development. Anyone involved in proposing reform of, or a more or less effective legal input into, the urban development process is then steering between Scylla and Charybdis – between the need to take account of existing political and societal realities and the desirability of proposing principled changes or reforms which would have as their objective bringing about changes in the existing political and societal realities. It is to aid that difficult navigational exercise that this chapter has been directed.

Notes

1. See Ola (1986) and Gihring (1976).
2. Kikuyu Development Plan PPAL (Tanzania Government 1977).
3. For example, *Olga Tellis* v *Bombay MC. AIR* (1986) SC180.
4. This was the pattern in the early years of the master plan. The services of the master planners were dispensed with by the beginning of 1981.

5. See Stevens (1955).
6. The proposals survived two abrupt changes to regime and were ultimately enacted into law as the first piece of legislation passed by the Parliament elected in 1980: Reconstruction and Development Corporation Act 1981.
7. In Calcutta I was informed that 'we in India have followed your planning laws mistake by mistake'.
8. (1988) AC 45.
9. An eruption of toxic gas from a storage tank at a chemical plant owned by Union Carbide, an American multinational company in Bhopal, India in December 1984 which caused the deaths of 2,000 residents and injured thousands more.

CHAPTER 10

Conclusions: assessing the new approaches

Carole Rakodi and Nick Devas

At the end of the 1980s, the time seemed to be right for a review of experience with respect to the planning and management of rapidly growing cities. Many of the traditional tools of urban planning and management had been tried in recent decades by countries in Asia, Africa and Latin America and proved wanting. Much of this book is a review of that experience. In some places, new approaches have been initiated and different institutional arrangements developed. Sufficient expertise has now accumulated for us to assert that many of the problems and issues are better understood, our approach is less naïve and promising tools can be identified. We characterise the emerging understanding as a 'new realism' and this forms the starting-point for our attempt to outline the characteristics of approaches to urban planning and management which rapidly urbanising countries might further adopt and develop in the 1990s and beyond.

The book does not pretend to be a comprehensive review of experience throughout the developing world, although each of the contributors has worked in a number of countries. They have also been able to draw on the experience of the larger group of practitioners, academics and consultants from both developing and developed countries, as well as representatives of donor agencies, who participated in the 1989 workshop. Nor does it attempt to suggest a universally applicable blueprint for future urban planning and management. Indeed, one of the main themes of every contributor is that the experience of countries, and even cities, with their widely differing economic, social, political and physical histories and characteristics, will be different. Thus the outcome of similar attempts to intervene in the process of urban development will also vary and we must explain not only what the outcome has been but also why. Following on from this, it is clear that we must evolve institutional arrangements and procedures, policies and means of implementation which are appropriate to a particular economic, political, social, cultural and physical context.

In a single volume, it is impossible to consider systematically all those issues with which urban planners and managers are concerned. In par-

265

ticular, it was decided to adopt an approach in which aspects of urban planning and management were discussed on a system-wide basis rather than sectorally. Most of the issues discussed in this book refer to more than one sector of urban activity and this has been explored quite explicitly by some contributors.

In some cases, a particular sector has, historically, attracted considerable attention from policy-makers, practitioners and analysts. Housing, in particular, comes into this category, with numerous studies, such as Skinner and Rodell 1983; Davidson and Payne 1983; Swan *et al.* 1983; Payne 1984; van der Linden 1986; Ha 1987; Skinner 1987; Amis and Lloyd 1990; Raj and Nientied 1990; Mathey 1990; Shidlo 1990. There have been a number of recent collections which review the issues involved in planning for a range of services (Richards and Thomson 1985; Roth 1987; Rondinelli and Cheema 1988; UNCHS 1989d) and more in-depth treatments of particular infrastructure elements (eg Kalbermatten *et al.* 1982, on sanitation; Dimitriou with Banjo 1990, on transport) or particular services (eg Furedy and Gotoh 1989, on solid waste management, and Harpham *et al.* 1988 and Tabibzadeh *et al.* 1989 on community health).

In the case of other sectors, while some analyses of aspects of sectoral development or policy interventions exist, these are partial and our understanding of issues of planning and management for the sector on a city-wide basis is imperfect. This particularly applies to the urban economy, including manufacturing and services. For example, although a recent compilation of work on retailing is available (Findlay *et al.* 1990), this is not set within an overall understanding of the supply and distribution systems of commodities, especially food (Drakakis-Smith 1990). In addition it does not provide much guidance for practitioners.

We have been concerned, therefore, to explore various characteristics of the urban development process, notably land markets, politics and household strategies. We have examined institutional arrangements for planning and managing this process. We have also raised issues to be considered in attempting to intervene in development, including efficiency, political and economic equity, gender, the needs of the poor, and so on. Such considerations may influence the choice of interventions, help to identify obstacles to appropriate new approaches and suggest how such obstacles might be overcome.

Some issues have been raised in passing but have not received in-depth attention. Movement, accessibility and planning for transport is one of these issues. The complex relationships between land use and transport, and the role which planning at the national and local levels might have in influencing the way in which the transport needs of cities are met, have not been discussed in this volume, although the case study of Curitiba (Box 6.1, p. 159) is relevant in this context. Urban environmental problems have been mentioned by many contributors but the issue of environmental sustainability has not been systematically addressed. Although environmental issues will be discussed briefly in this chapter, a short section cannot do justice to such a major issue. One problem is that the available information is limited. Another is that most attempts to deal with environmental problems in cities have been *ad hoc* responses to crisis situations, such as grossly contaminated water supplies or dangerous levels of air pollution. Environmental awareness must pervade all decision-making. In this, of course, it is not unlike other matters, such as gender, which cannot be relegated to sectoral concerns but have not yet been integrated into planning and managing for urban development (Rakodi 1991b).

In this concluding chapter, we shall not attempt a summary of all that has gone before. Instead, a number of key themes will be addressed, some of which are relevant to the wider national development process and not just to planning and managing urban development. In many cases, we can offer no definitive guidelines as to how the issues drawn out can be tackled. However, with respect to some of the key aspects of managing urban development, it is possible to identify promising approaches which may present a way forward. The enabling role of international donors will be discussed in this context.

Key themes

Four key themes have been identified: the role of cities in national development, population growth and manageability, the need for realistic and effective planning and management, and the institutional and political framework for urban governance. The purpose of this section is to draw together threads of discussions in earlier chapters which have revealed the importance of these issues.

The role of cities in national development

The first key theme concerns the role of cities in national development. Opposing views of cities as parasitic or productive have been outlined in Chapter 1. The belief that cities exploit their rural hinterlands and aid the penetration of large-scale and foreign capital underlay the 'urban bias' hypothesis of Lipton (1977) and the anti-urban policies of a country such as Tanzania. The rural neglect, to which development policies aimed at economic growth via industrialisation gave rise in the 1950s and 1960s, rightly resulted in an attempt to redress the balance in terms of policy emphasis and public expenditure.

The need for a balance to be reached between policy priorities (agriculture and other economic sectors, urban and rural areas, economic and social objectives, growth and basic needs satisfaction) is, of course, still valid and a matter for continuing political and policy debate in every country. However, the relative success of countries which have industrialised has given rise to increased attention to reducing the economic, physical and other constraints on industrial development and to creating conditions conducive to investment in manufacturing. To date, most emphasis has been given to national economic and fiscal conditions, and less attention paid to the constraints on industrialisation posed by international conditions including world terms of trade, rich country protectionism and so on. Increasingly, the costs of failing to provide a suitable and consistent operating environment for manufacturing (and services) are being recognised and this is leading to a renewed recognition of the importance of providing and managing the urban services necessary both for production and for living (Peterson *et al.* 1991).

At the same time, recognition of the economic and employment significance of the small-scale sector is increasingly leading government and city administrations to realise that discriminating against informal sector activities is counter-productive. Instead, programmes to support and diversify such activities are hesitantly being adopted in city after city. Many of these activities are in the services sector rather than manufacturing and this has led some analysts to regard them, and indeed all investment in welfare and other services, as lower priority and less desirable than investment in production and services directly relevant to business. However, more recent analyses have demonstrated the directly and indirectly productive effects of investment in sectors such as housing, health, and education and training. While perhaps valuing investment in manufacturing more highly, there seems no reason to undervalue services jobs *per se*.

Cities have a crucial economic role, and planners and managers are important in helping to produce a set of economic and physical conditions in which economic activities of all types and scales can flourish. However, we must be careful not to equate cities with the economic and political relationships of which they are the spatial expression. Cities in themselves are neither parasitic nor productive. The relationships of economic enterprises with their suppliers, the consumers of their produce and the people who work for them may be exploitative or they may be 'fair'. Those with whom they carry out transactions may live in the city, in its hinterland, or elsewhere in the world. The terms on which those transactions occur depend on the relative bargaining power of the parties involved.

Marxists would hold that all capitalist enterprises, by definition, exploit their workforces and that the dependent relationships between Third World economies and those of the rich world are also exploitative. Neo-classical economists, whose analysis informs most current choices by developing countries, believe that ultimately, economic growth based on relatively unfettered market forces will increase the welfare of all. In the mean time, however, they recognise that market forces are not fully developed in developing countries, and that state intervention is often necessary for them to be sustained and to develop further. In addition, and to varying extents, they recognise that the market does not produce all the conditions necessary to sustain life, especially in cities; the state, therefore, has a role to play, particularly in the provision of infrastructure and services and in ensuring that some balance is reached between social costs and private benefits of urban enterprise.

The outcome of economic relationships between enterprises in the city and elsewhere, of bargains between firms and those they employ, and struggles over collective consumption, will depend on the relative power of actors in the economic and political relationships involved. The urban built environment is one of the outcomes. It reflects the relative power over time of the many actors involved and may influence the nature of economic, social and political relationships in its turn. In a situation in which the newfound enthusiasm among some for the positive economic role played by cities is contrasted with the profound pessimism of others, we must remember that existing economic and political power structures are not unchanging.

The scope for intervention to increase the potential for economic growth and to change the distribution of its costs and benefits varies from place to place and from time to time. Thus, as we shall argue later, the ability to identify and respond to such windows of opportunity is a desirable attribute of an urban management system. Gut feelings about the positive or negative role of cities are insufficient: more empirical analysis of the process of economic development, political power relationships, social conditions and factors influencing the production of the built environment is essential.

Population growth and manageability

Population projections are notoriously difficult to get right at the city level. Rates and patterns of rural–urban (and indeed urban–urban) migration may change over time in response to changing national economic circumstances, or to the improvement or deterioration of economic opportunities and living conditions in both urban and rural areas. In addition, boundaries often bear little relationship over time to the extent of the built-up area. However, aside from phenomena such as AIDS in Africa and the recent cholera epidemics in Latin America, the effects of which are hard to predict, we can be reasonably sure that urban populations will continue to grow at least at the rate of natural increase.

There may be some scope for diverting migration flows to smaller urban centres and secondary cities, but however successful rural development programmes are, cities will continue to grow. As the proportion of national population which lives in urban areas increases, cities mature, and countries approach the demographic transition, rates of population increase may slow. However, the increase in population of large cities will continue to be very significant in absolute terms.

Because of their economic functions and continued population growth, therefore, it is important to improve the planning and management of cities. But are they unmanageable? Experience to date in cities such as those portrayed in Chapter 1 – Jakarta, São Paulo and Dar es Salaam – might lead us to this pessimistic conclusion. Our belief is that the answer to that question depends on what we desire to manage and how. If the aim is to produce cities in which land uses are tidily arranged according to an optimal pattern determined ten or twenty years before, in which all households have access to a private car and in which all areas are developed legally and with a full range of physical infrastructure, including waterborne sanitation, then they are undoubtedly unmanageable. But the contributors to this book have argued that, for a variety of reasons, this set of aims is inappropriate. Thus we must redefine both the goals of urban planning and management and the tools it employs.

The main areas of government intervention were identified in Chapter 1 as: protection of the public, regulating private sector activities, providing public services, promoting economic development, and redistribution of income and wealth. Goals have to be arrived at for these areas of intervention. In defining the goals, a realistic appraisal of the capacity of the public sector is vital. We have attempted to steer a middle way between two opposing positions: on the one hand, the traditional beliefs of the blueprint planners that the public sector, by regulation, control and direct investment, can determine the future shape of cities; and on the other, the apparently blind faith in market forces which led to monetarist calls for rolling back the state by deregulation and privatisation in the 1980s. Instead, the task for the 1990s is to define appropriate roles, in particular local situations, for the market and the private sector; for the state, both national and local; and for the third sector, known variously as the non-governmental, voluntary or popular sector.

Effective urban planning and management

A recurring theme of this book has been the need for realism in relation to the task of planning and managing urban development. Realism about the scale of the task involved, so that the solutions developed match the scale of needs. Realism about the limited resources – financial, skilled personnel, management capacity – available to tackle these problems, so that the best possible use can be made of those resources. Realism about, and a better understanding of, the position of the urban poor and their survival strategies, so that the policies adopted do not (intentionally or unintentionally) disadvantage them further. Realism about the capacity of governments to intervene effectively within complex urban systems, about the capacity of institutions to deliver what is required, and about both the motives and the competence of the actors involved – politicians, planners, managers.

All this implies the need to adopt more appropriate and affordable standards, and to intervene more selectively. Over-ambitious attempts to control not only lead to frustration and failure but also encourage corruption, as people seek ways around the controls. The benefits, such as they are, of such misdirected intervention are likely to accrue only to the privileged.

Lest it might appear that this 'new realism' implies wholesale deregulation and the abandonment of any attempt to manage urban growth, it is important to restate the case for government intervention. The realistic reappraisal of the failures of master planning and state intervention should not be replaced with a wholly unrealistic view of what unfettered market forces and individual initiative can achieve. The state, whether at the national or local level still has a clear role in providing the appropriate framework for development and acting to counteract inefficiencies, inequities and environmental damage. But the interventions need to be more selective, more strategic and more realistic.

The potential roles of urban planning and management must be defined in this context. In Chapter 2 we portray it as a cycle of activities designed to make planning (looking ahead), policy formulation (decision-making) and management (implementation and operation) more effective. In the unpredictable, rapidly changing, messy and complex context which is urban reality, a single blueprint plan or set of policies is unlikely to be either desirable or feasible.

At the disposal of the institutions concerned with urban management are technical knowledge, resources and access to power. Our ability to manage future urban growth depends on how these are deployed. First, in some areas, we have a considerable stock of technical knowledge and can expand this stock by drawing on experience elsewhere. However, our information tends to be imperfect and incomplete. Even if the implications of actions are explored, outcomes are not wholly predictable. Better information, to be able to predict more accurately the consequences of alternative courses of action (or failure to act) is a crucial prerequisite for effective planning and management. This is a point to which we shall return.

Second, the institutions which are attempting to manage the urban development process have at their disposal a variety of resources, including staff, their skills and expertise, institutional capacity to carry out certain functions and financial resources. All these resources are likely to be in limited supply. Thus, realistic appraisal of resource levels and needs, deliberate strategies to increase resource availability, and informed choices with respect to the most efficient way of deploying scarce resources are the hallmarks of effective management.

Third, as noted in Chapter 1 and further explored by Richard Batley in Chapter 7, the interests of many actors are in tension. Planners and managers must realise that there is no such thing as 'the public interest', in the service of which they can employ their professional expertise. City planning and management is an inherently political activity, involving choices and conflicts at every stage. It is part of the task of officers to make the implications of alternative actions explicit. Although this cannot ensure that the most appropriate decisions are taken, they are unlikely to be appropriate without such clarification. In the choice of criteria by which to judge alternative actions and the selection and presentation of relevant information, urban managers are, by definition, playing a political role.

Criteria must also be defined by which to assess whether institutional arrangements, policies and techniques have achieved their aims; this requires that systems of monitoring and evaluation are also established. Related to this is the need for criteria by which to judge whether solutions which have apparently been successful elsewhere can be transferred to a different national or local context.

How, then, do we assess whether a city is being managed effectively? Objectives and criteria by which to judge performance need to be defined at several levels. An attempt to do this was made in Chapter 2, in which we suggested five broad groups of goals and some more specific criteria under each heading. We recognise that not all the goals and objectives are compatible, and that priorities have to be set and conflicts resolved. Furthermore, criteria such as efficiency and equity are difficult to operationalise for the purposes of evaluating policy choices and outcomes. Nevertheless, urban planners must seek to make the choices and criteria explicit wherever possible.

In addition to specifying performance criteria, we need to identify the conditions which are necessary for planning and management to be made more effective. We can, from the foregoing chapters, identify some prerequisites for improved management of urban development. Unless these underlying needs are satisfied, it is unlikely that the more specific and practical ways forward identified in the subsequent section will be feasible. Here, we will restrict our discussion to two general preconditions for more effective urban administration.

Credibility and legitimacy

It is vital that local administrative systems are credible in the eyes of central government and the political power structure and legitimate in the eyes of local residents. Urban planners and managers, therefore, need an explicit strategy to build confidence in the system, so that it will be granted greater autonomy of decision-making and revenue generation, and so that its decisions will be respected by actors in the urban development process. This is unlikely to be achieved by the inefficient, arbitrary and corrupt administration of regulatory systems, such as development control, which to developers represent a hindrance to legitimate economic activities and to the majority of residents represent part of the restrictive system which prevents them obtaining access to land for housing and income-generating activities. It is more likely to be achieved by a mix of action programmes which directly meet the needs of various urban groups, including politicians and residents; by services which are directly paid for and efficiently provided; and by improved communication by means of consultation and participation. Consultation, in particular, is a way of improving the information available to planners and managers.

Information

The ability to make appropriate decisions and effectively administer services depends, amongst other things, on the availability of information. Essential flows of information needed by planners and managers include:

1 monitoring of demographic, social and economic characteristics of urban residents, trends in the urban economy, land-use changes and physical development
2 monitoring of ongoing operations and programmes for the purposes of day-to-day management
3 evaluation of the outcomes and impact of policies, plans and programmes in order to provide both better knowledge of how the urban system operates and a guide to further decisions

4 consultation with residents to obtain their views on priorities and proposals.

Equally important, as we noted in the previous section, are flows of information to urban residents. These may include information on the purpose and operation of regulatory procedures, and information on proposals for developments or improvements. Clearly, the volume of information passing between actors in the urban development process could be extremely large. However, the generation, channelling and dissemination of this information has resource costs. Part of the management task is to decide how much information is necessary, which information is most valuable, how it is to be used and how it can most efficiently be collected.

Institutional and political framework for urban governance

There are certain parallels between the new realism referred to above and the current agenda for 'good governance'. Whilst the good governance agenda has, at times, been associated rather too closely with the ideological right, it does raise important issues for management in the public sector. The need for greater accountability of governments and government agencies, for opportunities for electoral choice, for transparency in decision-making processes, especially over the allocation of resources, for greater efficiency and effectiveness in the provision of public services, are all central to improved urban management, and have been touched on by many of the contributors to this book.

The institutional system for managing urban development is based on a set of laws which provide a framework for decision-making, action, regulation and operation. The political basis for decision-making may also be based on law, depending on the political system of the country concerned at a particular point in time. Although dictatorships do not need legal backing and cities may be run by the appointees of national leaders who themselves are not politically accountable, it is our contention that accountability in both the political and institutional system for urban management is essential if that management is to be responsive not only to the needs of ordinary residents, but also to the needs of investors.

This accountability may be achieved in part through the market, but must also rely on the political system. Thus a water supply undertaking may provide a more efficient and cost-effective service if it depends on user charges to recover its capital and operating costs and if service provision is directly related to payments made by consumers. However, a political input into decisions about pricing policy and cross-subsidies, and political backing for enforcement of charges, are essential.

This is not to say that a multi-functional local government system based on directly elected councillors is always the most appropriate solution. It may have a number of advantages over other systems, but, as Kenneth Davey and Jim Amos both note (Chapters 6 and 5), a variety of other institutional arrangements are possible and may be both more feasible and more effective in certain political, economic and social circumstances. The prerequisites for effectiveness are, first, a positive mandate backed politically over as long a time scale as possible, and second, a set of institutions with clearly defined tasks, responsibilities and powers, together with the resources needed to achieve their objectives.

While changes in priorities and particular approaches may be called for in order to achieve this, it should not be taken to imply that radically new institutional systems or laws are needed. In most cases the best approach is to start with what is there already, building on its strengths and ensuring that changes are compatible with ongoing structures and procedures. One reason for this, stressed by Patrick McAuslan (Chapter 9), is that national laws, especially those related to land, are embedded in cultural and social attitudes and traditional legal systems. Another is the almost always unrecognised opportunity costs of change, as existing procedures are disrupted and new systems and institutions take months or years to become fully operational.

We have so far in this chapter drawn out a number of key themes from earlier chapters and discussed these in general terms. Some of the principles and prerequisites of effective urban planning and management have been established. However, we are, in respect of some aspects of planning and management, able to go further in terms of pointing out promising approaches which might be taken up much more widely in the 1990s. Drawing on the contributions in this volume, the next section will explore some ways forward.

New approaches for the 1990s

Inevitably, the issues discussed by authors of earlier chapters in this book have overlapped. Generally, authors are in agreement, occasionally not, in part because situations in the different parts of the world of which they have knowledge vary so widely. In this section, headings have been chosen which roughly coincide with the main contributions, namely land, services, institutions, finance, clients, laws and environmental sustainability.

Land and its development

Land, according to McAuslan (1985: 13) '– its use, abuse, control and ownership – is the central problem of the city'. In Chapter 4 Michael Mattingly adopts an holistic approach to urban land markets and policy. His analysis deals with tenure and ownership, regulation of use and the revenue generation potential of land and property. We shall not attempt to summarise his convincing analysis of inappropriate policies based on mistaken assumptions and poorly implemented procedures. Instead, we shall concentrate on identifying priorities for land policy and the means for its implementation.

Improving access to housing land for the poor
The constraints on access to land experienced by the urban poor must be

Plate 35 Land readjustment can be a useful mechanism where there are multiple owners: this piece of land on the fringe of Bandung, Indonesia, is in multiple ownership and is scheduled for a pilot land readjustment project.

alleviated. However, constraints on access to land by high- and middle-income groups result in competition for that land which is being made available, either legally or illegally, for the poor. Therefore, as increasing commercialisation of land supplies reduces the amount of free or cheap land available for squatting or illegal subdivision, measures directed at low-income groups may need to be accompanied by action to relieve bottlenecks in the supply of land for higher-income users. Accelerated subdivision and servicing of peripheral sites is one strategy which is being increasingly advocated. Projects to supply land for house construction in large quantities at low prices are in their infancy and monitoring of experience in, for example, Pakistan and Indonesia, is vital (UNESCAP 1988). Baross's hypothesis that a sequence of planning–occupation–building–servicing might be a more appropriate sequence for public sector intervention, increasing supply and keeping costs down, needs further testing (Baross 1990).

Ensuring access to affordable land for public sector activities
Public–private partnerships may be used to solve problems of illegal tenure and the need for renewal in already built-up areas, to assemble land where appropriate for redevelopment, and to develop land on the urban periphery. However, they should be used cautiously until their overall effect on land markets and access to land by the poor are understood. The experience of land readjustment as a technique for servicing

275

peripheral land in fragmented ownership has been positive, mainly in East Asia. Already, careful assessments are available of the conditions in which land readjustment may be appropriate and the factors governing the transfer of this technique to other countries (Acharya 1987; Masser 1987). It is, in the right circumstances, capable of providing plots for high- and middle-income housing in the formal land market and land for infrastructure and social facilities. However, it does not benefit low-income people, unless the local authority is able to incorporate specific provisions to ensure that it does so.

A new conventional wisdom seems to be pervading international agency statements and practice to the effect that individual freehold tenure is the preferred option. Mattingly draws attention to the need for care in improving land tenure, lest this renders areas too attractive to higher-income buyers. Presumably individual freehold is felt to be desirable because it encourages maximum levels of investment in land, gives owners a stake in society, provides a location for shelter and economic activity, and does not result in the problems of neglect which tend to occur towards the end of leases. However, as with other commodities in a capitalist economic system, inequalities in ownership exist and tend to widen over time, as a result both of speculative and entrepreneurial activity and inheritance. It is likely that many urban residents will never be able to get a foot on the land and home ownership ladder: are they to be permanently disadvantaged as squatters or tenants while other residents benefit to a greater or lesser extent from the increasing value of their landholdings? There is a need to evaluate the advantages and disadvantages of individual freehold tenure and to explore in theory and practice alternative forms of tenure.

Ceilings on the holding of vacant urban land have not worked where these have been introduced.[1] Nevertheless, advocating greater access to land for low-income housebuilders in addition to free access to land to all other buyers with funds for purchase or investment fails to face up to problems of sprawl and of inequity between urban dwellers. Arguably, the purchase of land over and above the buyer's own needs is justified if investment is going to take place in residential, commercial or other buildings on that land. However, in no circumstances can speculation in undeveloped land be justified. Hoarding vacant land which is ripe for development in anticipation of further price increases is inefficient. In addition, obtaining excessive profits as land purchased at agricultural prices is urbanised, with the assistance of public sector investment in infrastructure, is undesirable. Mechanisms used to prevent the re-emergence of inequalities in rural landownership, such as those used in Taiwan, should be studied in order to assess their potential applicability in urban areas. However, where direct controls are inappropriate, fiscal measures can be explored. These will be discussed further below.

Constraints on the supply of land include the legal and procedural arrangements for subdivision, issue of title, registration and transfer. In addition, unnecessarily high planning standards with respect to reservation of land for access and public uses and minimum plot sizes exacerbate shortages. Large-scale land banking is no answer, subject as it is to administrative delays, corruption, the use of inappropriate standards, and the risks of squatting. As both Mattingly and Amos note, even small-scale land banking of sites for public facilities is becoming more difficult as pressure on urban land increases and prices rise. Increasingly in future, public sector agencies must have the willingness and capacity to enter into negotiations with private sector landowners and developers, in order to produce development packages which are of benefit to both. In addition, there will continue to be a need to preserve sites for public facilities and to be less profligate and more efficient in the use of publicly owned land.

Extracting revenue from land and improvements
A third priority for urban land policy is the need to generate revenue from the ownership and increased value of land, an issue also discussed by Devas in Box 6.2 (p. 170). Although site value or property taxation has the disadvantage of being highly visible and thus politically sensitive, it is likely to continue to be a major source of revenue for local authorities as long as central government keeps the proceeds of less sensitive, more lucrative and more buoyant taxes for itself. Thus attempts to increase the revenue-generating capacity and efficiency of collection of land and property taxes will be important. These rest on the technological requirements of an up-to-date set of cadastral maps, efficient systems for registering title, regular reassessment of property values and collection of taxes, and sufficient central and local political backing for revisions of tax rates and enforcement (Davey 1983; Dale and McLoughlin 1988; Kent 1988; Dillinger 1991).

Attempts to capture increases in land value through betterment taxation are fraught with difficulty, at least in the absence of a sophisticated capital gains tax. Periodic reassessment of property values, while essential to maintain the real value of property tax revenues, does not in itself capture the capital gains made by landowners as a result of infrastructure provision or changes in land use. Local authorities should, at the least, seek to recover the costs of new infrastructure from benefiting landowners wherever possible. There are a variety of ways of levying development charges or valorisation taxes to achieve this. In favourable circumstances, land readjustment schemes should permit the recovery of some of the increase in land values over and above the recouping of infrastructure costs.

Land taxes may, of course, be used for purposes other than revenue generation. They may be designed to prevent speculation, in the sense of frequent transactions in pieces of undeveloped land, as in the case of Malaysia's Property Gains Tax Act 1976 (R S Smith 1979). Alternatively, they may be intended to inhibit hoarding. Thus vacant land taxes, providing they are set at sufficiently high levels, may encourage owners of land ripe for development to build on it. Land taxes may also be intended to stabilise land prices and, if graduated, to discourage concentration of land holding. Further evaluations of these hoped for effects of land taxation are needed (see Cho and Kim 1989 on Korea).

Implementing physical development strategies

Taxes may also be one of the mechanisms used to achieve the fourth of Mattingly's land policy priorities, the implementation of physical development strategies. The use of public sector capital investment programmes to guide urban development and lever private sector participation is advocated by several contributors. Where cash flow problems or restrictions on borrowing limit this option, valorisation taxes designed to raise capital funds for infrastructure installation or improvement, as mentioned above, have potential for wider use, despite their complexity. Traditionally, public landownership and/or development control have been the mechanisms to which land-use planners have turned to implement their plans. Large-scale land banking is unrealistic in most situations, although judicious use of land in public ownership and further purchases of land, preferably at agricultural values, may be both desirable and possible.

Land-use controls are generally acknowledged as necessary, but severely criticised both for their ineffectiveness and, somewhat contradictorily, for the constraints they impose on the development process. However, these assertions are based on remarkably few attempts to assess past performance or to evaluate future roles for them. Thus confusion abounds.

Most discussions of controls have been written by planners with either a British or an American background (for example, Courtney 1978; Rivkin 1978; McCoubrey 1988). The systems with which they are familiar are based on certain assumptions with respect to the role of plans and the relationship between plans and development control. However, these assumptions tend to be taken for granted and then implicitly to inform their analyses of development control needs elsewhere.

We have tended to dismiss master plans as being rigid and inflexible. Nevertheless, they form the basis for zoning systems, in which proposed development which complies with an approved plan and its associated regulations is guaranteed approval. Such a system may provide a climate of certainty within which development can occur, and may reduce the scope for speculation and corruption once a land use plan has been approved. A system in which land-use allocations on a plan do not give automatic entitlement to development permission, and in which decision-makers have discretion in deciding whether or not to approve a proposal and what conditions to impose on it, is said to be more flexible and responsive to changing needs and circumstances. However, it is also harder to understand, provides more opportunities for influence to be brought to bear on planners and decision-makers, and gives greater scope for both arbitrary decisions and corruption.

What should the balance be between plans which are binding on subsequent development control decisions and those which allow an element of discretion? Regulations and institutions governing use, zoning, subdivision and construction can be combined or separate. What are the merits and demerits of alternative arrangements? What are the prerequisites for a development control system to be effective? Are simplified systems feasible for countries which lack the political will, public support and administrative capacity to develop fully fledged control mechanisms? Alternatively, should differentiated degrees and types of controls be applied to different types of area and use, as advocated by Patrick McAuslan? The assumptions on which systems are based and the advantages and disadvantages of different planning/development control systems need to be more systematically discussed.

Clearly, with respect to urban land, many questions remain unanswered. Mattingly calls for a better understanding of the land market in which planners intervene. A methodology for large-scale land market assessments has been evolved and used, for example, in Bangkok, where the results illustrate features of a virtually unregulated market (Dowall 1989; 1991). However, characteristics of land markets cannot be understood by the exclusive use of neo-classical land rent theory and its associated analytical methods. These need to be complemented by analyses which are oriented towards the political economy of land delivery, and which focus on the agents involved in the production process. Despite the methodological difficulties, this broad approach should focus on analyses of land market operations in terms of land prices, as well as the quantity and location of land supplied and demanded by various users; on the land development process; and on the role of cultural and other factors in shaping property relations (Fitzwilliam Memorandum 1991).

Even in Thailand, it is impossible to consider urban land and housing as a free market, and this is even more so almost everywhere else. The operation of land markets and government attempts at planning and regulation are inextricably interwoven. Thus, investigations of the morass of different land administration systems are also needed, devising appropriate criteria by which to assess their achievements and shortcomings. While the ultimate aim is to understand the results of public sector interventions in land market processes, we cannot expect these to be encapsulated in simple indicators.[2] Appropriate methods for such analyses, which take into account the needs of policy-makers, are still being developed.

The institutional framework for planning and service provision

Land, of course, is of little value in either use or monetary terms unless it is provided with services. Of immediate relevance here are physical infrastructure services, including roads, water supply, sanitation, power supply and refuse disposal. However, social services, which are of high priority to urban residents, and business services, which are important to economic enterprises, also have land implications, as well as resource needs. In Chapter 5, Jim Amos is concerned less with the technical operation of urban services than with the prerequisites for their efficient provision: good information as a basis for planning, sufficient financial resources, suitable co-ordinating mechanisms, appropriate standards, and institutional arrangements for installation or initiation, operation and maintenance. Decisions with respect to many of these involve trade-offs, which are explored by both Amos and Davey.

Plate 36   Infrastructure upgrading work carried out by the Hyderabad Urban
Community Development Project, India; improvements to
infrastructure have stimulated residents to improve the houses on
the left but not yet those on the right.

For example, decisions about appropriate institutional arrangements
must consider whether the balance of advantage lies with a set of single
service agencies or with a multipurpose agency, often local government.
The former are limited purpose and thus have clear objectives. They
provide services for which consumers may pay directly and in which the
quality of service provided can be directly related to cost recovery.
Multipurpose agencies, in principle, promise improved co-ordination,
but are more complex to manage.

A further issue, both at the national level and within conurbations, is
the question of appropriate degrees of centralisation and decentralisation. Allocation of responsibility for decision-making, operation and
maintenance must balance the relative advantages of each. Thus central
government can ensure the achievement of uniform standards of service
provision country-wide, by exercising its regulatory and redistributive
roles. However, decentralisation is needed to ensure flexibility of response to local needs and problems, so many decisions and operational
functions should be decentralised to the lowest level which is feasible.

Appropriate allocations of responsibilities between the public and the
private sector, as well as between public sector agencies and local residents and community organisations, can be decided only in particular
local contexts. Further evaluation of the advantages and disadvantages
of privatised service provision is needed. Many urban services are
natural monopolies, and delivery by a private sector monopoly is unlikely to be any more efficient than a public sector monopoly. In the case

of other services, notably public transport, increased competition is likely to be beneficial. Where private and public services are both on offer, however, the ability of the rich to buy private sector services may have an adverse impact on the quality of public sector services and the latter need to be safeguarded (Stren and White 1989).

Reliance on inputs from local communities has been demonstrated to have considerable potential, provided these inputs are appropriately handled. But there are limits, resulting either from the unwillingness of public sector agencies to relinquish decision-making power or from constraints on the time and energy of residents (Rakodi 1990). In this context, feedback on the recent experiments with community maintenance of services will be useful.

While Amos is concerned with the service-providing capacity of 'agencies' in general, Davey explores the particular role of municipal government. This much neglected set of institutions has received increased attention lately, at least by the international agencies, as part of their general awareness of the need for strengthening institutional capacity. An enhanced role for local government can improve the efficiency of investment through greater local knowledge and choice, improve the execution of policies and programmes because of greater local accountability and increase recovery of the costs of infrastructure provided. Local government is, in principle, well suited for certain tasks. Its sectoral, formal, permanent, hierarchical organisation is suitable for certain tasks of urban management: in particular, efficient service delivery, infrastructure provision and regulatory activities (Sivaramakrishnan and Green 1986). Its local nature makes it more aware of local conditions and responsive to local needs and crises. However, metropolitan areas also need a conurbation-wide capacity for planning, implementation of policies and large-scale capital programmes, and delivery of certain services. This may be achieved, as Davey shows (Chapter 6), by a variety of political and institutional arrangements.

Within the institutions concerned with urban development, an integrated approach to planning and management is required, and we have used the terms in tandem throughout this volume. However, if a distinction is to be drawn, urban planning is concerned primarily with anticipating and preparing for the future, and particularly with the spatial and land-use dimensions of urban development, while urban management is concerned with a wider range of interventions, especially the day-to-day operations of the services needed to support urban economic activities and daily life. It is by no means new to advocate more future-orientated planning by service delivery agencies or more action-orientated planning by land-use planning institutions. Thus it is possible to envisage the evolution of a traditional physical planning agency or department to enable it to fulfil this wider role, as has been observed, for example, in many British local authorities.

The first stage in such an evolution is for the traditional physical planning department to adopt a programming function, in which it collects together and makes available information on the plans and programmes of all the other agencies involved in the urban development process. While a useful service in itself, this does not necessarily result in integrated and synchronised development programmes. The planning authority should, therefore, move towards a more active co-ordinating role by developing its capacity to anticipate future problems and needs, and thus to influence the future investment programmes of related agencies. An ability to accurately predict changes and the outcomes of policy interventions based on improved information, is an important factor in increasing the credibility of planning (Mumtaz 1983).

The need to deal with anticipated requirements and problems may then lead the planning authority to move even further away from its traditional regulatory role to one of enabling and facilitating attempts by a variety of public and private sector actors to meet urban needs. Ultimately, it may initiate policy interventions on its own behalf. The organisational and political conditions which are necessary for such a transformation to occur, and the demands it places on the organisation concerned, have yet to be systematically investigated.

For any institution to operate effectively, it must have the necessary staff resources and create an environment in which staff can discharge their responsibilities efficiently. To attract and retain staff, conditions of service which provide for career advancement are necessary. Where deficiencies are apparent, training programmes will be needed, and, as part of the further development of institutional capacity, training needs must be identified on an institution-wide basis. A capacity for institutional learning is also crucial for effective operation. There is a need for appropriate information flows, vertically between management and employees and horizontally, for co-ordination purposes. Not only should attention be paid to the generation of information, however, but self-evaluation by employees and institutions should be encouraged and rewarded.

It is not possible, as Davey and other contributors emphasise, to advance a blueprint for an institutional framework for the management of urban development or for the allocation of responsibilities to particular agencies within that framework. It is, however, possible to identify certain features which characterise effective government of growing cities. These include:

1   clear responsibility for the main elements which affect the well-being of the urban population and the efficient functioning of the city: roads and public transport, preventive health care, water supply and sanitation, land-use and development control, and residential area development
2   clear responsibility for constructing, operating and maintaining infrastructure and services
3   a clear focus of executive authority and well-defined allocation of administrative responsibilities to the agencies and departments concerned
4   access to adequate resources to discharge those responsibilities, notably buoyant revenues (discussed below) and skilled staff
5   accountability both in overall political terms and in terms of the

design of procedures for carrying out the policy formulation and implementation tasks

6 responsiveness, which implies both accountability and room for manoeuvre; the latter requires a capacity for independent action and the exertion of leverage on relevant points in the governmental system.

Finance

A recurrent theme in every chapter in this book has been the need for greater financial resources and improved financial management. Attention must be paid not only to revenue generation, but also to planning and budgeting and to cost recovery. Recent research, practical innovations and publications mean that we now have access to better information on which to base policy recommendations, and clearer guidance on good practice, especially in Asia (Cheema 1989; National Institute of Urban Affairs 1989; Prantilla 1988; McMaster 1991).

There is a great variety of means of generating revenue for urban development. No single revenue source is without disadvantages and it is impossible to identify an optimal set of sources. More important is to establish criteria by which the performance of different sources can be assessed. Crucial considerations in respect of revenue sources are: their potential yield, taking account of collection costs; their buoyancy in relation to inflation, population growth and increasing economic activity; their incidence, taking account of equity and redistribution objectives; and their effects on economic incentives and relative prices. Some revenue sources have inherent characteristics which affect ease of assessment and collection, buoyancy, progressivity and economic neutrality, but these can also be strongly influenced by the design of the tax or pricing policy.

Locally collected revenue derives from a wide variety of sources of differing significance from city to city. Mattingly and Devas both point to the almost universal, although problematic, use of property tax, which has been discussed above. Entertainment and vehicle taxes, as well as taxes on selected utilities, are useful and easily collected sources of local revenue which fall mainly on the rich. Full cost recovery for services by means of user charges has been increasingly advocated in recent years. However, this is by no means easy to institute. Some services, such as street cleaning and fire and ambulance services, should be available to all without requiring individual payment. Others should be available to all, even those who cannot afford to pay their full costs, because of the benefits to the urban population as a whole, for example, preventive health care, piped water supply, and so on. These represent a basic environmental sanitation package. Difficult decisions about funding out of general revenues or through cross-subsidies then arise, as well as issues of waste where services are communal or where there is no price mechanism to ration consumption.

Several contributors stress the need for attention to be paid to both capital and recurrent funds. Devas (in Box 6.2, p. 174) notes that agencies need access to loan funds for capital investment and, because of the need to rank capital expenditures in order of priority, an integrating device such as a medium-term capital investment programme is necessary. Both central government and the private sector may provide loan funds for local government, subject to considerations of borrowing capacity.

Revenue for recurrent expenditure, likewise, may be channelled from central government by means of grants or tax shares. While grants tend to appeal to central government because of their extreme flexibility, they make it harder for local government to budget properly for precisely the same reason. More desirable is a share of a buoyant tax, such as income, sales or excise taxes, although these may be problematic to collect even at national level in countries with a large informal economy.

A share of the revenue generated from urban economic activities and urban residents should be devoted to meeting the needs of the urban areas, although it is difficult to estimate what such a share should be. Cities should be able to finance their own development from internally generated resources and should not pre-empt more than their fair share of national resources. While locally collected revenue is relatively easy to quantify, estimating a fair share of national resources presents accounting and political problems. In practice, therefore, given the competing demands for general revenue, local government's ability to ensure itself a regular allocation will depend, among other things, on its political status.

To accompany improved revenue generation, improved financial planning and resource management are required. These processes need to be integrated with the overall system of urban planning and management. As identified in Chapters 5 and 6, they might include:

1 improved budgeting based on realistic estimation of revenues, and the use of demand projections, appropriate standards and unit costs of providing for the recurrent costs of expanding basic services
2 regular revision of user charge tariffs
3 improved systems of revenue administration including effective enforcement action against defaulters
4 decentralisation of budget management to operational levels, where service branches are likely to be more responsive to local needs and problems and be able to deploy resources more effectively
5 a greater concern with the cost-effective provision of services and with 'value for money'
6 clearly defined and measurable performance targets to which service managers and revenue administrators can be held accountable
7 greater transparency of decision-making over the allocation of financial resources and about the use of subsidies, with clearer identification of the costs of benefits of particular services and activities.

Clients

So far, in this review of promising approaches with respect to land, finance and the institutional framework for planning and service provision, we have been examining urban planning and management very much from the point of view of the institutions concerned. We have noted that institutional operations take place in political contexts, that decisions on priorities are political decisions and that, in order to operate better, agencies must be aware of the views of urban residents. However, we have not been very explicit with respect to the nature of political processes and the characteristics of urban residents which influence the way in which they relate to planning and management agencies.

For Richard Batley (Chapter 7) the essential question is to what extent urban decision-making processes can change the status quo, and this is related in turn to the role of urban managers *vis-à-vis* the political process. The nature of the political process at a particular time and place determines which interests are heard and which are excluded, and thus will also determine whether the new approaches to urban planning and management advanced in this volume are politically feasible.

Administrative systems develop in response to particular productive, technological and social conditions and it is necessary to be wary of imported ideas and techniques for that reason. Batley argues that a particular form of urban administration, based on master planning, regulation and standardised service delivery, was developed in the west to sustain large-scale factory production and a workforce predominantly employed as wage labour in manufacturing and later in services. This, he suggests, is giving way to action oriented and more innovative and market-led approaches. Reasons for these changes include the need for regeneration of built environments which are not only obsolete because of economic change but also because of their age. They are possible because system-wide regulatory and service provision mechanisms are in place, widely accepted and generally satisfactory, thereby permitting more fine-grained and flexible approaches to be initiated.

A bottom-up, local and participatory approach to planning and management, while appropriate to certain economic and social conditions and for some purposes in developing countries, is not sufficient. Where city-wide infrastructure provision, services and regulatory systems are not yet in place, there is a need for these to be planned and introduced by appropriate types of administrative agencies. The urban managers who are attempting to introduce and run these services operate in an urban environment in which there are a variety of more and less powerful actors. They need to perform the difficult balancing act of obtaining the support of the former while not allowing their interests to take total precedence over those without a political voice. For an administrative system to achieve an appropriate balance between efficient performance of technical tasks and accountability is difficult. More often, as Batley points out, professional judgement is politically subverted or a bureaucracy develops which exists to perpetuate itself rather than to respond to client priorities. Moreover, the dividing line between attempts to respond to particular political voices on the one hand and clientelism and corruption on the other is often far from clear.

Much of Batley's discussion is concerned with who controls urban planning and management, through what formal and informal organisational arrangements. He is also concerned, however, as is Rakodi, with the question of how the urban administration affects the relatively powerless, affecting their access to services and regulating their activities. In theory, bureaucracies, because of their impersonality and standardised procedures and products, are capable of supplying basic services 'as of right'. They could, if extended to incorporate the poor within their remit, be a great improvement on unregulated and clientelistic forms of supply. In practice, the conditions necessary for bureaucracies to function according to the formal rules are often not present. In the face of unresponsive, limited capacity and incomprehensible bureaucracies, clients are forced to appeal to the patronage of politicians and officials.

One result of the lack of access by powerless groups to formal consultative procedures via a party political system, or the possible distortion of their views in a clientelistic political situation, is that planners may have little understanding of how poor people gain a livelihood in the city. Similarly, planners typically have little understanding of the impact which institutional actions and procedures may have on the life chances of the poor. Physical and national economic planners, as well as middle- and upper-class urban residents and politicians, tend to have only a limited understanding of the coping strategies of low-income households, and the needs of small and micro-enterprises. Thus there is typically little empathy with poor people's experience of the formal service provision, planning and regulatory procedures which do not meet their needs and may make it more rather than less difficult for them to survive.

The neglect and discrimination which all poor people experience, is exacerbated for women, who have even less of a political voice than men. In addition, their means of livelihood and attempts to secure the well-being of their families are even less understood than those of men and run a greater risk of being jeopardised by inadequate and inappropriate management policies and procedures.

Other contributors to this volume have concentrated on ways in which the operation of institutions and administrative agencies can be improved, generally including greater accountability as a principle. Batley and Rakodi (Chapters 7 and 8) explore ways of making those institutions more client responsive. Administrative reform may improve the output of service providing agencies without necessarily making them more responsive. Political reform is essential for a less regulatory and more enabling, negotiated and participatory form of planning to occur.

One shape that this reform may take is devolution of real decision-making power to local government and not mere deconcentration of administrative functions. A second type of reform is to provide scope for greater participation by local residents. The term 'participation' has encompassed a variety of approaches, a variety of understandings of what is meant by participation and a variety of outcomes. Considerable experience of community self-help and participatory projects has now been documented and it is important for planners to learn from this in order to assess realistically the scope for involving residents and to ensure that the intended mechanisms are appropriate.

Plate 37   Low-income core housing in the Freedom to Build project on the outskirts of Manila, showing the flexibility to extend the core to suit households' needs.

Many of these do not in any sense increase the rights of residents, especially the poor, to have a say in decision-making. Even where participation has involved empowerment, naïve or cynical views of 'the community' as a homogeneous group, with all members having an equal say or benefiting equally, may result in further exclusion and control of the weak. More pragmatically, the constraints on participation imposed by inappropriate public sector procedures and attitudes, community characteristics, or the limited time and energy available to urban residents, are often unrecognised.

An enabling, participatory approach assumes the existence of effective providers of services, a relationship of trust and accountability between politicians and officials, and a willingness on the part of the powerful to share power. These are precisely what cannot be assumed, but they may be worked towards, more rapidly in some political circumstances than others. Planners and managers can help to create these conditions by administrative improvements, building up their negotiating capacity and broadening access to the fora in which decisions are taken on priorities for resource allocation. They can increase their understanding of urban residents' needs and make services more accessible. Neighbourhood offices and close working relationships with those officials, who, as service providers come into daily contact with urban residents can, for example, increase the physical and social proximity between residents and officials.

Efforts by planners and managers must be complemented by efforts by residents to make their views known. Their hand may be strengthened if alliances can be forged, for example, between lower- and middle-income residents, or if non-governmental organisations can play a role as intermediaries. A community-based participatory approach thus implies that communities must organise themselves in ways which facilitate working relationships with public sector agencies. The conditions in which this can occur are not always present, but the process of community organisation and involvement can be encouraged and facilitated.

NGOs have a role to play in expressing community needs, fostering community organisation, in acting as catalysts for action and change and, as suggested above, in acting as intermediaries. They may, in certain circumstances, become involved in direct service provision or project implementation instead of, or in addition to, the public sector. Some writers advocate a role for NGOs as a third sector in society. However, our assessment of their potential must be realistic: a supportive public sector is still necessary for the successful functioning of community self-help projects and for the continuing operation of NGOs. Certain urban planning and management functions are most appropriately provided or regulated by the public sector. While the performance of this sector is often lamentable, alternative relatively untried organisations should be seen as complementary to the public sector rather than a substitute for it.

Laws

Laws, McAuslan stresses in Chapter 9, are not neutral, technical instruments for guiding and regulating the urban development process. They reflect political priorities and cultural values and these affect their outcomes. While recognising that laws may be regarded as unnecessary by the powerful and an obstacle to survival by the poor, they are needed to safeguard the rights of people against governments, and local societies against foreign insensitivity or interference. However, new or additional laws may not be needed. In many cases, existing laws are not being properly used. Where a proliferation of overlapping and contradictory laws is the problem, simplification and clarification is likely to be the solution. In no circumstances can planning laws be devised or amended without reference to linked areas of public law and policy, especially in relation to other aspects of land, and to the local situation. Imported models are rarely appropriate.

McAuslan does, however, suggest two exceptions. The first is the case of building regulations applicable to large multi-storey and/or international buildings, such as airports, major hotels, office blocks or factories where large-scale manufacture or processes using dangerous raw materials occur. The second are pollution control regulations applicable to toxic and hazardous processes and waste. In these cases, he argues for sets of model, internationally applicable regulations, if necessary modified to suit local conditions. These could be made binding on all international contractors and UN expertise could be made available to countries lacking sufficient resources to enforce such regulations.

However, because a legal input into the urban development process is a matter of politics and policy and not just technicalities, because it involves costs for some and benefits for others, it is not desirable to propose checklists for model legislation. Instead, McAuslan outlines principles which might guide changes in the legal framework for urban development. To summarise these principles, law should be equitable, flexible, participative and easily manageable, simple, efficient, administratively fair and environmentally conscious. There are, of course, conflicts between these principles, and any laws must represent a compromise. In addition, reforms need to build on existing systems, to be implemented incrementally, to achieve balance between the regulative and facilitative functions of laws, and to explain the purpose of laws and procedural requirements to all the actors concerned. While a clear and integrated legal framework for urban development is not sufficient to produce economically healthy and well-ordered cities, it is an essential requirement.

Environmental sustainability

Urban development must be environmentally conscious and the law should facilitate the integration of environmental considerations into development processes. But, just as not too great a reliance should be placed on law alone as a mechanism to bring about fundamental change in the urban development process, so environmental regulation is only part of what must be a more integrated approach to managing the natural resources on which urban development depends.

Cities depend on a variety of environmental resource systems, both within the built-up area and for a considerable distance beyond it. Urban development places demands on supply systems for food, water, energy, building materials and so on, and these lead to economic, social and physical changes in the areas in which these are produced, areas which become more extensive as cities grow. In some instances, the changes may be beneficial to populations in the producing areas, as when urban demand for food or other agricultural products results in increased rural incomes. In other cases, urban users compete with local users for the same resource, such as water, trees or land, for example, when agricultural areas are flooded for reservoir construction.

At the same time, the urban development process has long-lasting and complex impacts on the physical characteristics of natural resource systems:

> The material demands of the urban population are the cause of profound changes in the physical characteristics of the city and its surroundings. Modification of the natural flows of energy, water and materials goes hand in hand with the creation and maintenance of artificial flows of the same commodities. The character of the land surface changes, affecting the radiation balance, the rainfall-runoff relationship, sources and supplies of sediments and solutes,

infiltration and groundwater levels, soil chemistry and plant and animal habitats. (Douglas 1988: 220)

Urban activities generate wastes (solid, liquid and gaseous) which in turn affect the environment of the city and its surrounding area. Although public sector agencies attempt to operate waste disposal systems and emission controls, their resources are generally inadequate in relation to the need and their ability to enforce regulations is severely limited.

The flows of resources into the city and the use made of the environment within the built-up area together help to determine the living environment for urban residents. Here, our familiar criteria of efficiency, equity and sustainability are again relevant. Adequate and consistent flows of food, energy, water and so on, are necessary conditions for the efficient functioning of urban areas. Equitable access to the resources on which human life depends is rarely achieved. In practice, deficiencies in the supply and distribution of these resources, exposure to environmental hazards, and failure to provide safe and healthy living environments, are never evenly spread. Whole cities may be short of energy or water, while air and water pollution may affect all residents. Invariably, however, environmental costs are borne disproportionately by the poor.

Inequalities in ability to purchase food, energy, water and land lead to malnutrition, illegal construction of houses on marginal and often dangerous sites, and illegal tapping into electricity or water supplies. Alternatively, the poor may depend on cheaper but less efficient and dirtier fuels, costly water purchased from vendors, or polluted water from wells and streams. Often, the marginal land they occupy is liable to landslips or flooding, is near polluting activities, including factories and waste disposal sites, and is not provided with even a minimum level of services. Indeed, it may be land which has not been developed precisely because it is topographically unsuitable or difficult to service. In Quito, Ecuador, for example, the mountain slopes above the contour to which piped water can currently be pumped are occupied by increasing numbers of low-income people.

While the environmental base for whole cities may be deficient and unsustainable, therefore, the impacts tend to be uneven. Powerful residents may have sufficient political influence to ensure the enforcement of high standards and efficient service provision, or have the resources to provide their own. Meanwhile, industrialists can flout regulations dealing with working conditions and emissions of pollutants and wastes with impunity. The health and welfare impacts of an unsatisfactory urban environment tend to fall disproportionately, although not exclusively, on the poor (Hardoy and Satterthwaite 1989a).

Awareness of the natural resource requirements of cities is growing. Increasingly the adverse environmental impacts of current urban development patterns and processes are being documented, and experience is accumulating of various ways of tackling environmental problems.[3] However, none of these is yet adequate. While we are able to give some pointers as to the way forward, one of the priority tasks for the 1990s will be to incorporate environmental concerns into urban planning and management.

The natural resource requirements of urban development have widespread impacts and thus need to be dealt with at the national and regional as well as the local level. National policies with respect to agricultural development, industrialisation and energy, for example, must have regard to the needs of urban as well as rural areas. The immediate needs of cities for food, energy, water, building materials and waste disposal must be incorporated into regional development planning for the cities and their hinterlands.

For particular resources, and ultimately for whole cities, environmental audits are needed, dealing with demand, resource use, and disposal of waste products. For example, cities often waste large quantities of water in leakages from poorly maintained reticulation systems or illegal connections. Meanwhile, water supply investment is typically planned to match projected demand, with little or no attention paid to reducing leakages or conservation. Water-use conflicts arise from competition between sectors for the allocation of water, upstream–downstream linkages, the lack of co-ordinating mechanisms in planning water supplies and water quality deterioration. An audit of this resource would need to examine (UNCRD and East–West Center Environment and Policy Institute 1989):

1   how the development of a city has affected water use in the wider region
2   the projected water needs of different sectors
3   the trade-offs between quality and quantity and between investment in long- and short-term capacity
4   the organisational framework (including pricing policies)
5   cultural aspects, including perceptions of the value of water and established processes of conflict resolution
6   the hydrological consequences of urban development (Douglas 1988)
7   sources of pollution to water supplies and pollutants in waste water
8   disposal of waste water, including alternative methods of sanitation and their financial and resource costs
9   the potential of waste water (together with human and other waste) as a resource, by reuse and recycling.

Within cities, a co-ordinated set of policies for land allocation and development, infrastructure provision and services operation is needed, which takes into account the need for environmental sustainability as well as administrative and financial sustainability. This does not necessarily imply the need for new agencies. Instead, the emphasis should be to increase the environmental awareness of existing agencies and to ensure that environmental impacts and sustainability are incorporated as criteria against which all policies can be evaluated.

There is a need, as we have emphasised already, for positive and facilitating action as well as regulation. Rees (1988), reviewing the tools available to government, concluded that a combination of regulation, monitoring and persuasion is needed for pollution to be tackled success-

Plate 38   Public sector/informal sector interaction: informal sector garbage
pickers reclaiming materials for recycling on a municipal dump in
Philippines.

fully. Pollution control legislation is problematic to enforce because of
industrial resistance, lack of alternative fuels and lack of capacity to treat
waste or to instal adequate disposal systems.

In São Paulo State, controls on industrial pollution were introduced in
1985, together with a programme to enlist public support, and technical
and financial assistance for pollution monitoring and the introduction of
cleaner industrial processes (World Bank 1990a). These have now been
supplemented with attempts to reduce pollution from vehicle emissions. The latter include commitments to produce cars which emit fewer
pollutants and to develop a stable, cleaner lead-free fuel, in which alco-
hol is mixed with gasoline, for petrol engined cars. In addition, the
State's Environmental Secretariat has installed a city-wide air pollution
monitoring system, regulations to prohibit the use of private cars in the
city centre when emergency levels of pollution are reached, fines for
commercial vehicles using diesel fuel which fail to satisfy standards and
experimental use of methane from refuse disposal in State-owned trucks
(Wilheim 1990).

Measures to deal with pollution and other environmental issues need
to be underpinned both by scientific and technological knowledge and
by political support. With respect to the former, there is a possibility that
self-interest in the rich countries might encourage greater transfer of
technology on clean industrial processes, waste disposal and so on, to
developing countries. Experience with methods for assessing the implications of proposed development, such as Environmental Impact

Assessment, should be disseminated, although perhaps with less emphasis on visual aspects than is typical in western countries and more on socio-economic impacts. Further research and exchange of scientific knowledge between southern countries is necessary. In addition, evaluations are needed of the outcome of attempts to solve particular environmental problems, such as those in São Paulo, and of attempts to incorporate environmental issues into urban planning and management.

Because the upper- and middle-income groups also suffer from poor water quality, traffic congestion and pollution, this political lobby is likely to become increasingly important, as it has in the west. Such political pressures may force public agencies to tackle certain environmental problems. That is not to say that these will be the environmental problems of greatest concern to the poor. Although a shift of investment from private to public transport and improved enforcement of pollution and waste control regulations will benefit the poor, more direct action is needed to tackle the problems of their inadequate living environment. Here, however, we know what is needed to produce healthier conditions. The technology of basic services provision is relatively straightforward, although further dissemination of appropriate technologies is necessary. In addition, there is now considerable accumulated experience, as we have discussed in the book, of installing and operating appropriate infrastructure and services and of ways of working with low income communities. What is required is to put these into practice.

Agenda for donors

In developing and adopting some of the new approaches to urban planning and management which we have discussed in this book, the key actors are, of course, the politicians, planners, managers, enterprises and residents of rapidly growing cities themselves. The resources which multilateral or bilateral donors have devoted to urban development in the past or are likely to make available in the future are a very small proportion of the total resources needed. Nevertheless, such donors have a potentially catalytic role because of their ability to fund experimental approaches, training programmes, research and policy evaluation, and dissemination of experiences. For this reason, we devote the final section of this chapter to exploring some of the issues for donors which have been raised by our discussion.

In this book we have advocated an integrated approach to management of the urban development process, in which physical planning is not divorced from resource planning, and operation and maintenance of infrastructure and services is not divorced from their installation or construction. Any integrated approach needs good co-ordinating mechanisms and appropriate arrangements for debating and making choices about priorities. We are realistic about the political and administrative obstacles to achieving such an integrated approach. In practice, even if co-ordination is good, institutional frameworks are likely to be complex, with responsibility for the many functions necessary for urban management divided up between a large number of agencies. Even if an overall statement of corporate policy and a guiding strategy for development are prepared, these will have to be expressed in terms of short and medium term programmes and projects to be undertaken by particular agencies, in order to be manageable. Thus there will still be scope for donor assistance to programmes and projects planned and implemented by one or a number of agencies.

However, experience in the 1970s and 1980s has shown that a project by project approach often fails to institutionalise sector or area-wide improvements in capacity (Rakodi 1991c). Project-based lending has a role to play, particularly in trying out new approaches, for example, pilot residential area development projects in which land, infrastructure, income generation and environmental issues are tackled in innovative ways.

In general, however, the perceived need is for the development of planning and management capacity. This implies the development of greater administrative and financial sustainability and thus the need for programmes of institutional support and development. The transfer of new technology, for example, in relation to the development of computerised information systems for planning, *management* and land administration, may form part of such programmes. However, as we have consistently stressed, the management of information is more important than technology in improving institutional operations. Donors should be wary of the 'technological fix' and of technical assistance resulting in the introduction of inappropriate techniques, laws and procedures imported from elsewhere.

The development of administrative capacity is a long-term process and thus greater continuity of donor input is required. Often, in the past, donor involvement has been short term, and schedules for project planning and implementation have been tied to the needs of aid agencies to fulfil disbursement targets rather than the needs of local institutions. The first stage of an institutional development programme might be a process of working with existing managers (and politicians where appropriate) to assess institutional support needs, with a guarantee that agreed needs would be met over a sufficiently long period.

Training, at all levels in the organisation, will often be the first priority. Such training programmes would include high-level workshops for managers and policy-makers; training associated with the introduction of new technology, new policy aims or new procedures; and training to consolidate and upgrade existing skills. There is scope for both in-house and on-the-job training and for externally based courses and exchanges of experience, especially at a mid-career level. Training can also be provided as part of long term technical assistance and consultancy, enabling ongoing support to be provided to trainees to improve their job performance. Consultants with expertise in the design and implementation of training courses will be needed. A vital training need which is rarely tackled is that of local politicians. Involvement of politicians from western countries, who have themselves experienced training, might be a way of creating a climate in which appropriate training is accepted as necessary by the men and women concerned.

In addition, the supply of equipment and development of a capacity to fully utilise and maintain that equipment may be appropriate, as may be technical advice on laws, regulations and procedures. Continued reliance on donor financial support for ongoing operations would be considered undesirable and assistance should be directed at developing sustainable revenue generation and cost recovery mechanisms.

We have referred in this chapter to the need for institutional learning. This may be achieved by establishing monitoring and evaluation systems and the management's willingness to learn from its own mistakes. However, recipient institutions are certainly not likely to undertake or reward self-evaluation unless donor agencies are also willing to admit their mistakes and to demonstrate the use of monitoring and evaluation procedures in their own operations.

In the past, donors' experience in a range of countries has sometimes been a liability, as solutions have been transferred wholesale from one context to another, often quite inappropriately. However, comparisons between the outcome and impact of interventions in different contexts can be valuable in assessing which policy components succeed or fail and why. For such learning to occur, in-house monitoring and evaluation as well as independent research are necessary. Donor agencies are in a good position to fund evaluations of similar programmes and projects in different contexts, and to disseminate the findings.

They would also gain in credibility by funding independent research, both policy evaluation studies and research into the nature of the urban development processes in which they seek to intervene. City-wide research is needed into, for example, land and housing markets, natural resource systems and environmental issues, political and institutional capacity, and the urban economy. In addition, more specific research is needed into the outcome of particular policies or projects; into the influence of specific actors, such as intermediaries in land and housing markets, on the urban development process; and into household strategies and how these are affected by urban policies.

Conclusion

Many of the topics which have been discussed in this book with respect to urban planning and management are, of course, not only relevant to urban areas. Indeed, this review of experience, and many of the new approaches we advocate bear a close resemblance to wider issues of 'good governance'. Many of the approaches to city planning and management which we have suggested should be experimented with, extended and replicated, incorporating elements of what is held to constitute good governance at every level.

However, we do not wish to fall into the trap of much current policy conditionality – that of imposing a new conventional wisdom on developing countries which, it soon becomes apparent, is no more appropriate than older imported solutions. To conclude, we reiterate the belief of all the contributors to this volume that, while principles for urban planning and management may be transferable, institutional, legal, technical and practical solutions must be based on a thorough appreciation of local political, social, economic and cultural contexts and how these are changing over time. Such knowledge, and thus the ultimate responsibility for the design of institutions, procedures and policies, rests with the politicians, officials and residents of each country and city.

Notes

1. South Korea's recent (1990) attempt to impose a ceiling of 660 sq m on residential land ownership in Seoul and a limit on real estate profits on specified projects should be monitored (Choe 1991).
2. A recent review of twenty-eight studies which have attempted to measure the effects of zoning regulations in the USA concludes that few definite conclusions could be reached, largely because of the lack of large data sets and methodological shortcomings (Pogodzinski and Sass 1991). Care must be taken that the World Bank's proposed research programme on the effects on land markets of development regulation does not fall into the trap of assuming complex relationships can be adequately summarised in a few indicators (Bertaud 1992).
3. Hardoy and Satterthwaite (1989b) document many of the environmental problems, and suggest actions at individual and household, neighbourhood, city and national levels to address environmental health issues (see also World Commission on Environment and Development 1987: chapter 9). UNCHS has long been concerned with environmental sanitation in relation to housing and residential areas and this is a more recent concern of the WHO (1987). UNCHS has recently turned its attention to energy issues (UNCHS 1984d; 1989e) and in 1987, together with UNEP, produced a set of guidelines for incorporating Environmental Planning and Management in Settlements Planning and Management at regional and metropolitan levels (UNEP and UNCHS 1987). USAID has incorporated environmental assessments of varying degrees of sophistication in its project appraisal requirements since the later 1970s (USAID 1989; Hyman 1990). As regards the World Bank, 'Until recently, environmental considerations received little attention in the World Bank's work plans and policy statements concerning urban development, and most of its internal attention was devoted to industrial pollution' (Hyman 1990: 204). However, protecting and upgrading the environment has been incorporated among the Bank's urban development priorities since 1989 and it is one of the components of the joint UNDP/ World Bank/UNCHS Urban Management Program.

Bibliography

Abrams C (1964) *Man's struggle for shelter in an urbanizing world*. Cambridge, Mass, MIT Press

Abrams C (1966) *Housing in the modern world*. London, Faber and Faber

Acharya B P (1987) The transferability of land pooling/readjustment techniques. *Habitat International* 12 (4): 103–17

Aguilar A G (1987) Urban planning in the 1980s in Mexico City. *Habitat International* 11 (3): 23–38

Ahmed N (1989) Managing urban growth in Karachi. Paper presented to the Workshop on Planning and Management of Urban Development in the 1990s, Birmingham, September 1989 and forthcoming in *Habitat International* 1992

Aina T A (1990) Petty landlords and poor tenants in a low-income settlement in Metropolitan Lagos, Nigeria. In: Amis P and Lloyd P (eds): 87–102

Altaban Ö and **Güvenç M** (1990) Urban planning in Ankara. *Cities* 7 (2): 149–58

Amis P (1984) Squatters or tenants: the commercialisation of unauthorised housing in Nairobi. *World Development* 12 (1): 87–96

Amis P (1989) African development and urban change: what policy makers need to know. *Development Policy Review* 7: 375–91

Amis P (1990) Introduction: key themes in contemporary African urbanisation. In: Amis P and Lloyd P (eds): 1–31

Amis P and **Lloyd P** (eds) (1990) *Housing Africa's urban poor*. Manchester, Manchester University Press

Amos F J C (1986) Plans, policies and pragmatism: a view of a century of physical planning. *Habitat International* 10 (4): 135–46

Amos F J C (1989a) Strengthening municipal government. *Cities* 6 (3): 202–8

Amos F J C (1989b) The relationship between urban planning and the management of urban services. Paper presented to the Workshop in Planning and Management of Urban Development in the 1990s, Birmingham, September 1989

Anderson M (1964) *The Federal bulldozer*. Cambridge, Mass, MIT Press

Angel S (1983a) Upgrading slum infrastructure: divergent objectives in search of a consensus. *Third World Planning Review*, 5 (1): 5–22

Angel S (1983b) Land tenure for the urban poor. In: Angel S *et al*. (eds): 110–42

Angel S and **Pornchokchai S** (1990) The informal land subdivision market in Bangkok. In: Baross, P and van der Linden, J (eds): 169–92

Angel S, Archer R, Tanphiphat S and **Wegelin E** (eds) (1983) *Land for housing the poor*. Singapore, Select Books

Angel S *et al*. (1987) *The land and housing markets of Bangkok: strategies for public sector participation*. Washington, DC: PADCO

Anker R and **Hein C** (eds) (1986) *Sex inequalities in urban unemployment in the Third World*. London, Macmillan

Annis S (1987) Can small-scale development be a large-scale policy? The case of Latin America. *World Development* 15, Supplement: 129–34

Appalraju J and **Safier M** (1976) Growth centre strategies in less developed countries. In: Gilbert A (ed) *Development planning and spatial Structures*. Chichester, John Wiley

Archer R W (1984) *Bibliography on urban land management*. Bangkok, Asian Institute of Technology, Human Settlements Division

Archer R W (1987) *Transferring the urban land pooling/readjustment technique to the developing countries of Asia*. Bangkok, Asian Institute of Technology, Human Settlements Division, Working Paper 24

Archer R W (1991) *Review of the PB Selayang land consolidation project in Medan, Indonesia*. Bangkok, Asian Institute of Technology, Human Settlements Division, Working Paper 37

Ariffin J (1984) Migration of women workers in Peninsular Malaysia: impact and implications. In: Fawcett J T, Khoo S E and Smith P C (eds): 213–26

Armstrong A (1987) Master plans for Dar es Salaam, Tanzania. *Habitat International* 11 (2): 133–45

Armstrong W and **McGee T G** (1985) *Theatres of accumulation: Studies in Asian and Latin American urbanization*. London and New York, Methuen

Arnstein S R (1969) A ladder of citizen participation. *Journal of the American Institute of Planners* 35

Ashe J (1985) *The PISCES II experiment: Local efforts in microenterprise development*. Washington, DC, US Agency for International Development

Auty R M (1990) The impact of heavy industry growth poles on South Korean spatial structure. *Geoforum* 21 (1): 23–4

Aylen J (1987) Privatisation in developing countries. *Lloyds Bank Review* Jan: 15–30

Bahl R W and **Linn J F** (1992) *Urban public finance in developing countries.* Oxford, Oxford University Press

Bailey F (1977) *Strategems and spoils: a social anthropology of politics.* Oxford, Basil Blackwell.

Bannerjee T K (1989) Issues in financial structure and management: the case of Calcutta metropolitan area. *Regional Development Dialogue* 10 (1): 61–70

Barnekov T, Boyle R and **Rich D** (1989) *Privatism and urban policy in Britain and the United States.* Oxford, Oxford University Press

Baross P (1983) The articulation of land supply for popular settlements in Third World cities. In: Angel S *et al.* (eds): 180–210

Baross P (1990) Sequencing land development: the price implications of legal and illegal settlement growth. In: Baross P and van der Linden J (eds): 57–82

Baross P (1991) *Action Planning*. Rotterdam, Institute for Housing and Urban Development Studies, Working Paper 2

Baross P and **van der Linden J** (eds) (1990) *The transformation of land supply systems in Third World cities*. Aldershot, Avebury

Batley R A (1971) An explanation of non-participation in planning. *Policy and Politics* 1 (2): 95–114

Batley R A (1981) *Empleo y necesidades basicas: acceso a servicios urbanos y contratos publicos*. Santiago, PREALC

Batley R A (1985) The allocation of public contracts in Lima and Caracas. In: Bromley R (ed) *Planning for small enterprises in Third World cities*. Oxford, Pergamon: 309–18

Batley R A (1989) London Docklands: an analysis of power relations between UDCs and local government. *Public Administration* 67 (2): 167–87

Batley R A (ed) (1990) Generating economic development in smaller towns in Gujarat, India. *Papers in the Administration of Development* 36, DAG, University of Birmingham

Batley R A and **Devas N** (1988) The management of urban development: current issues for aid donors. *Habitat International* 12 (3): 173–86

Batley R A and **Stoker G** (eds) (1991) *Local government in Europe, trends and developments.* London, Macmillan

Bendix R (1966) *Max Weber: an intellectual portrait.* London, Methuen University Paperbacks

Bengali K, Ghaus A and **Pasha H A** (1989) Issues in municipal finance and management: the case of Karachi. *Regional Development Dialogue* 10 (1): 81–110

Benson J K (1980) *Interorganisational networks and policy sectors: notes toward comparative analysis.* Columbia, Miss, University of Missouri

Berg E (1989) The Dutch experience: lessons for the UK. Conference on European Local Government, INLOGOV, University of Birmingham

Bertaud A (1992) The need for a methodology for evaluating the impact of land use regulations on land supply. *Regional Development Dialogue* 13 (1): 35–40

Bilsborrow R E, Oberai A S and **Standing G** (1984) *Migration surveys in low income countries.* London, Croom Helm

Blair T L (1985) *Strengthening urban management: international perspectives and issues.* New York, Plenum Press

Blore I C (ed) (1989) Making decentralisation work: a management performance study of four Municipalities in the Calcutta Metropolitan Area. *Papers in the Administration of Development* 33, DAG, University of Birmingham

Bolaffi G (1989) Urban planning in Brazil: past experience, current trends. Paper presented to the Workshop on Planning and Management of Urban Development in the 1990s, Birmingham, September 1989 and forthcoming in *Habitat International* 1992

Boleat M (1987) Housing finance institutions. In: Rodwin L (ed): 151–78

Bracken I (1981) *Urban planning methods: research and policy analysis.* London, Methuen

Brett E A (1988) Adjustment and the state: the problem of administrative reform. *IDS Bulletin* 19 (4): 4–11

Briggs A (1963) *Victorian cities.* London, Odhams

Brindley T, Rydin Y and **Stoker G** (1989) *Remaking planning: the politics of urban change in the Thatcher years.* London, Unwin Hyman

Bromley R (ed) (1984) *Planning for small enterprises in Third World cities.* Oxford, Pergamon

Bromley R and **Gerry C** (eds) (1979) *Casual work and poverty in Third World cities.* Chichester, John Wiley

Brooke R (1989) *Managing the enabling authority.* Harlow, Longman

Brown C V and **Jackson P M** (1986) *Public sector economics.* Oxford, Basil Blackwell

Brown J (1981) Case studies: India. In: Farbman M (ed) *The PISCES studies: assisting the smallest economic activities of the urban poor.* Washington, DC, USAID

Brown L R and **Jacobson J L** (1987) *The future of urbanization: facing the ecological and economic constraints.* Washington, DC, Worldwatch Institute, Worldwatch Paper 77

Bruce J (1989) Homes divided. *World Development* 17 (7): 979–91

Brydon L and **Chant S** (1989) *Women in the Third World: gender issues in rural and urban areas.* Aldershot, Edward Elgar

Bubba N and **Lamba D** (1991) Local government in Kenya. *Environment and Urbanisation* 3 (1): 37–59

Bujra J M (1986) 'Urging women to redouble their efforts . . .': class, gender and capitalist transformation in Africa. In: Robertson C and Berger I (eds) *Women and class in Africa.* New York, Africana Publishing Company

Burgess R (1978) Petty commodity production or dweller control? A critique of John Turner's view on housing policy. *World Development* 6 (9): 1,105–33

Burgess R (1985) Progress in the classification of low income neighbourhoods in Latin America. *Third World Planning Review* 7 (4): 287–306

Buvinić M (1983) Women's issues in Third World poverty: a policy analysis. In: Buvinić M, Lycette M A and McGregory W P (eds) *Women and poverty in the Third World,* Baltimore, Md, Johns Hopkins University Press: 14–31

Buvinić M (1986) Projects for women in the Third World: explaining their misbehaviour. *World Development* 14 (5): 653 64

Cadman D and **Payne G** (eds) (1990) *The living city: towards a sustainable future.* London, Routledge

Cairncross S, Hardoy J E and **Satterthwaite D** (1990) *The poor die young: housing and health in Third World cities.* London, Earthscan

Campbell J (1988) Tanzania and the World Bank's urban shelter project. *Review of African Political Economy* 42: 5–18

Carley M (1980) *Rational techniques in policy analysis.* London, Heinemann

Castells M (1977) *The urban question: a Marxist approach.* London, Edward Arnold

Chambers R (1989) Vulnerability, coping and policy. *IDS Bulletin* 20 (2): 1–7

Chant S (1987) Domestic labour, decision-making and dwelling construction: the experience of women in Queretaro, Mexico. In: Moser C O N and Peake L (eds): 33–54

Cheema G S (ed) (1984) *Managing urban development: services for the poor*. Nagoya, United Nations Centre for Regional Development

Cheema G S (ed) (1989) Financial structure and management of Asian metropolises: issues and responses *Regional Development Dialogue* 10 (1)

Chenery H, Ahluwalia M S, Bell C L G, Duloy J H and **Jolly R** (eds) (1974) *Redistribution with growth*. Oxford, Oxford University Press

Cherry G (1974) *The evolution of British town planning*. London, Leonard Hill

Cherry G (1988) *Cities and plans: the shaping of urban Britain in the nineteenth and twentieth centuries*. London, Edward Arnold

Cho Y H and **Kim Y S** (1989) Land tax policy to control urban land speculation in the Republic of Korea. In: Costa A K, Dutt A K, Ma L J C and Noble A G (eds) *Urbanization in Asia: spatial dimensions and policy issues*. Honolulu, University of Hawaii Press: 367–86

Choe S-C (1991) Seoul: still a metropolis in the making. *UNU Work in Progress* 13 (3): 8

Choguill C (1985) *Third world shelter policy: solutions and problems for housing the poor*. Sheffield University, Department of Town and Regional Planning TRP55

CIUL (Council for International Urban Liaison) (1979) *The Urban Edge*. Washington, DC, February

CIUL (Council for International Urban Liaison) (1982) *The Urban Edge*. Washington, DC, April

Clarke G (1985) Jakarta, Indonesia: planning to solve urban conflicts. In: Lea J P and Courtney J M (eds): 35–60

Clarke G (1989) New approaches to urban planning and management in the 1990s: the role of UNCHS. Paper presented to the Workshop on Planning and Management of Urban Development in the 1990s, Birmingham, September 1989

Coit K (1986) Community participation, self management and self help in Third World countries. *Cities* 3 (4): 321–32

Conyers D (1982) *Introduction to social planning in the Third World*. Chichester, John Wiley

Conyers D and **Kaul M** (1990) Strategic issues in development management: learning from successful experience, Part I. *Public Administration and Development* 10 (2): 127–40

Coquery M (1990) Autopromotion de l'habitat et modes de production du cadre bâti: l'apport de recherches récentes en Afrique Noire Francophone. In: Amis P and Lloyd P (eds): 55–70

Cornia G, Jolly R and **Stewart F** (1987) *Adjustment with a human face* Vols 1 and 2. Oxford, Oxford University Press

Courtney J M (1978) Intervention through urban land use regulations. In: Dunkerley, H B (ed) Vol 2: 127–49

Cousins W J (1978) Urban community development in Hyderabad. In: de Souza A (ed) *The Indian city*. New Delhi, Manohar

Cracknell B E and **J E Rendall** (1986) *Defining objectives and measuring performance in aid projects and programmes*. London, Overseas Development Administration, Evaluation Department

Cullen M and **Woolery S** (1982) *World Congress on Land Policy, 1980*. Lexington, Mass, D C Heath

Cullingworth J B (1973) *Problems of an urban society, Vol 2: The social content of planning*. Canada, George Allen and Unwin

Cullingworth J B (1988) *Town and country planning in Britain*. London, Unwin Hyman

Dale P F and **McLoughlin J D** (1988) *Land information management: an introduction with special reference to cadastral problems in Third World countries*. Oxford, Oxford University Press

Davey K (1983) *Financing regional government: international experience and its relevance to the Third World*. Chichester, John Wiley

Davey K J (1988) *Municipal Development Funds and intermediaries*. Washington, DC, World Bank

Davey K (1989a) Municipal government in Brazil: a case study. Birmingham, Institute of Local Government Studies. Mimeo

Davey K J (1989b) *Strengthening municipal government: the Turkish case*. Washington, DC, World Bank

Davidoff P and **Reiner T A** (1962) A choice theory of planning. *Journal of American Institute of Planners* 28 (May)

Davidson F and **Payne G** (1983) *Urban projects manual*. Liverpool, Liverpool University Press

Devas N (1980) KIP: a case study of Indonesia's Kampung Improvement Programme. *Papers in the Administration of Development* 10, DAG University of Birmingham

Devas N (1983) Financing urban land development for low income housing: an analysis with particular reference to Jakarta, Indonesia. *Third World Planning Review* 5 (3): 209–25

Devas N (1989a) New directions for urban planning and management: conclusions from an international workshop on urban planning and management in rapidly urbanising countries. *Papers in the Administration of Development* 34, DAG, University of Birmingham

Devas N (1989b) *Financing local government in Indonesia*. Athens, Ohio: Ohio University Press Monographs in International Studies

Devas N (1989c) The evolution of urban housing projects in Lesotho: the tale of five schemes. *Land Use Policy*, July: 203–16

Dillinger W (1991) *Urban property tax reform: guidelines and recommendations*. UNDP/World Bank/UNCHS Urban Management Program Tool No 1

Dimitriou H with **Banjo G** (eds) (1990) *Transport planning in Third World cities*. London, Routledge

DKI Jakarta (1979) *Jakarta Dalam Angka 1979*. Jakarta, Kantor Statistik DKI Jakarta

DKI Jakarta (1986) *Jakarta Dalam Angka 1986*. Jakarta, Kantor Statistik DKI Jakarta

Doebele W (ed) (1982) *Land readjustment: a different approach to financing urbanization*. Lexington, Mass, Lexington Books

Doebele W (1983) The provision of land for the urban poor: concepts, instruments and prospects. In: Angel S *et al*. (eds): 348–74

Doebele W (1987) Land policy. In: Rodwin L (ed): 116–32

Dos Santos T (1970) The structure of dependence. *American Economic Review* 60: 231–6

Douglas I (1988) The rain on the roof: a geography of the urban environment. In: Gregory D and Walford R (eds) *Horizons in geography*. London, Macmillan: 217–38

Douglass M (1989) Environmental sustainability of development: co-ordination, incentives and political will in land-use planning for the Jakarta Metropolis. *Third World Planning Review* 11 (2): 211–38

Dowall D E (1989) Bangkok: a profile of an efficiently performing housing market. *Urban Studies* 26 (3): 327–39

Dowall D (1991) *The land market assessment: a new tool for urban management*. A joint UNDP/World Bank/UNCHS Urban Management Program Publication (no place of publication given)

Drakakis-Smith D (1981) *Urbanisation, housing and the development process*. London, Croom Helm

Drakakis-Smith D (ed) (1986) *Urbanisation in the developing world*. London, Croom Helm

Drakakis-Smith D (1990) Food for thought or thought about food: urban food distribution systems in the Third World. In: Potter R B and Salau A T (eds): 100–20

Dror Y (1983) *Public policymaking reexamined*. New Brunswick, NJ, Transaction Books

Dror Y (1986) *Policymaking under adversity*. New Brunswick, NJ, Transaction Books

D'Souza J B (1987) Bombay 2001. *Times of India*, Bombay, 16 Feb

D'Souza J B (1989) Will Bombay have a plan? Are planners and their plans irrelevant? Paper presented to the International University of Workshop on Planning and Management of Urban Development in the 1990s, Birmingham, September 1989 and forthcoming in *Habitat International* 1992

Dunkerley H B (ed) (1978) *Urban land policy: issues and opportunities*. Washington, DC, World Bank, Staff WP 283

Durand-Lasserve A (1987) Land and housing in Third World cities: are public and private strategies contradictory? *Cities* 4 (4): 325–38

El-Shakhs S and **Obudho R** (1974) *Urbanization, national development and regional planning in Africa*. New York, Praeger

Elson D (1988) The impact of structural adjustment on women: concepts and issues. In Onimode B (ed) *The IMF, the World Bank and the African debt: the social and political impact*. London, Zed Press: 56–74

Evans P B, Rueschelmeyer D and **Skocpol T** (eds) (1985) *Bringing the state back in*. Cambridge, Cambridge University Press

Evers H D (1989) Urban poverty and labour supply strategies in Jakarta. In: Rodgers G (ed) *Urban poverty and the labour market*. Geneva, International Labour Office: 145–72

Evers H D and **Korff R** (1986) Subsistence production in Bangkok. *Development: Seeds of Change* 4: 50–5

Fagence M (1977) *Citizen participation in planning*. Oxford, Pergamon

Faludi A (ed) (1973) *A reader in planning theory*. Oxford, Pergamon

Fawcett J T, Khoo S E and **Smith P C** (eds) (1984) *Women in the cities of Asia: migration and urban adaptation*. Boulder, Colo, Westview

Feldman L D (ed) (1981) *Politics and government of urban Canada*. Toronto, Methuen

Findlay A M, Paddison R and **Dawson J A** (eds) (1990) *Retailing environments in developing countries*. London, Routledge

Finquelievich S (1987) Interactions of social actors in survival strategies. The case of the urban poor in Latin America. *IFDA Dossier* 59 (May/June): 19–30

Fitzwilliam Memorandum (1991) International Research Workshop: Land value changes and the impact of urban policy upon land valorization processes in developing countries. *International Journal of Urban and Regional Research*, 15 (4): 623–8

Folbre N (1986) Cleaning house: new perspectives on households and economic development. *Journal of Development Economics* 22: 5–40

Frank A G (1966) The development of underdevelopment. *Monthly Review* 18 (4)

Franklin G (1979) Physical planning in the Third World. *Third World Planning Review* 1 (1): 7–22

Friedmann J and **Wulff R** (1976) *The urban transition: comparative studies of newly industrializing societies.* London, Edward Arnold

Fuchs R J, Jones G W and **Pernia E M** (eds) (1987) *Urbanization and urban policies in Pacific Asia.* Boulder, Colo, Westview

Furedy C and **Gotoh S** (eds) (1989) Solid waste management for metropolitan development. *Regional Development Dialogue* 10 (3)

Garilão E D (1987) Indigenous NGOs as strategic institutions: managing the relationship with government and resource agencies. *World Development* 15, Supplement: 113–20

Gerry C and **Bromley R** (eds) (1977) *Casual work and poverty in Third World cities.* Chichester, John Wiley

Ghai Y P, Luckham R and **Synder F G** (1987) *The political economy of law: a Third World reader.* New Delhi, Oxford University Press

Gihring T A (1976) From elitism to accountability: towards a re-formation of Nigerian Town Planning Law. *Quarterly Journal of Administration* (Ife) X, 4

Gilbert A (ed) (1976) *Development planning and spatial structure.* Chichester, John Wiley

Gilbert A (1987) Latin America's urban poor: shanty dwellers or renters of rooms? *Cities*, 4 (1): 43–51

Gilbert A (1989) Rental housing in developing countries: report for UNCHS. Mimeo

Gilbert A (1990) The costs and benefits of illegality and irregularity in the supply of land. In: Baross P and van der Linden J (eds): 17–36

Gilbert A and **Gugler J** (eds) (1982) *Cities, poverty and development: urbanization in the Third World.* Oxford, Oxford University Press

Gilbert A and **Varley A** (1990) Renting a home in a Third World city: choice or constraint. *International Journal of Urban and Regional Research* 14 (1): 89–108

Gilbert A and **Ward P** (1982) Low-income housing and the state. In: Gilbert A (ed) *Urbanisation in contemporary Latin America.* Chichester, John Wiley: 79–128

Gilbert A and **Ward P** (1984a) Community action by the urban poor: democratic involvement, community self-help or a means of social control? *World Development* 12 (8): 769–82

Gilbert A and **Ward P** (1984b) Community participation in upgrading irregular settlements. *World Development* 12 (9): 913–22

Gilbert A and **Ward P** (1985) *Housing, the state and the poor.* Cambridge, Cambridge University Press

Gosling D (1979) Brasilia. *Third World Planning Review* 1 (1): 41–56

Government of Indonesia (1985) *National Urban Development Strategy Project: Final Report.* Jakarta, Department of Public Works

Green H (1975) Is urban administration different? *International Review of Administrative Sciences* XLI (4): 351 60

Green S (ed) (1978) Comparative studies of migrant adjustment in Asian Cities. *International Migration Review* 12: 66–116

Griffin K B and **Enos J L** (1970) *Planning development.* London, Addison-Wesley

Grindle M (ed) (1980) *Politics and policy implementation in the Third World.* Princeton, NJ, Princeton University Press

Grindle M S and **Thomas J W** (1991) *Public choices and policy change: the political economy of reform in developing countries.* Baltimore, Md, Johns Hopkins University Press

Grown C A and **Sebstad J** (1989) Introduction: toward a wider perspective on women's employment. *World Development* 17 (7): 937–52

Guarda C G (1989) Is land use planning of any use to Third World countries? Paper presented to the Workshop on Planning and Management of Urban Development in the 1990s, Birmingham, September 1989

Gugler J (ed) (1988) *The urbanization of the Third World.* Oxford, Oxford University Press

Gutman P (1986) Feeding the city: potential and limits of self-reliance. *Development: Seeds of Change* 4: 22–6

Ha S-K (ed) (1987) *Housing policy and practice in Asia.* London, Croom Helm

Hai A (1981) The Third World view: planning consultancy in the developing world. *Third World Planning Review* 3 (2): 133–40

Hall P (1982) *Urban and regional planning.* London, Routledge

Hardoy J E and **Satterthwaite D** (1981) *Shelter need and response.* Chichester, John Wiley

Hardoy J E and **Satterthwaite D** (eds) (1986a) *Small and intermediate urban*

centres: their role in regional and national development in the Third World. London, Hodder and Stoughton

Hardoy J E and **Satterthwaite D** (1986b) Urban change in the Third World: are recent trends a useful pointer to the urban future? *Habitat International* 10 (3): 33–52

Hardoy J E and **Satterthwaite D** (1989a) *Squatter citizen: life in the urban Third World*. London, Earthscan

Hardoy J E and **Satterthwaite D** (1989b) Environmental problems in Third World cities: a global issue ignored? London, International Institute for the Environment and Development for Conference on Cities the Mainspring of Economic Development in Developing Countries, Lille, 6–10 November

Harper M (1984) *Small business in the Third World: guidelines for action*. Chichester, Wiley

Harpham T, Lusty T and **Vaughan P** (1988) *In the shadow of the city: community health and the urban poor*. Oxford, Oxford University Press

Harris J R and **Todaro M P** (1968) Urban unemployment in East Africa: an economic analysis of policy alternatives. *East African Economic Review* 4: 17–36

Harris N (1983) Metropolitan planning in the developing countries: tasks for the 1980s. *Habitat International* 7 (3/4): 5–18

Harris N (1984) Some trends in the evolution of big cities: studies of the USA and India. *Habitat International* 8 (1): 7–28

Harris N (1989) Aid and urbanisation: an overview. *Cities* 6 (3): 174–85

Harris N (1990) *Urbanization, economic development and policy in developing countries*. London, Development Planning Unit Working Paper No 10

Harriss B (1987) Poverty in India: micro-level evidence. Paper for the Workshop on Poverty in India, Queen Elizabeth House, Oxford, October 1987

Harriss J (1989) Urban poverty and urban poverty alleviation. *Cities* 6 (3): 186–94

Hart K (1973) Informal income opportunities and urban employment in Ghana. *Journal of Modern African Studies* 11: 61–89

Hauck Walsh A M (1969) *The urban challenge to government: an international comparison of thirteen cities*. New York, Praeger

Hayuma A M (1983) The management and implementation of physical infrastructure in Dar es Salaam city. *Journal of Environmental Management* 16: 321–34

Herbert J D (1979) *Urban development in the Third World: policy guidelines*. New York, Praeger

Heyzer N (1981) *Women, subsistence and the informal sector: towards a framework of analysis.* Brighton, Institute of Development Studies, Discussion Paper 163

Higgott R A (1983) *Political development theory: the contemporary debate.* London, Croom Helm

Hildebrand M (1987) Overview of urban management policy. Nairobi, UNCHS. Mimeo

Hogwood B W and **Gunn L A** (1984) *Policy analysis for the real world.* Oxford, Oxford University Press

Holnsteiner M (1977) People power: community participation in the planning of human settlements. *Assignment Children* (UNICEF) 40

Hong S (1984) Urban migrant women in the Republic of Korea. In: Fawcett J T *et al.* (eds): 191–210

Hosaka M (ed) (1988) *Case studies on metropolitan fringe development with focus on informal land subdivision.* Summary of Proceedings of UNESCAP Regional Workshop on Metropolitan Fringe Land Development, June 1988. Bangkok, UNESCAP

Hosken F (1987) Women, urbanisation and shelter. *Development Forum* May: 8–9

Hourani A H and **Stern S M** (eds) (1970) *The Islamic city.* Oxford, Bruno Cassirer

Howard E (1898 republished 1946) *Tomorrow: a peaceful path to real reform.* London, Faber

Hurley D (1990) *Income generation schemes for the urban poor* Oxford, Oxfam Development Guidelines 4

Hyland B (1989) Urban management: an assessment. Paper presented to the Cities and People Conference, London, September 1989

Hyman E L (1990) An assessment of the World Bank and AID activities and procedures affecting urban environmental quality. *Project Analysis* 5 (4): 198–212

Iliffe J (1987) *The African poor: a history.* Cambridge, Cambridge University Press

ILO (International Labour Organisation) (1972) *Employment, incomes and equality: a strategy for increasing productive employment in Kenya.* Geneva, ILO.

IMF (International Monetary Fund) (1990) *Government Financial Statistics.* Washington, DC, IMF

INSTRAW (1987) *Decent shelter is a women's right.* Santo Domingo, United Nations International Research and Training Institute for the Advancement of Women

Jakobson L and **Prakash V** (eds) (1974) *Metropolitan growth: public policy for South and Southeast Asia*. New York, John Wiley

James R W (1987) *Nigerian Land Use Act: policy and principles*. Ife

Jones G W (ed) (1984) *Women in the urban and industrial workforce*. Canberra, Australian National University, Development Studies Centre Monograph 33

Kaitilla S (1987) The land delivery mechanism in Tanzania. *Habitat International* 11 (3): 53–9

Kalbermatten J M, De Anne S J and **Gunnerson C G** (1982) *Appropriate sanitation alternatives: a technical and economic appraisal*. Baltimore, Md, Johns Hopkins University Press

Kammeier H D and **Swan P J** (eds) (1984) *Equity with growth? Planning perspectives for small towns in developing countries*. Bangkok, Asian Institute of Technology

Kasfir M (1976) *The shrinking political arena: participation and ethnicity in African politics, with a case study of Uganda*. Berkeley, University of California Press London.

Keeble L (1964) *Principles and practice of town and country planning*. London, Estates Gazette

Kelley A C and **Williamson J** (1987) What drives city growth in the developing world? In: Tolley G S and Thomas V (eds): 32–46

Kent R B (1988) Property tax administration in developing countries. *Public Administration and Development* 8 (9): 99–113

Khoo S-E, Bruce J, Fawcett J T and **Smith P C** (1984) Women in Asian cities: policies, public services and research. In: Fawcett J T *et al.* (eds): 397–406

Killick T (1986) Twenty-five years in development: the rise and impending decline of market solutions. *Development Policy Review* 4 (2): 99–116

Killick T (1989) *A reaction too far: economic theory and the role of the state in developing countries*. London, Overseas Development Institute

Killick T (1990) *Problems and limitations of adjustment policies*. London, Overseas Development Institute, Working Paper 36

Kim D-H (1989) Financial structure and management: the case of Seoul Metropolitan Region. *Regional Development Dialogue* 10 (1): 145–72

Kim I-J, Hwang M-C and **Doebele W A** (1982) Land readjustment in South Korea. In: Doebele W A (ed): 127–74

King A D (1977) Exporting planning: the colonial and neo-colonial experience. *Urbanism Past and Present* 5 (Winter): 12–22

King A D (1990) *Urbanism, colonialism and the world economy*. London, Routledge

Kirkby R J R (1985) *Urbanisation in China: town and country in a developing economy, 1949–2000.* London, Croom Helm (Reprinted 1990)

Kirkby R J R (1990) *Urbanisation in China: town and country in a developing economy, 1949–2000.* London, Routledge (1st printing 1985)

Knight G (1989) Urban planning and management in Jamaica: past experiences, issues and outlook. Paper presented to the Workshop on Planning and Management of Urban Development in the 1990s, Birmingham, September 1989 and forthcoming in *Habitat International* 1992

Koenigsberger O (1964) Action planning. *Architectural Association Journal* 74 Feb. Reproduced in Mumtaz B (ed) 1982: 2–9

Koenigsberger O (1975) Planning legislation in developing countries. In: *Proceedings of the Town and Country Planning Summer School 1975*

Korten D C (1987) Third generation NGO strategies: a key to people-centered development? *World Development* 15, Supplement: 145–59

Kreuger A O (1974) The political economy of the rent-seeking society. *American Economic Review* 64 (3)

Kulaba S (1986) *Urban growth and the management of urban reform, finance, services and housing in Tanzania: revised final summary report.* Dar es Salaam, Ardhi Institute, Centre for Housing Studies

Kulaba S (1989) Local government and the management of urban services in Tanzania. In: Stren R and White R (eds): 203–45

Lado D (1990) Informal urban agriculture in Nairobi, Kenya. *Land Use Policy* 7 (3): 257–66.

Lal D (1985) *The poverty of development economics.* Cambridge, Mass, Harvard University Press

Lea J P and **Courtney J M** (1985) *Cities in conflict: studies in the planning and management of Asian cities.* Washington, DC, World Bank

Ledogar R J and **Lungu E** (1978) *A nutrition survey of 60 households in Chawama complex, Lusaka, April 1977.* Lusaka, American Friends Service Committee (draft)

Lee G B (1991) *Urban planning in Malaysia: history, assumptions and issues.* Petaling Jaya, Tempo Publishing

Lee G B and **Siew T T** (1991) Urban land policies: towards better management of Asian metropolises: the case of Penang, Malaysia. Paper presented to the First International Workshop on Urban Land Policies, Penang, Malaysia, February 1991

Lee H-Y (1989) Growth determinants in the core-periphery of Korea. *International Regional Science Review* 12 (2): 147–63

Lee M (1989) Urban planning in the developing world: a personal, tangential note. Paper presented to the Workshop on Planning and

Management of Urban Development in the 1990s, Birmingham, September 1989

Lee R C T (1982) Land policy as a tool of social and economic development. In: Cullen M and Woolery S (eds): 41–57

Lee-Smith D, Manundu M, Lamba D and **Gathuru P K** (1987) *Urban food production and the cooking fuel situation in urban Kenya.* Nairobi, Mazingira Institute

Lerner J (1991) Urban transport and urban growth. *UNU Work in Progress* 13 (3): 5

Lessinger J (1990) Work and modesty: the dilemma of women market traders in Madras. In: Dube L and Patriwala R (eds) *Structures and strategies: women, work and family.* New Delhi, Sage: 129–50

Lewis W A (1954) Economic development with unlimited supplies of labour. *Manchester School* 22 May

Lichfield N and **Darin-Drabkin H** (1980) *Land policy in urban planning.* London, Allen and Unwin

Lichfield N, Kettle P and **Whitbread M** (1975) *Evaluation in the planning process.* Oxford, Pergamon

Linn J B (1983) *Cities in the developing world: policies for their equitable and efficient growth.* New York, Oxford University Press

Lipton M (1977) *Why poor people stay poor: a study of urban bias in world development.* London, Temple Smith/Harvard University Press

Little J, Peake L and **Richardson P** (1988) Introduction: geography and gender in the urban environment. In: Little J, Peake L and Richardson P (eds) *Women in cities: gender and the urban environment.* London, Macmillan: 1–20

Lloyd P (1979) *Slums of hope? Shanty towns of the Third World.* Harmondsworth, Penguin

Lodden P (1991) The 'Free Local Government' experiment in Norway. In: Batley R and Stoker G (eds): 189–209

Lomnitz L (1971) Reciprocity of favors among the urban middle class of Chile. In: Dalton G (ed) *Studies of Economic Anthropology.* Washington, DC, American Anthropological Association Studies 7

Low N P (1991) *Planning, politics and the state: political foundations of planning thought.* London, Unwin Hyman

Lufadeju E O (1989) Protecting and enabling the urban poor: resources support approach to planning: the cases of Lagos and Nairobi. Paper presented to the Workshop on Planning and Management of Urban Development in the 1990s, Birmingham, September 1989

Lugard F D (1919) *Instructions to political officers on subjects chiefly political*

and administrative: memorandum No. XI–townships. London, Waterlow & Sons

Lusagga-Kironde J M (1989) The underutilisation of allocated land in developing neighbourhoods in Tanzania, with examples from Dar es Salaam. Unpublished paper, Centre for Housing Studies, Ardhi Institute, Dar es Salaam

Mabogunje A K (1989) New initiatives in urban planning and management in Nigeria. Paper presented to the Workshop on Planning and Management of Urban Development in the 1990s, Birmingham, September 1989 and forthcoming in *Habitat International* 1992

McAuslan P (1985) *Urban land and shelter for the poor.* London, Earthscan

McAuslan P (1989) Law in development: a review of experience. Paper presented to the Workshop on Planning and Management of Urban Development in the 1990s, Birmingham, September 1989

McCallum D and **Benjamin S** (1985) Low-income housing in the Third World: broadening the economic perspective. *Urban Studies* 22 (4): 277–88

McCoubrey H (1988) The English model of planning legislation. *Third World Planning Review* 10 (4): 371–88

MacGaffey J (1988) Evading male control: women in the second economy in Zaire. In: Stichter S B and Parpart J L (eds) *Patriarchy and class: African women in the home and the workforce.* Boulder, Colo, Westview: 161–76

McGranahan G (1991) *Environmental problems and the urban household in Third World countries.* Stockholm, Stockholm Environment Institute

McKee W (1981) Is there a future for planning? *Town and Country Planning Summer School Proceedings.* London, Royal Town Planning Institute

McKie R (1971) *Housing and the Whitehall bulldozer.* London, Institute of Economic Affairs, Hobart Paper 52

McLoughlin J B (1969) *Urban and regional planning: a systems approach.* London, Faber and Faber

McMaster J (1991) *Urban financial management: a training manual.* Washington DC, World Bank

McNeil D (1985) Planning with implementation in view. *Third World Planning Review* 7 (3): 203–18

Macon J and **Mañon J M** (1977) *Financing urban development through betterment levies: the Latin American experience.* New York, Praeger

Majedi-Ardekhani H (1990) unpublished text in support of PhD studies, Development Planning Unit, University College, London

313

Malaysia: Ministry of Housing and Local Government (1988) *Local financial equalization system* (seminar proceedings). Kuala Lumpur.

Marcusen L (1990) *Third world housing in social and spatial development: the case of Jakarta*. Aldershot, Avebury

Marulanda L and **Steinberg F** (1991) *Land management and guided land development in Jakarta*. Rotterdam, Institute for Housing and Urban Development Studies (IHS) Working Paper 1

Masser I (1987) Land readjustment: an overview. *Third World Planning Review* 9 (3): 205–210

Mathey K (ed) (1990) *Housing policies in socialist Third World countries*. Oxford, Mansell

Matthaeus H (1989) *Bhaktapur/Nepal integrated urban renewal and development, Review of 12 Years development cooperation*. Eschborn, GTZ

Mawhood P N (ed) (1983) *Local government in the Third World*. Chichester, John Wiley

May R (1989) *The urbanisation revolution*. New York, Plenum Press

Meier G M (ed) (1983) *Pricing policy for development management*. Baltimore, Md, Johns Hopkins University Press/Economic Development Institute of the World Bank

Meikle S (1989) Reflections on the performance of planning projects in Egypt and Iraq. Paper presented to the Workshop on Planning and Management of Urban Development in the 1990s, Birmingham, September 1989 and forthcoming in *Habitat International* 1992

Menezes B O (1985) Calcutta, India: conflict or consistency. In: Lea J P and Courtney J M (eds): 61–80

Michl S (1973) Urban squatter organisation as a national government tool: the case of Lima, Peru. *Latin American Urban Research* 3: 155–78

Mingione E (1983) Informalisation, restructuring and the survival strategies of the working class. *International Journal of Urban and Regional Research* 7 (3): 311–19

Ministry of Housing and Local Government (1970) *Development Plans: a manual on form and content*. London, HMSO

Mishan E J (1981) *Economic efficiency and social welfare*. London, George Allen and Unwin

Misra B (1986) Urban development policies in India: focus on land management. In: Nagamine H (Ed) *Urban development policies and programmes: focus on land management*. Nagoya: UN Centre for Regional Development

Mitra B C (1990) Land supply for low income housing in Delhi. In: Baross P and van der Linden J (eds): 193–223

Moser C O N (1977) *The informal sector or petty commodity production: autonomy or dependence in urban development?* London, Development Planning Unit

Moser C O N (1978) Informal sector or petty commodity production: dualism or dependency in urban development? *World Development* 6, (9/10): 1041–64

Moser C O N (1987a) Women, human settlements, and housing: a conceptual framework for analysis and policy-making. In: Moser C O N and Peake L (eds) *Women, human settlements, and housing.* London, Tavistock: 12–32

Moser C O N (1987b) Mobilisation is women's work: struggles for infrastructure in Guayaquil, Ecuador. In: Moser C O N and Peake L (eds): 166–94

Moser C O N (1989a) Community participation in urban projects in the Third World. *Progress in Planning* 32 (2): 71–133

Moser C O N (1989b) Gender planning in the Third World: meeting practical and strategic gender needs. *World Development* 17 (11): 1,799–826

Mosha A C (1988) Slum and squatter settlements in mainland Tanzania. In: Obudho R A and Mhlanga C C (eds) *Slum and squatter settlements in Sub-Saharan Africa.* New York, Praeger: 145–57

Mumtaz B (ed) (1982) *Readings in action planning.* London, Development Planning Unit

Mumtaz B (1983) Reaction planning. *Habitat International* 7 (5 6): 97–104

Musgrave R A and **Musgrave P B** (1984) *Public finance in theory and practice.* New York, McGraw-Hill

Namur M (1989) Faculdade de Arquitetura e Urbanismo, Universidade de São Paulo, private interview, London, August 1989

National Institute of Urban Affairs (1989) *Urban management in Asia.* Delhi, UNCHS/Economic Development Institute of the World Bank/National Institute of Urban Affairs

Nelson N (1977) How women and men get by: the sexual division of labour in the informal sector of a Nairobi squatter settlement. In: Gerry C and Bromley R (eds): 283–302

Nepal: Legislative Study Team (1987) *Strengthening town government finances in Nepal.* Bhaktapur: GTZ

Nientied P and **van der Linden J** (1988) The 'new' policy approach to housing: a review of the literature. *Public Administration and Development* 8 (2): 233–40

Niskanen W (1971) *Bureaucracy and representative government.* Chicago, Aldini-Atherton

315

Obudho R A and **El-Shakhs S** (1979) *The development of urban systems in Africa*. New York, Praeger

O'Connor A (1988) The rate of urbanisation in Tanzania in the 1970s. In: Hodd M (ed) *Tanzania after Nyerere*. London, Pinter: 136–42

Offe C (1976) Political authority and class structures. In: Connerton P (ed) *Critical Sociology*. Harmondsworth, Penguin

Ogawa N and **Suits D** (1985) An application of the Harris-Todaro Model to selected ASEAN countries. In: Hauser P M, Suits D and Ogawa N (eds) *Urbanization and migration in ASEAN development*. Tokyo, National Institute for Research Advancement

Ola C S (1986) *Town and country planning law in Nigeria*. Ibadan, Oxford University Press

Omotola J A (ed) (1982) *The Land Use Act*. Lagos

Onimode B (ed) (1988) *The IMF, the World Bank and the African debt*. London, Zed Books, Vols 1 and 2

Overseas Development Administration (1988) *Appraisal of projects in developing countries: a guide for economists*. London, HMSO.

Pacione M (ed) (1981) *Problems and planning in Third World cities*. London, Croom Helm

Page E C and **Goldsmith M J** (eds) (1987) *Central and local government relations*. London, Sage

Pasteur D (1979) *The management of squatter upgrading: a case study of organisation, procedures and participation*. Farnborough, Saxon House

Paul S (1987) Community participation in development projects: the World Bank experience. *World Bank Discussion Papers* 6, Washington, DC, World Bank

Payne G (ed) (1984) *Low income housing in the developing world*. Chichester, John Wiley

Payne G (1989) *Informal housing and land subdivision in Third World cities: a review of the literature*. Oxford, Centre for Development and Environmental Planning, Oxford Polytechnic

Payne G K and **Cadman D** (eds) (1990) *The living city: towards a sustainable future*. London, Routledge

Peattie L (1979) Housing policies in developing countries: two puzzles. *World Development* 7 (11/12): 1,017–22

Peil M (1977) *Consensus and conflict in African societies*. London, Longman

Peters T and **Waterman R H** (1982) *In search of excellence: lessons from America's best-run companies*. New York, Harper and Row

Peterson G E, Kingsley G T and **Telgarsky J P** (1991) *Urban economics and*

national development. Washington, DC, USAID Office of Housing and Urban Programs

Planning Advisory Group (1965) *The future of development plans*. London, HMSO

Pogodzinski J M and **Sass T R** (1991) Measuring the effects of municipal zoning regulations: a survey. *Urban Studies* 28 (4): 597–621

Poshyananda K (1987) *Issues and opportunities in local taxation: the case of Thai local authorities*. New Delhi, National Institute for Urban Affairs

Potter R B (1985) *Urbanisation and planning in the Third World*. Beckenham, Croom Helm

Potter R B and **Salau A T** (eds) (1990) *Cities and development in the Third World*. London, Mansell

Pouliquen L Y (1970) *Risk analysis in project appraisal*. Baltimore, Md, Johns Hopkins University Press/World Bank

Prakash V (1988) Financing urban services in developing countries. In: Rondinelli D and Cheema G S (eds): 59–88

Prantilla E B (ed) (1988) *Financing local and regional development in developing countries*. Nagoya, United Nations Centre for Regional Development

Quade E S and **Carter G M** (1989) *Analysis for public decisions*. New York, North Holland

Raj M and **Nientied P** (eds) (1990) *Housing and income in Third World urban development*. London, Aspect Publishing

Rakodi C (1988) Urban agriculture: research questions and Zambian evidence. *Journal of Modern African Studies* 26 (3): 494–515

Rakodi C (1990a) Self-help housing: the debate and examples. *Habitat International* 13 (4): 5–18

Rakodi C (1990b) Can Third World cities be managed? In: Cadman D and Payne G (eds) *The living city: towards a sustainable future*. London, Routledge: 111–124

Rakodi C (1990c) Urban development planning in Tanzania, Zambia and Zimbabwe in the late 1980s: a review and research agenda. *Review of Rural and Urban Planning in Southern and Eastern Africa* 1: 78–110

Rakodi C (1991a) Women's work or household strategies? *Environment and Urbanization* 3 (2): 39–45

Rakodi C (1991b) Cities and people: towards a gender-aware urban planning process? *Public Administration and Development* 11 (6): 541–60

Rakodi C (1991c) Developing institutional capacity for meeting the housing needs of the urban poor: a review of experience in Kenya, Tanzania and Zambia. *Cities* 8 (3): 228–43

Rakodi C and **Schlyter A** (1981) *Upgrading in Lusaka: participation and physical changes.* Gävle, National Swedish Institute for Building Research

Ramirez R, Fiori J, Harms H and **Mathey K** (1991) *The commodification of self-help housing and state intervention. Household experiences in the 'barrios' of Caracas.* London, Development Planning Unit Working Paper 26

Rees J (1988) Pollution control objectives and the regulatory framework. In: Turner R K (ed) *Sustainable environmental management: principles and practice*, London, Belhaven and Westview: 170–89

Renaud B (1981) *National urbanization policy for developing countries.* London, Oxford University Press

Renaud B (1987) Urban development policies in developing countries. In: Tolley G S and Thomas V (eds): 60–72

Richards P J and **Thomson A M** (eds) (1985) *Basic needs and the urban poor: the provision of communal services.* London, Croom Helm

Rivkin M D (1978) Some perspectives on land use regulations and control. In: Dunkerley H B (ed) Vol 2: 85–126

Roberts B (1978) *Cities of peasants: explorations in urban analysis.* London, Edward Arnold

Rocha S (1988) *Linhas de pobreza para as regiões metropolitanas na primeira decada de 80.* São Paulo, IPEA/INPES

Rodgers G (ed) (1989) *Urban poverty and the labour market: access to jobs and incomes in Asian and Latin American cities.* Geneva, International Labour Organisation

Rodwin L (ed) (1987) *Shelter, settlement and development.* Boston, Mass, Allen and Unwin

Rodwin L and **Sanyal B** (1987) Shelter, settlement and development: an overview. In: Rodwin L (ed): 3–31

Rondinelli D A (1983) *Secondary cities in developing countries: policies for diffusing urbanization.* Beverly Hills, Calif, Sage

Rondinelli D A and **Cheema G S** (eds) (1983) *Decentralization and development: policy implementation in developing countries.* Beverly Hills, Calif, Sage

Rondinelli D A and **Cheema G S** (1988) *Urban services in developing countries: public and private roles in urban development.* Basingstoke, Macmillan

Rosser C (1970) Action planning in Calcutta – the problem of community participation. In: Apthorpe R (ed) *People planning and development studies.* London, Frank Cass

Roth G (1987) *The private provision of public services in developing countries.* New York, Oxford University Press

Rowat D C (1980) *International handbook on local government reorganization.* Westport, Conn, Greenwood Press

Ruland J (ed) (1988) *Urban government and development in Asia – readings in subnational development.* München, Weltforum Verlag

Sachs I (1986) Work, food and energy in urban ecodevelopment. *Development: Seeds of Change* 4: 2–11

Safier M (1974) Habitat for development: an action planning approach. *Report of Royal Town Planning Summer School 1974:* 72–9 (reproduced in Mumtaz B (ed) 1982)

Safier M (1983) The passage to positive planning. *Habitat International* 7 (5–6): 105–16

Safier M (1989) The improving hand: evolving approaches to urban planning: an overview of key issues. Paper to the Workshop on Planning and Management of Urban Development in the 1990s, Birmingham, September 1989

Salmon L E (1987) *Listen to the people.* New York, Oxford University Press

Samol F (1989) A summary of GTZ experience and present policies and priorities. Paper presented to the Workshop on Planning and Management of Urban Development in the 1990s, Birmingham, September 1989

Sandbrook R (1982) *The politics of basic needs: urban aspects of assaulting poverty.* London, Heinemann

Sanyal B (1981) *Urban agriculture: a strategy for survival in Zambia.* Los Angeles, University of California, unpublished PhD dissertation

Sarin M (1973) *Planning perspectives and the urban poor.* London, Development Planning Unit

Sarin M (1978) *Urban planning in the Third World: conflicts and contradictions in Chandigarh.* Oxford, Alexandrine Press

Sarin M (1983) The rich, the poor and the land question. In: Angel S *et al.* (eds): 237–53

Saunders P (1979) *Urban politics: a sociological interpretation.* London, Hutchinson

Sazanami H (1984) Keynote address. In: Cheema G S (ed): 3–9

Schaffer B B (1969) The deadlock in development administration. In: Leys C (ed) *Politics and change in developing countries.* Cambridge, Cambridge University Press

Schaffer B B (1980) Insiders and outsiders: insiderness, incorporation and bureaucratic politics. *Development and Change* 11 (2): 187–210

Schlyter A (1988) *Women households and housing strategies: the case of George, Lusaka*. Gävle: National Swedish Institute for Building Research

Schneider B (1988) *The barefoot revolution*. London, Intermediate Technology Publications

Schramm G (1987) Managing urban/industrial wood fuel supply and demand in Africa. *Annals of Regional Science* 21 (3): 60–79

Scott A M (1979) Who are the self-employed? In: Bromley R and Gerry C (eds): 105–29

Segal E S (1979) Urban development planning in Dar es Salaam. In: Obudho R A and S El-Shakhs (eds): 258–71

Serageldin I and **El-Sadek S** (1982) *The Arab city: its character and Islamic cultural heritage*. Riyadh, Arab Urban Development Institute

Shankland Cox Partnership (1977) *Third World urban housing*. Watford, Building Research Establishment/Department of the Environment

Sharma U (1986) *Women's work, class and the urban household: a study of Shimla, North India*. London, Tavistock

Shidlo G (ed) (1990) *Housing policy in developing countries*. London, Routledge

Shoup D C (1978) Land taxation and government participation in urban land development. In: Dunkerley H B (ed) Vol 2: 1–84

Shrestha C B and **Malla U B** (1991) Nepal. In Asian Development Bank/ Economic Development Institute (eds) *The urban poor and basic infrastructure services in Asia and the Pacific, Vol II*. Jan 1991 Manila, Proceedings of a Regional Seminar

Shrestha N R (1988) A structural perspective on labour migration in underdeveloped countries. *Progress in Human Geography* 12 (2): 179–207

Siddiqui T A and **Khan M A** (1990) Land supply to the urban poor: Hyderabad's incremental development scheme. In: Baross P and van der Linden J (eds): 309–24

Simmie J (1981) *Power, property and corporatism: the political sociology of planning*. London, Macmillan

Sims D (1982) Ismailia 1978–82: institution building for urban development. In: *British planners in the Canal Zone: the lessons of experience 1975– 82*. Development Planning Unit Working Paper 13, London

Singh A M and **Kelles-Viitanen A** (eds) (1987) *Invisible hands: women in home-based production*. New Delhi, Sage

Sivaramakrishnan K C and **Green T** (1986) *Metropolitan management: the Asian experience*. New York, Oxford University Press

Skinner R (1983) Community participation: its scope and organisation. In: Skinner R and Rodell M (eds): 125–50

Skinner R J (ed) (1987) *Shelter upgrading for the urban poor: evaluation of Third World experience*. Manila, Island Publishing House

Skinner R J and **Rodell M J** (eds) (1983) *People, poverty and shelter*. London, Methuen

Smith B C (1987) *Bureaucracy and political power*. Brighton, Wheatsheaf

Smith R S (1979) The effects of land taxes on development timing and rates of change in land prices. In: Bahl R W (ed) *The taxation of urban property in less developed countries*. Madison, University of Wisconsin Press: 137–62

So F S and **Getzeis J** (eds) (1988) *The practice of local government planning*. Washington, DC, International City Managers Association

Spengler J J (1967) Africa and the theory of optimum city size. In: Miner H (ed) *The city in Modern Africa*. London, Pall Mall Press: 55–89

Standing G (ed) (1985) *Labour circulation and the labour process*. London, Croom Helm

Steinberg F (1990) Cairo: informal land development and the challenge for the future. In: Baross P and van der Linden J (eds): 111–32

Stevens R M (1955) Planning legislation in the colonies. *Colonial Building Notes* 31

Stewart J (1983) *Local government: the conditions of local choice*. London, Allen and Unwin

Stewart J (1988) *Understanding the management of local government*. Harlow, Longman

Stewart J and **Holtham C** (1986) *Decentralised resource management: an issues paper*. Luton, Local Government Training Board

Stewart R (1989) Urban planning in the developing world: a personal perspective. Paper presented to the Workshop on Planning and Management of Urban Development in the 1990s, Birmingham, September 1989 and forthcoming in *Habitat International* 1992

Stoker G (1989) Creating a local government for a post-Fordist society. In: Stewart J D and Stoker G (eds) *The future of local government*. Basingstoke, Macmillan: 141–70

Strassman W P (1987) Home based enterprises in cities of developing countries. *Economic Development and Cultural Change* 36 (1): 121–44

Stren R E (1990) Urban housing in Africa: the changing role of government policy. In: Amis P and Lloyd P (eds): 35–53

Stren R E and **White R R** (eds) (1989) *African cities in crisis: managing rapid urban growth*. Boulder, Colo, Westview

Struyk R J, Hoffman M L and **Katsura H M** (1990) *The market for shelter in Indonesian cities*. Washington, DC, Urban Institute

Swan P J, Wegelin E A and **Panchee K** (1983) *Management of sites and services housing schemes: the Asian experience*. Chichester, John Wiley

Swindell K (1979) Labour migration in underdeveloped countries: the case of Sub-Saharan Africa. *Progress in Human Geography* 3 (2): 239–59

Tabibzadeh I, Rossi-Espaget A and **Maxwell R** (1989) *Spotlight on the cities: improving urban health in developing countries*. Geneva, International Labour Organisation

Tanzania, Government of (1977) *Kikuyu Development Plan PPAL*. Doudoma, Capital Development Authority

Taylor J L and **Williams D G** (eds) (1982) *Urban planning practice in developing countries*. Oxford, Pergamon

Teedon P (1990) Contradictions and dilemmas in the provision of low-income housing: the case of Harare. In: Amis P and Lloyd P (eds): 227–38

Thomson B (1989) ODA workshop on urbanization and British aid: a note on the discussion. *Cities* 6 (3): 171–3

Tinbergen J (1967) *Development planning*. London, Weidenfeld and Nicolson

Tinker I and **Cohen M** (1985) Street foods as a source of income for women. *Ekistics* 52 (310): 83–9

Tipple A G and **Willis K G** (1989) The effects on households and housing of strict public intervention in a private rental market: a case study of Kumasi, Ghana. *Geoforum* 20 (1): 15–26

Todaro M P (1989) *Economic development in the Third World*. London, Longman

Tolley G S and **Thomas V** (eds) (1987) *The economics of urbanization and urban policies in developing countries*. Washington, DC, World Bank

Town and Country Planning Organisation and **Institute of Local Government Studies** (1988) *The management of urban fringe land development in Bangalore*. Birmingham, Development Administration Group

Toye J (1987) *Dilemmas of development: reflections on the counter-revolution in development theory and practice*. Oxford, Basil Blackwell

Tullock G (1987a) *The politics of bureaucracy*. New York, University Press of America

Tullock G (1987b) *Democracy and public choice*. Oxford, Basil Blackwell

Turner A (ed) (1980) *Cities of the poor*. London, Croom Helm

Turner A (1989) Urban planning in the developing world: lessons from experience. Paper presented to the Workshop on Planning and Management of Urban Development in the 1990s, Birmingham, September 1989 and forthcoming in *Habitat International* 1992

Turner B and **Maskrey A** (1988) Baldia Soakpit Project, Karachi. In: Turner B (ed) *Building community: a Third World casebook*. London, Building Community Books: 53–8

Turner J F C (1969) Uncontrolled urban settlements: problems and policies. In: Breese G (ed) *The city in newly developing countries*. Englewood Cliffs, NJ, Prentice-Hall: 507–34

Turner J F C (1976) *Housing by the people: towards autonomy in building environments*. London, Marion Boyars

Turner J F C and **Fichter R** (1972) *Freedom to build: dweller control and the housing process*. New York, Macmillan

Turnham D, Salome B and **Schwarz A** (1990) *The informal sector revisited*. Paris, OECD

UN (United Nations) (1966) *Local government personnel systems*. New York, UN

UN (1976) *World housing survey 1974*. New York, UN

UN (1980) *Patterns of urban and rural population growth*. New York, United Nations Department of International Economic and Social Affairs, Population Studies 68

UN (1986) *Popular participation in selected upgrading programmes in urban areas*. New York, Department of International Economic and Social Affairs

UN (1988) *World population trends and policies: 1987 monitoring report*. New York, United Nations Department of International Economic and Social Affairs

UN (1989) *Prospects of world urbanization 1988*. New York, United Nations Department of International Economic and Social Affairs

UNCHS (United Nations Centre for Human Settlements – Habitat) (1981) *The residential circumstances of the urban poor in developing countries*. New York, Praeger

UNCHS (1982) *Survey of slum and squatter settlements*. Dublin, Tycooley

UNCHS (1984a) *Community participation in the execution of low income housing projects*. Nairobi, UNCHS

UNCHS (1984b) *Land for human settlements*. Nairobi, UNCHS

UNCHS (1984c) *A review of technologies for the provision of basic infrastructure in low income settlements*. Nairobi, UNCHS

UNCHS (1984d) *Energy requirements and utilisation in rural and urban low income settlements*. Nairobi, UNCHS

UNCHS (1985) *Population distribution and urbanisation: a review of policy options*. Nairobi, UNCHS

UNCHS (1986a) *Supporting the informal sector in low-income settlements*. Nairobi, UNCHS

UNCHS (1986b) *Rehabilitation of inner city areas: feasible strategies*. Nairobi, UNCHS

UNCHS (1987) *Global report on human settlements 1986*. Oxford, Oxford University Press

UNCHS (1988) *Global shelter strategy for the year 2000*. Nairobi, UNCHS

UNCHS (1989a) Appropriate forms of urban spatial planning. Unpublished discussion paper of the Urban Management Programme, Nairobi, May

UNCHS (1989b) Analysis of land markets. Unpublished discussion paper of the Urban Management Programme, Nairobi, May

UNCHS (1989c) Land development policies. Unpublished discussion paper of the Urban Management Programme, revised draft, Nairobi.

UNCHS (1989d) *Methods for the allocation of investments in infrastructure within integrated development planning: an overview for development planners and administrators*. Nairobi, UNCHS

UNCHS (1989e) *Use of new and renewable energy sources with emphasis on shelter requirements*. Nairobi, UNCHS

UNCHS (1989f) *Improving income and housing: employment generation in low-income settlements*. Nairobi, UNCHS

UNCHS (undated but known to be 1989) *Land for housing*. Nairobi, UNCHS

UNCHS (1992) Experiences with the project approach to shelter delivery for the poor. Forthcoming technical paper

UNCRD (United Nations Centre for Regional Development) (1982) *Small cities and national development*. Nagoya, UNCRD

UNCRD and **East–West Center Environment and Policy Institute** (1989) *Workshop on water-use conflicts*. Nagoya and Honolulu, UNCRD and the Institute

UNEP (United Nations Environment Programme) and **UNCHS** (1987) *Environmental guidelines for settlements planning and management*. Nairobi, UNEP and UNCHS, Volumes 1–3

UNESCAP (United Nations Economic Commission for Asia and the Pacific) (1988) Case studies on metropolitan fringe development with focus on informal land subdivisions. Paper to the Regional Workshop on Metropolitan Fringe Land Development, Bangkok, 6–10 June, UNESCAP

UNICEF (1991) *State of the world's children*. New York, Oxford University Press

Unikel L (1982) Regional development policies in Mexico. In: Gilbert A (ed) *Urbanization in contemporary Latin America*. Chichester, John Wiley: 263–78

Uphoff N *et al.* (1979) Feasibility and application of rural development participation: a state of the art paper. *Cornell University Monograph*, 3

USAID (United States Agency for International Development) (1989) *Urbanization and the environment in developing countries*. Washington, DC: Office of Housing and Urban Programs

van Binsbergen W M J and **Meilink H** (eds) (1978) Migration and the transformation of modern African society. *African Perspectives*, 1

van der Linden J (1982) Squatting by organised invasion in Karachi: a new reply to a failing housing policy. *Third World Planning Review* 4 (4): 400–12

van der Linden J (1986) *The sites and services approach reviewed*. Aldershot, Gower

van Westen A C M (1990) Land supply for low income housing in Bamako, Mali: its evolution and performance. In: Baross P and van der Linden J (eds): 83–110

Varley A (1989) Settlement, illegality, and legalisation: the need for reassessment. In: Ward P (ed) *Corruption, development and inequality*. London: 156–74

Viking N (1990) Royal Institute of Technology, Stockholm, Sweden, in a private interview, London, 9 March

Violich F (1987) *Urban planning for Latin America: the challenge of metropolitan growth*. Boston, Mass, Oelgeschlager, Gunn and Hain/Lincoln Institute of Land Policy

Volbeda S (1989) Housing and survival strategies of women in metropolitan slum areas in Brazil. *Habitat International* 13 (3): 157–71

von Einsiedel N (1989) Future directions of urban planning in the Philippines. Paper presented to the Workshop on Planning and Management of Urban Development in the 1990s, Birmingham, September 1989 and forthcoming in *Habitat International* 1992

Wade I (1986a) *City food: crop selection in Third World cities*. San Francisco, Urban Resource Systems Inc

Wade I (1986b) Food, transport and zoning. *Development: Seeds of Change* 4: 30–4

Wakely P (1988) The development of housing through the withdrawal from construction: changes in Third World housing policies. *Habitat International* 12 (3): 121–31

Wakely P (1989) Urban housing: the need for public sector intervention and international cooperation. *Cities* 6 (3): 195–201

Wakely P, Schmetzer H and **Mumtaz, B** (1976) *Urban housing strategies: education and realization.* London, Pitman

Wallis M (1989) *Bureaucracy: its role in Third World development.* London, Macmillan

Walsh A H (1969) *The urban challenge to government.* New York, Praeger

Walsh K (1991) *Competitive tendering for local authority services: initial experiences.* London, HMSO

Walton D (1989) Urban planning in the developing world: review and experience. Paper presented to the Workshop on Planning and Management of Urban Development in the 1990s, Birmingham, September 1989 and forthcoming in *Habitat International* 1992

Ward K B (1985) Women and urbanization in the world system. In: Timberlake M (ed) *Urbanization in the world economy.* Orlando, Florida, Academic Press: 305–23

Ward P (ed) (1982) *Self-help housing: a critique.* London, Mansell

Ward P M (1986) The politics of planning in Mexico. *Third World Planning Review* 8 (3): 219–36

Ward P (1990) The politics and costs of illegal land development. In: Baross P and van der Linden J (eds): 133–68

Ward P M and **Chant S** (1987) Community leadership and self-help housing. *Progress in Planning* 27 (2): 69–136

Waterston A (1965) *Development planning: lessons from experience.* Baltimore, Md, Johns Hopkins University Press

Watts K (1989) Planning and development since 1948: a personal memoire. Paper presented to the Workshop on Planning and Management of Urban Development in the 1990s, Birmingham, September 1989 and forthcoming in *Habitat International* 1992

Watts S J and **Watts S J** (1986) Morphology, planning and cultural values: a case study of Ilorin, Nigeria. *Third World Planning Review* 8 (3): 237–50

Wekwete K (1989) Planning and managing urban growth in the 1990s – the case of Zimbabwe. Paper presented to the Workshop on Planning and Management of Urban Development in the 1990s, Birmingham, September 1989 and forthcoming in *Habitat International* 1992

Werlin H (1987) On Calcutta: the challenge of urban misery. *Development International* 1 (2): 18–21

Werlin H (1989) The community: master or client – a review of the literature. *Public Administration and Development* 19 (4): 447–57

White L G (1987) *Creating opportunities for change: approaches to managing development programs*. Boulder, Colo, Lynne Rienner

Whyte M K (1988) Social control and rehabilitation in urban China. In: Gugler J (ed): 264–86

Wigglesworth M (1982) Planning legislation as a necessary charade. In: *Planning legislation*. Report of Proceedings of a Seminar in Cyprus, London, Commonwealth Association of Planners.

Wildavsky A (1980) *The art and craft of policy analysis*. London, Macmillan

Wilheim J (1989) Urban planning in the 1990s: the case of an ill-developed although modern country – Brazil. Paper presented to the Workshop on Planning and Management of Urban Development in the 1990s, Birmingham, September 1989 and forthcoming in *Habitat International* 1992

Wilheim J (1990) Curbing air pollution in São Paulo. *Cities* 7 (1): 78

Women and Geography Study Group of the Institute of British Geographers (1984) *Geography and gender: an introduction to feminist geography*. London, Hutchinson

Woods R I (1982) *Theoretical population geography*. London, Longman

World Bank (1983) *Indonesia: selected issues of spatial development*. Washington, DC, World Bank Report No. 4776–IND

World Bank (1985a) Bangladesh: urban government finance and management. Washington, DC, World Bank Urban and Water Supply Division. Mimeo

World Bank (1985b) *Social indicators data*. Washington, DC, World Bank

World Bank (1985c) *Urban Edge* 9 (6): 3

World Bank (1986) *Management options for urban services*. Washington, DC, World Bank

World Bank (1988) *World development report 1988*. New York, Oxford University Press

World Bank (1989) *Reaching the Poor through urban operations*. Washington, DC, World Bank, Infrastructure and Urban Development Department

World Bank (1990a) Pollution: two cities, two solutions. *Urban Edge* 14 (8): 1–6

World Bank (1990b) *World development report 1990*. New York, Oxford University Press

World Bank (1991) *Decentralisation and urban management in Mexico*. Washington, DC, World Bank

World Bank and **UNCHS** (1989) *Urban management program: overview of program activities*. Washington, DC, World Bank

World Commission on Environment and Development (1987) *Our common future*. Oxford, Oxford University Press

WHO (World Health Organization) (1987) *Improving environmental health conditions in low-income settlements: a community based approach to identifying needs and priorities*. Geneva, WHO, No. 100

World Health Organization and **UNEP** (1991) *Surface water drainage for low income communities*. Geneva and Nairobi, WHO and UNEP

Yahya S S (1990) Residential urban land markets in Kenya. In: Amis P and Lloyd P (eds): 157–74

Yeh A G-O (1986) Urban planning and development in Hong Kong now and in the 1990s. In: Choi P L-Y *et al.* (eds) *Planning and development of coastal open cities: Part Two: Hong Kong*. Hong Kong, University of Hong Kong, Centre of Urban Studies and Urban Planning: 1–23

Yeung Y-M (1987) Cities that work: Hong Kong and Singapore. In: Fuchs R J, Jones G W and Pernia E M (eds): 257–74

Yeung Y-M (1988) Agricultural land use in Asian cities. *Land Use Policy* 5 (1): 79–82

Index

329

land in 122
urban population of 7

Kampung Improvement Programme (KIP)
in Indonesia 81, 154, *82*
Kano, Nigeria
law reform in 257–8
Kano Urban Development Board
(KUDB) 239, 240, 241, 243, 249
Karachi, Pakistan
death rate in 9
Development Authority 154
housing in 207, 241
instability of 191
land in *84*
local government in 162, 167
projects for 223
taxes in 157
Kathmandu, Nepal 88
Kenya
agriculture in 235
city size in 8
in-migration in 23
local government in 156, 164
projects in 222
public expenditure in 35
Kikuyu Model Community 243
Kingston, Jamaica 97, 247
kinship networks 214–15
Korea 183 *see also* South Korea

labour market, 24, 25
Lagos, Nigeria
housing in 207
wealth gap in 94
Lahore, Pakistan 167
land
invasion of 83, 84
ownership/tenure/title 31, 106, 111–12,
119–20, 247–8, 251, 275–6
shortage of 23
subdivision of 83, 84
vacant 276
see also Guided Land Development;
housing land; public sector land; rural
land; urban land management
land access 23, 83–4, 97, 118–21, 227–8,
274–7, *57*
land allocation 65
land banking 276–7
land markets
assessment of 126–30, 279
definition of 103–4
formal and informal 106–8, 112, 119–20
intervention in 104–6, 108–9, 117–19,
130, 279
Marxist theory of 103–4
policies and *see* land policies
revenues from 116–17, 124–5, 277–9

land policies
government 108–9
income related 106–8
nationalisation of 109–10
ownership *see* land
prices and 109, 110, 115 *see also* land
values
revenue raising *see* land markets
supply related 110–13
land readjustment (pooling) 122–4, *122,
123*
land supply factors 110–13
land taxation 97, 105, 112, 124, 277–8
land use 44, 113–16, 259
land-use controls 69–70, 102, 113–16, 125–
6, 278
land values 109–10, 111, 115, 117, 120, 124,
129–30
Latin America
colonial style in 64
industrialisation of 36
land supply in 23, 83, 121, 127
local government in 162, 167, 189
low-income communities in 80, 215
participation in 221
population of 6, 269
professions in 196
law
as basis for planning 74, 220, 273–4
checklists 252, 289
justification of 239–45
local factors governing 249–52
role of, generally 236–7, 288–9
survey of 248–9
see also individual countries
law reform
acceptance and implementation of 261–
3, 289
application of 256–9
existing systems and 260–1, 274
holistic view of 259–60
principles for 252–6, 289
see also individual countries
Le Corbusier 70
Leeds, UK 169
legislation *see* law; law reform
Letchworth 67
Lever 67
Lima, Peru 223
livelihoods *see* employment and earnings;
urban poor
loan funds *see* financial resources
local conditions 185–8, 285, 296
local government
administration of 92–3, 158–62
alternative models of 165–8
housing and 67
land management and 102–3
planning role and functions of 68, 91,
140, 155–65, 182–3, 273–4, 281–2

local government – *cont.*
  planning tasks of 153–5
  reform of 168–9
  see also urban administration
London, UK
  Docklands 97, 201
  layout of 70
*Lopinot Limestone Ltd v AG of Trinidad and
    Tobago* 250
Los Angeles, USA 166
low-income groups 80, 81, 83, 106–8, 118–
    21
  see also urban poor
Lusaka
  housing plots in *107*
  projects for 222, *223*, *231*
  slum upgrading in 81–2

Madras, India
  planning law in 246–7
  women traders in 211
  Working Women's Forum 233
Madras Metropolitan Development
    Authority (MMDA) 246–7
Maiduguri, Nigeria 116
maintenance 138–9, 144–6, *139*
Malawi
  land values in 111
  planning law of 245–6
Malaysia
  employment in 208, 209
  Property Gains Tax 277
  socialism in 36
  structure planning in 85, *85–6*
  urban development of 126
Maldives 245, 255
management *see* environment; urban
    management
management skills and training 73, 93,
    152, 294
Manchester, UK 169, *66*
Manila, Philippines *32*, *147*, *287*
  Capital Investment Folio (CIF) 88, 116,
    89–90
  housing in 207
  land in 113
  local government in 156, 167, 190
  planning for 191
  wealth gap in 94
market mechanism 31–3, 37, 54–7, 69, 93–
    4, 96–8, 100, 113–14, 201
Marxism 34, 40, 78, 81, 103–4, 268
Masaka, Uganda 245
master planning 70–6, 86–7, 278, 285, *71–2*
  by foreign consultants 243–5
Mbarara, Uganda 244
metropolitan development initiatives 90–1
Mexico
  local government in 164, 166, 187

Mexico City
  land in 73
  local government in 156, 161
  size of 7
Middle East 65
migration 22–5, 27–8
migratory controls 28–30, 77, 269
models *see* urban management models
monitoring 45, 46, 93, 133, 252, 271–2, 295
monopolies 98
Mozambique 36
municipal government *see* government
    urban planning role; institutions; local
    government
municipal management *see* urban
    management

Nairobi, Kenya
  employment in 210–11
  land in 73
  local government in 164–5
  projects for 222
nationalisation 109–10
Nepal
  local action in 180–1
  sanitation in 9
  urban poor in 2, 13–14
Netherlands 187
'new convention' 178–81, 190, 206
'new realism' 100–1, 179, 265, 270
new towns 67, 77
newly industrialised countries (NICs) 26,
    208
Nicaragua 36, 223
Nigeria
  capitalism in 192
  foreign consultants in 243–4, 249
  Housing Corporation 154
  industrialisation of 184
  land in 124
  Land Use Decree 1978 110, 239
  local government in 156
  planning authorities in 167
  planning law in 238–9, 240, 244, 245,
    257–8
  political structure of 232
Nigerian Town and Country Planning
    Ordinance 1946 69
non-governmental organisations (NGOs)
    49–50, 91, 201, 222, 224–5, 232, 234,
    288
North America
  public expenditure in 35
  public sector management in 92
Norway
  Ministry of Local Government 187
Nyerere, President 77

Overseas Development Administration.
    (UK) (ODA) 98

urban management
  definition of 41, 271, 281
  effective 270–2
  influences on 76, 259
  origin of 42–3
  responsive 229–35
  see also colonial influences and
    inheritance; law; law reform
urban management models 92–4, 158–62,
    165–8
  see also colonial influences and
    inheritance; consultants; law
urban planning 217–20, 270–2, 281
  see also economic development;
    government urban planning; master
    planning; political factors; town
    planning
urban poor
  employment of 208–12, 226–8, 286
  households: housing 215–16
  households: management 212–15
  law and 254, 256
  needs of 206, 217, 219, 227–9, 274–5, 290
  policy towards 94–6
  see also low-income groups; urban
    poverty
urban population 1–7, 2, 3, 4, 5, 6
  see also city growth; city size
urban poverty 12–14, 33, 39, 13
  see also urban poverty
urban regeneration 97, 79
urban services
  access to 58, 217
  context of 133–46
  costs of 9, 56
  indicators 10–12
  land for 114–15
  managers of 74
  needs for 8–9, 11–12, 35, 94, 132–3, 140,
    219, 287, 10, 11
  provision of 31, 33–4, 97–8, 146–52,
    166–7, 228–9, 279–83
  studies of 266
urbanisation see city growth; government
    urban growth policies; urban
    population

United States Agency for International
    Development (USAID) 98, 180, 296
vested interests 49, 50, 74, 91, 93, 96, 191–
    4, 192
Vietnam 36
voluntary bodies see non-governmental
    organisations; private voluntary
    organisations

Washington, USA 70
waste see environment
water supplies 8–9, 11–12, 61, 132, 136,
    137, 138, 173
wealth
  inequalities of distribution of 32–3, 36,
    37, 57, 94
  redistribution of 34, 36, 57, 58
Welwyn, UK 67
Western Asia 7
women
  employment of 209, 210–11, 226, 286
  migrant 24
  role of 96, 221, 222, 226, 233, 286
working classes 66
World Bank 12, 13, 14, 37, 83, 93, 98, 100,
    107, 111, 127, 155, 202, 222, 296
World Health Organisation (WHO) 12
World Population Trends and Policies 30

Yogyakarta, Indonesia 127

Zaïre 211
Zambia
  agriculture in 235
  employment in 208
  housing in 216
  participation in 221
Zimbabwe 156
  colonial legacy in 64, 66
  employment in 208, 211
  housing in 81
  local government in 156, 160, 163
  planning in 191
  planning law of 237–8, 249
zoning 64–5, 101, 194, 218, 238, 249, 254,
    278, 296